THE REGULATION
OF THE
LEGAL PROFESSION IN IRELAND

THE REGULATION
OF THE
LEGAL PROFESSION IN IRELAND

MAEVE HOSIER

qTp

QUID PRO BOOKS

New Orleans, Louisiana

Published in 2014 by Quid Pro Books.

ISBN 978-1-61027-257-5 (pbk)
ISBN 978-1-61027-259-9 (ebk)

QUID PRO BOOKS

Quid Pro, LLC
5860 Citrus Blvd., Suite D-101
New Orleans, Louisiana 70123 USA
www.quidprobooks.com

qp

Publisher's Cataloging-in-Publication

Hosier, Maeve

The Regulation of the Legal Profession in Ireland / Maeve Hosier.

p. cm. — (Dissertation series)

Includes appendix and bibliographical references.

ISBN 978-1-61027-257-5

1. Lawyers—Ireland—History. 2. Law—Ireland—History. 3. Lawyers—Ireland—Regulation.
4. Law reform—Europe. I. Title. II. Series.

KDK156 .H423 2014

315'.04'239—dc22
2014234971

Front cover photograph of Four Courts, Dublin © by Susan Kennedy, Lensmen Photographic Agency, used by permission. Author photograph on back cover inset provided courtesy of George Nelissen.

CONTENTS

FOREWORD

The Great Recession of 2008 is largely blamed, and no doubt correctly so, on the bankers and their willingness to indulge in assembling complex financial instruments, which they sold to unwitting clients who then found themselves shorted against by those same institutions. While complicated derivatives and credit default swaps usually require PhD mathematicians to construct them, the documentation has to be drafted by the lawyers. Yet during the recession we have heard little of lawyers' roles in the run up to the awful events that still mire us. Were they merely the under-labourers working at the behest of the banks or are they accountable for their actions?

Maeve Hosier's study of the (re)regulation of the Irish legal profession is one of the first examinations of lawyers' roles in the period prior to the crisis, as well as the state's response to it. Indeed, it is the only study of the legal profession in Ireland that considers what lawyers did and didn't do. It is a cautionary tale that should force lawyers everywhere to reflect on their responsibilities and professionalism.

In Ireland the crisis came about because of the property bubble fuelled by loans to developers who were making sweetheart deals with finance and government. Since the recession there have been many bankruptcies and collapses of banks. Ireland became one of the three countries in the Eurozone to accept a bailout package from the Troika (European Central Bank, European Commission, IMF). Greece and Portugal also had to take bailouts from the Troika. The Irish Tiger was felled.

Rather like England and Wales, the Irish government had earlier probed the anti-competition activities of the professions in Ireland. It found there was much to remedy, but the professions resisted any incursion into their monopolies. The crisis changed that. As part of the Memorandum of Understanding between the government and the Troika, legal services, including the profession, had to be liberalised and externally regulated. The Troika saw the status quo as a barrier to economic recovery.

The result was that the Irish government drafted the Legal Services Regulation Bill 2011 (LSRB). Not only would it open up the legal profession, it would subject it to external regulation—a single regulator for solicitors and barristers. Over three years the legal profession has fought the government for reform of the bill. Concessions were made and now the bill is on the cusp of becoming formal law.

Hosier takes us through the process explaining the profession's views and why the government was committed to new forms of regulation. Even though in the MOU legal services is a relatively small part it has been among the most contentious. Hosier provides us with a history of the legal profession in Ireland which has deep roots in the early stages of Ireland, showing that lawyers grew up with a strong sense of self-governance and regulation. Of course with English imperialism the Irish legal profession became more like the English with separate barristers and solicitors, also with the same kinds of status ambiguities. Control of courts and control of clients was the resolution that gave them their respective monopolies. The Bar focused on Dublin and solicitors spread themselves throughout the country.

After joining the European Union, Ireland's development surged. Big law firms evolved as Ireland became a key player in the global financial markets and provided favourable tax harbours for many international businesses. Ireland was the "tiger" of Europe. Its banks lent money to property developers who were floating on one of the world's biggest asset bubbles. When the various subprime and other bubbles burst in the global recession, the banks went down and many of the assets on their books became toxic. By following the strictures of the Troika, Ireland has suffered much austerity but has become the first debtor country to emerge from this external bailout regime. Yet the LSRB 2011 has not passed. It soon will and its implementation will see huge changes in the legal services market. In both financial recovery and legal services reform Ireland has performed markedly better than Portugal or Greece, the two other Eurozone debtor countries.

It is tempting to see England and Wales as the model for regulatory change in legal services, in conjunction with Australia, which introduced incorporated legal practices and permitted publicly owned law firms (e.g. Slater & Gordon). The UK has a population of well over 60 million whereas Ireland's population is around 4.5 million. So Ireland's legal population is much smaller and its market tinier. Unlike the British, Ireland is introducing a single regulator for legal services, much to the horror of traditional solicitors and barristers. England's adoption of an oversight and eight frontline regulators is complex and follows the result of turf wars between the various parts of the legal profession. Only now are calls for a single regulator being heard so Ireland may lead the way for the English in this regard.

Ireland can learn from the English experience. The liberalising of the legal services market allowing Alternative Business Structures and multi-disciplinary practices (MDP) promised much. While around 300 ABS have been licensed, few MDPs have been created. Generally, the frontline regulators are slow to adapt to new markets and even though their analysis is meant to be risk-based, the degree of caution in their thinking is excessive. Thus seven years after the passing of the Legal Services Act 2007, the Solicitors Regulation Authority is now developing procedures for speeding up the introduction of MDPs. The UK legal profession still drags its feet over change. Legal services change is quite unlike the change in the financial services market of the 1980s. That was a "Big Bang" while in law it's more like a whimper. Ireland's single regulator has the potential to be more radical in its redesign of the market.

Both the UK and Ireland are part of the globalised world in commerce and legal services. They each have large law firms that are heavily involved in cross-border work and their legal systems share many features. Their promotion of common law puts them in the vanguard of jurisdictions. They are part of a small group of other countries that are rethinking their roles in the global legal services market, especially how they can capture more business for their courts, arbitration services, and lawyers. Canada, Hong Kong, and Singapore are relatively small jurisdictions that foresee value in liberalising their legal markets. It is not surprising that all of them have derived some, if not all, of their legal systems from England. All are ambitious to provide safe, enduring and stable harbours for foreigners to litigate and do business.

Few if any civil code countries have moved in the same direction—apart from France's earlier abortive move with the Darrois Commission, which proposed modernising ideas that never gained traction with the French legal profession. This perspective gives credence to Weber's portrayal of civil code countries lawyers as formally academic in nature while the common lawyers approached their profession as craftsmen willing to adapt their procedures according to the needs of the market rather than the dictates of the code and the state.

Any country that tries to alter the regulation of its legal profession and its attendant market faces huge obstacles. The legal profession is remarkable in its ability to resist change, much more than most other professions. Legal professions are adept at working both with and against the state. And it is a truism that legislatures are filled with lawyers. It is a further truism, but one that is usually obscured by professions, that self-regulation exists independently of the state. Professions in the last resort are endowed with the capacity to "self-regulate" only at the behest of the state. States therefore enjoy a big advantage in how they treat these endowments.

But even in the radical Thatcher years in the UK, government was unable to deregulate lawyers despite having tackled every other profession successfully. The most significant change of this period was the profession's loss of the conveyancing monopoly. This loss brought competition to a formerly closed and cosy market.

It was the twin tracks of complaints against lawyers—the rise of consumerism—and the move of anti-competition thinking—deregulating markets— converging into something that had to be challenged. These moves culminated in the passing of the Legal Services Act 2007. The renegotiation of the regulatory bargain between state and legal profession is now a continuing debate, which renders the situation impossible to imagine ever reverting to the status quo ante.

We see these forces reverberating around the world as I have outlined above. There was a vain attempt at forcing back the tide by the ABA and the CCBE. Both organisations sent a joint letter demanding that the IMF withdraw its ordered changes to the legal services markets of the Eurozone debtor countries. The changes would only result in undermining the sacred position of the legal profession within society. The IMF's rejection was terse.

Maeve Hosier takes us through the political and legal processes that are dramatically renegotiating the regulatory compact between the Irish state and the legal profession. She helps us navigate the "networks of governmentality" in which states and professions are enmeshed. We are now able to observe that many institutions are part of these networks and even their indirect inputs can force considerable change. The OECD's work on bringing money laundering to the fore has resulted in lawyers having to comply with strict regulations that directly impinge on the sanctity of the lawyer-client relationship. Anti-bribery rules are a further manifestation of these efforts. No doubt more such change will occur as more trade and security treaties are negotiated around the world in which legal services will be one of the services under discussion.

One other element should be included, namely the effects of technology on the delivery of legal services. Large parts of legal work can easily be commoditised and made accessible to machine delivery. As the law technology sector grows, lawyers' roles will alter from direct deliverers of services to providers of software that enable direct transmission to the client. Document creation has been largely automated and diagnostic services exist that provide immediate answers to legal problems, e.g. roadtrafficrepresentation.com gives answers to queries on speeding offences and others. Legal process outsourcing shifts activities like document reviews from humans to algorithms run by companies in India and elsewhere.

Hosier brings all these elements to mind as we join her journey through the reconfiguration of the Irish legal services market and profession. Even though her main task is the analysis of one country's regulatory reform, her brief takes in globalisation and more. Her comparative approach places Ireland's problems in context, which has the ability to make them simultaneously local and global. She has taken a defined period and subjected it to intense scrutiny: not for her the *longue durée*, but rather the penetrating analysis of a rupture in time. One that lawyers should read and ponder on.

JOHN FLOOD
McCann FitzGerald Professor of International Law and Business
UCD Sutherland School of Law
University College Dublin

Dublin, Ireland
August, 2014

PREFACE

I am delighted to have the opportunity to contribute to *Quid Pro*'s Dissertation Series, and hopefully, to bring the fruits of my research to a wider audience. This book is based upon my doctoral thesis entitled 'The Regulation of the Legal Profession in Ireland' which I completed in January 2014 at The National University of Ireland, Galway, under the supervision of Professor Laurent Pech, currently Head of the Law and Politics Department at Middlesex University, London.

Since I commenced my research in 2009, Ireland has undergone a period of profound change as a result of the economic crisis following the collapse of the property and banking sectors which began in 2008. The Troika bailout which was agreed between the Fianna Fáil Government and the International Monetary Fund, the European Central Bank and the European Commission came at a high social and economic price, given the extensive programme of austerity which was agreed in return for the bailout funds. The Legal Services Regulation Bill 2011 had its origins in the Troika programme for reform. In the Memorandum of Understanding on Specific Economic Policy Conditionality which was attached to the IMF/EU Letters of Intent of December 2010, it was agreed that Ireland would establish an independent regulator for the legal profession and that it would implement a programme to fundamentally reform the legal profession

Yet progress has been slow, and the legal profession has shown itself to be most resilient to the 'Troikaisation' process. The Legal Services Regulation Bill 2011 is presently making its sedate passage through the legislature. In the meantime the archaic regime of self-regulation continues to prevail. This book closely reflects the contents of the original thesis, current as of December 2013. However, I have altered Chapter 5, § 5.6 in order to include amendments to the Legal Services Regulation Bill 2011 which were agreed at Committee Stage, subsequent to the submission of my thesis. I have also included, as Appendix 1, an extensive extract of a paper examining the background of the economic crisis in Ireland and the actions of the Troika, a paper I previously presented in the United States at the Law and Society Association's annual meeting.

I would like to express my sincere appreciation to my research supervisor at the National University of Ireland, Galway, Professor Laurent Pech, for his enduring patience and support. Thanks are also due to Ms Ursula Connolly and Mr Tom O'Malley of my Research Committee, whose suggestions and comments have been invaluable. Dr Paul Wilson of the University of Wolverhampton provided assistance with the statistical aspects of my research, and Professor Dáibhí Ó Cróinín helped with my research into the early Irish legal system. Within the wider academic community, the work of Professor Richard Abel, Professor John Flood, Professor Andrew Boon, Professor Richard Moorhead, Professor Avrom Sherr and Professor Colin Scott has been inspirational in shaping the direction of my research. I am thankful to Osayomwanbor Enofe of University College Dublin for his advice regarding the comparative aspects of my research. Also, the contributions of Ken Murphy and Kevin O'Higgins of the Law Society of Ireland are most appreciated.

The support of my friends and colleagues in the School of Law at the National University of Ireland, Galway made my life as a researcher considerably easier, and I'd like to express my gratitude to them for their patient assistance, especially Ms Connie Healy, Dr Bernadette Gannon, Ms Anna-Louise Hinds, Dr Mary Keys, Trevor Conway, Hugo Kelly, Gabi Honan, Carmel Flynn, Geraldine O'Rourke and Tara Elwood. A special thank you is due to my lawyer Patrick Mullarkey of Campbell, Fitzpatrick & Co, Solicitors, Belfast, a fearless warrior, a great teacher and a wonderful inspiration. I could not have completed my research without the generous help of my friends Veronica, Douglas, Yvonne, John, Anne-Marie, Geraldine, Eamon, Jayne and Tommy. Finally, my eternal gratitude is due to my sister Hilary, and also to Zoe, Stella and George, for their patience, love and support.

MAEVE HOSIER
Lecturer in Law
Middlesex University
Mauritius Branch Campus

Vacoas, Mauritius
September, 2014

ABSTRACT

This study seeks to explore the regulation of the legal profession in Ireland and to identify whether changes ought to be made to the present regulatory regime. Against a background of economic collapse and Troika bailout, it critically evaluates the present regulatory framework and assesses whether the Legal Services Regulation Bill (LSRB) 2011 adequately addresses the shortcomings in the present system.

Ireland's complex, archaic regulatory framework is explored, and its various shortcomings are highlighted, including the role which the HSKI plays in the current system. The various international factors which affect the regulation of the Irish legal profession are identified, including the law of the EU and the Codes of Conduct of international representative bodies. The rationale behind regulation, and the importance of identifying regulatory objectives, are also examined.

The present self-regulatory framework is critically analysed. A quantitative study of solicitors' misconduct is included, which seeks to identify common features in patterns of misconduct and to provide insight into the efficacy of the present regulatory regime. The regulatory systems in other jurisdictions are examined with a view to informing suggestions for reform in the Irish context. The regimes in other bailed-out states, in particular Greece and Portugal, are considered, in order to ascertain whether Ireland has been subjected to a unique experiment at the hands of the Troika, or whether other bailed-out countries have been subjected to similar programmes of regulatory reform. A detailed account of the provisions of the LSRB 2011 is given, along with a consideration of the responses of key stakeholders to its publication. Further reform of the Bill is recommended in view of the study's findings, and measures beyond the enactment of legislation are also suggested.

THE REGULATION
OF THE
LEGAL PROFESSION IN IRELAND

INTRODUCTION

> Up to now, the legal profession has been self-regulated, and it is obvious that this has not worked.[1]

> One would need a JCB to get a file back from a solicitor who is not diligently attending to it. Many ordinary people have had this experience with members of the legal profession. It is that routine dereliction of duty that concerns me as much as the few bad apples in the barrel that have recently gained such notoriety.[2]

> As far as [the Benchers] were concerned ... they would not change and would continue for the next two hundred and fifty years as they continued for the last.[3]

The legal profession in Ireland is at a crossroads. It faces the prospect of radical reform in the shape of the Legal Services Regulation Bill (LSRB) 2011 which is set to revolutionise the provision of legal services and their regulation. Elements of the profession have set their face against the need for reform, and as a consequence, it has been in a state of unprecedented turmoil since the Bill's publication. The profession has felt pressure not only from the legislature, but it has also succumbed to the wider social and political pressures which Ireland has experienced since the spectacular collapse of its economy in 2008.

This study examines the regulation of the legal profession at a unique moment in Ireland's history, and seeks to understand how lawyers as *social actors* have contributed to the collapse of the Irish economy and responded to the challenge of 'Troikaisation' – the process of liberalisation which has characterised the structural reforms agreed between the Troika and bailed-out nations in return for bailout funds. The study also seeks to understand the impact of globalization and technological advancement upon the legal profession which, being entrenched in tradition prefers to depend upon tried and tested precedent rather than embrace innovative solutions.

Aims and Objectives

This study aims to critically review how the legal profession in Ireland is regulated, to consider the provisions of the Legal Services Regulation Bill (LSRB) 2011, to assess whether the Bill is an appropriate instrument to correct present regulatory failures and to identify what changes, if any, should be made

---

[1] 656 (1) *Dáil Debates* 47 (29th May 2008) Deputy Paul Connaughton
[2] 656 (1) *Dáil Debates* 55 (29th May 2008) Deputy Pat Rabbitte
[3] 440 (5) *Dáil Debates* 1211 (23rd Mar 1994) Deputy Desmond O'Malley

to the proposed new regulatory framework, to ensure that high quality legal services are readily available to the public at a reasonable cost. Having offered a comprehensive exposition of how the LSRB 2011 should be amended, the book also identifies what other steps, beyond the enactment of legislation, are required to attain a balanced and functional regulatory system.

In applying the law in the interests of justice, the legal profession performs a unique role in society. Lawyers defend the rights of citizens against the arbitrary use of state power. They seek to vindicate the rights of citizens when these are denied by means of unfair or incorrect decisions of the judiciary. They also act to curb the excesses of the legislature by facilitating the challenge of statutes and rules which fail to conform to the requirements of the Constitution. In entrusting the legal profession with these important functions society has vested considerable power and trust in it, in order to ensure it can carry out its duties. However, the state is the largest user of legal services in Ireland, and there is a considerable overlap between the legal and political community. These competing tensions give rise to particular ethical challenges for the profession, which must alternatively seek to please and challenge its political masters, lawyers being deeply embedded within networks of 'governmentality'.[4] As Abel has observed, the legal profession is located 'between market and state'.[5] Regulation of the profession is necessary to ensure that the societal trust which is necessarily placed in lawyers is not abused. However, what form should that regulation take? Too much regulation threatens to impede the functioning of a free market in legal services, with an undesirable impact upon service costs. On the other hand, too little regulation carries the risk of creating a race to the bottom amongst substandard practitioners, seeking to supply poor quality services at the lowest cost. To identify the correct regulatory balance for Ireland's legal profession must therefore be a fundamental aim of this study.

Regulation may be broadly defined as *control*, and a regulatory regime, whether it is of a biological, social or economic nature, consists of three elements:

(i) norms, standards or rules,

(ii) mechanisms for monitoring or feedback,

(iii) ways of correcting behaviour which deviates from the norms.[6]

The regulatory regime for the legal profession in Ireland consists of a complex array of authorities and instruments, both Irish and international.[7] These authorities use a variety of methods to either deter or correct lawyers' deviant behaviour. In the context of this study, the concept of 'profession' is understood

---

[4] M Davies, 'The Demise of Professional Self-Regulation? Evidence from the "ideal type" professions of medicine and law' (2010) *Professional Negligence* 5

[5] R Abel, *English Lawyers between Market and State: The Politics of Professionalism* (Oxford University Press 2010)

[6] Hood, Rothstein & Baldwin, *The Government of Risk* (OUP, 2001) in C Scott, 'Regulating Everything' UCD Geary Institute Discussion Paper Series. 26th Feb 2008, 7

[7] These authorities and instruments are described in detail in chs 1 & 2.

as a particular type of occupational control, commonly in the form of self-regulation.[8] According to MacDonald, '[p]rofessions aim for a monopoly on the provision of services of a particular kind, and as monopolies can only be granted by the state, professions have a distinctive relationship with the state'.[9] According to the terms of the bargain between the state and the profession, in return for ensuring expertise and appropriate behaviour from members, the profession gains monopolistic privileges from the state.[10] The acquisition of a specialised body of knowledge is a core aspect of the professional identity, and it is this command of special knowledge which allows the profession to achieve social closure and enhanced social status.[11] In controlling a particular body of knowledge, professionals are able to maintain *the means of production for their line of business in their heads.*[12] However, the twenty-first century presents considerable challenges for professional identities, not least to that of lawyers. Against the backdrop of the financial crisis and rapid technological change, there has been a dissipation of trust in professionals – an essential ingredient in securing the professional position – and lawyers, along with other professionals, have experienced challenges to the maintenance of their monopoly and status. This research was carried out in a period of social turmoil, both in Ireland and internationally, and the professions have not been immune from the winds of change.

The research objectives of this study are as follows:

• To provide an overview of the Irish regulatory framework for the legal profession

• To make clear that the Irish regulatory framework is affected by international and external norms

• To identify any weaknesses in the present system of regulation, in light of best practices derived from an overview of the regulation of the legal professions in other jurisdictions

• To critically examine the new regulatory framework contained in the LSRB 2011, and to suggest amendments for its improvement

• To critically assess the impact of the Troika upon the regulation of the legal profession in bailed-out countries, in particular; Ireland, Greece and Portugal

Research Methodology

In pursuing the aims and objectives which were identified above, a mixed methodological approach was used, consisting of both qualitative and quantitative methods. From a qualitative perspective, doctrinal research was the main

---

[8] M Davies, 'The Demise of Professional Self-Regulation' (FN 4) 4

[9] K McDonald, 'Professional Work' in M Korczynski et al, *Social Theory at Work* (OUP 2006) 367

[10] B Barber, *The Logic and Limits of Trust* (Rutgers University Press, 1983) in M Davies, 'The Demise of Professional Self-Regulation' (FN 4) 4

[11] Ibid 372

[12] Ibid 372, citing M Weber, *Economy and Society* (University of California Press, 1984)

approach adopted in order to identify those factors, both legal and non-legal which influence the current Irish regulatory framework and to explore the manner in which that framework is affected by international and external norms. Doctrinal analysis was used to identify the legal rules, and non-legal mechanisms which apply to the regulation of the legal profession in Ireland. It was also used to analyse the current regulatory framework with a view to identifying its strengths and weaknesses, to examine the provisions of the LSRB 2011 and to inform proposals for the reform of the regulatory framework.

The method was also used to investigate the place of primary sources of law in regulating the legal profession. Primary sources of Irish law which were studied included The Constitution of Ireland, statutes, statutory instruments and case law.[13] The primary sources of EU law which were examined were the Treaty on European Union, the Treaty on the Functioning of the European Union, directives, regulations and the case law of the European Court of Justice. At an international level, primary sources of law which were studied included the International Monetary Fund's Articles of Agreement, the Council of Europe's Recommendation regarding the Freedom of Exercise of the Profession of Lawyer, the United Nations' Basic Principles on the Role of Lawyers and the World Trade Organisation's Joint Statement on Legal Services.

Doctrinal analysis was also used to explore an extensive array of secondary sources of law over the course of the research. These included books, legal periodicals and accounts of parliamentary proceedings.[14] In the early phase of the research, an extensive literature review was carried out to identify both the main theoretical perspectives and the most significant methodologies which have been adopted by the academic community to explore the regulation of the legal profession. Throughout the conduct of the doctrinal research, extensive use was made of the online legal research databases of the James Hardiman Library at The National University of Ireland Galway.[15] In addition, the library's hard copy collection was a most valuable resource for both primary and secondary sources. During the research programme, I regularly participated in conferences in order to gain a greater understanding of the key discourses within the academic community which pertain to the regulation of the legal profession, and to participate in debates and discussions in that regard.

In order to better understand the perspectives of key stakeholders in the legal services market with regard to the regulatory *status quo*, and also to the proposed reforms contained in the LSRB 2011, interviews were sought with individuals within the main representative and regulatory bodies of the legal profession and also amongst the community of legal practitioners. A structured interview format was used to explore participants' views concerning issues such

---

[13] Other primary sources of Irish law which were examined included professional conduct guides of both branches of the legal profession.

[14] Other secondary sources of Irish law which were examined included newspapers and other media reports. The websites of key stakeholders in the legal services market were also regularly accessed. Accounts of debates in both the Dáil and Seanad, and also of the proceedings of Select Committees of the Dáil and Joint Oireachtas Committees were studied.

[15] The databases which were most frequently used were Hein on Line, Westlaw, Lexis Nexis, Justis, EurLex and SSRN.

as the strengths and weaknesses of the current regulatory regime, and also of the provisions in the LSRB 2011.[16] In several cases however, the initial structured interview was followed by a more wide ranging, unstructured conversation which provided a deeper insight into interviewees' perceptions of the rules pertaining to their activities as legal professionals.

The interview process was revealing not only in terms of the responses of participants, but also as a result of the behaviour of those stakeholders who declined or failed to participate in the interview process. A marked contrast emerged between the attitudes of the two branches of the legal profession towards participating in the interviews. Whilst the LSI was most accommodating in facilitating this aspect of the research, representatives of both the BCI and the HSKI did not take part. Furthermore, where individual members of the BCI did agree to facilitate me with an interview, they did so upon condition of anonymity. The interviewees' responses were helpful in identifying weaknesses in the current regulatory framework contained in Chapter 3, and in understanding attitudes within the legal profession to the proposed reforms contained in the LSRB 2011 which are discussed in Chapter 5. The interview process, although limited in scope, was most helpful in developing a greater sense of how lawyers as social actors perceive their role in society, and how legal professionals envisage recent socio-economic changes as impacting upon their activities.

A qualitative, comparative approach was used, to a limited extent, in order to explore the occurrence of professional misconduct in the US, England and Wales (Chapter 3) and also the regulation of the legal profession in Northern Ireland, England and Wales, Australia, Greece and Portugal (Chapter 4). The aim of these comparisons was to identify whether there are common patterns of lawyers' misconduct internationally; to facilitate an understanding of the similarities and differences between the regulatory approaches in the different jurisdictions and to identify possible solutions to rectify the shortcomings which

---

[16] A total of 10 interviews were conducted. Interview participants were asked the following questions:

1. What do you consider to be the strengths and weaknesses of the present regulatory regime for barristers/solicitors?

2. In light of the recently published committee amendments, what do you consider to be the strengths and weaknesses of the LSRB 2011?

3. What are your views on MDPs? Do you perceive any advantages for barristers/solicitors if they are introduced? What do you consider to be their main drawbacks?

4. Do you have any reservations about the recently amended definition of 'lay person' in section 2 of the Bill?

5. Given the provisions of section 30 of the Bill, what do you think about the possible unification of both branches of the legal profession, and also the possible creation of a new profession of conveyancer?

6. Do you have any concerns about the origins of the LSRB 2011, given that it appears to have been published in accordance with the terms of the Memorandum of Understanding which was agreed with the Troika in return for the bailout funds?

7. Given the rapid pace of technological change today, and also the process of globalization, do you think that the LSRB 2011 will equip the solicitors' / barristers' profession to fully participate in the global market for legal services in future? If not, what changes would you wish to see being made to the Bill?

were identified in the Irish regulatory system in Chapter 3. Given that five different jurisdictions were studied in Chapter 4, only a brief overview of their legal systems and frameworks for regulating the legal profession was possible. The jurisdictions of Northern Ireland, England and Wales were selected for comparison on the grounds that they have similar systems of common law and they have legal professional structures which are similar to Ireland. They also share common historical roots with Ireland, a fact which is reflected in their regulatory frameworks. The enactment of the Legal Services Act 2007 in England radically altered the regulation of the legal profession in England and Wales, and as such, it was particularly useful to consider the recent changes in that jurisdiction, and to reflect upon their possible merits from an Irish perspective. Australia was considered because it has been innovative globally in liberalising the provision of legal services by both incorporated entities and MDPs, and as such, it provided a useful perspective from which to consider the potential impact of the provisions of the LSRB 2011, and also to inform suggestions for amendment of the Bill.

The legal professions and the regulatory frameworks in Greece and Portugal were selected for comparison on grounds of the economic crises which those jurisdictions have experienced in recent years, and which have given rise to the necessity for Troika bailouts. Whilst constraints of financial and other resources, and also linguistic barriers precluded anything but the most superficial examination of these jurisdictions, their comparisons were valuable in shedding light on the role of the Troika in liberalising the provision of legal services in EU member states which are experiencing similar socio-economic challenges to Ireland. These comparisons also facilitated an understanding of whether the Troika has subjected Ireland to a unique experiment in terms of the liberalisation of professional services, as evidenced by the terms of the Memorandum of Understanding which was agreed between the Government of Ireland and the Troika, or whether this agreement, in fact, reflects the Troika's general *modus operandi* in bailed-out states.

In the early course of the research, I regularly consulted the summarised findings of the proceedings of the Solicitors Disciplinary Tribunal (SDT) in order to gain a deeper understanding of the nature of lawyers' misconduct. It soon became apparent that many of these cases displayed similar features, and this observation was the initial inspiration for conducting a quantitative study with a view to identifying dominant patterns of professional misconduct amongst solicitors in Ireland (Chapter 3, section 3.8). This study took the form of an analysis of one hundred consecutive cases of professional misconduct which were heard by the Solicitors Disciplinary Tribunal (SDT) between January 2008 and May 2010. The main aim of the study was to investigate the link between a finding of professional misconduct in a case by the SDT and the presence of a financial, dishonesty or property element in that case.[17]

---

[17] The study adopted a broad categorization which included dishonesty and breaches of undertakings. The study also sought to investigate the extent to which misconduct resulting in a striking off concerned all three elements of finance, dishonesty and property, and to establish whether a past history of misconduct involving all three of these elements was predictive of a solicitor being struck off in future. See Chapter 3 section 3.8 and Appendix 2 for further details

Given that both financial and time constraints where factors impacting upon the nature and scope of this study, it was decided that the construction of a database of the one hundred cases which indicated the presence or absence in each case of the discrete elements of finance, dishonesty and property by means of a binary code would provide the simplest and most effective basis for the further exploration of patterns of misconduct in the desired manner.[18] Accordingly, the Chi-Square Test was selected as the most appropriate means of ascertaining whether there was a link between the following discrete pairs of variables: finance and dishonesty; dishonesty and property and finance and property.[19] The database was analysed using the statistical software package Minitab.[20] Whilst the database was limited in terms of both the number of cases and also the discrete variables it contained, arguably it is a tool which may in future be usefully developed to provide a greater insight to patterns of solicitors' misconduct, and which may have a degree of predictive power in identifying those practitioners who are most likely to offend in future.

Thesis Outline

The first chapter of this study commences with a brief account of the history of the Irish legal profession, and then proceeds to examine its current system of regulation. It describes the main authorities which are responsible for the regulation of solicitors, including the Law Society of Ireland (LSI), its Complaints and Client Relations Committee and the Independent Adjudicator of the LSI. It also examines the place of the SDT within the regulatory framework and the regulatory role of the President of the High Court. In describing the regulation of barristers, it considers the role of the Bar Council of Ireland (BCI), its Professional Practices Committee, the Barristers' Professional Conduct Tribunal and the Barristers' Professional Conduct Appeals Board. It also considers the contribution of the Honorable Society of Kings' Inns, its Disciplinary Committee and the Special Meeting of the Bar to the regulation of barristers. The latter part of Chapter 1 examines the main regulatory instruments for the regulation of the legal profession in Ireland. These include the Constitution of Ireland, various statutes and statutory instruments and the professional codes of conduct. The chapter concludes by considering some non-legal regulatory mechanisms in-

---

of the study.

[18] Appendix 2 describes how the table of binary codes was compiled.

[19] The Chi-Square Test for the independence of two variables is also known as the test for contingency tables. It may be used to identify whether there is an association between two discrete variables. It involves a comparison between observed and expected values of the variables. Where two discrete variables are associated, the distribution of observed values for one will differ depending on the category (either 0/1) of the second variable. Where two discrete variables are independent, the distributions of observed values for one variable will be similar for both categories of the second variable. The test results are shown in Appendix 2. Observed counts are shown above the counts which would be expected if the pairs of variables were independent.

[20] The choice and application of the Chi-Square Test for the analysis of the database was made following consultations with the Statistics Department at NUIG in June 2010, and the assistance of Dr Paul Wilson with this aspect of the research is greatly appreciated.

cluding the role of insurance companies and the influence of internalised norms of conduct in controlling the professional activity of lawyers.

Chapter 2 examines those international bodies which impact upon the regulation of the legal profession in Ireland. It commences with an examination of the impact of EU law, particularly with regard to freedom of establishment, freedom to provide services and EU anti-corruption policy. It proceeds to consider the jurisprudence of the European Court of Justice (ECJ) in relation to multi-disciplinary practices (MDPs), minimum fee schedules and legal professional privilege. The European Parliament Resolution on the Legal Profession and the General Interest in the Functioning of Legal Systems is also discussed. The chapter then examines the impact of the Troika upon the regulation of the legal profession in Ireland, and offers a brief description of the origins of the economic crisis which gave rise to the necessity for the bailout. The impact of various international bodies on the regulation of the Irish legal profession is also considered, including the Council of Europe, the United Nations and the World Trade Organisation. Finally, the role of international representative bodies is examined, including the Council of the Bars and Law Societies of Europe (CCBE), the International Bar Association (IBA), the International Law Association (ILA) and the International Association of Lawyers (IAL). The chapter concludes with a consideration of the process of globalization and its impact upon the legal profession in Ireland.

Chapter 3 identifies the shortcomings of the present system for regulating the Irish legal profession. In order to comprehensively analyse the current regulatory system, the chapter utilises Laurel Terry's framework for assessing the strengths and weaknesses of regulatory regimes for the legal profession.[21] This framework is also helpful in identifying how the legal profession *ought* to be regulated in the context of a particular jurisdiction. The chapter commences with a consideration of the rationale for the regulation of the legal profession. The economic argument for regulation is considered, and the concepts of information asymmetry and externalities are explored. It proceeds to consider the issue of who should be responsible for the regulation of the legal profession from the perspective of various reports which have examined that question in the course of the last twenty years. The problems associated with self-regulation are also explored. The issue of which particular legal activities and entities should be the subject of regulation is considered, as is the question of whether regulation should be focused either upon the prevention of lapses, or upon the appropriate response following the detection of a lapse. Terry's framework also prompts reflection upon where regulation should occur, a question which is becoming increasingly relevant given the global dimension to the activities of both lawyers and clients alike. The increasingly virtual nature of legal service provision is also considered in this regard. The chapter proceeds to consider the question of how legal services should be regulated. In particular it looks at whether a similar regulatory approach is appropriate, regardless of whether a lawyer has corporate or private clients, or whether the regulatory response should be tailored to the

---

[21] L Terry et al, 'Trends and Challenges in Lawyer Regulation: The Impact of Globalization and Technology' (2012) 80 (6) *Fordham Law Review* 2661, 2663

differing needs of these cohorts. It also considers whether regulation ought to be either rules-based, or focused upon the attainment of specific outcomes. The chapter also offers an analysis of the current Irish framework for regulating the legal profession using the OECD General Principles for Regulatory Quality and Performance. It concludes with a case study into one particular aspect of regulation; that of professional misconduct, and presents the findings of an investigation into patterns of solicitors' professional misconduct, based upon the analysis of one hundred consecutive findings of misconduct in cases which were heard by the SDT.

Chapter 4 adopts a comparative perspective and looks at the manner in which the legal profession is regulated in other jurisdictions. It commences with an examination of the regulatory regime in our nearest jurisdictional neighbour, Northern Ireland. Its present regulatory system is described, and the recommendations of the Bain Report which sought to identify appropriate regulatory reform for Northern Ireland are also considered.[22] The chapter proceeds to examine the regulation of the legal profession in England and Wales which has undergone a revolution in recent years following the publication of the Clementi Report in 2004, and the subsequent enactment of the Legal Services Act 2007.[23] It then considers the regulatory regime in Australia which was the first country to permit the establishment of Alternative Business Structures (ABSs). Next, the regulation of the legal profession in Greece and Portugal, which both received bailout funds from the Troika is considered. In return for their bailout funds, these countries agreed to implement extensive programmes of structural reforms, including the liberalisation of their legal services markets. An examination of the regulatory regimes in these jurisdictions is instructive regarding the Troika's overall *modus operandi* in respect of bailed-out nations, and reveals whether its programmes are tailored to the needs of individual states, or whether a one-size-fits-all approach has been adopted in seeking to correct their economic problems. The chapter also looks at the response of the international representative bodies to the Troika's reform programmes in bailed-out countries, and concludes with an assessment of the extent to which Greece, Portugal and Ireland have actually implemented the agreed programmes to reform their legal service sectors.

The final chapter of this study, Chapter 5, examines the provisions of LSRB 2011. It commences by considering the background to the publication of the Bill, in particular; the commitments which were given to the Troika by the Irish Government in return for the bailout funds. The chapter proceeds to describe the main provisions of the Bill and also the new regulatory bodies which will be established following its enactment. The response of the legal profession's representative bodies and that of other stakeholders to the publication of the Bill is also examined. The chapter considers the response of the Minister for Justice,

---

[22] G Bain, 'Legal Services in Northern Ireland: Complaints, Regulation, Competition'. (2006). Available at: <http://www.dfpni.gov.uk/legal_services.pdf> Accessed 25/2/2013

[23] D Clementi, 'Report of the Review of the Regulatory Framework for Legal Services in England and Wales' (December 2004). Available at: <http://www.legal-services-review.org.uk/content/report/index.htm> Accessed 6/8/2014

Equality and Law Reform to the criticisms of the Bill, and describes amendments which have recently been agreed by the Select Committee on Justice, Defence and Equality.[24] It concludes by making suggestions for further amendment of the Bill, in light of the problems identified in the current regulatory framework in Chapter 3, and also the comparisons with other regulatory regimes contained in Chapter 4 of the study.

---

[24] The Select Committee's list of Amendments to the LSRB 2011 is available at:
<http://www.oireachtas.ie/viewdoc.asp?fn=/documents/bills28/bills/2011/5811/b5811d-dscn.pdf> Accessed 14/8/2013

1

THE REGULATION OF THE
LEGAL PROFESSION IN IRELAND

1.0 Introduction

The Irish legal profession is regulated by a complex framework consisting of the Constitution of Ireland, statutes, common law, codes of conduct devised by the professions themselves and non-legal regulatory mechanisms such as insurance and peer pressure. This chapter explains the origins of the current regulatory system by firstly examining the early legal profession and its regulation. A consideration of the legal profession as described in a collection of texts dating from the seventh century onwards provides valuable insight into those processes of continuity and change which have impinged upon the modern legal profession and its regulatory system. An understanding of the early legal system also helps to explain why today's regulatory system takes its current form, and illustrates the strong influence which tradition and history have had on the regulatory system. As stated by Carr, 'It is at once the justification and the explanation of history that the past throws light on the future, and the future throws light on the past.'[1] The chapter proceeds with a comprehensive examination of the current Irish regulatory framework. It examines the key regulatory bodies including the Law Society of Ireland (LSI), the Bar Council of Ireland (BCI) and the Honorable Society of Kings Inns (HSKI). It also looks at the main regulatory instruments including common law principles, The Constitution of Ireland and statutes. This is necessary in order to offer an informed judgment of what changes if any ought to be made to the current system of regulation, and also to analyse the impact upon it of the proposed changes contained in the Legal Services Regulation Bill (LSRB) 2011.

1.1 The History of the Legal Profession in Ireland

The arrival of St Patrick in Ireland in the fifth century and the introduction of Christianity saw the emergence of a written scholarly tradition in Ireland, and accordingly, the history of the Irish legal profession may be traced, by means of a body of written texts dating back to the early Christian period. In the period from the seventh to the twentieth century, the legal profession experienced major transformation, as Ireland changed from being a 'tribal, rural,

---

[1] E Carr, *What is History?*, 2nd ed (Palgrave McMillan, 2001) 117

hierarchical and familiar' society, to an aristocracy and finally to a democratic republic.[2]

1.1.1 The Early Irish Legal System

A large body of Early Irish legal material exists in the form of approximately eighty law texts, dating from between the seventh and ninth centuries, and this has provided a rich harvest for the student of Early Irish or 'Brehon' Law.[3] The texts, which were written in Early Irish, were composed in both prose and poetry. These sagas and stories were used to illustrate the application of various legal principles. This incredible historical record offers evidence of highly developed and self-contained system of Brehon law, consisting of a complex set of rules which applied to almost every aspect of social life, and which included the law relating to persons, property, offences, procedure and punishment.[4] Whilst some of the early texts are virtually complete, only small fragments of others remain, and there is evidence to suggest that other texts have been lost in their entirety.[5] Whilst the texts themselves originate from the seventh century onwards, the essential elements of the legal system they describe dates back 'at least as far as the Common Celtic period (c. 1000 B.C.).[6] According to Kelly:

> When the Christian missionaries arrived in Ireland in the 5th century they encountered a legal system which can be assumed to have developed from Celtic law with little or no outside influence. There could well have been some influence form pre-Celtic inhabitants of Ireland, but – in the absence of documentary evidence – one can only speculate about the legal ideas of these peoples.

> This pre-literate Irish legal tradition was presumably passed on by lawyers from generation to generation in the form of alliterative verse and legal maxims. The introduction of Latin letters revolutionized the transmission of legal material.[7]

The authorship of the Early Irish legal manuscripts has been the subject of much debate amongst historians, who have yet to reach consensus in this regard.[8] On the one hand, Binchy has argued that the justification of polygyny and the rules relating to divorce which are described in the manuscripts are indica-

---

[2] F Kelly, *A Guide to Early Irish Law* (first published 1988, Dundalgan Press Ltd 2001) 3. Citing D Binchy's 'Thomas Davis Lecture' 1953

[3] D Binchy, 'The Lingusitic and Historical Value of the Irish Law Tracts' The Sir John Rhys Memorial Lecture, British Academy 1937. (Milord, London) 107; F Kelly, 'Texts and Transmissions: The Law-Texts' in P Ní Chatháin & M Richter (Eds), *Ireland and Europe in the early Middle Ages: Texts and Transmission* (Quill, 2002)

[4] F Kelly, *A Guide to Early Irish Law* (FN 2) vii – xi; Interview with Professor D Ó Cróinín, Professor of History, The National University of Ireland Galway (14th June 2013) Much of the early manuscripts have been printed by Binchy. See D Binchy, *Corpus Iuris Hibernici* (CIH) I – VI (Dublin, 1978).

[5] D Binchy, CIH, VI 2103.12 in F Kelly, 'Texts' (FN 3) 230 – 231

[6] F Kelly, *A Guide to Early Irish Law* (FN 2) 231

[7] Ibid 232

[8] Ibid 233

tive of a non-clerical author. For instance, in *Corpus Iuris Hibernici* (CIH) there were detailed rules concerning the grounds for divorce:

> There are seven women in Irish law who, though their marriage contract is bound by enforcing surety and paying surety, are entitled to leave their marriage any time they like and what is given them in their bridewealth is theirs: a woman whose husband spreads slander about her, a woman whose husband inflicts humiliation upon her so that she becomes an object of derision, a woman on whom is inflicted the mark of beating, a woman who is repudiated and abandoned for another woman, a woman whose bed is spurned and whose husband prefers to sleep with boys unless he have cause, a wife to whom her husband gives charms while wooing her and excites her to fornicate, a woman who does not receive her needs in the marriage partnership, for every woman who is married in Irish law is entitled to her needs.[9]

On the other hand, it has been argued that the law tracts were produced by scholars who were equally well versed in both the ancient Irish legal tradition and also the scriptures, with the resultant texts being, 'a conscious and sophisticated compromise between the two'.[10]

According to Kelly, the early manuscripts were produced for the purpose of legal education of judges.[11] He has argued that whilst the exact location of the earliest centres for legal knowledge are unknown prior to the ninth century AD, when the monasteries of Cloyne, Cork and Slane were identified as legal centres, the Early Irish texts themselves provide evidence to support their role in educating the early practitioners of law. For instance, in one text, guidance is given to a judge who must deliberate in a matter concerning bee-keeping.[12] Kelly has stated that the collection of texts *Senchas Már* was most probably compiled at a law-school in the north midlands, a view which is based upon the frequent use in the texts of place names from that area.[13] Binchy has argued that another collection of texts, *Nemed*, originated in a politico-legal school which was possibly located in the Munster region.[14]

The texts of the *Senchus Már* describe three different types of advocate practising in Ireland.[15] A fettering advocate was skilled in enforcing on behalf of a court; 'including [taking] hostage-sureties and the driving of [distrained

---

[9] D Ó Corraín (ed), 'Early Medieval Law: c 700 – 1200' 28 (citing 6 – 44 CIH, 2230- 31) in A Burke, et al (eds), *The Field Day Anthology of Irish Writing Vol IV: Irish Womens' Writing & Traditions*. (Cork University Press, 2002)

[10] Ibid 233 – 234, citing D Ó Corraín in Pertita 3 (1984) 412

[11] F Kelly, *A Guide to Early Irish Law* (FN 2) 242

[12] Ibid 242, citing CIH 405.13. Bee-keeping was an activity which was the subject of a considerable amount of legal attention in the Early Irish period.

[13] Ibid 242. (*Senchas Már* means Great Tradition)

[14] Ibid 246, citing D Binchy, 'Ériu' 17 (1955) 4 – 6; 18 (1958) 44 – 54. (*Nemed* means holy or privileged)

[15] L Breathnach, 'Lawyers in Early Ireland' in D Hogan & W Osborogh (eds), *Brehons, Sergeants & Attorneys: Studies in the History of the Irish Legal Profession* (Irish Academic Press, 1990) 11

cattle]'.[16] A court advocate was able to take cases to court and plead them. After a case was related to him, the court advocate would plead it by the same time the following day. He did not accept a case unless he had determined the correct procedure for its resolution. The court advocate was also competent in all advocacy and enforcement, neighbourhood law, and the law of marital union. 'An advocate from whom judgment encounters' was the most senior ranking advocate in the early Irish system. He would take over the pleading of a case immediately prior to judgment, and was competent to plead on behalf of a judge or a king.

In the pre-Norman period there was a tradition of hereditary legal families where a body of knowledge was passed down within particular families. However, the prestige of such families was eroded within the Irish legal tradition by Gregorian reforms in the field of canon law, and also the Norman conquest, which saw a system of English appointments to bishoprics and abbeys, resulting in a gradual displacement of traditional Irish learning and a fading of the Brehon tradition. In the conflict between canon and secular law which was played out in the medieval period in Ireland, the poets were ostracised, and were legislated against at the provisional synod in Armagh in 1346, along with harpers, tympanists, mimers and jugglers.[17] Support for the extension of the use of English common law in Ireland on the part of the clergy also served to undermine the position of the Brehon tradition within Irish medieval society. In the later medieval period, the growing influence of foreign jurisprudence upon the Irish domestic legal system in the form of both canon and English common law undoubtedly presented challenges to the regulation and practice of law in Medieval Ireland. Yet notwithstanding such sustained external pressure, the Brehon tradition displayed considerable resistance.

By the late medieval period, the Brehon tradition had lost considerable ground to the English common law system.[18] In the sixteenth century, it was alleged that the ninth Earl of Kildare, when trying criminal cases, was apt to select either a Brehon judge or a judge of the common law, depending on the particular outcome he wished to achieve in a given case. This indicates a degree of flexibility in the use of the various legal approaches, which were for a time able to operate in parallel with one another. The adaptability of the Brehon tradition is also supported by the appointment, as late as 1591, of the Brehon Patrick MacAodhagain by the crown to prosecute and punish, by all means possible, 'malefactors, rebels, vagabounds, rymors, Irish harpers, idle men and women, and other unprofitable members.'[19] However, the use of parallel systems was not sustainable in the long term and ultimately the pressure to adopt the English system grew stronger.

---

[16] Ibid 11

[17] Citing D Chart (ed), *The Register of Primate John Swayne* (Belfast, 1935) in K Sims, 'The Brehons of Late Medieval Ireland' Ibid 54

[18] Ibid 75. The growing influence of the English common law system in the late medieval period is evidenced by the increasing use of terms and concepts such as 'heirs and assigns' and 'reversion'.

[19] Ibid 75, citing *Fiants Ire Eliz* nos 5528, 6658

The Introduction of English Law in Ireland

The introduction of the English system of law in Ireland can be traced to the realm of King John.[20] Efforts were made to achieve a uniform system of law in both England and Ireland, and this process was assisted when the offspring of the original English settlers in Ireland returned to London to further their legal education. Kenny has argued that whilst there is a dearth of categorical evidence on the point, it would appear that the English Inns had both a social and educational function as early as 1300.[21] However, in the fifteenth century prospective law students had to contend not only with a general hostility towards the Irish in England which manifested itself in 1413 in the form of a statutory exclusion, but also with a particular animosity towards those who aspired to obtain a licence in order to study at the London Inns of Court.[22] Some of those Irishmen who managed to obtain a licence in order to study law in Europe still had to suffer the indignity of a Lincoln's Inn order of 1513 that no Irishmen should be admitted without 'the assent of a Bencher'.[23] The sixteenth century English attitude towards their Irish neighbours was illustrated by a proclamation of 1594 which ordered all Irish people to go home as 'the discovery of Irish traitors can hardly be made when as many other vagrants of that nation haunt about the court.'[24] However, Irish law students were exempted from this particular diktat. Prospective law students often prepared themselves prior to travelling to the London Inns by studying under the authority of an experienced lawyer in Dublin, with a view to improving their educational, social and cultural skills.

Ultimately, the proclamation of King James I in 1605 that English law must be adopted throughout Ireland marked the beginning of the end of the Brehon tradition, and this was accompanied by the confiscation and plantation of Brehon lands. The sixteenth century saw the demise of the Brehon system of law which finally succumbed to the various external pressures. The evolution of law and its regulation is a continuous process, and canon and common-law disciplines continuously impacted upon the native Irish Brehon law tradition which was also subject to external cultural, political and religious forces. The end result of these relentless pressures was the demise of the Brehon tradition. The Irish law schools in Ireland continued to operate until the beginning of the seventeenth century. Many academic lawyers also practiced law, such as the Mac Aodhagains who acted as the legal representatives of most of the ruling families of West and Central Ireland during the fourteenth and fifteenth centuries.[25] The

---

[20] King John's realm was from 1199 until 1216

[21] Robert de St Michael went from Ireland to England to study law in 1292. P Brand, 'The Early History of the Legal Profession of the Lordship of Ireland, 1250- 1350' in D Hogan & W Osborough (eds), *Brehons, Sergeants and Attorneys* (FN 15) 25

[22] 1 Hen V c 8 (Irish Mendicants, etc)

[23] There was no necessity for an English legal scholar to require a Bencher's assent to join an Inn, and such an acquisition may have been problematic for many prospective Irish legal scholars.

[24] Harrison, 'An Elizabethan Journal' 288 (21 February 1594) in C Kenny, *King's Inns and the Kingdom of Ireland* (Irish Academic Press, 1992) 51

[25] F Kelly, *A Guide to Early Irish Law* (FN 2) 253

Elizabethan Wars from 1594 to 1603, and the subsequent Flight of the Earls in 1607 marked the end of the Brehon tradition. The Lords, who were both the Earls' allies also and the main employers of the legal families, were either banished or agreed to adopt English law.[26]

1.1.2 The Medieval Period: Moving towards a Split Profession

The two branches of the legal profession in England, Wales and Ireland have their origins in the emergence of a practice during medieval times which permitted one man, an attorney, to stand in the place of another in a legal matter, whereas it had long been traditionally accepted that one man should be free to seek the assistance of another, a serjeant, in legal proceedings.[27] Thus the precursor of today's solicitor was the attorney, whilst the serjeant was the forerunner of today's barrister. The Statute of Merton of 1235 contained a provision requiring the personal attendance in court of parties to legal proceedings. Initially, attorneys did not advocate on a client's behalf, but gradually they began to do so, receiving statutory authority to plead in 1285.[28] During the medieval period there was not a clear demarcation between the two branches of the legal profession, and professional separation only emerged towards the end of the sixteenth century. Holdsworth has described the separation process as follows:

> At the lower end we see a growing distinctness in the profession of the attorney, a growing separation between the attorneys and the barristers and the rise of three new classes in the legal profession – pleaders, conveyancers and solicitors – the first two of which approximate to the profession of barrister and the third to that of the attorney. At the upper end, the commanding position of the serjeants was modified by the growth of the preeminence of the law officers of the Crown and the rise of the new class of King's counsel. As the result of these changes the grouping of the legal profession begins to assume almost its modern form.[29]

The jurisdiction of the courts over solicitors and attorneys was established by statute in 1605.[30] Barristers did not perform administrative acts or engage with court officials, and consequently were not considered to be officers of the court. Their role was confined to the understanding and application of the law and the pleading of court cases.[31] The barristers' branch of the profession con-

---

[26] The Flight of the Earls marked the demise of Ireland's ancient aristocracy, as the Earls (the Irish Chieftans) left Ireland rather than face removal of their freedoms and the seizing of their lands by the Lord Deputy of Ireland, Sir Arthur Chichester. The Flight followed nine years of war from 1594 to 1603 during the reign of Elizabeth I, as the Earls fought against the English invaders.

[27] P Reeves, *Are Two Legal Professions Necessary?* (Waterlows Publishers Limited, 1986) 2, citing W Holdsworth, *A History of English Law* 3rd edition (1923) Vol II 312

[28] 13 Edw 1 St 1 c 10 1285

[29] W Holdsworth, *A History of English Law* (1923) Vol VI 436 (FN 27), in P Reeves, *Are Two Legal Professions Necessary?* (FN 27) 3

[30] An Act to Reform the Multitudes and Misdemeanours of Attornies (3 Jas 1 c 7)

[31] P Reeves, *Are Two Legal Professions Necessary?* (FN 27) 3

sisted of either aristocrats or members of families with wealth derived from success in trade or commerce.[32]

The seventeenth century saw an ongoing process of differentiation between the two branches with English attorneys and solicitors being finally excluded from the four Inns of Court in 1793, henceforth being confined to the Chancery Inns.[33] In England, The Society of Gentlemen Practisers (SGP) was established by attorneys and solicitors in 1739 in order to uphold professional standards of conduct amongst its members. With a view to protecting its members' economic interests the SGP insisted that barristers should not accept briefs directly from the public. Reeves has argued that this position was later approved and justified by the Bar as being necessary to protect the public interest, as barristers were not in a position to establish the facts of a matter, a task which fell instead to the instructing solicitor.[34]

According to Reeves:

> This illustrates the way in which rules of professional etiquette have arisen for the purpose of protecting sectarian interests and have later been justified on the grounds that they are fundamental to the public interest.[35]

In Ireland, the two subdivisions of the solicitors' branch of the profession, solicitors and attorneys were fused following the enactment of the Supreme Court Judicature Act (Ireland) 1877. Prior to the 1877 Act, attorneys were attached to the three courts of common law, which were the King's (or Queen's) bench, common pleas and exchequer, whilst solicitors were attached to the court of chancery. The 1877 Act brought about the merger of these four separate courts into a unified Supreme Court of the Judicature. The use of the title 'solicitor' was henceforth extended to include attorneys.[36]

1.1.3 The History of the Solicitors' Profession in Ireland

Whereas today, the Benchers of the HSKI confine their jurisdiction to the regulation of the barristers' branch of the profession, this was historically not the case, and from the middle of the sixteenth century, when the Society of Kings' Inns (SKI) was established, the Benchers who were comprised of senior barristers, serjeants, law officials and members of the judiciary also exerted their influence upon solicitors and attorneys, and exercised authority regarding admittance to practice in those capacities. In 1629 the Benchers ruled that the right to practice as an attorney was to be predicated upon admittance to the SKI.[37] The Benchers continued to exert regulatory authority over the entire legal profession until the end of the nineteenth century.[38] Statutory regulation of

---

[32] Ibid 3

[33] P Reeves, *Are Two Legal Professions Necessary?* (FN 27) 4, citing *Halsbury's Laws of England* 4th edition Vol 44 (1983) 5 para 1

[34] Ibid 4, citing R Webster AG, 'Law Times' 7th July 1888

[35] Ibid 4

[36] The Irish term for solicitor is 'aturnae'.

[37] C Kenny, *King's Inns and the Kingdom of Ireland* (FN 24) 100.

[38] The Solicitors (Ireland) Act 1898 greatly increased the role of the LSI in matters concerning entry to the solicitors' profession, and the education and discipline of solicitiors.

lawyers in Ireland commenced in earnest towards the end of the seventeenth century, when laws were enacted with the aim of confining the practice of law to members of the established church.[39] The 1698 statute recited that, 'papist solicitors have been and still are the common disturbers of the peace and tranquillity of his Majesty's subjects in general.'[40] Quite apart from rooting out disturbers of the peace in the form of Catholic solicitors, the 1698 statute also had the effect of limiting the right to provide legal services to a smaller more exclusive group of practitioners who would face less competition in the legal services market and increase their incomes accordingly.

In 1733 an Act was passed which was entitled 'An act for the amendment of the law in relation to papist solicitors; and for remedying other mischiefs in relation to the practitioners in the several courts of law and equity'.[41] Prior to its enactment, in order to be admitted as an attorney, it was necessary to obtain a placement with a practising attorney for a period, before applying to one of the courts of law for liberty to practise in that court. This judicial control of entry into the legal profession was a form of governmental interference and was contrary to the principle of the independence of the legal profession. The 1733 Act required that a period of five years' apprenticeship must be served, that indentures of apprenticeship must be enrolled and that an affidavit of due service must be sworn. The Act also set out the parameters of a solicitor's role which included the drawing of pleadings, transcription of depositions or other evidence for use in a suit at law or equity, and the direction or management of a suit or the defence thereof within the four courts. The regulations were amended and refined in 1773, and a system of 'moral examiners' was introduced whereby would-be attorneys were examined by a panel of court officers and the most reputable attorneys to ascertain whether they had the requisite moral and educational standards to be admitted as an attorney.[42]

The late eighteenth century saw the removal of the bar on Catholics being admitted to the legal profession.[43] The reign of George the III marked the beginning of a continuous process of relaxation of the penal laws against Irish Catholics.[44] This policy was motivated by the observation that Catholics being largely conservative in their political outlook would support the legislature in its opposition to revolutionary forces which were growing in the wake of the American and French revolutions. The late eighteenth century was a period of particular turbulence in Ireland, evidenced by the 1798 rebellion, when the native Catholic

---

[39] 10 Will III (1698) c 13 (Ir). The 1698 statute was enacted during the realm of King William III (1689 – 1702). He was also known as 'William of Orange'. Staunchly Protestant, William III was perceived as a champion of his faith. His Irish victory over the Catholic King James II at the Battle of the Boyne is still commemorated annually by the Orange Order on 12th July.

[40] D Hogan, 'The profession before the charter of 1852' in E Hall & D Hogan (eds), 'The Law Society of Ireland, 1852 – 2002' (Four Courts Press, 2002) 23

[41] 7 Geo II (1733) c 5 (Ir)

[42] 13 & 14 Geo III (1773) c 23 (Ir). The 1773 Act expressly gave the judiciary discretion regarding admission to practice in court.

[43] 32 Geo III (1792) c 21 (Ir).

[44] J Hill, 'The legal profession and defence of the ancient regime' in D Hogan and W Osborough (eds), *Brehons, Sergeants and Attorneys* (FN 15) 187

populace rose against the English planters. The gradual easing of the penal laws may be seen in this context as a move to placate the native Irish population. However, the question of Catholic rights in Ireland was extremely sensitive for the ruling Protestant elite, and nor were the English willing to cede governmental power of a judicial nature, so the exclusion of Catholics from the judiciary continued unabated until 1829.

The Law Club of Ireland was established in 1791, and this was akin to an early form of Law Society. It was comprised of the 'more substantial' members of the legal profession.[45] The Rules of the SKI published in 1793 declared that the Benchers had authority to make rules in respect of the admission and membership of attorneys, students and barristers to the society. All members had to satisfy the Benchers of their fitness for admission to the society and they were also obliged to pay fees. These were non-statutory requirements which derived their force from the fact that the Benchers included within their number the judiciary, whose authority extended beyond the confines of the society to the courts themselves.

The nineteenth century saw further refinements of the solicitors' regulatory system. The right to hold a practising certificate was subjected to a tax in 1816, with those practising in Dublin initially paying £8, whilst country practitioners paid a lesser rate of £3. The imposition of the practising certificate tax was resented by solicitors, and as a benefit in return, the profession was granted its lucrative monopoly upon the provision of conveyancing services. The monopoly of the conveyancing market was an important achievement for the solicitors' profession and has been assiduously guarded ever since, given that it represented an important source of revenue for many practitioners. The early nineteenth century also saw the emergence of a draft charter for the regulation of the solicitors' profession, which set out the requirements for the admission of solicitors to the profession, and also for their education.

In 1830 the Law Society of Ireland (LSI) was established. Its aim was to secure the rights and privileges of attorneys, to promote fair and honest practices, to suggest improvements to the rules and practices of the courts where circumstances required it, to adopt measures to prevent improper or unqualified persons from practising and to procure a hall for the use of solicitors. In its early years, the LSI moved from a system of membership based upon proposal and approval, to a voluntary system, which was considered to be more in keeping the society's representative role in respect of the profession. The voluntary system allowed prospective members to apply to join the LSI of their own volition and entry was no longer dependent upon securing a recommendation from an existing member. The LSI's most notable activities in its early days concerned its efforts to remove the power of the Benchers over the solicitors' profession. The LSI held a watching brief on applications to the SKI for admission to the solicitors' profession, and its views regarding applications appeared to carry some weight with the Benchers. The Benchers agreed to the LSI's request that it be given copies of the petitions and affidavits of prospective solicitors to facilitate their scrutiny for suitability for entrance to the profession.

---

[45] Ibid 28

The mid nineteenth century saw a failed attempt of the LSI to break free from the constraints of the SKI. Regulatory independence from the SKI for solicitors would ensure their professional status by creating the possibility for their self-regulation, a prerequisite for any aspiring profession. In 1838 and 1839 Daniel O'Connell introduced Bills to remove solicitors from the regulatory grip of the SKI, but these were not passed. In 1830 the LSI passed a resolution denouncing advertisements purporting to transact business at rates below 'legal and established fees', and in 1841, it set out new objectives for itself which included the provision of better education in laws and court practice, the establishment of a library and the preservation of the rights and privileges of the profession. The LSI was incorporated by Royal Charter in 1852 under the name of 'The Incorporated Society of Attorneys and Solicitors of Ireland'.

In the latter part of the nineteenth century, the LSI was primarily concerned with new efforts to seek independence of the solicitors' profession from the SKI. It was also concerned with establishing self-governance and with securing its representative and regulatory functions, endeavours which culminated in some success with the enactment of the Solicitors (Ireland) Act 1898. The LSI's representative aspirations were challenged by the fact that its membership during this time was confined to approximately one third of practising solicitors, as it was considered to be a Dublin dominated organisation. In 1846 a House of Commons Select Committee reported that the state of legal education in England and Ireland was extremely unsatisfactory, and new programmes of lectures for apprentices were recommended. The SKI was initially reluctant to acquiesce to the LSI's request for the introduction of such a programme, but following a LSI petition to Parliament in 1858, it conceded, and established a preliminary examination system for solicitors, and in 1866, under judicial supervision, the LSI assumed responsibility for solicitors' education.[46]

In seeking to strengthen its regulatory power over solicitors, the LSI sought to control not just educational matters, but also the professional activities of its members. The importance of conveyancing work for solicitors has been noted earlier and the introduction of the Torrens system of public title registration in the mid-nineteenth century posed a significant threat to solicitors' conveyancing incomes. This threat was due to the efficiency of the Torrens system of property transfer which relied upon registration of title to transfer property ownership rather than the conveyance of often lengthy deeds. The Record of Title (Ireland)

---

[46] Prior to the introduction of obligatory courses for articled clerks which were introduced after the Incorporated Law Society of Ireland became independent of SKI in 1866, the only form of legal examination in Ireland was of a judicial nature, and its purpose was to verify that a prospective candidate had been apprenticed for the correct period, and had paid the requisite fees. In 1838, the Select Committee on Foundation Schools and Education in Ireland (HC 1838, 701) recommended the establishment of four provincial colleges of higher education, with law schools to be founded either separately or in connection with them. The Report's recommendations influenced the Law Programme in the Queen's Colleges, which were designed to meet the requirements of both professional and non-professional students. The Queen's Colleges in Belfast, Cork and Galway were founded following the enactment of the Colleges (Ireland) Act 1845. The Law Faculty was one of the three original faculties at the time of the Colleges' foundation. L O' Malley, 'Law' in T Foley (ed), *From Queen's College to National University: Essays on the Academic History of QCG/UCG/NUI Galway* (Four Courts Press, 1999) 26

Act 1865 provided for the establishment of a registry of titles sold through the landed estates court. Solicitors' conveyancing fees which were once calculated upon the basis of the length of a deed, began to be based upon the value of the conveyed property, as the shortened Torrens conveyancing system made the old method of fee calculation unsustainable. Whereas the LSI failed to prevent the adoption of the Torrens system, they were more successful with regard to further legislative reform which abolished the necessity for a solicitor to pay fees to the SKI as a condition of admittance to the profession, and the LSI became the sole recipient of any fees payable by apprentices and solicitors. The Solicitors (Ireland) Act 1898 transferred control of education and some disciplinary functions from the supervision of the judiciary to the LSI. The beginning of the twentieth century saw the LSI with complete control of the education and examination of solicitors. It also bore responsibility for maintaining a roll of solicitors entitled to practice, and a committee of LSI Council members was established, which was responsible for the initial investigation of complaints of professional misconduct and for reporting upon these to the Lord Chancellor.

During the latter part of the nineteenth century, the LSI sought to protect and expand its representative functions and it vigorously defended its members' interests, and sought to preserve solicitors' incomes. It criticised perceived threats to the conveyancing monopoly; such as the policy of the Land Commission in 1893 which was to send forms to tenants, to assist them in compulsory registration of titles without the aid of a solicitor. It successfully rebuffed a proposal in 1895 for the appointment of a public trustee, which would have impacted negatively upon solicitors' fees for the administration of estates. It also objected to an 1893 Bill which would have permitted the official assignee of the court of bankruptcy to be generally appointed as liquidator and receiver of companies, a move which would have reduced the flow of solicitors' work and incomes accordingly.

The early part of the twentieth century saw the LSI less focused on regulatory and representative matters, but more embroiled in the political and civil disorder which occurred in the post World War I period prior to the establishment of the Irish state in 1922.[47] In 1920 the Courts of Dáil Éireann were established. However, there was a concerted effort by republicans to disrupt the established courts.[48] The 1920s was a particularly challenging time for the legal

---

[47] In the course of disturbances which occurred during the Easter week of 1916, the Four Courts were occupied by the Irish Volunteers and following the ensuing disorder during the Easter Rising, the Council of the LSI passed a resolution assuring the King of its continued loyalty. The Irish Volunteers were founded in the early twentieth century in order to fight for, and defend Home Rule in Ireland. They are considered to be the precursors of the modern Irish Republican Army (IRA) who continue to use the Volunteers' Irish title 'Óglaigh na hÉireann'. During the occupation of the Four Courts, significant property damage occurred when books and furniture were used to barricade the windows. In the first post-war election in Britain of December 1918, sixty-nine Sinn Fein members were elected to the Westminster parliament, and having failed to take their seats there, established the First Dail in Dublin.

[48] P Brand, 'The Early History of the Legal Profession' in D Hogan & W Osborough (eds), *Brehons, Sergeants and Attorneys* (FN 15) 70. The 'enemy courts' were to be 'rigorously boycotted' according to the Dail's Minister for Home Affairs in a 1921 Circular. The signing of the Anglo Irish Treaty in December 1921 may have signified the end of the Anglo Irish War,

professions in Ireland, not only as a result of the political upheavals which accompanied the foundation of the state in 1922, but also because of the volume of legislation enacted with which practitioners had to become acquainted following its establishment. The Courts of Justice Act 1924 provided for the establishment of the current court structure, consisting of Supreme Court, High Court, Circuit Court and District Court. The LSI was represented on the Judiciary Committee, which was established in 1923 to advise upon the administration of justice, the recommendations of which formed the basis of the 1924 Act. The LSI objected strongly to the Legal Practitioners (Qualification) Bill 1928 which required that legal practitioners must demonstrate by means of an examination 'a competent knowledge of the Irish language'. In spite of the LSI's protestations about this 'atrocious and tyrannical' measure, the Bill was enacted in 1929.[49] Between 1922 and 1950 the proportion of solicitors who were members of the LSI began to increase, and in 1948 it had attained a level of 80%. This increase in affiliation was most probably as a result of the LSI's emergence as an effective representative body for the profession, and the benefits which solicitors perceived from supporting a unified voice to negotiate with the state on its behalf. The LSI also offered the prospect of self-regulation which would secure the professional status of this branch of the legal profession.

The LSI's ambitions to put the self-regulation of the profession on a statutory basis bore fruit in the form of the Solicitors Act 1954. The 1954 Act was the result of a lengthy campaign on the part of the LSI to secure what it considered to be appropriate regulatory legislation for the solicitors' profession. In 1943 the LSI submitted a draft bill on the matter to the Department of Justice. This was aimed at ensuring that solicitors' accounts were properly maintained, enforcing strict discipline within the profession and making membership of the LSI compulsory for all practising solicitors. However, the government declined to accept the draft bill in the form presented, and stated that it should include provision for a fidelity bond to be taken out by solicitors. The government also stated that solicitors' accounts must be subjected to a system of auditing, and that membership of the LSI should not be compulsory. The LSI persuaded the Government that a fidelity bond or other means of compulsory insurance was not practicable, and that the Compensation Fund which had been established in 1948 was an adequate means of making amends to members of the public who suffered loss due to solicitors' dishonesty. The powers of the Disciplinary Committee of the LSI included the power to strike a solicitor from the roll where a case of misconduct had been established, but the constitutionality of this measure was promptly challenged following the enactment of the 1954 Act.[50]

---

however it did not see the end of unrest and disorder, as evidenced by the 1922 Irish Republican Army occupation of the Four Courts and their subsequent capture by government forces, events which resulted in serious damage to the Solicitors' Buildings.

[49] D Hogan, 'The Society from independence to 1960' (citing E Burne, President of LSI 1928) in E Hall & D Hogan (eds), 'The Law Society of Ireland (FN 40) 79

[50] For a full discussion of the constitutional difficulties which arose following the enactment of the 1954 Act, see ch 1 §§ 1.3.2, 1.3.3.1 and 1.3.3.2.

Critical Comments

The history of the solicitors' profession in Ireland reflects the development of the standard techniques which the profession relies upon in order to identify and maintain its exclusive area of competence for the provision of legal services. An early form of gatekeeping is apparent in the adoption of the religious barriers which served to exclude Catholics from the practice of law. This measure not only had the effect of securing the exclusivity of legal practice for those of the Protestant faith, it also had the effect of increasing practitioners' incomes by decreasing the level of competition in the market for service provision. The LSI's desire to attain professional autonomy was reflected in its power struggle with the SKI to maintain control over admission to the profession and also over the system of solicitors' education. The manner in which the LSI successfully fought to maintain reserved areas of practice in the face of statutory threats to establish a public trustee and an official assignee of the court of bankruptcy illustrates its efficiency as a representative body on the part of the solicitors' profession. The LSI also showed itself to be creative and flexible in the face of undesirable legislative changes; such as the introduction of the Torrens system of title registration, in response to which the LSI helped solicitors to preserve their conveyancing incomes by introducing a new system of fee calculation based upon the value of the conveyed property rather than the length of the conveyance documents.[51]

1.1.4 The History of the Barristers' Profession in Ireland

The history of the Bar in Ireland reflects the history of Ireland itself and the country's struggles since 1541 when the lordship of Ireland became a realm of King Henry VIII, a state of affairs remaining until the Act of Union in 1800 which saw the unification of the two realms. The SKI was also founded in 1541, and its status in comparison with the Inns of court in London was akin to a 'poor relation', just as Ireland's theoretical equality with England was really something of a 'polite constitutional fiction'.[52]

The SKI's original premises were situated on the site of the present Four Courts, which previously had been the site of the Blackfriars Dominican Abbey, and a lease for the premises was secured from government officials in Dublin. The SKI's inferiority to the English Inns of Court was evidenced by the fact that it lacked authority to admit persons to practice law, nor could it call individuals to the Bar. Prior to being called to the Bar by the Chief Justice in Ireland, a prospective barrister was obliged to reside for up to five years at one of the English Inns of Court. A further distinguishing feature of the Irish Inns from its English counterparts was that the judges and senior law officers of the realm known as the Benchers, were members of the SKI whereas in England such senior members of the legal profession maintained separate Inns known as the Serjeants' Inns which had no educational function, but which served as a

---

[51] For a full exposition of the economic argument for the regulation of the legal profession, see ch 3 § 3.1.

[52] C Kenny, *Kings' Inns and the Kingdom of Ireland* (Irish Academic Press, 1992) 1

meeting place for judicial conferences and chamber business.[53] Another important difference between the Irish and English Inns was that whilst the English Inns had the authority to both admit persons to practice by means of conferring the degree of barrister at law and also to call prospective barristers to the bar, the SKI could only admit persons to practice but lacked the authority to issue a call to the Bar, that being the prerogative of the Chief Justice in Ireland.[54] Even the right to admit prospective barristers to practice was restricted in Ireland as compared to England as they were obliged to attend an English Inn for several years and undergo examination there as a prerequisite for admittance to the Irish Bar, whereas the English Inns had full authority to admit suitable applicants.[55]

The Benchers were responsible for the SKI's most important decisions, such as admittance, maintenance of discipline and making decisions concerning the Society's betterment and also for its representation in dealings with external authorities. The Irish Inn's membership comprised not only of barristers, but it also included serjeants (senior barristers), judges and law officers. Attorneys were also either permitted or required to join, a fact which further served to distinguish it from its English counterparts. However, the SKI did serve a purpose in common with the English Inns which was to provide a meeting place where those who worked at the courts could enjoy meals in the common dining room, whilst also keeping up to date with current affairs. The society generally succeeded in avoiding becoming embroiled in the thorny issue of religious conformity, and in this regard it relied upon the rather technical distinction to be made between the Benchers and the judiciary, the latter whose role it was to ensure that the requirements of religious conformity were observed by legal practitioners in the penal era.

The SKI had a considerable gatekeeping role with regard to the barristers' profession having *de facto* control over admittance to the profession. As the Benchers included the members of the judiciary, it was not possible for a barrister to enjoy a right of audience in any court unless he was a member of the SKI, even though the formal power to call a person to the Bar was the prerogative of the Chief Justice. The SKI had a major regulatory role with regard to maintaining standards of discipline amongst the Bar, and it also served as a representative body. The SKI did not have a direct role in the education of barristers until the twentieth century, and in its early days its educative function was only to ensure that prospective members had served the requisite period at an English Inn of Court.

Thomas Cromwell, secretary to King Henry VIII was instrumental in the reform of legal education in the early sixteenth century, and he also had a keen interest in Irish affairs. On the monarch's behalf, he secured the leases of both Gray's Inn and the Inns of Temple from their previous ecclesiastical holders. Following a proposal for the establishment of a 'house of chaunsery' in Dublin

---

[53] Ibid 2, 36 – 37

[54] Ibid 2

[55] Ibid 2. The Statute of Jeofailles 1542 contained a provision requiring prospective Irish legal practitioners to reside in England for several years.

from Patrick Barnewall, the King's Serjeant in Ireland, who was held in high esteem by both Henry VIII and Thomas Cromwell, in due course the judges and law officers in Ireland acquired the aforementioned property at Blackfriars. The property had been vacated by the Dominicans following the suppression of religious houses during the Tudor period.[56] However, notwithstanding their best efforts, the lawyers were unsuccessful in their efforts to secure permanent possession of Blackfriars. Incorporation of the society was necessary for it to be able to obtain the freehold title of the property, and this was requested of Henry VIII in a petition from the lawyers in 1542. However, the lawyers failed to meet their objective and had to content themselves with two consecutive leases of 21 years.

The requirement that a period of residency at a London Inn was necessary for a person to practice law in Ireland was contained in The Statute of Jeofailles in 1542, and this requirement remained in force for the next three hundred years.[57] It had the effect of establishing control of Irish legal education firmly in England. Although in its early days the SKI had not aspired to assume responsibility for legal education in Ireland, the Statue of Jeofailles fettered any such future aspirations. A further difficulty for Catholics who wished to pursue a legal career in Ireland was the necessity for them to conform to the established church. There was to be no room at the English Inns of court for recusants – those who refused to conform – a group comprised exclusively of Roman Catholics.

Towards the end of the sixteenth century a growing animosity developed in Ireland between the 'New English' comprised of Protestant officials from England, and 'Old English' comprised of descendants of English and Norman settlers, which included the majority of Ireland's lawyers. The lawyers' opposition to the tax regime of the period did little to build bridges with government officials. The lawyers' differences with the government officials came to a head when the second lease at Blackfriars expired in 1584, and the title was transferred to Anthony Lowe. The lawyers were obliged to temporarily vacate the Blackfriars property. In the early seventeenth century, the Anglicisation of the Irish bench was achieved by means of a series of English appointments and the administration of the oath of supremacy to the newly appointed judiciary.

A revival of the SKI occurred in 1607 when the lawyers once more managed to secure the occupation of the Blackfriars property. The revival saw the society's membership increased by the admission of some of the most prominent lawyers and judges of the day, including the Lord Deputy Chichester, and leading members of the judiciary, such as Sir James Ley, chief justice of the King's Bench who was responsible for the issuance of mandates aimed at forcing recusants to conform. During a period of rapid expansion between 1607 and 1609, it would appear that the SKI extended membership without prejudice to Old English Catholics and New English Protestants alike.[58] However, in 1613 a general

---

[56] 28 Hen VIII c 16

[57] The London Inn residency requirement was repealed in 48 & 49 Vict (1885) c 20

[58] C Kenny, *King's Inns and the Kingdom of Ireland* (FN 52) 88. An exception to the non-admission of Irishmen was that of Sir Francis Shine who joined the SKI circa 1612.

prohibition of Catholic lawyers was introduced. This had a negative impact upon the SKI, as Catholics who were excluded from practice had little reason to frequent the inns, even if it was not directly responsible for the exclusion of recusants. The accession of Charles I to the throne led to an easing of restrictions upon Catholic lawyers, and several important concessions were made; in particular, those who had studied at the Inns in England for five years were to be admitted to practice law in Ireland, regardless of their religion.[59]

In 1629, the SKI ordained that membership of the society was compulsory for attorneys and counsellors (barristers) who wished to practice in the Dublin courts. This requirement was extended to all courts throughout Ireland in 1635. In 1638 the property of the SKI was transferred to a select group of trustees, who were chosen by Lord Deputy Wentworth. The rebellion of 1641 had a profound effect upon Irish society, but also upon the legal system, and the SKI was no exception, with only one member admitted between 1641 and 1649.[60] The administration of justice effectively ground to a halt, as the system for replacing judges was abandoned.[61] Nicholas Plunkett, a member of the SKI, was a leading Catholic figure in the rebellion. The rebels aspired to gain control of the administration of Ireland, and their plans included the establishment of a new Inn of court where the Irish gentry could receive training in law, and following protracted negotiations between the catholic confederates and the King, in 1645 the government was ready to concede on this issue. However, despite the government's having agreed to allow the building of a new Inn, in 1648 the continuing hostilities put paid to the plan. In 1649 the shift in power from the monarchy to the parliament in England which had culminated in the execution of Charles I, was to have dire consequences for Ireland.

The latter half of the seventeenth century was marked by wars and turmoil in Ireland. Oliver Cromwell commenced a nine month military campaign with his puritan army to put an end to the rebellion in 1649. The hostilities were protracted and the resultant turmoil left the administration of justice and the legal system in disarray, as the sitting of the Four Courts was suspended from 1649 – 1655. During this time the Inns of Court in Dublin (which were not referred to by their former 'Royal title') were used to adjudicate on claims concerning lands forfeited in the course of the Cromwellian campaign. In 1653 Cromwell, 'The Lord Protector', commenced a five year period of rule in England and Ireland until his death in 1658. His son Henry became the Lord Deputy of

---

[59] Ibid 98. The concession was in accordance with Article 15 of Charles I's 'Instructions and Graces'.

[60] The Irish Rebellion commenced with a failed coup by members of the Catholic aristocracy in Ireland, which was aimed at improving their circumstances under English rule. The attempted coup led to the outbreak of the Confederate Wars, as afterwards, hostilities broke out between Irish Catholics and English and Scottish Protestant settlers. A Confederation comprising of Catholic aristocracy and Catholic clergy formed a de facto government of Ireland which retained control of most of Ireland until the conquest of Ireland by Cromwellian forces in the 1650s.

[61] C Kenny, *King's Inns and the Kingdom of Ireland* (FN 52) 37. The Irish judiciary were appointed from amongst the more senior members of the legal profession including law officers and pleaders. This was different to the English system which made judicial appointments from the ranks of serjeants only.

Ireland, and in 1657 he was admitted to the Kings Inns. The society's Black book records indicate that several of Cromwell's associates were admitted during this period. However, there was reluctance amongst English lawyers to relocate in Ireland, in order to rectify a perceived lack of legal expertise in Ireland which had arisen. This was due not only to the disarray in Ireland following the Cromwellian campaign, but also to the ban on the practice of law 'by popish malignant or other delinquent persons'.[62]

The restoration of the monarchy in 1660 with King Charles II, saw the resumption in use of the old name of 'Kings Inns' for the Inns of Court in Dublin, and it also marked the beginning of another period of restoration for the SKI. The society's business was disrupted by the use of the premises for the holding of judicial tribunals and also as a court of claims. The latter was established to hear the cases of those whose land had been confiscated for the plantations under Cromwell.

The assent of the Catholic King James II to the throne in 1685 heralded an improvement in prospects for Catholics hoping to further their careers. In March 1689 James II came to Ireland, and summoned Parliament to meet at the Kings Inns. This event was shortly followed by the Battle of the Boyne in 1690 where James was defeated by William. The Catholic judiciary who had recently been appointed under James II's reign had their newfound employment cut short, as they were replaced with Protestants by William. The name of the King's Inns was changed once again, this time to 'Their Majesties Inns', in deference to both King William and Queen Mary. The realm of William and Mary saw the commencement of the persecution of Catholics on an unprecedented level, within both the legal profession where Catholics were to be completely excluded and also within society more generally. In accordance with penal legislation introduced from 1692 onwards, lawyers were required to take an oath in court prior to being permitted to practice. Whereas the seventeenth century had seen a decline in the social standing of the English Inns, the residency requirement for prospective Irish barristers was nonetheless rigidly enforced.

The penal age began in earnest with the ascent of Anne to the throne in 1702. The 'Queens Inns' was influential in ensuring that only those who conformed to the established church could practice law. Whilst in the seventeenth century The Society had generally left enforcement of the conformity rules to the judges, in the eighteenth century it assumed a more proactive role in this regard.

---

[62] C Kenny, *King's Inns and the Kingdom of Ireland* (FN 52) 131, citing Dunlop, *Caledonia State Papers Ireland 1647 – 1660* (Commonwealth i 2) 850. For an understanding of the challenges faced by Irish lawyers during this period, see L O'Malley, 'Patrick Darcy: Galway Lawyer and Politician: 1598 – 1668' in D O'Cearbhaill (ed), *Galway: Town and Gown: 1484 – 1984* (Gill & Macmillan, 1984). Born in Galway, Darcy was a prominent lawyer and politician, who was admitted to the Middle Temple, London, in 1617 and joined King's Inns in 1628. He came to public prominence as a result of his involvement in the campaign to prevent confiscation of land and the plantation of Connaught. As a Confederate, he was involved in the struggle for a just peace and an independent Irish Parliament, following the native rebellion of 1641. However, the arrival of Cromwell in 1649 marked an end to his political hopes, and he was declared a person 'liable to death and confiscation of his estates'. Following the Restoration, he was permitted to resume his legal career, but his lands were never restored. He is remembered as a constitutional statesman and untiring patriot.

In 1704 the Irish Parliament enacted a statute 'to prevent the further growth of popery' which established a sacramental test for public office.[63] On foot of this provision The Society devised a new test whereby admittance to the Bar required production of a certificate attesting that its recipient had received communion in the Church of Ireland. The Benchers were fastidious in their duties in this regard, and were known to make enquiries about the religion of applicants and their parents, and also in relation to the frequency of their church attendance. This policy had the effect of reducing membership of the Queen's Inns. It also led to a considerable decline in its finances.

During the sixteenth and seventeenth centuries the exclusion of Catholics from the legal professions and the implementation of the anti-Catholic rules by the SKI served as a crude yet effective gatekeeping instrument, whereby the power and prestige of the legal profession was reserved for an elite group of largely English aristocrats. This had the effect of protecting the incomes of practitioners, as the pool from which prospective lawyers were selected was very small, and given its history of war and civil unrest, Ireland was not a career destination of choice for many aspiring legal professionals of English origin. A rather interesting description of life at the SKI during this period has survived in the form of this account from *The Dublin Weekly Journal* of a day at King's Inns in 1725:

> Thursday last, being St John's day, Patron of the Most Ancient and Right Worshipful Society of FREE MASONS; they met about Eleven O' the Clock, at the Yellow Lion in Warbroughs Street, where there appeared above a 100 Gentlemen. After some time spent, in putting on their Aprons, White Gloves, and other parts of the *Distinguishing* Dress of that Worshipful Order, they proceeded over Essex-Bridge to the Strand, and from thence to King's Inns ... When they came to the [King's] Inns, they marched up to the Great Hall ... After marching round the Walls of the Great Hall, with many important Ceremonies, the *Grand Lodge*, composed of the *Grand Master*, Deputy Master, (who was absent) Grand Wardens, and the Masters and Wardens of all the Lodges, performing the *Mystical Ceremonies* of the *Grand Lodge* which are held so feared, that they must not be discovered to a Private Brother; they proceeded to the Election of a new *Grand Master* ... [T]he Proxy of Senior Grand Warden acquainted the Society, that the *Grand Lodge* had chosen the Rt Hon Earl of ROSS, *Grand Master* for the year ensuing, and Sir *Thomas Prendergrass,* and *Mark Morgan* Esq, Grand Wardens: and that the *Grand Master* had appointed the Hon *Humphrey Buttler* Esq, Deputy *Grand Master*. At the naming of each of these, the Society gave their Approbation, by three Huzzas, then the Officers of the Order, &c. went to the *Grand Lodge Room*, and conducted this new *Grand Master* in great State to the Head of the *Mystical* Table, and Mason King at Arms hung the Gold Trowel by the Black Ribbon about his Neck.[64]

---

[63] 2 Anne c 6 (Ir)

[64] *The Dublin Weekly Journal*, Saturday 26th June 1725. The 1st Earl of Lanesborough, Humphrey Butler, was firstly appointed Deputy Grand Master of the Grand Lodge of Ireland in 1723.

The reigns of George I and George II saw a period of mismanagement and decline at King's Inns.[65] The society lapsed into financial disarray due to non-payment of members' dues and a failure to secure a viable income from rented properties at the Blackfriars site. In 1736 concerns about the veracity of the society's accounts gave rise to a demand on the part of barristers to be permitted to inspect The Society's books. Incredibly, it appears that due to the loss of deeds and the demise of trustees, The Society's entitlement to the grounds upon which the King's Inns was located had become questionable. The remedy sought in the face of this dilemma was the passage of a private act of parliament to rectify the defect in title. The Society was initially unsuccessful in this endeavour in 1743, but a subsequent attempt in 1752 bore fruit, and the trustees and their successors were incorporated to a limited extent under the act, but only in respect of the ownership of the properties at King's Inns. Whilst this gave The Society the power to sell or lease the property on the King's Inns site, the limited nature of its incorporation was to prove problematic when The Society was unable to pursue publishers for breach of the Copyright Act of 1801.[66] Notwithstanding their new powers under incorporation, The Society received no compensation when a large part of its ground was used for the construction of the Four Courts and a new records office. The Society suffered further indignity at the hands of prostitutes and thieves who were rumoured to frequent its chambers during the early famine years of 1740 and 1741.[67] It is not surprising that the Society ceased to provide commons in 1742 given the general demise of its fortunes and property at the time.

The eighteenth century saw a decline in the standards of legal education provided at the English Inns. This was offset to some extent by the emergence of law as a university subject. A chair in the common law of England was established at Oxford in 1758, to be held by William Blackstone, and in 1761 Francis Sullivan was appointed professor of 'feudal and English law at Trinity College Dublin (TCD). During the latter part of the eighteenth century, there was a reduction of the time period for which a prospective Irish lawyer was obliged to reside at the English Inns. Whilst it was still necessary for a prospective member of the SKI to have his name registered with an English Inn five years prior to admittance to the Irish Bar in accordance with the provisions of a 1782 statute, it was possible to comply with the requisite keeping of eight terms of commons within a shorter two year period.[68] This statute also required students to keep a

---

He was also appointed High Sheriff for Co Cavan in 1727 and High Sheriff for Westmeath in 1728, and as a consequence of these positions he was most probably also a member of the Society of King's Inns. Given the HSKI's motto *nolumus mutari*, and also the comments of the Benchers to Desmond O'Malley, Minister for Justice from 1970 – 1973 (ch 1, § 1.2.3.1), the question arises whether similar cavorting might still be expected to occur at King's Inns on St John's day.

[65] George I 1714 – 1727, George II 1727 – 1760

[66] The Copyright Act of 1801 entitled the SKI to receive a free copy of every newly published book. It would appear that various publishers had failed to provide a free copy of newly published books as required under the Act and that the SKI lacked *locus standi* to pursue the matter at law as it was not an incorporated body.

[67] C Kenny, *King's Inns and the Kingdom of Ireland* (FN 52) 173

[68] 21 & 22 Geo III c 32

further four commons, either in Dublin or London. The difficulty posed by the fact that King's Inns had declined to the point where there was no facility to provide commons there was overcome by allowing that the payment of a guinea per term could be made in lieu of the keeping of the four extra commons. The 1782 statute also provided a concession for graduates of Oxford, Cambridge and Trinity College Dublin, who were required to enrol with King's Inns only three years prior to admittance as opposed to the usual five years for non-graduates.

The reduction of the time period which aspiring Irish lawyers had to spend in England may have arisen on foot of a recognition of the lack of rigour in the education and training to be received there, but it may also have reflected a new independence of mind developing amongst Irish Protestants. A programme of legislative reform which was adopted by the Irish parliament in the latter half of the eighteenth century is illustrative of this newfound independence of the Irish judiciary and of the administration of justice in Ireland. However, age-old religious intolerance towards Catholics was still manifest, and the 1782 statute which concerned the regulation of the legal profession professed to exclude Catholics from admittance to King's Inns as students, by confining eligibility for membership to those of the Protestant religion.[69] The introduction of the Stamp Duties Act 1783 provided for the levying of a £5 duty upon admission of a student or barrister to the SKI, and this represented an important source of income to provide for the Society's future financial needs, and in particular, to fund the construction of new premises.[70] The end of the eighteenth century saw the society adopt more rigorous standards of professionalism. In 1790 the Benchers declared that all rules concerning admission to the Society were to be strictly observed. The tightening of professional standards was evidenced by the disbarrment by the council of one barrister for alleged perjury, and the 'vacation' of the call to the bar of an aspiring barrister for unprofessional conduct.[71]

In 1792 the SKI received its royal charter, an event which marked its revival. Under the charter, the judges were to refrain from acting as Benchers, and instead were to become its 'board of visitors' with the power to 'amend, reform and correct every error, evil practice and abuse ...'.[72] The receipt of the charter was swiftly followed by the publication of some controversial bye-laws by the Benchers with the aim of introducing a much more complex and demanding system of education and training for Irish law students. Both the charter and the bye-laws met with an unprecedented level of opposition in the face of which the Benchers found it necessary to revisit their planned reforms. The charter was revoked in 1793 and the proposed bye-laws also lapsed. However, the Benchers did not delay in issuing a modified set of regulations, for the first time in a printed form. These provided for the lodging of a certificate of attendance at one of the English Inns, which indicated performance of the requisite exercises, by those wishing to be admitted to the degree of barrister in Dublin. The new rules

---

[69] Ibid

[70] 23 & 24 Geo III c 3 §§ 1, 12

[71] 'Admission of Benchers 1741 – 1792' (Kings Inns Manuscripts) 156 in C Kenny, *King's Inns and the Kingdom of Ireland* (FN 52) 194 – 195

[72] 'Kings Inns Charter' 6

also provided for the payment of deposits for chambers by all barristers and attorneys. Notwithstanding their frequent subsequent amendments, the rules of the profession concerning entry and education which were set down in 1793 form the basis for the regulatory code for the barristers' profession which survives to the present day.

The last decade of the eighteenth century saw the rise of the United Irishmen, a revolutionary group inspired by the American and French revolutions, and which sought Catholic emancipation and other social reforms. Association with the United Irishmen was sufficient to secure disbarment from the SKI, a fate which befell several members.[73] The Rebellion of 1798 marked the onset of one of Ireland's most terrible outbreaks of violence. The passage of the Acts of Union in 1800 signalled the end of the independence which had been afforded to the Protestant ascendancy in Ireland, elements of which had been instrumental in seeking common cause with Catholics, and which led to the establishment of the United Irishmen.

The Acts of Union brought about the unification of the separate kingdoms of Great Britain and Ireland. The prospect of this unification was not welcomed by the Irish legal profession who feared it would lead to a diminution in status for the Irish courts.[74] Whilst a few Irish barristers were vocal in their opposition to the Union, the Benchers were more circumspect.[75] Their silence was no doubt influenced by the politics of the day, and it is notable that the pro-Union Lord Chancellor Fitzgibbon laid the foundation stone to the present King's Inns building on 1st August 1800, which was also the date upon which the Act of Union received its royal assent.

The first half of the nineteenth century saw political reform in both England and Ireland against an international background of revolution in France and America. The course of Catholic emancipation was championed in Ireland by the barrister Daniel O'Connell. Whilst the right to freedom of worship had been established following the 1782 repeal of the penal laws, political rights proved more elusive. The central argument for the denial of such rights was based upon Catholic allegiance to the pope which was deemed to be at odds with the supreme authority of the Monarch as enshrined in the English Constitution. Many senior figures in the Irish legal profession were vociferous in their objection to Catholic emancipation during this period.[76] In 1829 George IV gave

---

[73] C Kenny, *King's Inns and the Kingdom of Ireland* (FN 52) 259. Thomas Addis Emmet (brother of Robert Emmet) and Arthur O'Connor were disbarred due to their association with the United Irishmen.

[74] The unification of the kingdoms of Great Britain and Ireland would also lessen the chances of prospective members gaining a seat in Parliament, as this goal was easier to attain when the Houses of Commons and Lords sat in Dublin. It would not be so easy to achieve a seat in Parliament at Westminster.

[75] C Kenny, *King's Inns and the Kingdom of Ireland* (FN 52) 261. Daniel O'Connell was the head of a group of Catholic barristers who opposed the Union.

[76] Members of the legal profession who objected to Catholic emancipation during the eighteenth century included Isaac Butt, Patrick Duigenan, William Saurin, Henry Joy, Thomas Lefroy and Francis Blackburne. O'Connell also sought municipal reform in Ireland which would allow Catholics to join corporations and thereby participate in local government, a campaign which was finally successful in 1840 with the introduction of the Municipal Corporations (Ireland) Act

assent to the Roman Catholic Relief Act which permitted Catholics to hold parliamentary seats and high public office. Remaining restrictions on Catholics were limited to the position of monarch and a few high public offices.[77]

The beginning of the nineteenth century saw the SKI concentrate its efforts on its new building project at Constitutional Hill having secured two leases at that location at the end of the eighteenth century. The Constitutional Hill building project appears to have consumed the energy and attention of the SKI and as a consequence by 1866 the Benchers had lost a large measure of the powers they had once exercised over attorneys and solicitors who established their own society, the LSI, in 1850 and which received its royal charter in 1852.[78] A Bar Committee was established in the 1880s, which assumed a representative function on behalf of the Bar, and which lobbied on issues such as the state of courthouses and the need to improve facilities at the Law Library. This was the forerunner of the Bar Council of Ireland (BCI) which was formed in 1897 following a General Meeting of the Bar, the establishment of which took place against a background of disharmony between the members of the Bar on the one hand, and the SKI and its Benchers on the other, and which also served to further erode the status of the SKI as a professional body. The General Meeting of the Bar was constituted by the coming together of practising barristers *en masse* to make decisions on matters of concern to its members. The Bar was of the view that its governing body's constitution was inappropriate and that the SKI was ineffective as a representative body for the barristers' profession. In 1869, barristers were dissatisfied with the proportion of practicing barristers on the bench of the SKI which was considerably less than the prescribed number set down in the Rules of 1793.[79] Initially the Bar Committee focused its energies upon securing improvements in the Law Library, and in representing the Bar in discussions with the Benchers, the LSI and Government bodies. The Committee's lobbying regarding the need to improve library facilities was successful, and following the enactment of the Four Courts Library Act in 1894, a new Law Library was built in 1897 on the site of the Four Courts. The requirement for Irish barristers to attend English Inns of court was finally abolished by statute in 1885.[80]

The BCI was henceforth to be the 'accredited representative of the Bar', with the responsibility to deal with all matters affecting the profession.[81] After a rather slow start, the BCI was reconstituted in 1907, whereupon it adopted a more modern format, with the Attorney General at its head. Rule 2 of the BCI's Regulations set out its functions:

1840. J Hill, 'The Legal Profession and the Defence of the Ancien Regime' 183. In D Hogan & W Osborough (eds), *Brehons, Sergeants and Attorneys* (FN 15)

[77] Ibid 201.

[78] 29 & 30 Vict (1866) c 84

[79] D Hogan, *The Legal Profession in Ireland 1789-1922* (The Incorporated Law Society of Ireland, 1986) 60

[80] 40 & 41 Vict (1866) c 20

[81] D Hogan, *The Legal Profession in Ireland* (FN 79) 65

The Council shall be the accredited representative of the Bar, and its duties shall be to consider and report upon, and to make such representations as may be necessary in all matters affecting the profession, and particularly concerning the conduct and arrangement of the business of the
profession, etiquette and professional practice, the relation between the
Inner and Outer Bars, the relations between the Bar and the Judicial
Bench, right of audience, and claims of the Bar in relation to the maintenance and disposal of offices, legislation, or alterations in the system of
administration, and all the matters in which the Irish Bar is professionally
concerned.[82]

In its early years, the BCI directed its efforts to lobbying on behalf of the profession on issues such as the appointment of non-lawyers as resident magistrates, and the making of rules relating to junior counsel's privileges. The lobbying on the issue of resident magistrates was an attempt to establish reserved
areas of practice for the legal profession. However, the establishment of the BCI
did not replace the General Meeting of the Bar, which provided the BCI with its
mandate to represent barristers and to lobby on their behalf, and which remained the higher authority, with the ultimate power to adopt schedules of
minimum fees. Whilst the General Meeting of the Bar retained the ultimate
authority in many key areas of decision-making, the BCI was assiduous in
endeavouring to protect members' incomes from threats. In 1914 The BCI
objected to Treasury plans to reduce barristers' remuneration for assisting in the
revision of the Electoral Register.[83] In 1908 it also circulated a recommended
scale of fees for conveyancing and High Court work, which when endorsed by a
General Meeting of the Bar in 1920, had the joint effect of reducing price competition and inflating prices for the provision of legal services.

The twentieth century saw further erosion in status for the SKI, as it lost its
unique position as the only Irish Inn of court with the establishment of a second
Inn of court in Northern Ireland. This occurred shortly after the adoption of the
Constitution of the Free State in 1922, whereupon Northern Ireland was established as a separate jurisdiction.

Critical Comments

There has been non-statutory regulation of the bar in Ireland since its origin
470 years ago, and today its regulatory framework remains deeply entrenched in
traditional practices. The judiciary historically played a major role in the regulation of the Irish bar as evidenced by their activities as Benchers in the SKI
whereby judges, along with senior law officers and members of the bar controlled entry to the profession and also the education, conduct and discipline of
barristers. The SKI was a strong conservative force in Ireland and was used as a
tool by the kingdom of England to maintain the aristocratic social order in
Ireland, but given the troubled nature of Irish history during the lifetime of the
SKI, it is clear that the bar was not a particularly effective means of exerting
social control. The SKI was not willing to implement the penal laws, a function

---

[82] Ibid 65
[83] Ibid 66

which was reserved exclusively for the judiciary in the course of their courtroom activities.[84] The fact that the SKI was weaker in terms of its authority and control of the Irish bar than its English counterparts most probably facilitated its manipulation by the English monarchical and executive authorities. Kenny has observed in relation to the SKI that:

> [J]ust as the kingdom of Ireland was never to enjoy complete independence from that of England, so too did the new inn fail to match fully, in the role it came to discharge, the societies that already existed across the Irish sea.[85]

The historical record shows little evidence of an independent bar prior to the establishment of the Irish state, and post-1922, the Irish judiciary have continued to exert a significant level of authority over the functioning of the bar.

1.2 The Key Regulatory Bodies of the Legal Profession in Ireland Today

The regulatory framework of the legal profession in Ireland is both archaic and complex and has undergone little in the way of meaningful reform in the last fifty years. There are various bodies who share responsibility for the regulation of the Irish legal profession. These are illustrated in Diagram 1 and are discussed further below.

1.2.1 The Law Society of Ireland (LSI)

Established in 1830, the LSI has a tripartite role in relation to the regulation of solicitors, having responsibility for the education, regulation and representation of its members. It consists of four departments which are overseen by the Director General.[86] The departments are: Policy Communication and Member Services, Regulation, Education and Finance and Administration.

The Policy Communication and Member Services Department is concerned with the LSI's representative role. Whereas the Council of the Society is charged with setting policy, this department is responsible for its implementation. It also seeks to represent the interests of both the profession and the public in its interaction with the Government and its agencies, the legislature and other professional bodies. It carries out its communication functions by means of the monthly publication of the *Law Society Gazette*, the publication of an 'ezine' (electronic bulletin system), the maintenance of the LSI website and the provision of a library service for solicitors.

The Regulation Department oversees the compliance of members with their statutory obligations. It also administers applications for grants from the Compensation Fund. The Compensation Fund was established in accordance with the Solicitors Act 1954 in order to compensate clients who suffer financial loss

---

[84] C Kenny, *King's Inns and the Kingdom of Ireland* (FN 52) 4
[85] Ibid 3
[86] Mr Ken Murphy is currently the Director General of the LSI

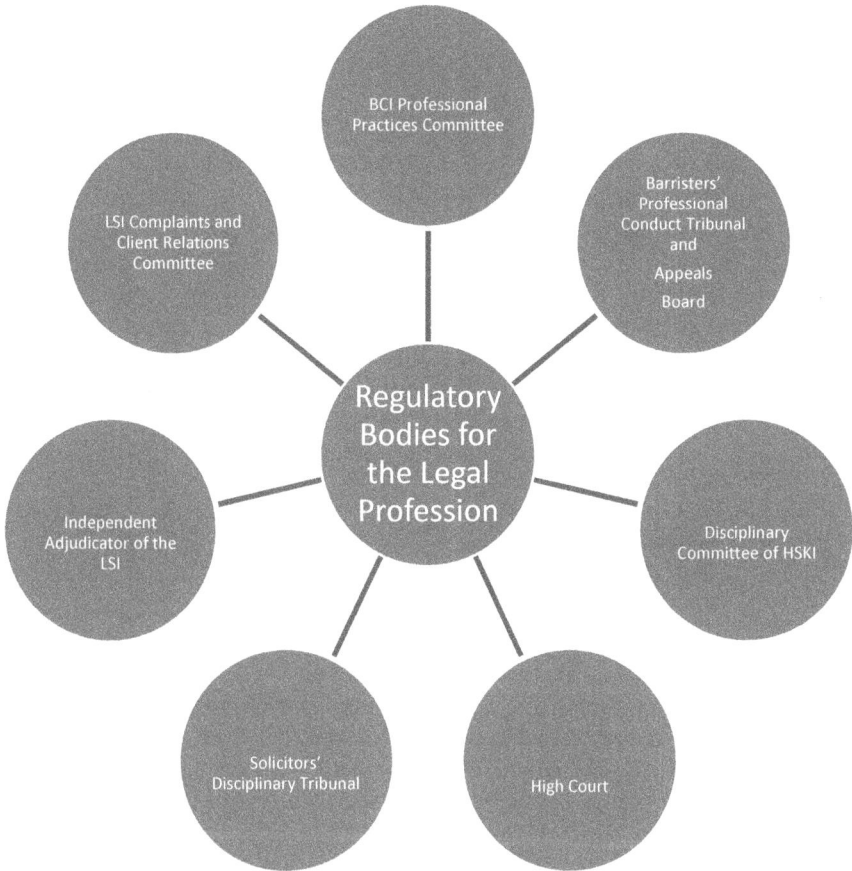

Diagram 1. Key Regulatory Bodies for the Legal Profession in Ireland

due to dishonesty on the part of a solicitor or his/her employees.[87] The Regulation department is also responsible for the investigation of complaints from clients, the public and from solicitors themselves through its Complaints and Clients Relations Committee. Its litigation section ensures that the LSI is represented where necessary in proceedings before the Solicitors' Disciplinary Tribunal and the courts. It is also responsible for the issuance of practising certificates and the orderly closure of practices.

The Education Department has a law school which provides courses for both trainee and qualified solicitors. It also offers a Continuing Professional Development programme for practising solicitors. The Financial and Administration Department oversees the Society's accounts, and is responsible for IT matters. It

---

[87] Solicitors Act 1954 §§ 69, 70 provide for the establishment of the Compensation Fund and for the making of annual contributions by practising solicitors to the Fund.

is also in charge of the LSI's administrative and commercial activities. Its Accounts and Finance sections manage the LSI's financial affairs.

The Council of the LSI consists of thirty-five members, either elected or nominated. It is responsible for the ruling and governance of the LSI. It is also the vehicle which carries out the LSI's statutory functions as set out in the Solicitors Acts 1954 – 2011. Thirteen of the Council members are nominated from amongst the membership of the Law Society of Northern Ireland, the Dublin Solicitors' Bar Association and the Southern Law Association. The remaining twenty-two members are elected from the LSI's countrywide membership. Its key statutory functions concern education, admission, regulation, discipline and client protection. Its work is carried out by various committees, with the standing committees taking care of statutory duties and the non-standing committees looking after non-statutory matters. Recently, the LSI has lobbied strongly for changes to be made to the LSRB 2011.[88]

1.2.1.1 The Complaints and Client Relations Committee (CCRC) of the LSI

The LSI's Complaints and Client Relations Committee (CCRC) may investigate complaints of misconduct, inadequate provision of legal services or the levying of excessive fees on behalf of clients. Where client complaints cannot be resolved by the Complaints and Client Relations Section of the LSI's Regulation Department, they may be referred to the CCRC for investigation. The CCRC consists of both solicitors and lay members with the latter being in the majority.[89] Where there is a finding by the CCRC of provision of inadequate professional services by a solicitor or that excessive fees have been levied, the CCRC may either order a solicitor to reduce or waive a fee, direct a solicitor to rectify an error or deficiency in services or require a solicitor to take any other measure it deems necessary in the client's interest. It may also order a solicitor to make a payment of up to €3,000 towards CCRC investigation costs and that a similar sum be paid to a client where financial or other loss has occurred due to the inadequacy of legal services which were provided. The CCRC may also direct a matter for investigation to the SDT.[90] The CCRC received 2,813 new complaints in 2012 of which 2,453 were deemed to be admissible. 85% of admissible complaints concerned allegations of misconduct, with allegations of inadequate professional services and excessive fees forming 11% and 4% of complaints respectively.[91] The most common areas of work giving rise to allegations of

---

[88] D Binchy, 'Serious Concerns' (2012) 106 (4) LSG 1. The LSI's lobbying in relation to the LSRB 2011 has met with some success, with the Minister for Justice indicating a willingness to make some amendments in line with the society's recommendations. In particular; the Bill will be amended to provide for the introduction of limited liability partnerships and corporate entities for solicitors' practices. There will be amendments to ensure the independence of the new Legal Services Regulatory Authority and to permit the LSI to maintain control over the operation of the compensation fund. For more information and a full discussion of the LSRB 2011 and the response of the professional bodies to its publication, see ch 5 § 5.3.

[89] Annual Report of the Independent Adjudicator of the Law Society of Ireland (2012) 7. Available at: <http://www.independentadjudicatior.ie/pdfs/independent-adjudicatio-annual-report.pdf> Accessed 20/5/2013

[90] Ibid 7

[91] Ibid 12

overcharging concerned litigation, matrimony and conveyancing.[92] Complaints about delay, shoddy work and failure to adequately communicate with clients formed the basis for most claims of inadequate provision of professional services. 83% of complaints of solicitors' misconduct concerned breaches of undertakings.[93]

1.2.1.2 The Independent Adjudicator (IA) of the Law Society of Ireland

The Office of IA was established by statutory instrument in 1997.[94] The Independent Adjudicator (IA) of the LSI has responsibility to ensure that complaints about solicitors are dealt with by the LSI efficiently and effectively. She is also responsible for reviewing the manner in which claims to the LSI Compensation Fund are dealt with and for making recommendations for changes to the LSI's system for responding to complaints and claims. The IA has the power to direct the LSI to re-examine its response to a complaint or to make an application to the SDT. She may also require the LSI to re-examine its decision regarding an application to its Compensation Fund. She does not have authority to award compensation to aggrieved clients. Last year the IA examined 132 complaints the majority of which concerned conveyancing, civil or probate matters.[95]

1.2.1.3 Solicitors Disciplinary Tribunal (SDT)

The Solicitors Disciplinary Tribunal (SDT) is an independent statutory tribunal which is appointed by the President of the High Court.[96] The SDT's function is to consider complaints of solicitors' misconduct. Such complaints may be brought directly to the SDT by a solicitor's client, or alternatively the CCRC of the LSI may make an application to the SDT in respect of alleged misconduct of one of its members.[97] The SDT is comprised of thirty members, twenty of whom are solicitors of at least ten years' experience in practice and ten lay members who are neither solicitors nor barristers. The SDT sits in panels of three members with a two thirds majority of solicitors being maintained on each panel.[98] Upon receipt of an application for an inquiry into alleged misconduct of a solicitor, with an accompanying affidavit setting out the basis of the complaint, the SDT decides if a *prima facie* case for the holding of an inquiry has been made out. The SDT forwards a copy of the complaint and affidavit to the LSI and the respondent solicitor. The respondent solicitor may file a response in affidavit

---

[92] Ibid 13

[93] Ibid 15

[94] Solicitors (Adjudicator) Regulations 1997 (SI 406/1997) and Solicitors (Adjudicator) (Amendment) Regulations 2005 (SI 770/2005)

[95] Annual Report of the Independent Adjudicator of the Law Society of Ireland (2012) 27

[96] The SDT is constituted in accordance with the provisions of the Solicitors (Amendment) Act 1960 § 6, as substituted by the Solicitors (Amendment) Act 1994 § 16, amended by the Solicitors (Amendment) Act 2002 § 8, as cited in the Civil Law (Miscellaneous Provisions) Act 2008 § 35.

[97] SDT 'About the Tribunal'. Available at: <www.distrib.ie> Accessed 20/5/2013

[98] Given that the Tribunal has a two thirds majority of solicitor members, its claim of being 'wholly independent' from the LSI lacks credibility. See Solicitors Disciplinary Tribunal Annual Report (2008) 1. Available at: <www.distrib.ie/documents/Solicitors_Disciplinary_Tribunal _CM508.pdf> Accessed 20/5/2013

form. The SDT decides on the basis of the documentation whether there is a *prima facie* case for an inquiry, and where this is established the parties are notified accordingly. The Tribunal has the power to subpoena witnesses to hear oral evidence and also for the purposes of cross-examination.[99] Upon conclusion of the inquiry the SDT will consider the evidence and record its findings regarding each specific complaint which the applicant raised. Where no misconduct is found, the applicant has a right of appeal to the High Court. Where the SDT finds there has been misconduct, it may make an order either to advise, admonish or censure the respondent solicitor, or it may direct the payment of up to €15,000 to the LSI Compensation Fund. It may also direct that the costs of any party including the LSI be paid by the respondent solicitor. In appropriate cases the SDT may refer its findings to the High Court with recommendations to either suspend or strike off the respondent solicitor from the Roll of practicing solicitors.[100] Summaries of the SDT's findings are published in the *Law Society Gazette*.[101]

1.2.1.4 President of the High Court

Following High Court receipt of a SDT report in relation to solicitors' misconduct, such report to be brought before the High Court by the LSI, the High Court may exercise its jurisdiction over a solicitor in several ways. [102] It may strike the solicitor's name from the roll, suspend the solicitor for a specified period, prohibit him/her from acting as a sole practitioner or partner, restrict him/her from acting in particular areas of work or censure him/her and require payment of a sum of money.[103] The High Court may also require a solicitor to disclose all information concerning accounts held in his/her own name, jointly with third parties or in that of his/her firm, to make restitution to third parties as the Court thinks fit or direct a solicitor to refrain from representing himself/herself as being a solicitor or from holding himself/herself out as being connected with his/her former practice without Court permission.[104] The nature of the High Court jurisdiction over the practice of solicitors was explored in the

---

[99] 'A Guide to Applicants on How to Make an Application to the Solicitors Disciplinary Tribunal for an Inquiry into Alleged Misconduct of a Solicitor'. Available upon Request from the Solicitors Disciplinary Tribunal, The Friary, Bow Street, Smithfield, Dublin 7.

[100] The Tribunal requires an applicant to establish his/her case to the criminal standard of proof, beyond all reasonable doubt (*The Law Society of Ireland v Andrew Walker* unreported, 21st July 2006 HC). This is somewhat stringent as in many cases the wrongdoing complained of falls more naturally within the civil realm, such as minor breaches of accounting regulations.

[101] Solicitors Disciplinary Rules. Rule 59 requires publication of both SDT orders and case summaries. Available at: <www.distrib.ie/documents/Solicitors_Disciplinary_Tribunal_Rules_2003.doc> Accessed 20/5/2013

[102] Such report from the SDT to the HC to be made in accordance with the provisions of the Solicitors (Amendment) Act 1960 § 7 as substituted by the Solicitors (Amendment) Act 1990 § 17 as amended by the Solicitors (Amendment) Act 2002 § 9

[103] Solicitors (Amendment) Act 1960 § 8 (1) (a) (i) (I) – (V), as substituted by Solicitors (Amendment) Act 1994 § 18 and amended by Solicitors (Amendment) Act 2002 § 10

[104] Solicitors (Amendment) Act 1960 § 8 (a) (iii), (c) (i) (viii), as substituted by Solicitors (Amendment) Act 1994 § 18 and amended by Solicitors (Amendment) Act 2002 § 10

case of *Re O'Farrell and the Solicitors Act 1954*, discussed further below.[105]

1.2.2 The Bar Council of Ireland

Established in 1897, the BCI has twenty-five members, twenty of whom are elected members and four of whom are co-opted members. The head of the BCI is the Attorney General. The twenty elected members are chosen by the Law Library, membership of which is compulsory for barristers and is almost synonymous with practice at the Bar.[106] The BCI's current functions have been described as follows;

> The Bar Council sets and enforces professional standards for barristers. The Council is also responsible for admitting people to the Bar. The leader of the Irish Bar is the Attorney General. It is a private, non-statutory body.[107]

The BCI presently has a predominantly representative role with respect to barristers but it also exercises a degree of regulatory authority. It also plays a role in relation to the education of barristers as evidenced by its Continuing Professional Development Programme and its link with the Law Library which it operates.

Complaints from fellow members of the Bar regarding a barrister's conduct are considered by the BCI's Professional Practices Committee (PPC), whilst complaints regarding a barrister's conduct from a member of the public, a solicitor or a client are considered by an independent body, the Barristers Professional Conduct Tribunal (BPCT).

1.2.2.1 The Professional Practices Committee (PPC) of the BCI

The PPC was established in accordance with the Disciplinary Code of the BCI and follows a non-binding resolution procedure for complaints relating to barristers' conduct which are made by fellow barristers or members of the judiciary.[108] Where the PPC considers it appropriate to so do it may refer a matter to the BPCT for investigation and adjudication.[109] Information relating to the adjudication of complaints is shared between the PPC and the BPCT.

---

[105] [1961] 95 ILTR 167. The case of *O'Farrell* is discussed further in ch 1 § 1.3.2, § 1.3.3.1 and § 1.3.3.2

[106] *Murdoch's Dictionary of Irish Law* 'Bar Council'. Available at: <http://milcnet.lendac.ie/NXT/gateway.dll/02dict-30.nfo/01v00706.htm/1lv00768.htm> Accessed: 21/4/2012

[107] Department of Taoiseach. *Bodies in Ireland with Regulatory Powers as of February 2007.* (Better Regulation Unit. February 2007) 54 Available at: <http://www.taoiseach.gov.ie/attached_files/Pdf%20files/Bodies%20in%20Ireland%20with%20Regulatory%20Powers.pdf > Accessed 22/3/2012

[108] 'The Disciplinary Code of the Bar Council of Ireland adopted by a General Meeting of the Bar of Ireland on Monday 5th July 2010' para A4. Available at: <http://www.lawlibrary.ie/viewdoc.asp?fn=/documents/barristers_profession/disciplinarycode.htm&m=3> Accessed 21/5/2013

[109] The Barristers Professional Conduct Tribunal Annual Report (2012) 5. Available upon request from The Secretary, Barristers Professional Conduct Tribunal, 145/146 Church Street, Dublin 7

*1.2.2.2 The Barristers Professional Conduct Tribunal (BPCT) and the
Barristers Professional Conduct Appeals Board (BPCAB)*

The BPCT was established in 1996 by a General Meeting of the Bar in order to investigate and adjudicate upon complaints of misconduct against barristers.[110] It is authorised to receive complaints from members of the public, the BCI and also the PPC of the BCI and it has a lay majority. Appeals of its decisions may be made to the Barristers' Professional Conduct Appeals Board (BPCAB).[111] The aim of the BPCT is to uphold the BCI's Code of Conduct and to ensure adherence to proper professional standards.[112] The BPCT has the power to either uphold or reject a complaint, or alternatively to recommend mediation between the parties. It also has the power to admonish barristers, to issue fines, order the repayment of fees to clients, suspend membership of the Law Library or remove a barrister from the register of practising barristers for a specified term or until a specified act has been performed.[113] In 2012 the BPCT dealt with one hundred new cases, the most common complaint concerning the following matters:

- Undue pressure to settle or compromise
- Delays with paperwork
- Not following instructions
- Conflict of interest
- Serious rudeness (*sometimes good advice robustly delivered*)
- Improper cross examination (*this charge is often made against the opposing barrister but the Tribunal points out that the complainant's own barrister should bring it to the attention of the Judge if it is so bad*)
- Excessive fees (*for the taxing master, not the Tribunal except where there has been serious overcharging*)
- Knowingly misleading the court (*allegation often made against the opposing barrister*).[114]

Since 2007 the BPCT has made a total of fifteen findings of misconduct against one or more barristers. Fines to the value of €30,000 have been issued and the total period of suspensions made since then was thirty months. Since 2007 two recommendations for disbarment were made to the Disciplinary Committee of the HSKI.[115]

---

[110] The Tribunal has nine members from whom panels of three are selected to hear complaints from members of the public or the BCI.

[111] The Barristers Professional Conduct Appeals Board was also established by a General Meeting of the Bar Council of Ireland in 1996. Its constitution and procedures are governed by 'The Disciplinary Code of the Bar Council of Ireland adopted by a General Meeting of the Bar of Ireland on Monday 5th July 2010' paras E, F. (FN 108)

[112] The Barristers Professional Conduct Tribunal Annual Report (2012) 1 (FN 104)

[113] Ibid 2

[114] Ibid 3

[115] Ibid 1

1.2.3 The Honorable Society of Kings Inns (HSKI)

Barristers in Ireland today are regulated by the HSKI as well as the BCI. The HSKI is comprised of members of both the judiciary and the bar. Entry of barristers into the profession is controlled by the HSKI. Holders of an approved law degree are eligible to apply for the Degree of Barrister-at-law. A list of approved degrees is available on the HSKI website.[116] Those without an approved degree must obtain a Diploma in Legal Studies from the HSKI, and will then be eligible to apply for the Degree of Barrister-at-Law. The HSKI therefore also plays a significant role in the education of prospective barristers.

Until recently, only one barrister had been struck off for professional misconduct by the Benchers of the HSKI in its entire 470 year history.[117] However, on the 11th of January 2012, the HSKI disbarred Patrick Russell, who was found guilty of "disgraceful acts of professional misconduct". It was found that Mr Russell had behaved in a manner which was fundamentally dishonest from beginning to end. He deceitfully accepted money for services he had not provided, having created a fictitious Supreme Court appeal and lied to his client, falsely claiming he had received offers in settlement of the client's claim. However, following *O'Farrell* it would appear that the HSKI ruling concerning Mr Russell is unconstitutional on the grounds that disbarment is an administrative act of justice which should be reserved to the judiciary. [118]

1.2.3.1 Disciplinary Committee of the HSKI and the Special Meeting of the Bench

> As Minister for Justice … I asked the representatives of the Benchers of the Kings Inns to come and see me but they refused. I continued to send requests and finally after about six months they deigned to come. Two elderly gentlemen arrived and I said my piece to them for five or ten minutes. They told me they had received their charter and motto from Queen Anne in 1703 which reads *nolumus mutare*. They said, in case I was not a Latin scholar, that it could be read transitively or intransitively. It meant that they were unwilling to change and unwilling to be changed. As far as they were concerned I could take it either way because they would not change and would continue for the next 250 years as they continued for the last.[119]

The above comments of Deputy O'Malley aptly illustrate the staunchly guarded independence of the Benchers of the HSKI who sit on the Disciplinary Committee (DC) as far as their regulatory functions are concerned. The rules relating to the constitution, powers and procedures of the DC of the HSKI are contained in

---

[116] The website may be accessed at: <http://www.hski.ie> Accessed 1/6/2012

[117] See ch 1 § 1.1.4 for a discussion of this case.

[118] *Re O'Farrell and the Solicitors Act 1954* (FN 105). See ch 3 § 3.2.1 for a discussion of *O'Farrell* and the constitutional issues it raises in relation to the Disciplinary Committee of the HSKI, The *O'Farrell* case is also discussed in ch 1 § 1.3.2.

[119] Solicitors (Amendment) Bill 1994 (Second Stage Resumed) *Dáil Debates* 23rd Mar 1994 Vol 440 (5) Cols 1210 – 1211. Deputy O'Malley

the General Rules of the HSKI.[120] The DC was established in order to inquire into complaints of professional misconduct on the part of barristers.[121] It may receive complaints from the BCI, BPCT or the BPCAB.[122] The DC is composed of three judicial Benchers.[123] The DC itself determines the procedures to be adopted by it and these shall be in accordance with the requirements of constitutional and natural justice.[124] The DC makes a decision upon a case by case basis in relation to the need to hold an oral hearing regarding a particular complaint and may elect to hear evidence either orally, by means of live video link, by video recording or other mode of transmission.[125] Barristers who are the subject of a complaint before the DC may elect to be legally represented in the course of the DC proceedings which are held in private.[126] The DC has authority to direct a barrister to make a written apology to an individual or to advise him/her in relation to conduct.[127] The DC may also admonish or censure a barrister, impose the payment of a fee or order its return by a barrister or impose a fine to be paid to the BCI.[128] Following a finding of professional misconduct the DC may also suspend a barrister from practice or disbar him/her.[129] Where the DC makes a finding of professional misconduct, it submits a report of its findings to the Benchers; a transcript is available from the Under Treasurer for inspection upon request.[130]

Where a barrister is the subject of a Report of the DC he/she may within three weeks of the date of the decision against him/her apply for the convening of a special meeting of the Benchers seeking cancellation of the decision.[131] All Benchers are notified of such a special meeting and twelve shall form a quorum, with decisions being made by a two thirds majority.[132] The special meeting shall be held in accordance with the requirements of constitutional and natural justice. Where cancellation of the DC decision is not sought, the DC Report shall

---

[120] Rules 30 – 38 of the General Rules of the Honorable Society of Kings Inns pertain to the Disciplinary Committee. Available at:
<http://www.kingsinns.ie/website/current_students/diploma/pdfs/Rules%2030%20-38.pdf>
Accessed 23/5/2013

[121] The General Rules of the Honorable Society of Kings Inns Rule 31 (1)

[122] Ibid Rule 32 (1)

[123] Ibid Rules 31 (2). The Disciplinary Committee has jurisdiction to hear complaints relating to barristers notwithstanding the fact that they are no longer members of the Law Library or the HSKI. Ibid Rule 31 (5)

[124] Ibid Rule 33 (1)

[125] Ibid Rule 33 (4)

[126] Ibid Rule 33 (9) and (10)

[127] Ibid Rule 34 (b) (i) (ii)

[128] Ibid Rule 35 (1)

[129] Ibid Rule 35 (2). The Order for disbarment is in the following form: 'That ____ be removed from the Register of Members and be expelled from the Honorable Society of Kings Inns and be prohibited from practice as a barrister and from enjoyment of all rights and privileges granted to him or her by virtue of being a barrister and be prohibited from holding himself/herself out as being a barrister and that ____ be hereby disbarred." (Rule 35 (2) (ii))

[130] Ibid Rule 34 (3), (5)

[131] Ibid Rule 36 (1))

[132] Ibid Rule 36 (6), (7)

be confirmed by the Benchers in the absence of good reasons to the contrary.[133] Thus the ultimate jurisdiction to disbar lies with the Benchers rather than the DC. Decisions to either disbar or suspend barristers shall be published either on a website maintained by the HSKI or other suitable publication.[134] Notices in respect of complaints of professional misconduct which have been confirmed by the Benchers are sent to senior judiciary, the Attorney General, the Chairman of the BCI, the President of the LSI and any other appropriate persons.[135] The jurisdiction of the DC of the HSKI extends to European lawyers who are registered to practice in Ireland as advocates.[136] The General Rules of the HSKI excluding Rules 30 to 38 are private and are not available for public perusal, the author having been refused access to same from the HSKI.[137]

1.3 The Main Regulatory Instruments of the Irish Legal Profession

Diagram 2 shows the main regulatory instruments of the Irish legal profession to be considered in this section.

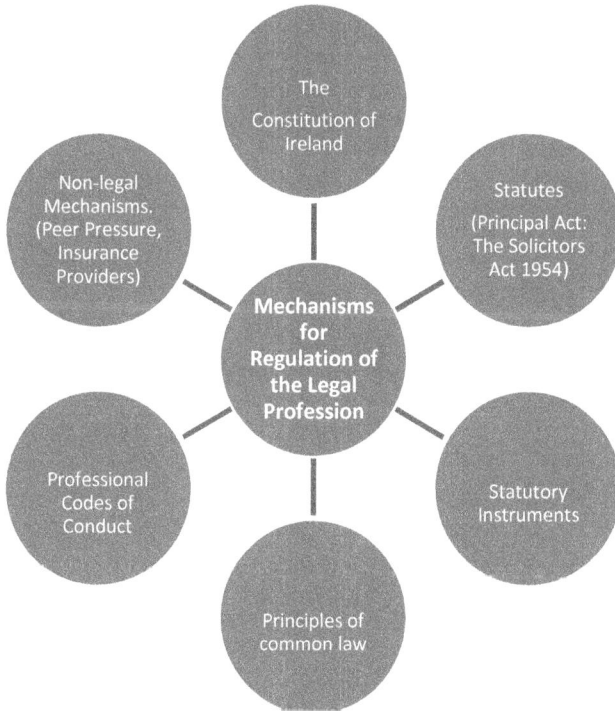

Diagram 2. The Main Regulatory Instruments for the Irish Legal Profession

[133] Ibid Rule 36 (11)

[134] Ibid Rule 37 (3)

[135] Ibid Rule 37 (4)

[136] Ibid Rule 38 (1), (2) In accordance with the provisions of the EC (Lawyers' Establishment) Regulations 2003 Regulation 6 (3) (b)

[137] Email from Under Treasurer of HSKI to Author (23rd May 2013)

The principles of common law pertaining to the practice of law are a well-established source of regulatory authority for both branches of the legal profession. The Constitution of Ireland has also significantly impacted upon the regulation of the legal profession, particularly in the case of *Re O'Farrell*, in which the Supreme Court held that due to the severity of the consequences which accompanied the striking of a solicitor from the roll, the exercise of such a power was judicial in nature, and should not be entrusted to those outside of the judiciary.[138]

The solicitors' profession is also regulated in part by statutes and statutory instruments, whilst the Bar is currently regulated only by non-statutory mechanisms.[139] However, the enactment of the LSRB 2011 will finally put the regulation of the Bar on a statutory basis. The enactment of The Solicitors Act 1954 consolidated the LSI's position as the key regulatory and representative entity for the solicitors' profession in Ireland, and represented an important milestone for the LSI which had long sought such statutory recognition. The position of the Bar with regard to statutory regulation is somewhat more complex. Whilst on the one hand, the BCI has been vociferous in its objections to the LSRB 2011, on the other hand the HSKI has been silent with regard to the contents of the Bill, no doubt due to the fact that the judiciary who constitute a significant part of the HSKI cannot be seen to try to exert influence upon the workings of either the executive or legislative arms of the state, without infringing the doctrine of separation of powers. Finally, the professional codes of conduct for each branch of the profession play a part within the overall regulatory framework which applies to the Irish legal profession today.

1.3.1 The Influence of the Common Law on the Regulation of the Legal Profession

The legal profession is governed by the principles of common law, which have had a considerable role in shaping modern practice. The bulk of the case law relates to solicitors, probably as a result of their direct contractual relationship with clients. Many aspects of a solicitor's privileges, rights and responsibilities have been the subject of judicial scrutiny. In *Mulligan v Corr* it was held that public policy required the maintenance of the highest possible standards of "conduct and honour" even if this resulted in the restriction of membership of the profession.[140] A solicitor has a dual role; as an officer of the court he/she has duties and responsibilities to assist the court in the proper administration of

---

[138] *Re O'Farrell and the Solicitors Act 1954* 167 (FN 105)

[139] 750 *Dáil Debates* 582 (16 December 2011). Alan Shatter stated that the Government would not be appointing anyone to the office of Legal Services Ombudsman. The non-statutory nature of the Bar's regulatory framework was altered in theory by the enactment of the Legal Services Ombudsman Act 2009 which made provision for the appointment of an Ombudsman with powers to oversee both branches of the profession. However, no one has actually been appointed to the position of Ombudsman, and the provisions of the 2009 Act have been rendered largely superfluous with the publication of the LSRB 2011, following which the Minister of Justice subsequently abandoned plans for the appointment of a Legal Services Ombudsman

[140] [1925] 1 IR 169. For a full account of the common law regulation of solicitors, see P O'Callaghan, *The Law on Solicitors in Ireland* (Butterworths 2000)

justice, and he/she also has a duty to advocate on behalf of his/her client.[141] The Superior Courts may exercise summary, inherent jurisdiction over solicitors as court officers in order to control misconduct and to prevent the contempt of court.[142] The contract of retainer has been considered at common law, and it has been established that an estoppel may arise in respect of a client who seeks to deny that a solicitor is his/her agent where he/she has allowed or acquiesced in a representation to that effect.[143] A solicitor may terminate a retainer where a client does not defer to his/her judgment regarding the best way to conduct a case.[144] Common law principles have also been established regarding the manner in which a contract may be terminated, either by a solicitor or a client. It was held in *The People (DPP) v Healy* that the court's permission is necessary for the termination of a retainer with a client who is being held in custody.[145] However, a client may dismiss his/her solicitor if he/she so wishes, and the solicitor is entitled only to receive reasonable costs and disbursements for services provided in those circumstances.[146]

The solicitor-client relationship is governed by the principles of both contract and agency. A solicitor's authority is limited to the extent of a client's express and implied instructions.[147] There also exists a fiduciary relationship between a solicitor and client which demands that the solicitor always acts with good faith, in the client's interests, and that all matters within the solicitor's knowledge pertaining to the client's retainer must be disclosed to the client.[148] The solicitor's duty of confidentiality to a client arises on foot of the fiduciary relationship.[149] The rules of privilege permit free communication between a solicitor and client and are necessary to protect the confidential nature of that relationship, in the interests of the proper administration of justice.[150] The privilege attaches to communications occurring either during the course of a retainer or with a view to its establishment. The privilege, which is that of the client, extends beyond the conclusion of the retainer.[151]

Where a conflict of interest arises between a solicitor and client or between two clients of a solicitor in the context of a non-contentious matter, a solicitor may sometimes be able to select which of the clients he/she wishes to continue to represent and which must seek independent advice. Good professional prac-

---

[141] *Lloyd v Nagle* (1747) 1 Dick 129

[142] In *Marsh v Joseph* [1897] 1 QB 217, compensation was awarded by the Court to a person who had suffered loss as a result of a solicitor's misconduct. In *Re K* (minors) (Incitement to Breach of Orders) [1992] 2 FLR 108, a solicitor incurred liability for aiding and abetting another person in a contempt of court.

[143] *Culhane v O'Maoileoin* HC unrep 17 November 1988. It was held by Murphy J that a retainer had arisen due to acquiescence in the issuance of legal proceedings.

[144] *Chance v Tanti* (1901) 35 ILTR 126, 127, Fitzgibbon LJ.

[145] [1990] 2 IR 73, Finlay CJ

[146] *Re Lane Joynt* [1920] 1 IR 228

[147] *Gordon v Gordon* [1904] P 163

[148] *Mouat v Clarke Boyce* [1994] 1 AC 428

[149] *McMullen v Carty* Supreme Court unreported 28th January 1998

[150] *Duncan v Governor of Portlaoise Prison* [199] 1 IR 558, Kelly J

[151] *Sheehan v McMahon* SC unreported 29th July 1993, Egan J

tice requires both clients to have independent legal advice on the issue before proceeding.[152] Where a solicitor wishes to do business with a client or a former client, an extremely high standard is required, and he/she must act in an open and fair manner. There will be a presumption of undue influence where a solicitor enters into a transaction with a client.[153] It is prohibited in any circumstances for a solicitor to benefit from his/her fiduciary relationship with a client, even where no particular regulation has been breached.[154]

An undertaking is a promise made during a retainer to act in a specified fashion, and its binding nature extends to promises given by members of a solicitor's staff.[155] A solicitor is personally liable for the failure to abide by the terms of an undertaking, even where the undertaking was given on behalf of a client. The court can exercise its summary jurisdiction over a solicitor as an officer of the court, to secure performance of an undertaking.[156]

In the course of a retainer, a solicitor may owe a range of different duties to a client, such duties arising upon the basis of either contract or tort law. In other circumstances a fiduciary or restitutionary duty may arise. The nature of the duty owed in a particular case may vary in accordance with the level of a client's experience. Concurrent duties in tort and contract may also arise.[157] The solicitor's primary duty to a client is based upon the contract which contains an implied term that services will be provided with reasonable skill, care and diligence.[158] Where breach of a fiduciary duty is established, the right to a fee is forfeited. Where tortious liability is established on the part of a solicitor who is a partner in a firm, the principles of joint and several liability apply.[159]

The standard of care which must be met by a solicitor was set out in *Roche v Pellow*:

> [A] person cannot be said to be acting reasonably if he automatically and mindlessly follows the practice of others when by taking thought he would have realised the practice in question was fraught with peril for his client and was readily avoidable or remediable. [160]

A solicitor must ensure he/she is acquainted with the real nature of a client's problem, rather than unquestioningly following a client's instructions, and all reasonable enquiries should be made prior to offering legal advice.[161] Where a solicitor professes to have expert skills, a higher standard of care should apply

---

[152] In the context of a conflict of interest relating to a contentious matter, good professional practice requires the solicitor to decline to act for either client. Rule 1.2 *A Guide to Professional Conduct of Solicitors in Ireland* (LSI 2002)

[153] *Wright v Carter* [1903] 1 Ch 27 (CA)

[154] *Boardman v Phipps* [1967] 2 AC 46

[155] *Young v Power* (1862) 14 Jur 388

[156] *United Mining and Finance Corporation Ltd v Becker* [1910] 2 KB 296; 303

[157] *Henderson v Merrett Syndicaes Ltd* [1994] 1 AC 428

[158] Sale of Goods and Supply of Services Act 1980 § 39

[159] Partnership Act 1890 § 12

[160] [1986] ILRM 189; 196

[161] *McMullen v Farrell* [1993] 1 IR 163

than that of a reasonably competent solicitor.[162] Particular difficulties may arise in relation to conveyancing, given the complexity of the conveyancing system. A duty of care in the tort of negligence may arise in respect of a client vendor, and also in respect of a third party purchaser. A solicitor must ensure that the client understands the exact nature of the title being purchased.[163] Prima facie, there will be a breach of duty for omission to recommend an independent inspection by a qualified person of a prospective purchase property.[164] The usual principles of remoteness and causation apply to actions for negligence; a plaintiff must show that the breach of duty caused the damage complained of and that the damage was reasonably foreseeable as likely to occur in the circumstances of the particular breach of duty.

The relative lack of case law concerning the regulation of barristers in comparison to the amount of case law concerning solicitors is accounted for by a barrister's immunity from suit in the performance of courtroom duties and in the preparation of litigation, as a duty of care is not owed by a barrister to his/her client in these contexts.[165] The immunity is justified on the grounds that it permits a barrister to perform his/her duty in an independent manner, and also to discharge his/her higher duty to the court.[166] Furthermore, if clients were permitted to sue their barristers it would have the effect of prolonging litigation, which would not be in the public interest. There is also the fact that a suit in negligence being taken by a client against his/her barrister would open up the possibility of a collateral attack upon the judgment of the court, and such uncertainty could bring the administration of justice into disrepute.[167] In *Saif Ali v Sydney Mitchell & Co (a firm)* the extent of the advocate's immunity was considered, and it was held that it did not include a failure to advise a client to sue a potential defendant within the limitation period. However, this case saw the advocate's immunity extended to include a solicitor advocate. Following *Hall v Simon* the House of Lords moved away from the total immunity from suit in relation to the conduct of litigation which advocates enjoyed.[168] The reason for the departure from the principle established in *Rondel v Worsley* was that the immunity was not compatible with the provisions of Article 6 of the European Convention on Human Rights. Following *Hall*, it may be argued that whereas an advocate owes a duty of care in negligence to a client, the nature of the duty owed is tempered by his/her duty to assist the client in the administration of justice.[169] It is not certain to what extent the Irish courts will follow the House of Lords' decision in *Hall*, however the comments of Fennelly J in *Beatty v Rent Tribunal* are notable, where he observed that, 'formerly, barristers enjoyed

---

[162] *Duchess of Argyll v Beuselinck* [1972] 2 Lloyd's Rep 172

[163] In *Tuohy v Courtney* [1994] 3 IR 38, it was held to be negligent of a solicitor to fail to explain to a client he was acquiring a leasehold title rather than a freehold title.

[164] *O'Connor v First National Building Society* [1991] ILRM 204

[165] *Rondel v Worsley* [1969] 1 AC 191

[166] Ibid 231 – 232

[167] *Saif Ali v Sydney Mitchell & Co (a firm)* [1980] AC 198 at 222 – 223 Ld Diplock

[168] *Hall (Arthur JJ) & Co v Simons* [2000] 3 All ER 673

[169] B Mc Mahon & W Binchy, *The Law of Torts* (3rd ed Tottel Publishing, 2005) 402

complete immunity from suit by their clients in respect of their conduct of proceedings.'[170] Also, in *W v Ireland (No 2)* a duty of care was not imposed in relation to the discharge of advocacy functions.[171]

It is clear from the significant body of case law which has been amassed over the last two hundred and fifty years that the common law is an important means of regulating the practice of legal professionals by clarifying the circumstances under which a lawyer owes a duty of care to either a client or a third party and also by establishing the boundaries of what constitutes the provision of a reasonable level of service. Whilst in recent years the Client Compensation Fund which is administered by the LSI has reduced the necessity for some aggrieved clients to litigate in order to obtain redress for losses arising as a result of a solicitor's dishonesty, the limited nature of the scheme means that the courts will continue to play a key role in the regulation of legal practice for the foreseeable future.[172]

1.3.2 The Constitution of Ireland

The Constitution of Ireland, the nation's supreme legal instrument was adopted in 1937 and reflects both European and American liberal democratic constitutional traditions.[173] It provides for the exercise of legislative powers by a democratic parliament, the exercise of executive powers by a democratic government and the exercise of judicial powers by an independent judiciary.[174] The constitutional provisions concerning the exercise of judicial powers have impacted significantly upon the regulation of the legal profession having been cited by the Supreme Court in order to justify the undermining of legislative attempts to place the regulation of solicitors on a statutory footing.

In the case of *Re O'Farrell*, the Supreme Court reversed the decision of Maguire CJ and held that in striking the names of Mr O'Farrell and his co-appellant and partner in legal practice Mr O'Gorman from the roll of solicitors, the Law Society's Disciplinary Committee was exercising a judicial power.[175] Maguire also held that the Committee's powers which were conferred upon it by the Solicitors Act 1954, were powers of a limited nature within Article 37 of the Constitution, and that the 1954 Act was not repugnant to the Constitution. In accordance with section 18 of the Solicitors Act 1954, the Disciplinary Committee had the power to strike a solicitor from the roll where the Committee found that he/she had been guilty of professional misconduct. A client of Mr O'Farrell and Mr O'Gorman made a complaint to the Law Society in relation to financial wrongdoing, alleging that they had withheld monies which should rightfully

---

[170] 2 IR 191, 212

[171] [1997] 2 IR 141 (HC)

[172] Compensation from the LSI Compensation Fund up to €700,000 is available to clients who have suffered losses as a result of a solicitor's dishonesty (Solicitors (Amendment) Act 1960 § 21 (6), as amended by Solicitors (Amendment) Act 1994 § 22, as amended by Solicitors (Amendment) Act 2002 § 16 (a).

[173] The 1937 Constitution of Ireland replaced the 1922 Constitution of the Irish Free State. Preface, The Constitution of Ireland (Government Publications Sale Office, Dublin).

[174] Ibid. Preface, The Constitution of Ireland.

[175] *Re O'Farrell and the Solicitors Act 1954* (FN 105)

have been paid to the client. The two solicitors failed to cooperate with the Society's inquiry into the matter, nor did they attend the enquiry, or arrange for a representative to do so on their behalf. Following the enquiry, the Disciplinary Committee ordered that Mr O'Farrell and Mr O'Gorman's names should be struck from the roll, and it was this decision which was upheld upon appeal to the Chief Justice in the High Court.

Article 34.1 of the Constitution of Ireland states:

> Justice shall be administered in courts established by law by judges appointed in the manner provided by this Constitution, and save in such special and limited cases as may be prescribed by law, shall be administrated in public.

Furthermore, Article 37 of the Constitution of Ireland states:

> Nothing in this Constitution shall operate to invalidate the exercise of limited functions and powers of a judicial nature, in matters other than criminal matters, by any person or body of persons duly authorised by law to exercise such functions and powers, notwithstanding that such person or such body of persons is not a judge or a court appointed or established as such under this Constitution.

In delivering the judgment of the Supreme Court, Kingsmill Moore J described the key legal point at issue to be whether the Disciplinary Committee's powers involved the 'administration of justice' which did not fall within the saving provisions of Article 37 concerning, 'the exercise of limited functions and powers of a judicial nature'. He observed that the decisions of the Disciplinary Committee

> ... may determine the guilt or innocence of persons charged with offences against a code not indeed directly imposed by the State but recognised and authorised by it primarily in the interest of its citizens, and may inflict severe penalties for breaches of it, and may determine in a final manner rights and obligations in dispute between parties, which determination will be enforced by the authority of the State.... The decisive test in the opinion of the Court lies in the orders which by *section 18* the Committee is empowered to make... [The Committee] may order the making by the solicitor of such restitution or satisfaction to any aggrieved party as the committee may think fit. [T]he Court is unable to distinguish the power given to the Committee from the power given to a Court.... It seems to the Court that the power to strike a solicitor off the rolls is, when exercised, an administration of justice, both because the infliction of such a severe penalty on a citizen is a matter which calls for the exercise of the judicial power of the State and because to entrust such a power to persons other than judges is to interfere with the necessities of the proper administration of justice.[176]

The Supreme Court ruled that the far-reaching nature of the Disciplinary Committee's powers were not 'limited', and thus could not be saved by Article 37 of

---

[176] *Re O'Farrell and the Solicitors Act 1954* (FN 105) 167 Kingsmill Moore J

the Constitution. The Committee's powers were therefore unconstitutional, and the right to appeal its decisions to the Chief Justice was insufficient to restore their constitutionality.

The Supreme Court's ruling in *O'Farrell* gave rise to the necessity for further legislation to remedy the constitutional defects of the 1954 Act, and accordingly, the Solicitors (Amendment) Act 1960 was enacted. The 1954 and 1960 Acts together provided the basis for the regulation of the solicitors' profession for a generation of practitioners.[177]

The citing of the Constitution of Ireland in *O'Farrell* has effectively fettered the self-regulatory powers of the legal profession and deprived the solicitors' branch of the profession of the power to remove a solicitor's right to practice. The *O'Farrell* ruling has arguably had a similar fettering effect upon the HSKI regarding the right to disbar a barrister. However, the position with regard to barristers has never been tested in the courts given the extreme reluctance of the HSKI to disbar its members from practice under any circumstances. Whilst the Disciplinary Committee of the HSKI is partially comprised of judiciary, its judicial members arguably are not engaged in 'the administration of justice' when considering disciplinary cases before the Committee, as the administration of justice is a function which is exclusively confined to the precincts of the Courts. In *O'Farrell*, the Constitution of Ireland was interpreted in a manner which removed control over its membership from the LSI, and in this regard the decision arguably damaged the integrity and standing of the legal profession in the public eye.

In the later case of *Re Solicitors Act 1954, and D, a Solicitor*, a distinction was made between the temporary suspension of a solicitor and his/her striking off from the roll.[178] The former penalty which was issued by the Disciplinary Committee of the LSI was amenable to an appeal to the Chief Justice, and although the Supreme Court reversed the order of Maguire CJ in the case, it did not see fit to consider the constitutional aspects of the suspension decision.[179] According to Hogan and Whyte, in subsequent cases involving Articles 34 and 37 of the Constitution, it is possible to detect a degree of judicial unhappiness with the Solicitors' Act 1954 test as enunciated in *O'Farrell*, with some cases seeking to confine the ruling in *O'Farrell* to its particular facts, and other cases declining to apply *O'Farrell* by analogy.[180] For instance, in *Keady v Garda Commissioner*, O' Flaherty J reasoned that the test should be strictly limited in its application.[181] O'Flaherty J distinguished the facts in *Keady* from *O'Farrell* on the grounds that the former involved the removal of a person's employment, whereas the latter involved the removal of a qualification.

---

[177] D Hogan, 'The Society from Independence to 1960' in E Hall & D Hogan (eds), *The Law Society of Ireland* 96 (FN 40)

[178] (1961) 95 ILTR 60

[179] G Hogan & G Whyte, *J M Kelly: The Irish Constitution* 4th ed (LexisNexis Butterworths, 2003) para 6.4.90

[180] Ibid, para 6.4.96

[181] [1992] 1 IR 197. Ibid, para 6.4.98.

1.3.3 Legislation and Statutory Instruments

As far as the regulation of the solicitors' profession is concerned, the key statutory development of the last sixty years was the introduction of The Solicitors Act 1954 (which is referred to in subsequent amending legislation as the Principal Act, reflecting its central role in the regulation framework), which contains the most fundamental provisions regarding the regulation of the solicitors' profession.[182] The 1954 Act also had the effect of repealing earlier statutes which pertained to the regulation of the profession. The other main statutes concerning the regulation of the profession are the Solicitors (Amendment) Act 1960, The Solicitors (Amendment) Act 1994, the Solicitors (Amendment) Act 2002, the Civil Law (Miscellaneous Provisions) Act 2008 and the Civil Law (Miscellaneous Provisions) Act 2011.[183] The Legal Practitioners (Irish Language) Act 2008 and the Legal Services Ombudsman Act (LSOA) 2009 have also been enacted. Table 1 contains a brief description of the key legislative measures for the regulation of the legal profession and legal services in Ireland which are also described in more detail below.

Table 1. Key Legislative Provisions for the Regulation of the Legal Profession

Solicitors Act 1954	The Principal Act for the regulation of solicitors' admission to the profession, and also their enrolment and professional conduct
Solicitors (Amendment) Act 1960	An Act to amend the constitutional flaw in section 18 of the 1954 Act concerning the power of the LSI Disciplinary Committee to strike a solicitor from the roll, and to enhance the protection of the public from the activities of dishonest solicitors
Solicitors (Amendment) Act 1994	An Act providing for the advertisement of solicitors' services, to increase LSI powers to investigate complaints against solicitors and to impose sanctions for the levying of excessive fees
Solicitors (Amendment) Act 2002	An Act to improve the regulation of advertising by solicitors especially with regard to personal injuries claims and to facilitate lawyers' freedom of establishment within the EU
Civil Law (Miscellaneous Provisions) Acts 2008 and 2011	Part III of the 2008 Act referred to solicitors. It increased the availability of apprenticeships and classified the levying of excessive charges as professional misconduct. Section 58 of the 2011 Act increases the power of the Registrar of the LSI in responding to complaints of solicitors' misconduct
Legal Practitioners (Irish Language) Act 2008	An Act to promote the better use of Irish amongst solicitors and barristers and to enhance the provision of legal services in Irish
Legal Services Ombudsman Act 2009	The 2009 Act provided for the establishment of an Office of Legal Services Ombudsman responsible for independent investigation of complaints concerning both solicitors and barristers

---

[182] Henceforth referred to as the 1954 Act.

[183] Henceforth referred to as the 1960, 1994, 2002, 2008 and 2011 Acts respectively.

1.3.3.1 The Solicitors Act 1954

The 1954 Act provided for the admission, enrolment and control of solicitors and other connected matters. Its enactment followed a lengthy process of scrutiny and debate of a private Bill which was firstly brought forward in 1942 by the LSI, and which was later adopted by the Government as part of its legislative reform proposals. It is clear from the Oireachtas debates that there was a considerable amount of unanimity amongst members across the political spectrum regarding the proposed legislation. This was reflected in the remarks of the then Taoiseach, Mr John Costello who stated; 'I think I can say that complete agreement has been reached on a variety of topics and on the Bill as a whole between the Present Government and Incorporated Law Society'.[184] These sentiments were largely shared by the opposition of the day, as evidenced by the comments of Mr Boland, who joined him in paying tribute to the "public spirit" of the LSI in introducing the proposed legislation. The reason for this somewhat unusual level of cross party consensus regarding the regulation of the profession may arguably be found in the concluding remarks of the Taoiseach in the Oireachtas debate on the Bill of 24th November 1954 where he stated that; 'All my colleagues here on the Front Bench at the moment, with the exception of the Attorney-General are all ex barristers for the moment at any rate'.[185]

The 1954 Act gave The Law Society power to make regulations generally in relation to any matter referred to in the Act, the purpose of such regulations being to implement the provisions of the Act.[186] These regulations were to be laid before the Oireachtas as soon as possible after the making thereof.

Part II of the 1954 Act contained provisions concerning both the Registrar of solicitors and the roll of solicitors. It provided for the appointment of a Registrar who was responsible for compiling a register of solicitors.[187] The conditions for admission and enrolment were set out whereby an application for admission as a solicitor was to be made to the Chief Justice, and following this, an application could then be made to the Registrar to have one's name entered on the roll.[188]

Part III of the 1954 Act concerned the Disciplinary Committee and established the rules for the appointment of its members.[189] It prescribed the nature of applications which could be made to the Disciplinary Committee, including an application by a solicitor to remove his name from the roll, or an application by another person or the Society to strike a solicitor's name from the roll, or an application alleging misconduct, including conduct which would tend to bring the solicitors' profession into disrepute.[190] It outlined the procedure which the Disciplinary Committee had to follow where a charge was made against a solicitor.[191] Where there was a *prima facie* case against the solicitor

---

[184] 147 *Dáil Debates* 993 (24 November 1954)

[185] 147 *Dáil Debates* 1018 (24 November 1954)

[186] Solicitors Act 1954 § 5 (1)

[187] Solicitors Act 1954 §§ 8, 9

[188] Solicitors Act 1954 § 10

[189] Solicitors Act 1954 § 13

[190] Solicitors Act 1954 § 14

[191] Solicitors Act 1954 § 16

concerned, the Disciplinary Committee required the solicitor to send an affidavit and any supporting documents to the Disciplinary Committee within a specified time. It described the orders the Disciplinary Committee could make, including the dismissal of an application, the admonishment of a solicitor, suspension from practice, removal or striking off from the roll, payment by a solicitor of a party's costs and the making of restitution to an aggrieved party, where the Disciplinary Committee considered it appropriate.[192] It was the provisions of section 18 of the 1954 Act concerning the power of the Disciplinary Committee to strike off a solicitor from the roll which gave rise to the successful challenge to its constitutionality in the *O'Farrell* case.[193] The 1954 Act gave the Disciplinary Committee power, with the Chief Justice's concurrence, to make rules regulating applications to the Disciplinary Committee and it set out the filing, effect and notice of an order of the Disciplinary Committee.[194] It provided for the publication in *Iris Oifigiúil* of an order to either remove or strike off a solicitor from the roll. The Registrar was obliged to keep two specified files. File A was to contain the names of all those solicitors who had been removed or struck off by the Disciplinary Committee. File B was to contain a list of all other orders of the Disciplinary Committee.

Part IV of the 1954 Act concerned requirements for qualifying for admission as a solicitor or as an apprentice including the need for evidence of good character.[195] It also set out the rules relating to indentures and their registration, assignment, discharge and transfer, and the requirement to serve a bona fide apprenticeship. The Act also prescribed details of education, examination and associated matters, in relation to solicitors and apprentice solicitors.[196]

Part V of the Act set out the rules regarding applications for Practice Certificates and their issuance. It outlined the circumstances where a direction to refuse a Practice Certificate may arise, for instance; where over twelve months had passed since the solicitor held a Practice Certificate which was in force or where a period of suspension from practice had expired.[197] A Practice Certificate might also be refused where the applying solicitor was a person in respect of whose person or property any provision of either the Lunacy Regulation (Ireland) Act 1871, or any amending or extending Act of the 1871 Act, relating to the management and administration of property might apply. A direction to refuse a Practice Certificate might also arise where a solicitor failed to give the LSI an explanation in respect of a matter concerning conduct, having been invited to so do, where an order of attachment was made against a solicitor or where he/she had been adjudicated bankrupt.

Part VI of the 1954 Act concerned practice and set out the necessary qualifications for acting as a solicitor.[198] The solicitor's name must be on the roll.

---

[192] Solicitors Act 1954 § 18

[193] *Re O'Farrell and the Solicitors Act 1954* (FN 105)

[194] Solicitors Act 1954 §§ 20, 21

[195] Solicitors Act 1954 §§ 24, 25, 27

[196] Solicitors Act 1954 §§ 40 – 44

[197] Solicitors Act 1954 § 49

[198] Solicitors Act 1954 § 54

He/she must not have been suspended from practice and must have been either in the full-time service of the state or have held a practice certificate which was in force. The 1954 Act prohibited an unqualified person from acting as a solicitor, and provided for up to two years' imprisonment upon indictment, or, for up to six months' imprisonment upon summary conviction, and it also prohibited the drawing of documents by an unqualified person, except in certain circumstances, including; where such work was done at no cost, or where the work was performed either by a barrister or a public officer acting in the course of his/her duty.[199] It provided that where a solicitor acted whilst not qualified to so do then no costs were recoverable.[200] The Act also prohibited the employment by a solicitor of a person who had been struck off the roll, or suspended from practice, except with the express permission of the LSI.[201]

Part VII of the Act set out the rules regarding solicitors' accounts and provided for the introduction of regulations, with the concurrence of the Chief Justice regarding the opening and keeping of accounts by solicitors for client or trust money; the keeping of accounts by solicitors with particulars of monies received, held or paid by the solicitor either for or on account of clients, or held by a solicitor on a trust basis.[202] It also allowed for clients or those persons with interests in a trust to have priority of claims to clients' monies, over the State or any other person.[203] Part VIII of the Act concerned the Compensation Fund which was to be established for the benefit of clients who had incurred loss due to a solicitor's dishonesty, and set out the conditions whereby contributions to the fund were to be made.[204] Finally, Part IX of the Act allowed for the making of regulations regarding the professional practice, conduct and discipline of solicitors.[205]

1.3.3.2 The Solicitors (Amendment) Act 1960

The 1960 Act which amended the 1954 Act was enacted as a result of the judiciary's willingness to permit 'extra-judicial' regulation of the solicitors' profession to only a limited extent. That is to say, the judiciary carefully preserved their exclusive right to exercise their 'judicial' power to strike a solicitor from the roll. The legislative reform in the shape of the 1960 Act was necessary as a result of the Supreme Court decision in *O'Farrell*, where the provision in section 18 of the 1954 Act which permitted The Disciplinary Committee of the LSI to strike off an errant solicitor was rendered unconstitutional on the basis that the LSI could not exercise such a 'judicial function' which was the sole preserve of the judiciary.[206]

---

[199] Solicitors Act 1954 § 55, 58

[200] Solicitors Act 1954 § 57

[201] Solicitors Act 1954 §§ 58 – 60

[202] Solicitors Act 1954 § 66

[203] Solicitors Act 1954 § 68

[204] Solicitors Act 1954 §§ 69, 70. The Fifth Schedule to the Act contained provisions relating to the Compensation Fund, and set out the conditions under which grants could be made, at the discretion of the LSI.

[205] Solicitors Act 1954 § 71

[206] *Re O'Farrell and the Solicitors Act 1954* (FN 105)

A second aim of the 1960 Act was to strengthen the protection of the public from the actions of dishonest solicitors. In the Debate on the Second Reading of the Solicitors (Amendment) Bill in Dáil Éireann on 26th October 1960, the possibility of a dishonest solicitor working in conjunction with a dishonest accountant was considered by Deputy Ryan and Mr Haughey, the Minister for Justice. When it was suggested by Deputy Ryan that there was nothing in the proposed legislation to protect the public from the harm which such an unfortunate partnership could cause, his concerns were dismissed by the Minister who observed, 'There is no such thing as a dishonest accountant'.[207] However, this assertion was rejected by Deputy Ryan who observed that many accountants had a fondness for "codding" the income tax authorities. He also called for the dishonesty of a solicitor regarding a client's funds to be made a criminal offence which should carry a mandatory minimum penalty of a least seven years' penal servitude. Deputy Ryan observed, 'If that were on the statute books, the very small minority who are inclined to disregard their obligations to their clients might think twice before doing so'.[208] It is notable that the Minister proceeded to reject the Deputy's proposal to allow for unannounced accountant's inspections of solicitors' records, which he dismissed as, 'almost a form of police supervision' of an honest and honourable profession.[209]

Part II of the 1960 Act contained provisions regarding the Disciplinary Committee and allowed for its establishment by the President of the High Court, to consist of between seven and ten members.[210] Either a member of the public or the LSI could apply for an inquiry by the Disciplinary Committee into alleged misconduct by a solicitor.[211] The Disciplinary Committee would bring a report before the High Court where it found misconduct had occurred, and the Committee could indicate its opinion regarding a solicitor's fitness to practice. The 1960 Act permitted the High Court, upon consideration of the report from the Disciplinary Committee, to make orders including the following: striking the solicitor's name from the roll; suspending a solicitor from practice for a specified period; censuring a solicitor or imposing a monetary fine.[212] The High Court could also order the solicitor to make restitution to an aggrieved party. Furthermore, it could direct that no bank could, without its leave, make any payment out of a bank account in the name of a solicitor or his firm. The High Court also had power to restore the name of a solicitor to the roll where he/she had previously been struck off by High Court order.[213]

The 1960 Act gave the Disciplinary Committee powers, rights and privileges vested in the High Court for the purposes of their inquiries to be held in accordance with the provisions of the Act.[214] The Disciplinary Committee could enforce

---

[207] 184. *Dáil Debates* 144 (26 October 1960)

[208] Ibid 145

[209] Ibid 156

[210] Solicitors (Amendment) Act 1960 § 6

[211] Solicitors (Amendment) Act 1960 § 7

[212] Solicitors (Amendment) Act 1960 § 8

[213] Solicitors (Amendment) Act 1960 § 10

[214] Solicitors (Amendment) Act 1960 §§ 7, 9, 15

the attendance and examination of witnesses under oath, and it could compel the production of documents. It provided for the filing of High Court and District Court orders, and for the publication of a notice in *Iris Oifigiúil* where an order of the Disciplinary Committee concerned the striking off or suspension of a solicitor.[215]

Part III of the Act referred to the control of solicitors' property. It provided for the compensation of clients in certain cases and gave the LSI power to require production or delivery to a person of their appointment, all or any documents in the possession or control of a solicitor or his firm, where it was of the opinion that either a solicitor or his/her clerk or servant had been guilty of dishonesty in connection with the solicitor's practice, or a trust of which the solicitor was trustee.[216] It gave the LSI power to take control of solicitors' bank accounts where they were satisfied there had been dishonesty in a practice.[217] The Act also provided for compensation from the Compensation Fund for loss caused by the dishonesty of a solicitor, his/her clerk or servant.[218] Finally, it provided for contributions to be made by solicitors to the Compensation Fund prior to issuance of practice certificates.[219]

1.3.3.3 The Solicitors (Amendment) Act 1994

In its initial form, the Solicitors (Amendment) Bill of 1994 promised to introduce far-reaching reform in the provision of legal services through the opening up of the conveyancing market to solicitors employed as in-house lawyers by banks and financial institutions. However, these pro-consumer measures were abandoned following concerted pressure from a powerful legal lobby in Dáil Eireann.[220] The 1994 Act contained wide ranging provisions to amend and extend the 1954 and 1960 Acts including the granting of power to The Society to admit as an honorary member any person whom it so wishes.[221] Ultimately however, the most controversial aspect of the 1994 Act was its provision for the advertising of solicitors' services where such advertising would not bring the profession into disrepute, be in bad taste, reflect unfavourably on other solicitors, be false or misleading or be contrary to public policy.[222] This relaxation of the strict prohibition upon the advertising of legal services was credited with encouraging the growth of a 'compensation culture' in Ireland and giving rise to the undesirable practice of 'ambulance chasing' by less scrupulous members of the solicitors' profession.[223]

---

[215] Solicitors (Amendment) Act 1960 § 17

[216] Solicitors (Amendment) Act 1960 § 19

[217] Solicitors (Amendment) Act 1960 §§ 19, 20

[218] Solicitors (Amendment) Act 1960 § 21

[219] Solicitors (Amendment) Act 1960 § 22

[220] 440 (5) *Dáil Debates* 1197 (Deputy Allen)

[221] Solicitors (Amendment) Act 1994 Preface, §§ 4, 6

[222] Solicitors (Amendment) Act 1994 § 69 (3), (4) (a) – (g)

[223] 156 (13) *Dáil Debates* 1092 – 1093 (15th October 1998). Deputy Connor stated; '[A] small section of the profession engaged in aggressive advertising of the worst possible type. The phrase "ambulance chasing" entered into common use'.

Part III of the 1994 Act referred to the investigation of complaints and granted power to the LSI to investigate complaints against solicitors and to take various remedial measures, including placing a limit on the amount of costs if any, which a solicitor may claim in respect of the provision of legal services.[224] The LSI was permitted to require a solicitor to rectify at either his own or his firm's expense any error, omission or other deficiency arising in connection with the legal services which were provided by his/her practice. It was granted powers to impose sanctions on solicitors who were deemed to have charged excessive fees in respect of legal services and to require a solicitor to produce for inspection any documents in his/her possession or control, where there had been a complaint concerning misconduct, the provision of inadequate legal services or overcharging.[225] The Minister for Justice was empowered to require the LSI by means of regulation, to establish, maintain and fund a scheme allowing for the investigation of complaints against the LSI by an independent adjudicator.[226] The 1994 Act also specified the conditions in accordance with which the High Court may restore to the roll the name of a solicitor who has been struck off, having been involved in an act or acts of dishonesty and it required the LSI to annually publish general information on the number and nature of complaints it received, and also to publish the outcome of the investigations of the SDT in respect of any complaints which it may refer to the SDT.[227]

Part IV of the 1994 Act contained provisions for the protection of clients including a requirement that solicitors must obtain professional indemnity cover.[228] There was also provision for the compensation of clients who have incurred loss due to a solicitor's dishonesty, and for the making of contributions by solicitors to the Compensation Fund.[229] The 1994 Act also contained various requirements regarding qualification for admission as a solicitor and the issuance of practising certificates, their suspension, and the imposition of conditions upon their issuance.[230]

1.3.3.4 The Solicitors (Amendment) Act 2002

The 2002 Act amended the 1954 to 1994 Acts, and placed restrictions on the nature of advertising by solicitors regarding personal injury litigation following the scandal of 'Army Deafness' claims.[231] This was a series of almost seventeen thousand personal injury claims arising from hearing loss caused by inappropriate protective equipment being issued to army personnel, which commenced in

---

[224] Solicitors (Amendment) Act 1994 § 8

[225] Solicitors (Amendment) Act 1994 § 9, 10

[226] Solicitors (Amendment) Act 1994 § 15

[227] Solicitors (Amendment) Act 1960 § 10, as amended by Solicitors (Amendment) Act 1994 §§ 19 and 22

[228] Solicitors (Amendment) Act 1994 § 26

[229] Solicitors (Amendment) Act 1994 §§ 29 & 30

[230] Solicitors (Amendment) Act 1994 Parts V & VI

[231] J Drennan, 'Army deafness saga finally nears an end: Over €100 m paid out in legal fees since first claims 20 years ago', *Independent.ie,* 24th January 2010. Available at: <http://www.independent.ie/irish-news/army-deafness-saga-finally-nears-an-end-2665717.html> Accessed 6/6/2013

1990 and continued until 2010. The Army Deafness claims resulted in approximately €100 million being paid to lawyers which amounted to over a third of the total costs arising from these claims.[232] The 2002 Act also facilitated practice of the solicitors' or lawyers' profession throughout the European Economic Area and the Swiss Confederation.[233]

The 2002 Act explicitly stipulated the information which may be contained in a solicitor's advertisement, which is the name, address, phone number, facsimile number, place or places of business and details of electronically accessible information concerning services provided by a solicitor.[234] Also, details of a solicitor's professional qualifications may be given along with factual information regarding the services he/she provides and the areas of law to which those services relate, such information being subject to further restrictions contained in the Act.[235] Advertising in inappropriate locations, or which refers to personal injury claims, their outcome or the provision of services in relation to such claims, is prohibited.[236]

The 2002 Act also set out conditions to be considered by the LSI in considering whether to withdraw a practice certificate, including the nature and number of complaints against the holder of the certificate.[237] It identified the conditions to be complied with by a solicitors' practice upon attendance there by an Authorised Person from the LSI.[238] It allowed for the establishment of the SDT by the President of the High Court and set down the conditions under which the SDT could hold an enquiry.[239] The 2002 Act also provided for the implementation of Directive 98/5/EC which required EU member state lawyers practising in Ireland to take out professional indemnity insurance and to contribute to the Compensation Fund.[240]

1.3.3.5 Civil Law (Miscellaneous Provisions) Acts 2008 and 2011

The Solicitors Acts 1954 to 2002, Part III of the Civil Law (Miscellaneous Provisions) Act 2008 and section 58 of the Civil Law (Miscellaneous Provisions) Act 2011 are collectively referred to as The Solicitors Acts 1954 to 2011.[241] In its initial form, the Civil Law (Miscellaneous Provisions) Bill of 2006 provided for the appointment of a Legal Services Ombudsman whose role would be to inves-

---

[232] Ibid. The total cost of the Army Deafness claims was approximately €288 million.

[233] Preface to the 2002 Act.

[234] Solicitors (Amendment) Act 2002 § 4 (3) (a)

[235] Solicitors (Amendment) Act 2002 § 4 (5)

[236] Solicitors (Amendment) Act 2002 § 4 (3) and 3 (2) (f), (h)

[237] Solicitors Act 1954 § 44 (1) as amended by Solicitors (Amendment) Act 2002 § 2

[238] Solicitors Act 1954 §§ 66, as amended by Solicitors (Amendment) Act 2002 § 3

[239] Solicitors (Amendment) Act 1960 § 6 (1), as amended by Solicitors (Amendment) Act 2002 §§ 8, 9

[240] Solicitors (Amendment) Act 2002 § 20. Directive 98/5 EC of the European Parliament and of the Council of 16 February 1998 to facilitate practice of the profession of lawyer on a permanent basis in a Member State other than that in which the qualification was obtained [1998] OJ L 77/36

[241] The Civil Law (Miscellaneous Provisions) Act 2011 § 1 (7)

tigate complaints of solicitors' and barristers' misconduct.[242] However, the provisions relating to the Ombudsman were removed prior to the Bill's enactment to a separate Bill which was exclusively devoted to the establishment of the Office of Legal Services Ombudsman.[243] The remaining provisions of Part III of the 2008 Act were introduced in response to the revelation that many solicitors had overcharged victims of institutional abuse for legal services which had been provided in relation to the pursuit of their cases through the Residential Institutions Redress Board.[244]

Part III of the 2008 Act made various minor amendments to the preceding Solicitors Acts. It reduced the period of full-time practice necessary to have been undertaken from five to four years, following which a solicitor may take an apprentice.[245] It also provided for a greater degree of participation for non-lawyers on Committees of the Law Society.[246] It explicitly acknowledged the constitutional rights of solicitors and apprentices being investigated by the LSI in respect of alleged professional misconduct, and limited the effect of legislation relating to its investigative powers in order to avoid conflict with such constitutional rights.[247] The 2008 Act also empowered the LSI to make recommendations to the High Court regarding the question of a solicitor's fitness to practice, and the SDT's recommendations regarding appropriate sanctions in relation to findings of misconduct.[248] It provided for compensation to be paid to a client up to the amount of €3,000 where it has been established that they have suffered loss due to the provision of inadequate professional services, such amount to be increased by the Minister for Justice in accordance with the rate of inflation.[249] It explicitly acknowledged that the charging of excessive costs may constitute misconduct, and provided for complaints to be made to the LSI by its Registrar where he/she is of the view that a solicitor has acted in a manner tending to bring the profession into disrepute.[250]

Finally, Part III of the 2008 Act referred to contractual terms purporting to limit a solicitor's civil liability to a client, and it provided that such limitation cannot fall below the minimum level of cover as specified by the LSI in the

---

[242] 624 (5) *Dáil Debates* 1697, 1705 (5th October 2006)

[243] 658 (1) *Dáil Debates* 63 (1st July 2008)

[244] 624 (5) *Dáil Debates* 1702 (5th October 2006)

[245] Solicitors Act 1954 § 29, as inserted by Solicitors (Amendment) Act 1994, § 44, as amended by The Civil Law (Miscellaneous Provisions) Act 2008 § 33

[246] Solicitors Act 1954 § 73, as amended by Solicitors (Amendment) Act 1994, § 7, as amended by The Civil Law (Miscellaneous Provisions) Act 2008 § 34 (3) (b), (4A)

[247] Solicitors (Amendment) Act 1960, § 6A, as inserted by The Civil Law (Miscellaneous Provisions) Act 2008 § 36

[248] Solicitors (Amendment) Act 1960 § 8, as inserted by Solicitors (Amendment) Act 1994 § 18, as amended by Solicitors (Amendment) Act 2002 § 10, as amended by The Civil Law (Miscellaneous Provisions) Act 2008 § 37 (b)

[249] Solicitors (Amendment) Act 1994 § 8, as amended by The Civil Law (Miscellaneous Provisions) Act 2008 § 39 (a) (b)

[250] Solicitors (Amendment) Act §§ 14A, 14B as amended by The Civil Law (Miscellaneous Provisions) Act 2008 §§ 41, 42

Professional Indemnity Insurance Regulations.[251] Finally, section 58 of the Civil Law (Miscellaneous Provisions) Act 2011 confers broader powers upon the Registrar of the LSI in responding to complaints of solicitors' misconduct and in bringing these to the attention of the LSI for further investigation.

1.3.3.6 Legal Practitioners (Irish Language) Act 2008

The main aim of the Legal Practitioners (Irish Language) Act was to enhance the knowledge of Irish amongst legal practitioners and to improve the provision of legal services in Irish. It provided for the establishment of registers to be maintained by both the HSKI and the LSI to assist the general public in identifying legal professionals who are capable of providing legal services in Irish, and also for the introduction of courses to increase the proficiency of legal practitioners when providing legal services in Irish.

1.3.3.7 The Legal Services Ombudsman Act (LSOA) 2009

In 2008, the rationale for the appointment of a Legal Services Ombudsman was described by Dermot Ahern, Minister for Justice as follows:

> The Government is anxious that regulation of the legal professions is improved and strengthened. The enactment of this Bill, in addition to existing forms of oversight, will ensure that the highest standards are maintained in the legal professions. The provisions in this Bill for an independent review of the operation of the legal professions' complaints system by way of the legal services ombudsman is the way to proceed, consistent with the need for better regulation.[252]

The aim of the Legal Services Ombudsman Act (LSOA) 2009 was to provide for a new instrument to regulate the legal professions, which would rectify the shortcomings of the existing system that was perceived to lack efficacy as a result of its emphasis upon self-regulation.[253] The LSOA 2009 provided for the establishment of the Office of Legal Services Ombudsman and allowed for the appointment of an individual to that office.[254] It set out the functions of the Ombudsman which were to receive and investigate complaints about members of the legal profession.[255] He/she was also required to review the complaints handling procedures of both the LSI and the BCI. The Ombudsman had all the requisite powers to enable performance of his/her duties and was to be independent in carrying out his/her official functions.[256]

---

[251] Solicitors (Amendment) Act 1994 § 26A, as amended by The Law (Miscellaneous Provisions) Act 2008 § 44

[252] 644 (4) *Dáil Debates* 791 (28th May 2008), Minister for Justice, Mr Dermot Ahern

[253] 656 (1) *Dáil Debates* 47 (29th May 2008). Deputy Connaughton: 'Up to now the legal profession has been self-regulated and it is obvious that this has not worked'.

[254] Legal Services Ombudsman Act 2009 Part II

[255] Legal Services Ombudsman Act 2009 § 9

[256] Legal Services Ombudsman Act 2009 §§ 9 (2), 10.

Unfortunately, no appointment was ever made to the office of Legal Services Ombudsman on the basis that the provisions of the Legal Services Regulation Bill 2011 if enacted, will provide an alternative, improved system for the investigation of complaints concerning the legal profession.[257] Given that the LSRB 2011 provides for the repeal of the Legal Services Ombudsman Act 2009, no further consideration of its provisions are warranted.

1.3.3.8 Statutory Instruments

Statutory instruments (SIs) allow for the appropriate regulation of legal practice in light of the prevailing professional and economic climate. The LSI is empowered to introduce SIs, the adoption of which are subject to Ministerial approval.[258] They govern all the key areas of legal practice such as the requisite standards to be met by prospective entrants to the profession, the level of apprentices' examination fees and the requirements for solicitors to obtain professional indemnity insurance (PII) cover. Over one hundred and fifty regulations in the form of statutory instruments have been brought into effect since the 1954 Act came into force. Table 2 contains a sample of the statutory instruments which have been adopted over the last sixty years and it illustrates the role which they have played and continue to play in the regulation of solicitors' practice.

Table 2. Some Key Statutory Instruments for the Regulation of Solicitors

Solicitors Act 1954 (Apprentices Fees) Regulations 1954, Solicitors Act 1954 (Apprenticeship and Education) Regulations 1955 (SI 300/54, 171/68)	Established the level of apprentices' examination fees. Specified areas of law to be included in the Preliminary Examination for Apprentices
Solicitors Acts 1954 (Professional Practice, Conduct and Discipline) Regulations 1955 (SI 151/55)	Requirements for the charging of specific rates by solicitors for the performance of certain tasks
Solicitors Accounting Regulations 1984 (SI 204/84 and 304/84)	Procedures to be followed by solicitors when handling client or trust funds and for the recording of transactions
Solicitors (Advertising) Regulations 1984 (SI 344/88)	Requirements and restrictions to be observed in relation to the advertisement of solicitors' services including prohibition of fee comparison and adverse comment in relation to another solicitor's practice
Solicitors Acts 1954 to 2002 (Professional Indemnity Insurance) Regulations 2007 (SI 617/07)	Provided for the establishment of the LSI Professional Indemnity Insurance (PII) Committee with responsibility for administration of the Assigned Risk Pool (ARP) and for the review of minimum terms and conditions of qualifying insurance. The ARP provides insurance for those unable to obtain it elsewhere.

[257] LSRB 2011 § 5 provides for the repeal of the Legal Services Ombudsman Act 2009. Chapter 5 contains a detailed discussion of the LSRB 2011.

[258] Solicitors (Amendment) Act 1994 § 73 empowers the LSI to introduce SIs

Financial Emergency Measures in the Public Interest (Reduction of Payments to State Solicitors) Regulations 2009 (SI 159/09)	SI introduced by the Minister for Finance in accordance with Financial Emergency Measures in the Public Interest Act 2009, § 10. Provided for an 8% reduction in the remuneration of state solicitors
Solicitors Acts 1954 to 2008 (Professional Practice, Conduct and Discipline – Secured Loan Transactions) Regulations 2009 (SI 211/09)	Prohibition of the issuance of an undertaking where a solicitor/connected person has a beneficial interest in the secured loan transaction in the absence of notice to a lending institution
Solicitors Acts 1954 to 2008 (Professional Indemnity Insurance) (Amendment) Regulations 2009, Solicitors Acts 1954 to 2008 (Professional Indemnity Insurance) (Amendment (No 2) Regulations 2009 (SI 384/09, 441/09)	Increased cost of PII insurance obtained via the ARP. Provided for the exclusion from cover of liability in respect of commercial property transactions. Provided for temporary suspension of the ARP and reduction in requirement to obtain run-off cover upon cessation of practice
Solicitors Acts 1954 to 2008 (Professional Indemnity Insurance) (Amendment) Regulations 2011 (SI 409/11)	Provided for establishment of a Special Purpose Fund (SPF) consisting of the ARP and a Run Off Fund (ROF), to provide cover for firms ceasing to practice, in respect of liabilities arising after expiry of their PII cover. Provided for ARP to provide contingency cover for firms whose qualified insurer becomes insolvent, or who are unable to provide cover for other reasons.
Solicitors Acts 1954 to 2011 (Professional Indemnity Insurance) (Amendment) Regulations 2012 (SI 452/12)	The current regulations covering PII requirements for solicitors. Requirement to provide LSI with evidence of qualifying insurance. Requirement for payment of an ARP default premium by a firm which fails to obtain qualifying insurance, at a rate calculated by SPF manager

1.3.4 Professional Conduct Guides

Both the LSI and the BCI have published guides to professional conduct which impact significantly upon the regulation and practice of law in Ireland.

1.3.4.1 A Guide to Professional Conduct of Solicitors in Ireland

The LSI's 'A Guide to Professional Conduct of Solicitors in Ireland', the most recent edition of which was issued in 2002, sets out the function of a solicitor in society and identifies the profession's core values of independence, confidentiality and the avoidance of conflicts of interest.[259] It describes how the rules of

---

[259] LSI '*A Guide to Professional Conduct of Solicitors in Ireland*' (2002) Rule 1.1. Henceforth referred to as 'The Guide'. The lawyer's function is to serve the interests of justice as well as asserting and defending his client's interests. He must also act as his client's advisor. It is understood that a new *Guide to Professional Conduct* will be published by the LSI in October

professional conduct are to be enforced, either by the Complaints Committee of the LSI or the SDT of the High Court. It covers all areas of practice, including the acceptance of instructions, the maintenance of proper standards of legal services and the rules relating to the exercise of a solicitor's lien. It also addresses the appropriate response to conflicts of interest which may arise between a solicitor and client, or between two clients of a solicitor. Attention is also given to the area of property transactions and the issues which may arise in the context of these, especially between vendors and purchasers of newly constructed residential units.[260] The Guide sets out the rules relating to litigation, and it also gives a detailed description of the professional duty of confidentiality which a solicitor owes to his/her clients. Exceptions to the rules of privilege and confidentiality are identified; in particular, where a client is endeavouring to commit a crime or a fraud, or where there is a real risk of death or serious injury occurring as a result of non-disclosure.[261]

The Guide also contains the rules governing a solicitor's relationship with both the Court, third parties, other solicitors and counsel. It sets out comprehensive rules governing all areas of practice, including advertising, professional indemnity insurance and accounting regulations. It also contains the rules relating to legal charges. Overcharging is expressly prohibited, as is the calculation of charges as a percentage of damages.[262] Fee sharing with non-solicitors or solicitors who do not hold a current practising certificate is also prohibited.[263]

1.3.4.2 Code of Conduct of the BCI

The BCI has adopted a Code of Conduct for the Bar which sets out the minimum standards of professional conduct to be adhered to by practising barristers, in order to protect clients' interests and to ensure the sound administration of justice. In accordance with the Code, barristers must refrain from conduct which is likely to bring the profession into disrepute.[264] Failure to comply may lead to an investigation by the PPC or by the BPCT. In more serious cases of misconduct, a member may be suspended or excluded from the Law Library, and may be referred to the Benchers of the HSKI. The latter sanction may lead to admonishment, suspension or disbarment.[265] Barristers owe an overriding duty to the court to ensure the proper administration of justice in the public interest, and they must assist the court in that regard, refraining from either deceiving or misleading the court.[266] The Code sets out the type of work which a barrister may engage in, and permits part-time work in any occupation which is consistent with the Code of Conduct. It requires barristers to carry insurance against

---

2013. (Interview with Mr Ken Doherty, Director General, LOI, Dublin, 13th September 2013)

[260] Ibid. Rule 3.3 of The Guide recommends that such transactions should not generally be facilitated by the same solicitor or solicitors' firm.

[261] Ibid, Rules 4.1 & 4.2

[262] Ibid, Rules 10.2 & 10.3

[263] Ibid, Rule 10.8

[264] The Bar Council of Ireland 'Code of Conduct for the Bar of Ireland' 25 July 2011. Rule 1.2 (b)

[265] Ibid Rule 1.3

[266] Ibid Rule 2.2

professional negligence claims in accordance with the minimum standard stipulated by the BCI.[267] Barristers are obliged to maintain client confidentiality at all times except where disclosure may occur either in the course of an enquiry by the BPCT, the BPCAB or by the DC of the HSKI. The Code of Conduct sets out standards of behaviour to be observed regarding barristers' relations with solicitors, the courts, other bodies with quasi-judicial functions and the public at large. It also sets out requisite standards of behaviour vis à vis other barristers, and also foreign and registered lawyers.

1.3.5 Non-legal Regulatory Mechanisms

A corollary of the fact that it is a requirement for solicitors and barristers to carry Professional Indemnity Insurance (PII) in order to be eligible to practice is that insurance providers play a significant role in determining the eligibility of solicitors to practice. In this regard, Scott has identified insurance providers as significant players in the overall regulatory framework which shapes many aspects of modern behaviour.[268] W. Bradley Wendel has also identified the role of factors such as codes of honour and the phenomenon of shaming as being influential in shaping the behaviour of legal professionals, who are sensitive to the potential reaction of colleagues to behaviour patterns which fail to adhere to socially accepted norms within a professional community.[269]

1.3.5.1 The Role of Insurance in Regulating Legal Practice

Scott has cited insurance as an example of the fragmentation of the regulatory process in modern society whereby regulators are no longer confined to the ranks of legislators and other formal administrative institutions, but instead become diffused throughout society.[270] The powerful regulatory influence of the insurance industry upon the legal profession has been illustrated in recent times by the fact that where a solicitor's firm is unable to obtain insurance, its right to provide services is effectively negated. In this way, insurance providers become an effective means of regulating practitioners, and of ensuring compliance with desired behavioural standards. In recent years, practitioners have seen a steep rise in the cost of obtaining PII, with the average increase in premiums in 2010 being of the order of 56%.[271] This unprecedented rate of increase in insurance costs is due to an extremely high rate of insurer loss ratios for Irish solicitors, due to the conglomeration of a 'lethal cocktail of events' in Ireland, which resulted in an unsustainably high level of claims, and the virtual collapse of many legal practices.[272] There were several factors which contributed to this situation, but the main reason for it was that many solicitors had assumed the total risk associated with property transactions through the issuance of unqualified undertak-

---

[267] Ibid Rule 2.18

[268] C Scott, 'Regulating Everything', UCD Geary Institute Discussion Paper Series (Geary WP 24/2008)

[269] W Bradley Wendel,'Nonlegal Regulation of the Legal Profession: Social Norms in Professional Communities' (2001) 54 (6) *Vanderbilt Law Review* 1955

[270] C Scott, 'Regulating Everything' (FN 268)

[271] J O'Mahoney, "PII Survey Reveals Average Cost Increase of 56%" (2011) 105 (4) LSG 12

[272] A Neary, 'Cause and Effect' (2011) 105 (7) LSG 33

ings to financial institutions in respect of which there was an omission to perform the most basic forms of risk analysis.

The legal profession, like many sectors of business and industry, fell victim to the economic collapse which Ireland has experienced in recent years. An over-inflated property market led to the collapse of the Anglo Irish Bank, and caused severe stress in other key financial institutions in Ireland. It is estimated that 70% of PII claims against solicitors are related to property transactions.[273] PII providers have suffered extraordinary loss ratios ranging from 180% to 1,100%, the latter figure being reported by the (Solicitors Mutual Defence Fund) SMDF for the year 2008/2009.[274] It is little wonder that the SMDF was declared insolvent in 2011, leading to a further undesirable degree of consolidation within a rapidly decreasing legal insurance market, which recently saw the withdrawal of the key players Quinn Insurance and RSA from the market.[275] There are currently ten insurance providers remaining in the PII market.[276]

Neary has identified a problem with the certificate of title system which was instrumental in the development of 'the lethal cocktail of events', whereby the traditional three solicitor system was replaced with a two solicitor system, for the closing of residential property transactions. The two solicitor system saw the purchaser's solicitor provide an undertaking to the lending institution to the effect that its security would be duly registered. The purchaser's solicitor also certified that the title to the property was good. This arrangement resulted in a considerable cost saving for lending institutions, which no longer found it necessary to engage their own legal representative to attend to their interests, as was the case under the old three solicitor system. The introduction of the two solicitor system saw a diminution in the lending institutions' due diligence with regard to its loan portfolios, with a tendency for the institutions to rely upon the solicitors' undertakings as an 'insurance' against potential problems. The increase in commercial property transactions during the Celtic Tiger years saw many solicitors dabble in this area of conveyancing without the requisite expertise, leading to an increased exposure in the property market which in time led to an elevated level of claims against some firms. Further pressures in the property market developed as a result of the trend in lending institutions to base loan rates upon property values instead of a lender's ability to make repayments. When problems in the securitization of such loans began to emerge as property prices began to decrease, lenders looked to solicitors for compensation if any defect in security documentation could be identified. This process was exacerbated by the establishment of The National Assets Management Agency (NAMA) which had the effect of crystallising banks' property losses and accelerating the above processes. Security documentation is currently being scrutinised in the

---

[273] A Neary & F O'Toole, *The Blueprint Report: A Review of the Legal Profession in Ireland and a Vision for Irish Law Firms* (Anne Neary Consultations, 2011) 9

[274] Ibid 131

[275] The ensuing market instability resulted in the temporary suspension of the Assigned Risk Pool for a period at the end of November 2009.

[276] A list of authorised insurance providers is available on the LSI website. Available at: <http://www.lawsociety.ie/Documents/committees/PII/Insurers_2012-2013.pdf> Accessed 6/6/2013

course of due diligence examinations which are taking place within financial institutions.[277] Competition within the conveyancing market combined with the economic downturn were the final ingredients that Neary identified which helped to create the perfect storm for solicitors, who were heavily involved in conveyancing, and which in turn has given rise to such extreme pressures within the Irish PII market.[278]

In the future, firms which have robust risk management strategies in place, and which routinely engage in comprehensive business and financial planning, will benefit from reduced insurance costs. Neary has also identified the need for solicitors' firms to move away from risk analysis strategies based upon an individual's practice, towards a firm-based risk analysis strategy that will identify weaknesses in the firm's overall practice that may give rise to potential claims, and which may not be apparent upon examination of an individual practitioner's work.[279]

Baker and Swedloff have identified the tools which liability insurers use to regulate their insureds and to mitigate problems of adverse selection and moral hazard.[280] Adverse selection refers to the process whereby individuals most likely to be found liable for damages as a result of professional negligence are more likely to obtain liability insurance. Moral hazard in the context of liability insurance refers to the process whereby insureds are less likely to exercise caution in relation to their activities given the knowledge that they are protected from personal loss as a result of their insured status. Baker and Swedloff have identified seven mechanisms which insurers may use to reduce the impact of adverse selection and moral hazard upon the activities of insureds. These are risk-based pricing of policies, underwriting, contract design, claims management, loss prevention services, research and education and engagement with public regulators.[281] Baker and Swedloff have concluded that lawyers' professional liability insurers impact significantly upon the way in which insured lawyers practice law, notwithstanding their traditional resistance to risk management.[282] They have also cautioned that risk management techniques may reduce lawyers' individual responsibility for making moral decisions as ethical decision-making becomes the function of a centralised domain, such as a conflicts committee or a general counsel.[283] There is also the possibility that lawyers may abandon their roles as ethical decision-makers if they envisage risk management as an obstacle to be avoided. Further research is required to better understand the role of

---

[277] *Dáil Debates,* Joint Committee on Finance and the Public Sector Debate: NAMA and NTMA: Discussion with Chief Executives 13th April 2010. Brendan McDonagh (Chief Executive of NAMA).

[278] A Neary & F O'Toole, *The Blueprint Report* (FN 273) 8 – 9

[279] Ibid 139 – 140

[280] T Baker & R Swedloff, 'Regulation by Liability Insurance: From Auto to Lawyers Professional Liability' University of Pennsylvania Law School. Institute for Law and Economics Research Paper No 13.4. 1 Available at: <http://ssrn.com/abstract=2202314> Accessed 6/6/2013

[281] Ibid 6 – 7

[282] Ibid 35 – 36

[283] Ibid 37

lawyers' liability and lawyers' liability insurance in the creation of a culture of risk management, and the impact of such a culture on lawyers' practice.[284]

1.3.5.2 Internalised Norms of Conduct

Bradley Wendel has argued that formal regulatory codes cannot of themselves be expected to achieve an ideal regulatory framework for the legal profession. His analysis reminds us that lawyers are human beings first and foremost, and are subject to social pressures in common with all social actors. Thus whilst some within the legal profession may not welcome Wendel's comparison between the informal codes which govern their profession and those which pertain within La Cosa Nostra (the Mafia), he has brought an insightful and fresh perspective to the maintenance of social order within communities, and has highlighted the crucial role of social norms in the regulation of the legal profession.[285]

Wendel's analysis of the advantages and disadvantages of community based sanctioning of lawyers on the one hand, and of formal methods of sanction on the other, has provided a valuable framework for considering how these two different methods may be most usefully combined to attain the optimum system of regulation of the legal profession.[286] In Wendel's opinion, there is general agreement within the legal ethics academy that formal ethical codes which apply sanctions for ethical breaches are an ineffective means of addressing the problem of misbehaving lawyers.[287] Proposals for the adoption of aspirational ethical codes, which do not provide for the imposition of formal sanctions, have met with little enthusiasm as a means of improving the efficacy of lawyer regulation. Critics of such formal, aspirational ethical codes point to a powerful array of institutional forces which lead to unethical conduct on the part of lawyers, including competitive market forces, a falling level of client loyalty toward particular firms and the growth in lawyer malpractice litigation 'which causes lawyers to cover their proverbial behinds' regardless of the content of ethical codes.[288] The growth in the bureaucratization of legal practice in the US, and the fear that aspirational codes may be 'highjacked' by the judiciary to penalise lawyers who are disliked, notwithstanding the fact that such codes do not provide for the imposition of sanctions, are further factors which may serve to undermine the efficacy of such aspirational codes. The question therefore arises to what extent can informal sanctions fill this void, and provide the means for more effective regulation of the legal profession?

From Wendel's perspective, the informal regulation of a misbehaving lawyer may be enforced by his/her peer group because if Lawyer X acts like a jerk, he/she will be treated as such by colleagues. Other lawyers will not extend the normal courtesies of working practice, and they will be uncooperative in administrative matters with him/her. Lawyer X may also suffer social ostracism, and

---

[284] Ibid 38
[285] W B Wendel, 'Nonlegal Regulation' (FN 269) 1971
[286] Ibid 1955
[287] Ibid 1955 -1957
[288] Ibid 1958

may be excluded from referral networks or denied the opportunity to participate fully in bar association activities. The net effect of such informal sanctions will be costly for Lawyer X on both an economic and professional level, as the cost for him/her of completing legal transactions will become higher, and he/she will also endure the loss of professional development opportunities.

The idea of a community of lawyers is at the heart of Wendel's analysis, and is prevalent in much academic literature on the subject of the legal profession. Alongside the rules of professional discipline and the spectre of professional negligence litigation, regulation of lawyers is effected by means of lawyers' internalised norms of conduct which are regularly reinforced by the monitoring and criticism of other lawyers. From an economic perspective, the use of community-based sanctions accords with the idea of a reputational market. Where an individual lawyer is known for a commitment to straight dealing and fair play, he/she will be rewarded economically, as clients perceive him/her to be honest and trustworthy. Thus the straight dealing lawyer may be seen to have an economic advantage over meaner and nastier colleagues. The American Bar Association's (ABA) Model Rules of Professional Conduct acknowledge the regulatory role of reputational markets in stating that lawyers should be guided by the approbation of their professional peers.[289] The idea of 'community' as a means of enforcing informal mechanisms of social control has some resonance with the proposition that 'legal ethics is a matter of professional judgment', and is not simply a question of blindly following a set of rules.[290]

A key element in models of community social control is that of the 'social norm', and Bradley Wendel has considered this from three different perspectives. He identifies these as the honour/shame model, the rational choice model and the civic republican model. The role of informal social norms in shaping behaviour in many areas of life has been well documented.[291] The historical use of honour/shame to control behaviour in many small, homogenous societies has been extensively documented. A considerable body of historical and anthropological literature may thus be drawn upon to enhance our understanding of how honour/shame is used within the legal community to enforce social norms. Wendel cites the example of the Mafia as an organisation which adheres to its own strict code of honour.[292] In order to make a meaningful distinction between their code of honour and that of the American Military for example, one must step beyond both codes and resort to a meta-language that transcends each of the honour codes, in order to make a logical statement about the relative qualities of either code. Each code in and of itself may be coherent and claim validity. It is only when we compare them to one another that we are faced with the paradox of their incompatibility.

---

[289] Ibid 1961, citing 'ABA Model Rules of Professional Conduct' Preamble; 6

[290] Ibid 1961

[291] Ibid 1961. Wendel cites the example of both the grain and diamond industries as areas where social norms as opposed to formal rules are used to control the behaviour of participants. (See L Bernstein, 'Merchant Law in a Merchant Court: Rethinking the Code's Search for Immanent Business Norms' [1996] 144 *University of Philadelphia Law Review* 1765)

[292] W B Wendel, 'Nonlegal Regulation' (FN 269) 1971

Rational choice theory provides a useful framework for enhancing our understanding of informal mechanisms of community social control, even in cases where such mechanisms coexist with the possibility of the imposition of more formal means of sanctioning. From this perspective, social actors engage in a cost benefit analysis to inform their decisions regarding the desirability or otherwise of various courses of action. The cost attached to the imposition of informal sanctions will be taken into account in just the same manner as the imposition of more formal sanctions, and the benefits of adhering to social norms will be just as relevant in informing the actor's choices as are the benefits of acting in accordance with the formal rules. Thus when reflecting upon the prospect of reputational damage for example, or the termination of a favourable commercial relationship, a social actor will be equally mindful of the influence of both informal and formal sanctions when engaging in decision-making.

In contrast to the utilitarian model of rational choice theory, the idea of civic republicanism has been revived in response to the modern perception of a legal community which is blighted by 'pernicious individualism and selfishness'.[293] From this perspective, lawyers are duty bound to act in accordance with the greater public good, and to offer moral advice to clients where their instructions would appear to conflict with same. Lawyers must act with moral authority and in accordance with the requirements of social justice. They must remain independent from both their clients and the state in order to effectively protect moral values for the public good. In identifying what exactly the public good consists of in any particular case, civic republicanism points to the need for public dialogue, which must be able to take place without recourse to threats or deception on the part of participants. However, it must be said that the republican lawyer is a rare species indeed, as described by Wendel as follows:

> Republican lawyers are not shysters or sophists – they are a "virtuous elite" or "policy intelligentsia," who facilitate deliberation about the public good and who, if necessary, restrain their clients' selfish ambitions to conform with the social purpose of the law.[294]

Wendel was concerned to identify the correct balance between informal and formal sanctions in establishing an optimal system for the regulation of the legal profession. Having acknowledged the power of informal means of sanctions, which can, in some cases, act to undermine the efficacy of formal regulatory mechanisms, and also their financial attractiveness as a means of obtaining compliance with social norms, Wendel has cautioned against overestimating their potential to single-handedly control the unethical behaviour of lawyers, and draws attention to their lack of predictability and stability in comparison to formal regulatory codes. The use of informal sanctions may give rise to feuds within the legal community, and there is also the risk that inappropriate or abhorrent social norms may develop within communities which have a toxic effect both within and beyond the community. Wendel has noted that the larger and more heterogenous a community is, the less effective will be the use of

---

[293] Ibid 1967
[294] Ibid 2008

informal sanctions in controlling behaviour. In concluding that both formal and informal sanctions have a role to play in the regulation of the legal profession, Wendel has argued that the challenge of regulation consists in the identification of the appropriate balance between external and internal normative stances.[295]

1.4 Concluding Remarks

This chapter commenced with an examination of the history of the legal profession in Ireland, beginning with the earliest available written records which date back to the seventh century AD. It then explored the history of the regulatory bodies of both barristers and solicitors, beginning with the HSKI which was established in 1541, the LSI which was established in 1830, and the BCI which was established in 1897. The modern regulatory framework was then examined, including today's regulatory bodies: the BCI's PPC, the BPCT and BPCAB; the HSKI's DC; the LSI's CCRC and IA; the SDT and the High Court. Formal sources of regulation, including the principles of common law, The Constitution of Ireland, statutes, statutory instruments and Professional Codes of Conduct were also examined. Non-legal regulatory mechanisms such as requirements imposed upon practitioners by insurance providers and the influence of internalised behavioural norms were also considered.

It is clear from this examination that the regulatory framework of the Irish legal profession is both archaic and complex. The solicitors' profession has undergone little meaningful reform since the enactment of the Principal Act in 1954.[296] The barristers' profession has a deeply traditional regulatory system, lacking in transparency and accountability, which is strikingly similar today in terms of its key regulatory mechanisms as it was at the time of the HSKI's establishment in 1541. One may say that the HSKI has been true to its motto *nolumus mutari*.[297] Seven bodies and five types of legal instruments combine to form a complex regulatory array which presents challenges for both practitioners and clients alike.

The following chapter will look beyond the boundaries of the Irish regulatory framework and will identify and explore the various international influences which impinge upon the practice of Irish lawyers.

---

[295] Ibid 2055
[296] Solicitors Act 1954
[297] 'We will not be changed' or 'We will not change'.

2

INTERNATIONAL FACTORS WHICH AFFECT THE REGULATION OF THE LEGAL PROFESSION IN IRELAND

2.0 Introduction

Whereas Chapter 1 focused upon the Irish system of regulation for the legal profession, this chapter takes a wider view and looks at the regulation of the legal profession from transnational, international and global perspectives. The need to adopt a broader view takes account of the fact that modern legal practice is often of a transnational or international nature, and also that law is subject to social, cultural, political and economic forces which frequently transcend national boundaries. Within a couple of decades, modern communications have revolutionised our ability to develop new business and personal links. In many ways, the world has become a smaller place. This reality has presented law firms with both challenges and opportunities. Clients more frequently present with problems having a transnational or international dimension, with lawyers being asked to advise clients who are based outside Ireland regarding Irish law, or to advise clients within Ireland regarding international legal matters. New social media also present novel methods of contacting and communicating with clients and creating new business opportunities.

This chapter examines the contribution of key international institutions and professional associations to the regulation of the legal profession. It begins by looking at the role of European Union (EU) law which has had a significant impact upon the regulation of the legal professions as lawyers increasingly avail of the opportunities presented by the European single market, and the fundamental freedom of establishment and the freedom to provide services throughout the Union. Irish lawyers have also had to embrace the challenges presented by new layers of regulation applying as a result of EU membership which impinge upon both their activities and those of their clients.

More recently, the EU Commission and the European Central Bank (ECB) and the International Monetary Fund (IMF), collectively known as 'The Troika' have played a major role in altering many practices throughout Irish business and financial sectors. The Troika's intervention followed the unprecedented economic crisis that Ireland experienced in recent years following the collapse of the Irish banking sector which arose as a result of its massive overexposure to the commercial property market.[1] In return for the bailout funds received from

---

[1] Appendix 1 contains an extract from a paper by the author, entitled 'The Legal Profession in

the Troika in December 2010, Ireland agreed to implement widespread reforms in many sheltered sectors of the economy, including the legal services market, which the EU Commission historically has viewed as anticompetitive. The impact of the Troika upon the regulation of the Irish legal profession is evidenced by the publication of the LSRB 2011, which was a direct consequence of The Troika's financial intervention following the collapse of the Irish economy in 2010.

The Council of Europe has also exerted a soft regulatory influence upon the practice of law in its members' jurisdictions in the form of its Recommendation on the Freedom of Exercise of the Profession of Lawyer which aims to establish a working environment for lawyers that respects and protects their independent function in society. The United Nations has also made a valuable regulatory contribution to the legal profession on an international level through the adoption of its Basic Principles on the Role of Lawyers. On a more general level, this chapter will examine the role of the World Trade Organisation in regulating the global trade in professional services and will consider the effect of its Joint Statement on Legal Services.

Having examined the role of the institutions in the international regulatory framework, the chapter proceeds to examine the place of international professional associations of lawyers in the regulation of the legal profession. The regulatory role of the IBA will be examined, including its General Principles for the Legal Profession, which attempt to establish an internationally accepted Code of Conduct for legal practitioners. The CCBE has a significant regulatory impact upon European lawyers, and its authority in representing almost three quarters of a million lawyers is recognised both by EU institutions and throughout the EU member states. It has adopted a Charter of Core Principles of the European Legal Profession, and also a Code of Conduct, both of which impact upon the regulation of the legal profession in the EU and beyond, and which will be examined in this chapter. The International Law Association has issued the Hague Principles on Ethical Standards for Counsel Appearing before International Courts and Tribunals which provide guidance to assist in the resolution of tensions facing lawyers practising in these fora. The International Association of Lawyers has adopted the Turin Principles of Professional Conduct for the Legal Profession in the Twenty-first Century which whilst recognising the unique role of lawyers in securing the proper administration of justice, aims to achieve the highest possible standards of ethical practice for the legal profession.

Laurel Terry argues that both the legal profession and its regulators must respond to a global environment where changes to the regulatory framework in one jurisdiction often influence the regulatory climate in other jurisdictions.[2] She cites the example of the UK and Australian rules on Alternative Business Structures (ABSs) which have given rise to non-lawyer owned law firms, the public issuance of shares and corporate ownership of law firms. These develop-

---

Troikaland: Before and After the Irish Bailout', which gives an account of the origins of Ireland's economic crisis. Available at: <http://ssrn.com/abstract=2262083>.

[2] L Terry et al, 'Trends and Challenges in Lawyer Regulation: The Impact of Globalization and Technology' (2012) 80 (6) *Fordham Law Review* 2661

ments present regulatory challenges to legal services regulators in jurisdictions outside of Australia and the UK where Multi Disciplinary Practices (MDPs) are currently permitted.[3] Legal service regulators must also grapple with the difficulties presented by issues such as the differences in the rules in various jurisdictions concerning conflicts of interest. Terry states that lawyers and their regulators everywhere face similar challenges as a result of globalization and technological advances. These advances have given rise to common trends and challenges in lawyer regulation. As a consequence, legal regulators are not alone when struggling to respond to the rapidly changing environment, and may usefully look to their counterparts in other jurisdictions, and adopt a comparative perspective when looking for solutions to many problems.

The process of globalization which is variously fueled by unifying or fragmenting forces has impacted upon national cultures on a worldwide basis, Ireland being no exception. It is necessary to consider what impact if any this process has had upon the regulation of the legal profession in Ireland, given that technological advances are capable of facilitating instantaneous transactions across the world, and as such, have presented new opportunities and challenges for Irish citizens on both a business and personal level. Whilst technological advances such as cloud computing may present Irish legal practices with efficient and cost effective options in terms of business systems, they also present challenges and hazards from a regulatory point of view in terms of security of data and the duty of client confidentiality.

The chapter concludes with a consideration of Global Anti-Corruption Instruments and how they impact, directly and indirectly, upon the practice and regulation of lawyers. It will be seen that organisations such as the United Nations, the Organisation for Economic Co-operation and the Council of Europe have not only had a role in opening up markets in professional services to international competition, but they have also been active in preventing corrupt practices, and in so doing have impacted upon the regulation of the legal profession internationally. Diagram 3 offers an overview of the main international bodies which contribute to the regulation of the legal profession.

2.1 The Impact of EU Law

The EU Treaty provisions concerning the free movement of persons provide important opportunities for lawyers to extend the parameters of their practice beyond their traditional national boundaries to encompass the entire territory of the EU. Whilst the fundamental rights of freedom of establishment and freedom to provide services are contained in Articles 49 – 62 TFEU, these have been complimented by various Directives and Regulations, and also by a body of case law from the Court of Justice.[4]

---

[3] A MDP provides a combination of legal and other professional services such as estate agency or accountancy. An Alternative Business Structure (ABS) is a professional law firm or a company that provides reserved legal services, such as conveyancing, litigation and probate, as either part or all of its services. The first English ABS was licenced to operate in October 2011 after provision was made for their introduction in the LSA 2007. Non-lawyers may either own or partly own an ABS. A MDP is a form of ABS which does not offer legal services in isolation.

[4] The fundamental rights and freedoms of EU citizens have also been codified in the EU Charter

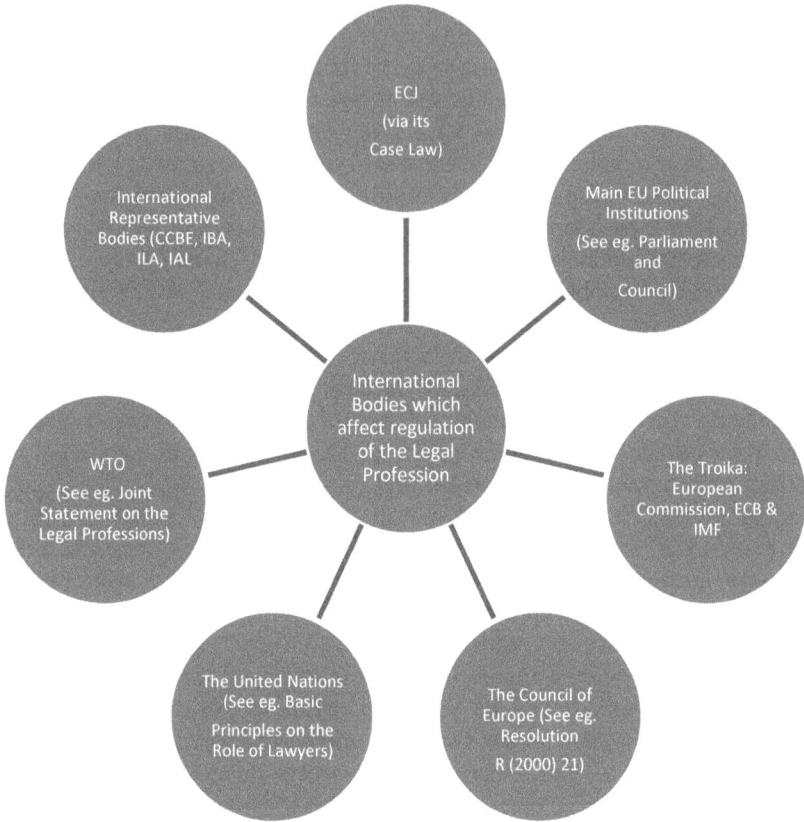

**Diagram 3: Key International Bodies whose Activities Tend
to Affect the Regulation the Legal Professions**

The Treaty Articles relating to establishment and freedom to provide services confer rights upon legal professionals who are either self-employed or employed by firms to pursue their activities in host member states under the same conditions as apply to nationals of the host member states. Where an Irish lawyer, either a solicitor or barrister, wishes to practice on an ongoing basis in an EU member state outside of Ireland, he/she can avail of his/her rights to freedom of establishment, whereas if the legal services to be provided are of a

---

of Fundamental Rights (EUCFR) which became legally binding in December 2009 with the coming into force of the Lisbon Treaty. Article 45 of the EUCFR provides every Union citizen with the right to move and reside freely within the territory of the Member States. Art 45 (2) EUCFR states that freedom of movement and residence may be granted, in accordance with the Treaties, to nationals of third countries legally resident in the territory of a Member State.

temporary or occasional nature, the lawyer may avail of the freedom to provide services provisions.

Establishment

Article 49 TFEU refers to the right of establishment as the right to enter another member state and to stay on either a long-term or permanent basis in order to pursue activities as a self-employed person, and to set up and manage undertakings. Establishment was described in *Factortame* (No 2) as 'the actual pursuit of an economic activity through a fixed establishment in another Member State for an indefinite period'.[5]

In *Gebhard*, establishment was characterised as the right of a community national to participate on a stable and continuous basis in the economic life of a member state other than his or her own (whereas 'services' are of a temporary, precarious and discontinuous nature).[6] Article 49 TFEU contains a prohibition upon the restriction of the freedom of establishment of nationals of member states in the territory of other member states. It was held in the case of *Reyners* that Article 49 TFEU is directly effective.[7] The case concerned a Dutch national who wished to gain access to the Belgian Bar, but was refused access on grounds of his nationality. The Court of Justice held that nationality should not be a barrier to appropriately qualified lawyers who wished to enter a member state to practise, and that Directives merely facilitated the right to free movement rather than establishing it, the right being established by the Treaty itself.

Services

The provision of services, in accordance with Article 56 TFEU envisages a temporary state of affairs, and an appearance in the host state, if at all, for a limited period of time in order to provide specific services. There is no permanent presence, either personal or professional in the host state, nor is there a necessity to reside there. A service provider need not necessarily move from his/her home state, as services may be provided via modern methods of communication, such as phone or email.[8] Article 57 TFEU defines services as 'provided for remuneration, in so far as they are not governed by provisions relating to freedom of movement of goods, capital and persons.'[9] This includes the activities of professionals.[10] In *Commission v Germany (Lawyers' Services)*, it was held that whereas local rules are acceptable, they should not go beyond the strict requirements of Community law so as to become a hindrance to free movement. The German requirements that a lawyer from another member state must have a local lawyer alongside him/her at all times, and also that a lawyer must live locally when providing services were deemed to be too restrictive, and

---

[5] Case C-221/89 *Factortame* (No 2) [1991] ECR I-3905

[6] Case C-55/94 *Gebhard v Milan Bar Council* [1995] ECR I-4165

[7] Case C-2/74 *Jean Reyners v The Belgian State* [1974] ECR 631

[8] Case C-384/93 *Alpine Investments* [1995] ECR I-1141; C-17/00 *De Coster* [2001] ECR I-09445

[9] Article 57 TFEU

[10] Article 57 (d) TFEU

could not be justified.[11] The Court held that the national rule should not be applied to activities of a temporary nature being carried out by lawyers who were established in another member state. Article 56 TFEU prohibits restrictions on the freedom to provide services in respect of member state nationals who are established in a member state other than that of the recipient of the services in question. In *Van Binsbergen* the Court of Justice held that Article 56 TFEU was directly effective, that the freedom to provide services was not conditional upon the issuance of a subsequent Directive relating to specific professions, and nor was it dependent upon the acquisition of a residence requirement.[12] The case concerned a Dutch lawyer, resident in Belgium, who was refused Dutch court audience rights. The professional rule that advocates must be resident within a court's jurisdiction for professional purposes in order to provide services was deemed not to be objectively justifiable, or proportionate to its aims.

EU Anti-Corruption Policy

Some Treaty Articles indirectly impact upon the regulation of lawyers, such as Article 67 TFEU (ex Article 29 TEU), which concerns the EU anti-corruption policy. The Union's main instruments for the prevention of corruption are the Convention on the Protection of European Communities' Financial Interests and the Convention against Corruption involving European Officials or Officials of Member States of the EU.[13] The Convention on the Protection of European Communities' Financial Interests was agreed following an Act of the European Council of 26 July 1995, and is aimed at addressing fraud which impacts upon the financial interests of the EU. It requires that fraudulent behaviour concerning both expenditure and revenue must be the subject of effective, deterrent, criminal penalties throughout the EU. It also provides for extradition and custodial sentences in cases of serious fraud. Where a criminal fraud concerns more than one member state, the relevant countries must co-operate to ensure an effective investigation takes place, by providing mutual legal assistance, extradition, transfer of proceedings or enforcement of sentences passed within the EU. The Convention against Corruption involving European Officials or Officials of Member States of the EU was agreed following an Act of the European Council of 26 May 1997. This Convention requires member states to take steps to ensure that both active and passive corruption involving officials of the EU is a criminal offence. It also requires instigation of such activity, or participation in it, to be punishable as a crime, and provides that serious offences should incur a custodial sentence and extradition where appropriate. Member states

---

[11] Case C-427/85 *Commission v Germany (Lawyers' Services)* [1988] ECR 1123

[12] Case 33/74 *Van Binsbergen* [1974] ECR 1299

[13] Convention on the Protection of the European Communities Financial Interests OJ C316/48 27th November 1995. Available at:
<http://europa.eu/legislation_summaries/fight_against_fraud/protecting_european_communitys_financial_interests/l33019_en.htm> Accessed 28/8/2012; Convention against Corruption involving European Officials or Officials of Member States of the European Union OJ C/195 25th June 1997. Available at:
<http://europa.eu/legislation_summaries/fight_against_fraud/fight_against_corruption/l33027_en.htm> Accessed: 28/8/2012

must also cooperate with one another to ensure that offences are effectively dealt with where they involve the jurisdiction of more than one member state. A fuller consideration of global anti-corruption instruments and their impact upon lawyers' activities is given in section 2.12 below.

Regulation of Irish Lawyers wishing to practise in a host member state on a permanent basis

An Irish lawyer who wishes to become established in another member state may do so most easily in accordance with the provisions of Directive 98/5 EC.[14] He/she must produce evidence of registration with an Irish professional body, either the Bar Council of Ireland or the Law Society of Ireland, to the relevant professional body in the host member state.[15] The Irish lawyer must practise in the host member state under his/her Irish professional title of either 'solicitor' or 'barrister'.[16] He/she must also confine his/her professional activities to the law of the home state, the host state, EU law and international law, whilst observing any rules of the host state regarding reserved activities.[17] The Irish lawyer will be bound by the rules of professional conduct which apply to practice in Ireland, and also those which apply to the profession in the host member state.[18] Where an Irish lawyer has practiced effectively and regularly in a host member state for at least three years, he/she may apply to be exempted from the provisions of Article 4(1)(b) of Directive 89/48 EEC with a view to gaining full admission to the profession in the host state.[19] This provision requires such an applicant to either complete an adaptation period of two to three years, or to take an aptitude test.

In the cases of *Wilson v Conseil de L'Ordre des Avocats du Barreau de Luxembourg* and *Commission v Grand Duchy of Luxembourg* the ECJ held that the protectionist rules of Luxembourg which required EU lawyers wishing to become established there to 'be proficient in the language of statutory provisions as well as the administrative and court languages' and also to submit to an examination to determine their linguistic proficiency, to be unlawful.[20] The ECJ took the view that such a linguistic test posed barriers to the free movement of EU lawyers, and that the protectionist rules were contrary to the terms of Directive 98/5.[21]

---

[14] Directive 98/5 EC of the European Parliament and of the Council of 16 February 1998 to facilitate practice of the profession of lawyer on a permanent basis in a Member State other than that in which the qualification was obtained [1998] OJ L 77/36

[15] Ibid Art 3

[16] Ibid Art 4

[17] Ibid Art 5

[18] Ibid Art 6

[19] Council Directive 89/48 EEC of 21 December 1988 on a general system for the recognition of higher education diplomas awarded on completion of professional education and training of at least three years' duration [1989] OJ L 19

[20] Cases C-506/04 and C-193/05 respectively. A-L Hinds & L Pech, 'When the Public Interest Masks Lawyers' Interests: Luxembourg's Failure to Adhere to Directive 98/5' (2007) 14 (1 & 2) 14 *Irish Journal of European Law* 161

[21] Ibid

Where an Irish lawyer wishes to practice in an EU member state other than Ireland under the same conditions as a lawyer who qualified in the host member state, he/she may opt to avail of the provisions of Directive 2005/36 EC.[22] This allows the Irish lawyer to comply with 'compensatory measures' consisting of both an adaptation period whereby the Irish lawyer practices under the supervision of a qualified legal professional in the host member state, and also an aptitude test, based upon a comparison of the applicant lawyer's qualifications with those required of a legal professional in the host member state. The test must take account of the fact that the applicant is a qualified professional in his/her home member state.[23] Where a lawyer meets either of these requirements, he/she is entitled to practice under the title used in the host member state. Where an Irish lawyer wishes to provide services in the host member state, he/she is exempt from a requirement to register with the relevant professional organisation in the host member state.[24] A lawyer wishing to avail of freedom to provide services within the EU should also be cognisant with the provisions of the Directive which facilitate the effective exercise by lawyers of their freedom to provide services.[25] This dispenses with the need for either residence or registration in order to represent a client in legal proceedings.[26] Lawyers providing services in judicial proceedings must observe the rules of professional conduct in both the home and host states.[27] Where justifiable, the same rules apply to those who are providing services in a host state as apply to nationals of that state.[28] The Directive also provides that a member state may require a lawyer representing a client in legal proceedings to work in conjunction with a lawyer who practices before the judicial authority in question, and who would, where necessary, be answerable to that authority.[29]

It is apparent that the regulation of the provision of legal services throughout the EU on a temporary rather than a permanent basis presented much less of a challenge for legislators, as evidenced by the adoption of initial legislation in respect of service provision as early as 1977 whilst agreement in respect of establishment was not reached until 1998. However, EU legislation concerning the provision of legal services has also frequently been influenced by the decisions of the ECJ, as will be seen from the examination below of some of the leading case law on the matter.

---

[22] Directive 2005/36/EC of the European Parliament and of the Council of 7 September 2005 on the recognition of professional qualifications [2005] OJ L 255/22

[23] Dir 2005/36/EC Art 3 (h)

[24] Dir 2005/36 EC Art 6

[25] Council Directive 77/249/EEC of 22 March 1977 to facilitate the effective exercise by lawyers of freedom to provide services [1977] OJ L 78/17

[26] Ibid Art 4 (1)

[27] Ibid Art 4 (1), (2)

[28] Ibid Art 4 (4)

[29] Ibid Art 5

The Jurisprudence of the European Court of Justice concerning member states' rules for regulating competition in the provision of lawyers' services

The European Court of Justice has ruled upon a range of issues relating to the practice of law within the EU. In two of its most significant rulings concerning the legal profession, the Court of Justice considered whether or not the rules of member states concerning the regulation of the legal profession were compatible with EU competition rules. These cases were heard on the same day by the ECJ, which set out the circumstances in which the regulation of individual member states will be subject to EU antitrust principles.

Multi-Disciplinary Practices

In the case of *Wouters* the ECJ struck down a challenge to a Dutch ban upon MDPs between lawyers and accountants.[30] The court held that the Dutch rule was subject to the competition provisions of Art 101 TFEU, and although the rule had the effect of restricting competition, and was likely to affect trade between individual member states, it did not violate Art 101 TFEU because the rule could reasonably be considered necessary in order to ensure the proper practice of the legal profession as it was organised in Holland. The Court of Justice further held that the Dutch rule was not subject to Art 102 TFEU, and that it did not violate Treaty provisions on the freedom of establishment.

Minimum Fee Schedules

In the *Arduino* case, the Italian rules for minimum and maximum fee schedules were upheld by the ECJ.[31] *Arduino* was a criminal case in which the Defendant, Mr Arduino having been involved in a car accident was sued for damages by the other party who was involved in the accident. In awarding costs against Mr Arduino, the trial court omitted to apply the Bar fee schedule, and failed to give reasons for its omission. Following the setting aside of its judgment by the Supreme Court of Cassation, the trial court referred two questions to the Court of Justice regarding the matter. It enquired whether the fee schedule came within the EU Treaty provisions and if so, whether it was covered by an Art 101 (3) TFEU exception. The Court of Justice concluded that the schedule did not violate Treaty competition provisions, on the basis that it was not compulsory, and required ministerial approval prior to its adoption. Also, the question of the appropriate fees in any given case was a matter for the courts, which could depart from the schedule where reasons for that departure were made known.

The cases of *Wouters* and *Arduino* taken together reflect the reluctance of the ECJ to apply competition law to the regulation of the legal profession.[32] This reluctance is partly due to traditional differences in how the legal profession operates across the member states, and also due its unique role in both the

---

[30] Case C 309/99 *Wouters v Algemene Raad van de Nederlandse Orde van Advocaten* [2002] ECR 1577

[31] Case C 35/99 *Arduino* [2002] ECR I-1529

[32] I Forrester, 'Where Law Meets Competition: Is Wouters Like a Cassis de Dijon or a Platypus?' In C Ehlermann and I Atanasiu (eds), *European Competiton Law Annual 2004: The Relationship between Competition Law and (Liberal) Professions* (Hart Publishing, 2006) 10

administration of justice, and the preservation of the rule of law throughout the member states. The ECJ's reluctance to intervene in the national regulation of legal services in these cases marks a departure from long-established principles of competition law and may well encourage other professions in seeking exemption from the application of such principles.[33] After all, if lawyers may lawfully apply minimum tariff scales, why should architects and accountants not do so?[34]

The matter of fee scales was revisited in 2006. In *Cipolla* the Court considered the issue of whether set scale fees impede the free movement of services, or whether such trade restrictions may be justified.[35] The court acknowledged that the imposition of a set scale of fees prevented lawyers from other member states from competing more effectively with lawyers who were already established within Italy. The use of set fee scales also diminished choice for users of legal services who were denied the opportunity to avail of legal services from providers outside the EU who were willing to provide their services at a lower price. However, the Court recognised that consumer protection and the safeguarding of the proper administration of justice were objectives which were capable of justifying the use of scale fees, in circumstances where excessive competition may lead to the provision of substandard legal services, and may also impact negatively upon the administration of justice. The ECJ held that it was for a national court to decide whether a less restrictive regime might meet the same requirements. The ECJ thus adopted a market-specific approach to the issue of proportionality and maintained the principle which was established in *Arduino*.

Legal Privilege

The parameters of legal professional privilege (LPP) was the subject of litigation in the cases of *AM & S* and *Akzo Nobel and Akros Chemicals Ltd*.[36] In *AM & S* the company wished to rely upon attorney privilege as its justification for withholding documents from the European Commission. The documents in question were memoranda from the in-house counsel of AM & S to the company's employees, and would have enjoyed privilege before the UK courts. However, the Court of Justice held that any such privilege which might be relied upon in the context of European Commission proceedings was limited to communications between clients and EU counsel, and did not extend to US counsel. In seeking to limit the extent to which LPP should be acknowledged, the Court of Justice sought to extend the powers of EU institutions to investigate breaches of competition and other EU rules. The ruling in *AM & S* illustrates how judgments or regulations in one jurisdiction can impact upon the nature of legal practice in other jurisdictions. In *Akzo Nobel and Akros Chemicals Ltd*, the Court of Justice held that LPP is confined to communications between independent lawyers and

---

[33] Ibid 15

[34] Ibid 15

[35] Joined cases C-94/04 & C-202/04 *Federico Cipolla & Others v Rosaria Fazari, nee Portolese & Roberto Meloni* [2006] ECR I-11421

[36] Case 155/79 *AM & S Europe Ltd v Commission of the European Communities* [1982] ECR 1575 and Case T-125/03 *AKZO Nobel Chemicals Ltd and Akros Chemicals Ltd v Commission of European Communities* [2003] ECR II-4471.

their clients, and does not extend to communications between clients and in-house counsel.

In *Akzo Nobel Chemicals v Commission* [2007], the Court of First Instance (CFI) held that the decision of Commission officials to annexe documents which the defendant had argued were covered by LPP and which were seized in the course of investigations was a reviewable act for the purposes of an annulment action.[37] The ruling rendered the Commission's decision in that regard as amenable to direct judicial supervision. The judgment failed to reformulate the AM & S test for LPP and left undisturbed the existing discrepancy between in-house and independent legal counsel, but it ensured continuity with ECJ case law and provided legal certainty regarding the extent of LPP.[38] However, Andreangeli has argued that the ruling does not fully accord with the case law of the ECHR, which favours a more positive approach to defining the concept of lawyers' independence, and which does not consider the existence of a relationship of employment between a client and lawyer as a definitive factor in deciding whether the protection of the ECHR should apply in the circumstances.[39]

To conclude on the importance of EU law and the EU courts' influence, it is clear that EU law, as interpreted by the European Court of Justice, has had considerable impact upon the regulation of the legal profession throughout the member states. This impact has developed as a result of the prominence given to the protection of the fundamental freedoms of both establishment and the provision of services and also the promotion of competition within the Union in the Treaties. In addition there is also the impact of secondary legislation in the form of Directives and Regulations to facilitate lawyers wishing to avail of such freedoms and the rulings of the ECJ in deciding whether the regulatory frameworks of individual member states are either anti-competitive or justifiable, given the unique role of lawyers in society in upholding and defending the rule of law. The liberal professions, not least the legal profession, present particular challenges for the EU institutions when striking a balance between the promotion of unfettered competition between member states and the establishment of a common market within the Union on the one hand, and the justifiable restriction of the activities of lawyers given the privileges they enjoy, including the right to represent parties in legal disputes, commence litigation, prosecute claims against the state, defend accused persons and hold client funds on the other.[40] The ECJ has shown itself to be singularly willing to depart from free market philosophy and competitive principles when adjudicating upon the regulation of the legal profession in the EU. In so doing Forrester has argued that when considering the lawfulness of member states' regulatory measures for the liberal professions in future, the ECJ should apply a test which considers the

---

[37] Joined Cases T-125/03 and T-253/03 *AKZO Chemicals Ltd v Ackros Chemicals Ltd v Commission* [2007] ECR II-3523. A Andreangeli, 'Joined Cases T-125/03 and 253/03 *AKZO Chemicals Ltd and Ackros Chemicals Ltd v Commission,* Judgment of 17 September 2007, not yet reported (under appeal)' [2008] *European Business Law Review* 1158

[38] Ibid 1160

[39] Ibid 1152. Citing Appl No 31611/96 *Nikula v Finland* [2004] 38 EHRR 45, paras 53-55; Appl No 37328/97 *AB v Netherlands* [2003] 37 EHRR 48, para 86.

[40] I Forrester, 'Where Law Meets Competition' (FN 32) 4

reasonableness of the measures; whether they discriminate against professionals on grounds of nationality; whether the rule or its variant is common to more than one member state; whether it is proportional for achieving its stated aim and whether it is an efficient means of reaching that aim.[41]

2.2 European Parliament Resolution on the Legal Profession and the General Interest in the Functioning of Legal Systems

The European Parliament is one of the main institutions of the EU and it is said to represent the peoples of the EU. It is a key law-making institution, along with the Council of the EU.[42] Its function is to debate and enact laws in conjunction with the Council, to examine other EU institutions, including the Commission to ensure they are functioning in a democratic fashion and along with the Council, to debate and approve the EU's budget. Pech has argued that the impact of the Lisbon Treaty upon the Parliament's powers and composition has been somewhat limited, with the most significant parliamentary reform being the renaming of the co-decision procedure to the 'ordinary legislative procedure' and the extension of the procedure's use to areas such as agriculture, energy policy, immigration and EU funds.[43]

In March 2006 the European Parliament adopted a non-binding Resolution on the legal professions and the general interest in the functioning of legal systems.[44] The adoption was welcomed by the CCBE as it recognised the fact that reform of the legal professions had an impact beyond the realm of competition law, and that it also impacted upon broader areas such as freedom, security and justice.[45] The Resolution was also welcomed for its recognition that reform of the legal profession should be carried out at a national level, because the authorities of individual member states are best placed to identify the rules which should apply to their respective legal professions.

The Resolution recognises the crucial role played by the legal professions in a democratic society in ensuring respect for fundamental rights, the rule of law and providing security in the application of the law, by representing clients in court and also by giving legal advice.[46] It also recognises the need to establish a relationship of trust between legal professionals and their clients.[47] The value of

---

[41] Ibid 15-17

[42] Article 13 TEU provides for the establishment of the EU Parliament, along with the European Council, the Council, and the Commission. In accordance with Article 14 TEU the European Parliament shall, jointly with the Council exercise legislative and budgetary functions, and exercise political control and consultation, as exemplified in the Treaties.

[43] L Pech, 'The Institutional Development of the EU Post-Lisbon: A Case of Plus ça Change...?', UCD Dublin European Institute Working Paper 11 – 5, December 2011

[44] European Parliament Resolution on the legal profession and the general interest in the functioning of the legal system, 23rd March 2006 OJ C292 E/105

[45] CCBE Press Release 'CCBE Welcomes European Parliament Resolution on Legal Professions' 24th Mar 2006. Available at:
<http://www.ccbe.eu/fileadmin/user_upload/NTCdocument/pr_0106_enpdf1> Accessed 12/7/2013

[46] European Parliament Resolution on the Legal Profession, 23rd March 2006, Art 1 (FN 44)

[47] Ibid Art 3

legal rules in ensuring the competence and integrity of the legal profession, and also in securing the role of the legal profession in providing a high quality of service, in the best interests of both clients and society in general, is reaffirmed in the Resolution.[48] It welcomes the European Commission's acknowledgement that reform of the rules pertaining to the legal professions ought to take place at national level, as the legislative bodies of individual member states are best placed to define appropriate rules for their own circumstances.[49] It also notes that the Court of Justice affords national legislatures and professional associations a margin of discretion regarding what is appropriate and necessary in order to safeguard the proper functioning of the legal professions in each member state.[50]

The Resolution acknowledges that from a competition perspective, each activity of a professional body must be considered in isolation, and that competition rules must only be applied where an association is acting exclusively in its own interest, and not in the general interest.[51] The Commission is reminded in the Resolution that the aims of the rules governing the legal professions are safeguarding the public interest; preserving security through the application of the law and guaranteeing rights of defence and access to justice. As a consequence of these aims, such rules cannot be tailored to a client's degree of sophistication.[52] In order to safeguard the sound administration of justice, the Resolution encourages professional bodies and associations of legal professionals to establish codes of conduct at a European level.[53] These should include rules regarding organisational issues, qualifications, professional ethics, liability and communications. It invites the Commission, whilst promoting the principle of "less regulation, better regulation" to consider the specific role of legal professions in a society which complies with the rule of law, and also to perform a detailed analysis of how markets in legal services operate.[54] It states that there is no EU wide public interest test which can be applied generally, and that where the public interest overrides EU competition principles, such considerations must be rooted in the legal system of an individual member state in which a particular rule has been queried regarding its potential to be anti-competitive.[55]

The Resolution urges the Commission not to apply competition rules to issues which, according to the EU constitutional framework fall to the jurisdictions of individual member states, such as access to justice, and matters concerning fee schedules to be applied by courts when liquidating lawyers' fees.[56] It states that fee schedules or similar compulsory tariffs for lawyers do not breach Article 101 of the TFEU (ex Art 81 EC), as long as their use is justified by the

---

[48] Ibid Art 4
[49] Ibid Art 5
[50] Ibid Art 6
[51] Ibid Art 7
[52] Ibid Art 8
[53] Ibid Art 9
[54] Ibid Art 10
[55] Ibid Art 12
[56] Ibid Art 13

pursuit of a legitimate matter of public interest, and where the relevant member state actively supervises the involvement of private operators in the decision making process.[57] Finally, the Resolution encourages professional organisations to further develop their roles in the field of legal aid, in order to ensure that all persons have the right to receive legal advice and representation.[58]

The terms of the Resolution reflect a degree of tension between the Commission and Parliament as far as the future of the legal services market within Europe is concerned. On the one hand, the Commission has a vision of a more integrated market for legal services within the EU, to be achieved by a process of deregulation following the programme of research it initiated in recent years. On the other hand, the Parliament's Resolution would appear to reflect the objections of representatives of the legal profession to the Commission's deregulatory plans. The Resolution emphasizes the diversity of the various national legal markets of the individual member states and also the need to maintain their discretion to regulate for the effective functioning of their national legal professions. On balance, the Resolution would appear to have been drafted with the interests of legal professionals in mind rather than those of the consumers of their services.

The economic crisis which has afflicted many EU member states in recent years, and the Troika bailouts which were agreed in Greece, Portugal and Ireland have given the Commission a renewed opportunity to further its stated aim of increasing competition in the provision of legal services in Europe. The impact of the Troika on the regulation of the EU legal profession will be considered below.

2.3 The Impact of the Troika

Arguably, the most significant international influence upon the regulation of the Irish legal profession in recent times has been 'the Troika', a tripartite body consisting of the European Commission, the European Central Bank (ECB) and the International Monetary Fund (IMF). The emergence of the Troika as a significant regulatory force followed the meltdown of the Irish economy in 2010, which necessitated a bailout of €67.5 billion from the Troika.[59] In December 2010 the Memorandum of Understanding which was attached to the letter of intent to the IMF from the Irish Government and the Central Bank of Ireland

---

[57] Ibid Art 15

[58] Ibid Art 19

[59] Department of Finance 'Government Statement: Announcement of EU-IMF Programme for Ireland'. Available at: <http://www.finance.gov.ie/viewdoc.asp?DocID=6600> Accessed 27/6/2013; IMF 'Joint Statement on Ireland by EU Commissioner Olli Rehn and IMF Managing Director Dominique Strauss-Kahn' Press Release No 10/461. 28th Nov 2010. Available at: <http://www.imf.org/external/np/sec/pr/2010/pr10461.htm> Accessed 16/7/2013; P Nyberg (2011) *Misjudging Risk: Causes of the Systemic Banking Crisis in Ireland: Report of the Commission of Investigation into the Banking Sector in Ireland*. Dublin. Available at: <http://www.bankingenquiry.gov.ie/Documents/Misjudging%20Risk%20-%20Causes%20of%20the%20Systemic%20Banking%20Crisis%20in%20Ireland.pdf> Accessed 27/10/2012

committed Ireland to the implementation of a series of economic policies.[60] These included the downsizing and reorganization of the banking sector, and also a programme of structural reforms aimed at achieving a sustainable budget position. The Memorandum of Understanding committed Ireland to the introduction of legislative changes to remove restrictions to trade and competition in sheltered sectors of the economy including the legal profession, by the third quarter of 2011. The section of the agreement between the Troika and Ireland which relates to the legal profession is as follows:

> (Actions to be completed by the end of Q3 – 2011) Structural Reforms. To increase growth in the domestic sector. Government will introduce legislative changes to remove the restrictions to trade and competition in sheltered sectors including: - the legal profession, establishing an independent regulator for the profession and implementing the recommendations of the Legal Costs Working Group and outstanding Competition Authority recommendations to reduce legal costs.[61]

The publication of the Legal Services Regulation Bill (LSRB) in October 2011 contained the Government's proposals to make good their undertakings as set out in the above section of the Memorandum of Understanding. The three bodies which make up the Troika are deserving of a brief description.

The European Commission

The European Commission is one of the central EU institutions which represents and safeguards the interests of the EU in general. It consists of twenty-eight commissioners, each having responsibility for a particular area of policy. The role and functions of the Commission are set out in the EU Treaties.[62] It is responsible for promoting the general interest of the Union and for taking appropriate initiatives in the general interest.[63] It is responsible for overseeing the application of EU law under the control of the ECJ.[64] It is also responsible for the external representation of the EU.[65] It is independent in the performance of its functions and member states must respect its independence.[66] The Commission acts by a majority of its members.[67] It is most active in the area of competition law policy and in the management of the Common Agricultural and Com-

---

[60] The Memorandum of Understanding between the Troika and Ireland may be accessed at: IMF Ireland: Letter of Intent, Memorandum of Economic and Financial Policies, and Technical Memorandum of Understanding 3rd Dec 2010. Available at: <http://www.imf.org/external/np/loi/2010/irl/120310.pdf> Accessed 14/6/2012

[61] Ibid 27. Copies of these Ireland/ IMF documents were sent to the ECB and the European Commission, the copies being attached to the above documentation.

[62] Art 17 TEU and TFEU Arts 244 – 250

[63] Art 17 (1) TEU

[64] Ibid

[65] Ibid. The Commission is responsible for external representation of the EU except in relation to foreign and security policy and other matters as set out in the Treaties.

[66] Art 17 (3) TEU, Art 245 TFEU

[67] Art 250 TFEU

mon Customs Policies.[68]

The President of the EU Commission has faced a difficult task in bolstering global confidence in the euro in light of the series of sovereign debt crises which have afflicted the eurozone in recent times. He has identified the eurozone crisis as being due to an illusory belief on the part of eurozone members that a common currency and single market are compatible with individual national approaches to economic and budgetary policy:

> For the euro to be credible – and this is not only the message of the federalists, this is the message of the markets – we need a truly community approach. We need to really integrate the euro area, we need to complete monetary union with real economic union.[69]

The European Central Bank

Based in Frankfurt, the ECB is an EU institution which is responsible for the management of the euro and for maintaining price stability within the eurozone.[70] It is responsible for the supervision of both the EU financial markets and its financial institutions and also for establishing policy in relation to the euro and eurozone interest rates. Along with the Parliament, European Council, the Commission and the other EU institutions it is responsible for ensuring the effectiveness and continuity of Union policies.[71] Together with the Central Banks of member states it constitutes the European System of Central Banks (ESCB), the primary objective of which is to maintain price stability.[72] The ESCB is governed by the decision-making bodies of the ECB.[73] The ECB and the Central Banks of member states whose currency is the euro constitute the Eurosystem, which is responsible for conducting the Union's monetary policy.[74]

The International Monetary Fund

The IMF and the World Bank were established following the Breton Woods Conference in 1944 when 44 nations reached agreement on an enduring plan for the international economy after World War II.[75] Today, the IMF is an organization comprised of 188 nations and its primary function is to assist its member states to achieve financial stability alongside growth, by making resources available for purposes in keeping with its Articles of Agreement.[76] The purposes of the IMF include *inter alia* the promotion of international monetary co-

---

[68] N Foster, *EU Law: Directions* 2nd ed (Oxford University Press, 2010) 42

[69] EU Commission President Jose Manuel Barrosso's Speech to the EU Parliament, 28th Sept 2012. Available at:
<http://www.irishtimes.com/newspaper/breaking/2011/0928/breaking40_pf.html> Accessed 30/9/2011

[70] N Foster, *EU Law* (FN 68) 60

[71] Art 13 TFEU

[72] Art 282 (1) TFEU

[73] Art 282 (2) TFEU

[74] Art 282 (1) TFEU

[75] A Lowenfeld, *International Economic Law* (Oxford University Press, 2002) 502

[76] IMF Articles of Agreement are available at:
<http:////www.imf.org/external/pubs/ft/aa/pdf/aa/pdf> Accessed 28/6/2013

operation through a permanent institution that provides the machinery for consultation and collaboration on international monetary problems and to facilitate the expansion of the balanced growth of international trade.[77] The Managing Director of the IMF presides over its staff, a board of governors and an executive board.[78] The Board of Governors is empowered to make decisions in relation to all matters which are not otherwise delegated within the Articles of Agreement. However, it delegates much of its decisions-making power to the Executive Board.[79] The IMF functions as a 'centre for the collection and exchange of information on monetary and financial problems' and in this regard its members must provide it with detailed information regarding their monetary and financial problems.[80] However, some commentators have argued that the IMF has moved away from the principles which informed its establishment. As economist Joseph Stiglitz has stated:

> Over the years since its inception, the IMF has changed markedly. Founded in the belief that markets often worked badly, it now champions market supremacy with ideological fervour. Founded on the belief that there is a need for institutional pressure on countries to have more expansionary economic policies – such as increasing expenditures, reducing taxes, or lowering interest rates to stimulate the economy – today the IMF typically provides funds only if countries engage in policies like cutting deficits, raising taxes, or raising interest rates that lead to a contraction of the economy. Keynes would be rolling over in his grave were he to see what has happened to his child.[81]

The Origins of Ireland's Economic Crisis

Whilst economists and politicians differ regarding the cause of Ireland's financial crisis, commentators universally acknowledge that a banking crisis arose in part as a result of an overheated property sector.[82] In the Letter of Intent from the Irish Government and the Central Bank of Ireland to the IMF, the Minister for Finance and the Governor of the Central Bank identified the problem as emanating from the banking sector:

> At the root of the problem is a domestic banking system, which at its peak was five times the size of the economy, and now is under severe pressure.

---

[77] IMF Articles of Agreement Art 1 (i)

[78] Ibid Art XII (3) (b)

[79] A Lowenfeld, *International Economic Law* (FN 75) 504

[80] IMF Articles of Agreement Art VIII (5), A Lowenfeld *International Economic Law* (FN 76) 506

[81] J Stiglitz, *Globalization and its Discontents* (The Penguin Press, 2002) 12 – 13

[82] P Nyberg (2011) *Misjudging Risk* (FN 59); K Regling and M Watson (2010) *Preliminary Report on the Sources of Ireland's Banking Crisis* Dublin, Government Publications Office, 5 <http://www.bankingenquiry.gov.ie/Preliminary%20Report%20into%20Ireland's%20Banking%20Crisis%2031/%20May%202010.pdf> Accessed 27/10/2012; M Hosier, 'The Legal Profession in Troikaland: Before and After the Irish Bailout' 2 – 11. Reprinted in Appendix 1. Available at: <http:///ssrn.com/abstract=2262083 Accessed 1/7/2013>. This article gives a more detailed account of the origins of the economic crisis.

> The Irish owned banks were much larger than the size of the economy. The fragility of the banking sector is undermining Ireland's hard-earned economic credibility and adding a severe burden to acute public finance challenges.[83]

The dramatic fall of over 18% in one week in March 2008 of the Anglo Irish Bank (Anglo) share price marked the first public sign of the beginning of the economic collapse which was to follow.[84] Following a run on the bank in September 2008 the Government guaranteed all the liabilities of the seven major Irish banks to a total of €37.5 billion.[85] However, the situation failed to stabilise, notwithstanding the nationalization of Anglo and the Government policy of bank recapitalization over the course of the following two years. By the autumn of 2010 the situation had become unsustainable, and having found itself unable to borrow on the international financial markets at viable rates, the Irish Government sought relief in the form of a bailout from the Troika.[86]

It is against this background that far reaching economic and structural reform of the Irish economy is currently occurring. Ireland has experienced a deep recession as the Government adheres to the reform program and implements the fiscal measures based upon free market ideology which were agreed with the Troika.[87] It remains to be seen whether Ireland will return to sustainable economic growth on foot of these policies. In the following section, the impact of the Council of Europe upon the regulation of the Irish legal profession will be considered.

2.4 The Council of Europe

The Council of Europe (COE) encompasses almost all of Europe, and has forty-seven members. Founded in 1949, it aims to promote the rule of law, democracy and respect for human rights. In order to protect and realise the common ideals and principles of its members, and to facilitate their economic and social progress, the COE pursues its aim of achieving greater unity between its members:

> ... through the organs of the Council by discussion of questions of common concern and by agreements and common action in economic, social, cultural, scientific, legal and administrative matters and in the maintenance and further realisation of human rights and fundamental freedoms.[88]

---

[83] IMF Ireland: Letter of Intent 3rd Dec 2010 (FN 60)

[84] P Nyberg, *Misjudging Risk* (FN 59) 151

[85] Ibid 152

[86] See Appendix 1, reprinting in extract M Hosier, 'The Legal Profession in Troikaland: Before and After the Irish Bailout' (FN 82)

[87] J Stiglitz, *Globalization and its Discontents* (FN 81) 18. Joseph Stiglitz has argued that the agreements which the IMF makes in return for the receipt of funds are shaped by its free market ideology.

[88] Statute of the Council of Europe (CETS 1), Art 1 paras a & b. Available at: <http://conventions.coe.int/Treaty/Commun/QueVoulezVous.asp?NT=001&CM=1&CL=ENG>

The Committee of Ministers is the main decision-making body of the COE, and is made up of either the Ministers of Foreign Affairs of the member states, or their permanent representatives at Strasbourg. Along with the Parliamentary Assembly which is the Council of Europe's forum for debate, the Committee of Ministers is responsible for safeguarding the fundamental values of the COE, and for seeing that member states comply with their commitments. It also regularly adopts recommendations such as the one examined.

Recommendation No R (2000) 21 of the Committee of Ministers to Member States on the Freedom of Exercise of the Profession of Lawyer

On the 25th October 2000 the Council of Ministers adopted Recommendation No R (2000) 21 of the Committee of Ministers to Member States on the Freedom of Exercise of the Profession of Lawyer.[89] The Recommendation was adopted as a result of an ongoing discussion at the COE regarding the quality of judicial and legal practices in member states.[90] The discussion recognised the role of an independent legal profession in the administration of justice and in safeguarding the rights of citizens in democratic societies which are enshrined in the European Convention on Human Rights.

The first principle of the Recommendation states that the freedom of the profession of lawyer should be protected and promoted by all necessary means, without discrimination or interference from the authorities.[91] It requires that decisions concerning authorisation to practice as a lawyer should be made by an independent authority, and subject to review by an independent judicial authority. It further states that lawyers should have freedom of belief, expression and association, and they should be free to participate in public debates about the law and legislative reforms.[92] The Recommendation also addresses the issues of legal education, training and entry into the legal profession, and states that these should not be influenced by a person's sex, sexual orientation, race, colour, ethnicity, religion, political persuasion, social position, property, birth or physical disability.[93] It also states that all necessary steps should be taken to ensure a good standard of legal training and morality as a condition of entry to the profession and to allow for the ongoing education of lawyers.

The Recommendation also refers to the role and duty of lawyers.[94] It states that bar associations and codes of conduct should require lawyers to act independently, diligently and fairly in the cause of defending their clients' legitimate

---

Accessed 16/7/2013

[89] Recommendation No R (2000) 21 of the Committee of Ministers to Member States on the Freedom of Exercise of the Profession of Lawyer. Adopted by the Committee of Ministers on 25th October 2000 at the 727th meeting of Ministers' Deputies.

[90] The debate on quality of judicial practice gave rise to the adoption of Recommendation No R (94) 12 of the Committee of Ministers to the Member States on the Independence, Efficiency and Role of Judges.

[91] Recommendation No R (2000) 21 of the Committee of Ministers to Member States on the Freedom of Exercise of the Profession of Lawyer, Principle 1

[92] Ibid

[93] Ibid, Principle II

[94] Ibid, Principle III

rights and interests. Lawyers should also respect the principle of professional secrecy as required by internal laws, regulations and professional standards. A lawyer's duty towards his/her client should include giving advice on the client's rights and obligations in law, and the probable outcome and consequences of a case, including its cost. A lawyer must strive to settle a case amicably where possible, and must take legal action to protect and enforce his/her client's rights and interests. Conflicts of interest must be avoided, and a lawyer should respect the judiciary and perform court duties in a fashion that respects domestic legal rules and professional standards. The Recommendation also addresses the issue of access to lawyers for all persons.[95] It requires that all necessary measures are taken for all persons to have access to legal services from independent lawyers, that lawyers should be encouraged to provide legal services to impoverished persons, and that member states' governments should ensure access to justice for such persons, especially where they are deprived of their liberty.

The Recommendation states that lawyers should be encouraged to form and join both national and international associations of lawyers, which are charged with strengthening professional standards and protecting lawyers' independence and interests.[96] It also states that bar associations and law societies should be self-governing and independent of both the authorities and the public. The role of such associations in protecting their members and defending their interests should be respected. Such associations should be encouraged to ensure lawyers' independence, to fearlessly promote the cause of justice, to defend the role of lawyers in society and to safeguard their honour, dignity and integrity. They should also promote lawyers' participation in programmes aimed at providing access to justice for impoverished persons in need of legal aid and advice. Associations of legal professionals should also promote and support law reform and debate concerning proposed legislation. They should co-operate with lawyers abroad to promote the role of lawyers, by considering the work of international lawyers' organisations and international intergovernmental and non-governmental organisations. Associations of legal professionals should take all necessary steps, including defending lawyers' interests, where a lawyer is arrested or detained, where a decision is made which calls a lawyer's integrity into question, where a lawyer or his/her property is searched or where there is a seizure of his/her documents or materials.

Disciplinary proceedings are also addressed in the Recommendation which requires that where lawyers fail to maintain professional standards as set down in the relevant codes of conduct, appropriate measures should be taken, including disciplinary proceedings, and that associations of legal professionals should be involved in the conduct of such proceedings.[97] Disciplinary proceedings should be in accordance with the requirements of the European Convention on Human Rights, including the right of the lawyer concerned to take part in the proceedings, the outcome of which should be subject to judicial review. Finally,

---

[95] Ibid, Principle IV
[96] Ibid, Principle V
[97] Ibid, Principle VI

in the determination of sanctions where disciplinary offences have been established, the principle of proportionality must be observed.

The Recommendation has been valuable in informing the debate at both national and international levels regarding the role and function of the legal profession. It serves as a useful framework with which to assess proposed changes to the regulation of lawyers and it highlights the particular role which lawyers' associations have in protecting their members' interests, contributing to debates regarding proposed legislative changes which may impact upon lawyers and the services they provide, and in particular; in the disciplinary process which pertains to their members. The Recommendation provides an alternative perspective on the regulation of the legal profession from the EU model which has focused primarily upon the legal services market and which emphasizes the role of competition in making legal services more readily available at a lower price for Union citizens. The following section will consider the impact of the United Nations upon the regulation of the legal profession.

2.5 The United Nations

Founded in 1945, and with a membership consisting of 193 member states, the United Nations (UN) is an organisation which is committed to the maintenance of international peace and security, the establishment of good relations between nations, ensuring social progress, the protection of human rights and encouraging respect for the rights and freedoms of others. The Preamble to the UN Charter states that the member states have determined 'to establish conditions under which justice and respect for the obligations arising from treaties and other sources of international law can be maintained.'[98] The UN therefore sees the maintenance of international law and order as a primary purpose of the organisation. The Charter establishes the International Court of Justice as the principal judicial organ of the UN.[99] All member states are subject to the Court's authority, in accordance with Article 94 of the Charter.[100]

The UN recognises that the promotion of the rule of law at both a national and international level is fundamental to its ethos.[101] It has defined the rule of law as:

> a principle of governance in which all persons, institutions and entities, public and private, including the state itself, are accountable to laws that are publicly promulgated, equally enforced and independently adjudicated, and which are consistent with international human rights norms and standards. It requires as well, measures to ensure adherence to the principles of supremacy of law, equality before the law, accountability to the law, fairness in the application of the law, separation of powers, participa

---

[98] The UN Charter is available at: <http://www.un.org/en/documents/charter/> Accessed 16/7/2013

[99] Charter of the United Nations, Art 92. Available at: <www.un.org/en/documents/charter/> Accessed 16/7/2013

[100] Ibid, Art 94

[101] UN Rule of Law Website. Available at: <http://www.un.org/en/ruleoflaw/> Accessed 16/7/2013

tion in decision-making, legal certainty, avoidance of arbitrariness and procedural and legal transparency.[102]

The centrality of the rule of law concept to the UN mission is evidenced by its website dedicated to the Rule of Law.[103] The UN has affirmed that 'human rights and the rule of law and democracy are interlinked and mutually reinforcing and that they belong to the universal and indivisible core values and principles of the UN'.[104]

The Basic Principles on the Role of Lawyers

The Basic Principles on the Role of Lawyers were adopted in 1990 by the Eighth UN Congress on the Prevention of Crime and the Treatment of Offenders in Havana, Cuba.[105] In accordance with the Basic Principles everyone is entitled to the assistance of a lawyer of their own choice in order to protect and establish their rights, and for the purpose of defending them throughout criminal proceedings.[106] Governments must ensure that persons within their territories have effective and equal access to lawyers, regardless of factors such as race, colour, sex, religion, politics or other opinion, property, birth, economic or other status.[107] They must ensure that poor and other disadvantaged persons shall have access to legal services. It also requires professional associations of lawyers to co-operate in organising and facilitating such services.[108] The public must be informed by Governments and professional associations of lawyers regarding their rights and responsibilities according to the law, and also about the role of lawyers in safeguarding their fundamental freedoms.[109] The General Principles also require special help to be given to poor and disadvantaged persons in asserting their rights.

The Basic Principles include special safeguards in matters of criminal justice, and provide that arrested or detained persons must be informed forthwith regarding their right to legal representation, and that where necessary, they are assigned a lawyer of suitable experience and competence, given the nature of the charges against them.[110] Access to a lawyer should be provided no later than 48 hours from the time of arrest. Detained persons should also be given the oppor-

---

[102] UN *Report of the Secretary-General on the Rule of Law and Transitional Justice in Conflict and Post-Conflict Societies* (S/2004/616). Available at: <http://www.un.org./en/ruleoflaw/> Accessed 16/7/2013

[103] <www.unrol.org>

[104] UN Resolution (A/RES/67/97) on The Rule of Law at the National and International Levels. Adopted by the General Assembly [on the report of the Sixth Committee (A/67/471)] 14th December 2012. Available at: <www.un.org/ga/serarch/view_doc.asp?symbol=A/RES/67/97> Accessed 17/7/2013

[105] The Basic Principles on the Role of Lawyers adopted by the Eighth UN Congress on the Prevention of Crime and the Treatment of Offenders, Havana, Cuba 27th August to 7th September 1990. <http://www2.ohchr.org/english/law/lawyers.htm> Accessed 10/7/2012

[106] Ibid, Art 1

[107] Ibid, Art 2

[108] Ibid, Art 3

[109] Ibid, Art 5

[110] Ibid, Arts 5 – 8

tunity to consult with their lawyer confidentially, although such meetings may be within sight, not hearing of a law enforcement official. Lawyers are required to have appropriate education and training, to be acquainted with the ideals and ethical duties of lawyers, and also with human rights and fundamental freedoms in accordance with national and international law.[111] Discrimination against a person wishing to enter the legal profession is prohibited on grounds including race, colour, sex, ethnic origin, religion, political or other opinion, property, birth and economic or other status.[112] However, a requirement that a lawyer must be a national of a particular country is not discriminatory. [113]

The Basic Principles state that where there are groups, communities or regions in a country whose needs for legal services have not been met, especially where such groups have distinctive cultures, traditions or languages, or have suffered previous discrimination, governments, professional associations of lawyers and educational institutions should take special measures to guarantee candidates from such groups have the opportunity to enter the legal profession, and that they receive training appropriate to their needs. Lawyers must uphold the honour and dignity of the profession, as these are necessary for the proper administration of justice.[114] Duties to their clients include giving advice about legal rights and duties, and the functioning of the legal system, assisting clients and taking legal action to protect their interests.[115] Lawyers also have a duty to assist their clients as necessary before courts, tribunals and administrative authorities. In the course of safeguarding clients' rights and promoting the cause of justice, lawyers shall endeavour to protect human rights and fundamental freedoms in accordance with national and international law, and shall act in accordance with the ethical standards established by the legal profession and in accordance with the law and recognised norms.[116]

The Basic Principles on the Role of Lawyers also set out necessary guarantees for the proper functioning of lawyers. Governments must ensure that lawyers can carry out their professional functions free from intimidation or improper interference, and that they can travel and consult with clients freely both at home and abroad.[117] Nor shall lawyers be prosecuted or threatened with prosecution or administrative, economic or other sanctions for actions taken in the course of their professional obligations. Where lawyers' security is threatened in the course of carrying out their obligations, adequate protection must be made available by the authorities.[118] Where a court recognises counsel's right to appear before it, the court must not deny that counsel the right to appear unless he/she has been disqualified in accordance with national law and practice.[119]

---

[111] Ibid, Art 9
[112] Ibid, Art 10
[113] Ibid, Art 11
[114] Ibid, Art 12
[115] Ibid, Art 13
[116] Ibid, Art 14
[117] Ibid, Art 16
[118] Ibid, Art 17
[119] Ibid, Art 19

Lawyers shall also be immune from civil and penal immunity in relation to statements made in good faith in either written or oral pleadings before a court, tribunal or other legal or administrative authority.

The General Principles require relevant authorities to grant lawyers access to appropriate information, files and documents in their possession or control promptly, in order to facilitate the efficient provision of legal assistance to clients.[120] Governments shall respect the confidential nature of communications and consultations between lawyers and their clients.[121] The General Principles also assert lawyers' freedom of expression, belief, association and assembly, and require that lawyers must be at liberty to participate in public debates about the law, the administration of justice, the promotion of human rights and to join or form organisations at a local, national and international level without being subject to restrictions upon their professional practice.[122]

The General Principles refer to professional associations of lawyers, and provide that lawyers should be at liberty to form such associations, and to join them in order to represent their interests, provide for their ongoing education and training and to protect their professional integrity.[123] These associations will co-operate with Governments so that lawyers are permitted to counsel and assist their clients in accordance with the law and recognised standards of professionalism and ethics. Finally, the General Principles address the issue of disciplinary proceedings.[124] Codes of professional conduct must be established by the legal profession.[125] Charges or complaints about lawyers shall be expeditiously dealt with in a fair manner, in accordance with appropriate procedures. Lawyers have a right to a fair hearing, and to have assistance from a lawyer of their choice. Disciplinary proceedings must be brought before either an impartial committee established by the legal profession, an independent statutory authority or a court. Such proceedings must be subject to judicial review. All disciplinary proceedings must be determined in accordance with the relevant professional code of conduct, other recognised standards and the ethics of the legal profession. They must also be in accordance with the Basic Principles on the Role of Lawyers themselves.

The UN's Basic Principles on the Role of Lawyers represent an important commitment on the part of the UN's members to respect the rights and requirements of lawyers in the exercise of their professional duties. They recognise the role of lawyers in maintaining civic order and protecting the rights of citizens in the course of their interactions with state authorities. They also reflect the fact that the work of lawyers is crucial in furthering many aspects of the UN's agenda, especially in relation to human rights, international law, peace and security. The following section will consider the impact of the World Trade Organisation (WTO) on the regulation of the legal profession.

---

[120] Ibid, Art 21
[121] Ibid, Art 22
[122] Ibid, Art 23
[123] Ibid, Arts 24, 25
[124] Ibid, Arts 26 – 29
[125] Ibid, Art 26

2.6 The World Trade Organisation

Whilst the WTO does not directly regulate the legal profession, the provision of legal services is included in the General Agreement on Trade in Services (GATS) which is a set of rules governing the international trade in services. It was agreed during the Uruguay Round of Negotiations (from 1986 to 1994), in response to the exponential rate of growth which the service sector has experienced in recent years.[126] The WTO organisation is primarily responsible for facilitating trade globally, and it also acts as a vehicle for international negotiations concerning trade. It facilitates the resolution of trade disputes, monitors the implementation of trade agreements and national trade policies and liaises with other international organisations on matters pertaining to trade. The GATS was established in 1995, almost fifty years after the establishment of the General Agreement on Tariffs and Trade in 1947. The WTO currently consists of 155 countries, and the EU countries are included in its membership. The WTO recently announced a growth in the global export of commercial services of 3% in the first quarter of 2012, and the services sector increasingly plays a central role in all aspects of the WTO's agenda.[127] The WTO Director General recently acknowledged the fundamental role of the export of services in facilitating the process of globalization:

> The global economy is becoming transformed at an unprecedented speed and at the heart of that transformation is the services economy. Services underpin every part of the production process, from research and development to design, engineering, financing, transportation, distribution and marketing.[128]

The principles which govern the international trade in legal services are contained within GATS. Parties who are signatories to the Agreement confer 'most favoured nation' status on other parties to it. This means that they must accord treatment which is no less favourable to the services and service providers from any individual signatory than that which it accords to those of other signatories. There is also a requirement for transparency, and all relevant laws and regulations must be published. Restrictive business practices should be the subject of consultation with a view to effecting their removal. The Agreement provides for an ongoing process of liberalisation in the services sector, to be achieved by a series of rounds of negotiations and the development of national schedules containing commitments on services liberalisation which go beyond the general obligations contained in GATS. Some of the national schedules provide for the

---

[126] A Lowenfeld, *International Economic Law* (FN 75) 113

[127] WTO services export data for 2012 is available at:
<www.wto.org/english/news_e/news12_e/stss_13Jul12_e.htm> Accessed 2/8/2012. The total value of global commercial services (excluding government services) exports in 2012 was almost $ 4, 347 billion (WTO statistics available at: <stat.wto.org/StatisticalProgram//WSDBViewData.aspx?Language=E> Accessed 17/7/2013).

[128] Pascal Lamy, Speech. China International Fair in Trade in Services, Beijing, 28th May 2012. A transcript of the speech is available at:
<http://www.wto.org/english/news_e/sppl_e/sppl233_e.htm> Accessed 2/8/2012

removal of limitations upon the type of legal entity or joint venture which can provide services.[129]

According to Terry, international trade agreements such as GATS have had a strong impact upon the regulation of lawyers in the US and elsewhere:

> these international trade agreements have affected the vocabulary, *landscape* and *stakeholders* involved in lawyer regulation. These agreements, coupled with globalization and pressure from lawyers and law firms engaged in transnational practice have led to fundamental changes that I believe will only increase in the future.[130]

WTO Joint Statement on Legal Services

In 2005 a group of WTO members, including the European Communities, issued a Joint Statement on Legal Services, setting out points of convergence which were agreed in the course of discussions held by the WTO's Informal Friends Group on legal services.[131] The Joint Statement declared that IBA resolutions concerning Principles for the Establishment and Regulation of Foreign Lawyers, and in Support of a System of Terminology for Legal Services for the Purposes of International Trade Negotiations should serve as valuable reference points in WTO discussions on both the regulation of foreign lawyers by means of either full or limited licensing approaches and also on the establishment of terminology to be used when referring to the international trade in legal services.[132] The Joint Statement acknowledged the right of members to impose qualifications or licensing requirements for providers of legal services. It also recognised the tension that may exist at times between the principle of progressive liberalisation on the one hand, and the needs of individual members on the other hand. Accordingly, the Joint Statement acknowledged members' rights to avail of the flexibility afforded in GATS to schedule their commitments in the area of legal service provisions in a manner in keeping with their domestic circumstances.

It further recognised that the practice of host country law and the practice of international and foreign law are subject to different regulatory regimes dealing with matters such as qualifications and licensing requirements, and that those differing areas of practice also tend to be subject to different levels of liberalisation, as far as market access is concerned. The Joint Statement proposed that the ability of foreign law firms to develop commercial associations with host country

---

[129] The GATS schedule which applies to EU countries refers to 'legal advice on home country law and public international law'; it also shows exceptions to the General Agreement, such as the reservation to home lawyers on the drafting of legal documents which applies in France and Portugal. (GATS/SC/31 GATS European Communities and their Member States: Schedule of Specific Commitments 15th April 1994, 12)   Available at: <www.wto.org/English/tratop_e/serv_e/telecom_e/sc31.pdf> Accessed 17/7/2013

[130] L Terry, 'From GATS to APEC: The Impact of Trade Agreements on Legal Services' [2010] 43 *Akron Law Review* 875, 969

[131] The WTO Joint Statement on Legal Services is available at: <http://trade.ec.europa.eu/doclib/docs/2008/september/tradoc_140347.pdf > Accessed 10/8/2012

[132] Links to these IBA resolutions are available at: <http://www.ibanet.org/About_the_IBA/IBA_resolutions.aspx> Accessed 26/8/2012

law firms should be encouraged, in order to accommodate the needs of clients who wish to avail of legal services covering multiple disciplines (domestic, foreign and international).

Finally, the Joint Statement suggested some common terminology to be used by WTO members, to facilitate communication and negotiations between members, including activities which consist of legal advisory services; legal representational services; legal arbitration and conciliation or mediation services. In accordance with the Joint Statement, in the context of WTO scheduling commitments, 'domestic law' is defined as the law of a given member; 'foreign law' is defined as the law of territories of the WTO and other countries, excluding the law of the particular member who is scheduling its commitments and 'international law' is defined as the body of law established by international treaties and conventions, as well as customary law.

The WTO is currently holding ongoing negotiations regarding the legal services market in the course of the Doha Round of Trade Talks.[133] The following sections will consider the impact of lawyers' international representative associations upon the regulation of the legal profession.

2.7 The Council of the Bars and Law Societies of Europe

The Council of the Bars and Law Societies of Europe (CCBE) is a non-profit making organisation which is responsible for the representation of European bar associations and law societies when interacting with European and other international organisations. It represents almost 750,000 European lawyers from forty one states, thirty one of whom are full members, with the remaining ten being observer countries. An individual's membership of the CCBE is effected by virtue of the membership of the national law society or bar association to which he/she belongs. The organisation was established in 1960, in light of the influence of the EEC upon the practice of lawyers. The CCBE portrays the views of European lawyers and seeks to defend the key principles underpinning democracy and the rule of law. It is considered to be the authentic voice of the European legal profession by both the EU institutions and also by individual law societies and bar associations. It also liaises with legal organisations globally.

The CCBE's objectives are to defend the rule of law, human rights and democratic values. It places particular emphasis upon the right of access to justice and client protection through the defence of core professional values. It concerns itself with the effect of competition law upon lawyers' core values and the interrelationship between lawyers' duties and the duties of governments to provide security for citizens. The organisation also takes an active interest in both the effects of globalization and market liberalisation upon legal practice. The CCBE works to coordinate and harmonise the practice of law within its member states. In 1979 the European Court of Justice permitted the CCBE to intervene in a case concerning legal professional privilege for in-house counsel, and subsequently it established a permanent delegation to the Court of Justice.[134] In 1988 the organi-

---

[133] Track #1 of the Doha Round concerns the liberalization of the trade in legal services. Track #2 concerns Disciplines in Domestic Regulation. L Terry, 'From GATS to APEC' (FN 130) 940

[134] Case 155/79 AM & S Europe Ltd v Commission of the European Committees [1982] ECR

sation established its Code of Conduct which regulates the cross-border activities of lawyers.

The CCBE functions through the work of Delegations. These are national bodies consisting of six elected individuals who together form the Standing Committee of the CCBE, its main executive body. Delegation members also participate in the work of specialist committees and working groups which research and report to the association on matters concerning the legal profession in Europe such as professional ethics, competition and its impact on the legal profession, the free movement of lawyers and the international trade in legal services. Following the publication of a European Union Commission initiative which may affect either the legal profession or users of its services, the relevant committees may produce a CCBE position paper where they perceive this to be necessary.[135]

The CCBE Code of Conduct

The CCBE Code of Conduct was adopted in recognition of the increasing harmonisation of the market for legal services within the European Economic Area (EEA).[136] The CCBE was of the view that the public interest required the establishment of a set of rules concerning cross-border practice which were common to all lawyers within the EEA, regardless of their member state of origin. Cross border activities, for the purposes of the Code of Conduct include professional contacts between lawyers in member states other than the lawyer's own member state, and professional activities of a lawyer in a member state other than his/her own, regardless of whether the lawyer is actually present in the host member state.

The Code begins by setting out the general principles of conduct which a lawyer must obey. He/she must remain independent in the course of his/her duties and avoid influences due to either his/her own personal interest or external pressure.[137] Professional standards must not be compromised for clients, third parties or the court. A lawyer has a professional obligation to ensure that his/her personal honour, honesty and integrity are beyond reproach.[138] The maintenance of confidentiality is both a fundamental right and a core duty for a lawyer, given that he/she is the recipient of highly personal information from clients, which would not normally be divulged.[139] A lawyer must respect the rules of other bar associations and law societies when practising in a host state and must ensure he/she is familiar with the relevant rules.[140] A lawyer must be mindful of the fact that certain occupations are in-

---

1575

[135] For further details of the CCBE's policy making process, see:
<www.ccbe.eu/index.php?id=288&L-O> Accessed 4/7/2012

[136] Both the CCBE Code of Conduct and the Charter of Core Principles of the European Legal Professions are available at: <www.ccbe.eu/fileadmin/user_upload/NTCdocument/ EN_Code_of-conductp1_1306748215.pdf > Accessed 31/7/2012

[137] CCBE Code of Conduct, Art 2.1.1

[138] Ibid, Art 2.2

[139] Ibid, Art 2.3.1

[140] Ibid, Art 2.4

compatible with his/her ability to function as a lawyer with the requisite level of independence, and to observe the rules in relation to incompatible occupations when practising abroad.[141] When informing the public about services, a lawyer must ensure the information given is accurate, honest and in accordance with obligations which arise from the core professional values, including confidentiality.[142] A client's interest must be paramount, subject to the rule of law and professional conduct, and must take precedence over a lawyer's own interests, or those of his/her colleagues in the legal profession.[143] Liability towards a client may be subject to limits, in accordance with the rules of professional conduct of both home and host member states.[144]

In the course of dealings with clients, a lawyer shall ensure he/she only accepts instructions either directly from a client, another lawyer or from a competent assigning body.[145] He/she shall be prompt in giving advice and making representations on behalf of clients, and must be personally responsible for discharging instructions and for keeping clients informed of progress.[146] He/she must not accept instructions in a matter where he/she lacks the requisite competence unless he/she co-operates with a lawyer who is competent in the relevant field.[147] He/she must not withdraw from a case in a manner that may compromise a client's case, or which may give rise to prejudice being suffered by a client.[148] A lawyer must avoid conflicts of interest, and where there is a significant risk of a conflict arising between the interests of two or more clients, he/she may not advise, represent or act on their behalf in relation to the same matter.[149] A lawyer must stop acting for both or all clients where a conflict of interest arises between them, or where his/her independence may be compromised.[150] A lawyer may not make a *pactum de quota litis* with a client.[151] He/she must fully disclose all fees to the client, and these must be fair and reasonable, and in conformity with the law and rules of conduct which govern the lawyer's behaviour.[152] Fee sharing with non-lawyers is prohibited, unless an association with such a person is permitted by both the law and the rules of professional conduct which apply to the lawyer concerned.[153]

---

[141] Ibid, Art 2.5

[142] Ibid, Art 2.6

[143] Ibid, Art 2.7

[144] Ibid, Art 2.8

[145] Ibid, Art 3.1.1

[146] Ibid, Art 3.1.2

[147] Ibid, Art 3.1.3

[148] Ibid, Art 3.1.4

[149] Ibid, Art 3.2.1

[150] Ibid, Art 3.2.2

[151] Ibid, Art 3.3.1. A *pactum de quota litis* is an agreement between a client and lawyer made before the end of a matter concerning the client whereby the client agrees to pay the lawyer a share of the result achieved upon finishing the matter.

[152] Ibid, Art 3.4

[153] Ibid, Art 3.6.1

A lawyer must seek to provide the most cost-effective resolution of a client's issue, and should advise as appropriate regarding a client's rights and upon the merits of seeking a settlement in a matter.[154] The Code of Conduct also specifies the manner in which client funds should be handled, and provides that they should be held in a designated client account unless other arrangements have been made with the client.[155] Full and accurate records concerning client accounts must be maintained.[156] Funds cannot be transferred from client accounts for the purpose of paying lawyers' fees without firstly informing the client in writing.[157] A lawyer must also be insured to a reasonable level against civil liability resulting from his/her legal practice, in light of the nature of the risks associated with his/her activities, and where this is not feasible, the client must be informed of the potential consequences.[158]

The Code of Conduct also sets out rules concerning a lawyer's relationship with the courts. A lawyer must abide by the rules of the court or tribunal before which he/she appears, and must respect the fair conduct of proceedings.[159] He/she must also be courteous and respectful of the court in the course of his/her actions or representations on a client's behalf.[160] He/she must never give false or misleading information to the court.[161]

As far as relations between lawyers are concerned, the Code requires lawyers to maintain relationships of trust and co-operation between lawyers, and to avoid unnecessary litigation and other behaviour which would impact negatively upon the profession.[162] Lawyers from other member states should be treated fairly and courteously as professional colleagues.[163] Where a lawyer is approached by a colleague from another member state to take instructions in a matter in relation to which he/she is not competent to offer advice, he/she must decline to accept the instructions and must instead assist the colleague to identify a lawyer who is competent to provide the services being sought.[164] Fees or commission must not be asked for, or accepted, in return for referring or recommending a lawyer to a client, nor may a lawyer pay such a fee in return for receiving a client referral.[165] A lawyer is prohibited from communicating directly with a person he/she knows to be represented by another lawyer without that lawyer's knowledge and consent.[166] He/she must also ensure that his/her skills are maintained and that he/she is fully acquainted with the European dimension

---

154 Ibid, Art 3.7.1
155 Ibid, Art 3.8.1
156 Ibid, Art 3.8.2
157 Ibid, Art 3.8.5
158 Ibid, Art 3.9
159 Ibid, Arts 4.1 & 4.2
160 Ibid, Art 4.3
161 Ibid, Art 4.4
162 Ibid, Art 5.1.1
163 Ibid, Art 5.1.2
164 Ibid, Art 5.2.1
165 Ibid, Art 5.4
166 Ibid, Art 5.5

of legal practice.[167] Disputes amongst lawyers from different member states must be resolved where possible between the lawyers themselves, and where this is not possible, with the assistance of their respective law societies or bar associations.[168]

Charter of Core Principles of the European Legal Profession

In 2006 the CCBE adopted a Charter of Core Principles of the European Legal Profession, which compliments the Code of Conduct adopted in 1988. The Charter is directed at all of Europe, and is not confined merely to countries which are members of the CCBE. It contains ten principles which apply to both national and international rules regulating the legal profession. It aims to assist bar associations in establishing and protecting their independence and to elucidate for lawyers the essential social function they perform. The Charter is directed at lawyers, decision-makers and the general public.

The Core Principles are as follows:

(a) the independence of the lawyer, and the freedom of the lawyer to pursue the client's case;

(b) the right and duty of the lawyer to keep clients' matters confidential and to respect professional secrecy;

(c) avoidance of conflicts of interest, whether between different clients or between the client and the lawyer;

(d) the dignity and honour of the legal profession, and the integrity and good repute of the individual lawyer;

(e) loyalty to the client;

(f) fair treatment of clients in relation to fees;

(g) the lawyer's professional competence;

(h) respect towards professional colleagues;

(i) respect for the rule of law and the fair administration of justice; and

(j) the self-regulation of the legal profession.[169]

The CCBE impacts both directly and indirectly upon the regulation of the legal profession throughout Europe. It impacts directly by virtue of both its Code of Conduct and its Charter of Core Principles. It has also impacted indirectly through its lobbying at a governmental level regarding proposed legislative reforms which it considers are likely to adversely effect either the legal profession or the recipients of its services. The Code of Conduct's broad and somewhat aspirational contents reflect the difficulty attributed to gaining agreement

---

[167] Ibid, Art 5.8

[168] Ibid, Art 5.9

[169] The Charter of Core Principles of the European Legal Professions is available at: <www.ccbe.eu/fileadmin/user_upload/NTCdocument/EN_Code_of-conductp1_1306748215.pdf> Accessed 31/7/2012

amongst the numerous national law societies which comprise the CCBE regarding what precise standards are appropriate, given the diverse structures of the various legal professions and the wide variety of traditions and practices involved.

Given its generality, the Code of Conduct may offer a somewhat limited solution to the problem of double deontology whereby a lawyer engaged in international practice must abide by the Codes of Conduct of both his/her home state and also that of the host states. However, it does provide a useful reference point for national law societies to refer to when considering amendments to their national codes of conduct and in that way, the potential difficulties associated with double deontology may be reduced over time. The role of the International Bar Association in regulating the legal profession will be considered in the next section.

2.8 The International Bar Association

The International Bar Association (IBA) is the paramount organisation representing international lawyers, bar associations and law societies. It was established in 1947 by thirty-four bar associations which met in New York in order to further the establishment of law and the administration of justice globally. The association is influential in matters of international law and it directs the development of the legal profession on a global level. It has over 45,000 individual lawyer members and over 200 affiliated bar associations and law societies.

The principal aims and objectives of the IBA include facilitating the exchange of information between legal associations on a global level; supporting the independence of the judiciary and upholding the right of lawyers to practice independently and free from duress. It is also active in the promotion of human rights for lawyers via its Human Rights Institute. The association provides services for individual lawyers by means of its divisions and committees. It also supports the activities of both established and developing bar associations and law societies.

The association has two main divisions: The Legal Practice Division and The Public and Professional Interest Division. The Legal Practice Division promotes information and opinion exchange between members regarding lawyers' practice and professional responsibilities. It also facilitates communication between members and presents opportunities for members to participate in activities such as debating and discussing legal practice through its various committees, fora and special projects. The Public and Professional Interest Division aims to promote the exchange of ideas concerning the public and professional interest activities of lawyers globally. It is active in the promotion of the rule of law and human rights protection, and it also facilitates debate between division members and member organisations through its Bar Issues Commission (BIC) and other fora. The role of the BIC is to provide members of the IBA with a forum to discuss issues concerning law at an international level. For instance at the 2012 IBA annual conference held in Dublin, the BIC programme included sessions on the regulatory response to alternative business structures and the nature of legal services, and it also hosted a symposium on the rule of law.[170] The BIC section of the IBA website also has a link to a website dedicated to the regulation of the legal profession which provides further links to Codes of Conduct for legal professionals in many countries whose law societies and bar associations are affiliated to the IBA.[171]

The IBA has several task forces and action groups dedicated to furthering understanding and facilitating problem resolution in areas of difficulty for lawyers internationally, such as the global financial crisis, illicit financial flows and the rule of law. The task force on the financial crisis has suggested that political and economic proposals aimed at alleviating the crisis, or at preventing a similar occurrence in future must ultimately be implemented into law and regulation to be effective, a process which will give rise to complex legal issues. The task force is of the view that lawyers should therefore contribute to debates concerning the financial crisis and the measures to be implemented in its wake. It also aims to critically analyse the views of others who have put forward proposals for regulatory reform, and to defend the rule of law as a fundamental principle and a prerequisite for the facilitation of free trade. The task force held a consultative forum meeting in April 2012, at which revised standards for the financial action task force were agreed. The financial action task force is the global standard setting body for anti-money laundering and for combating the financing of terrorism.[172]

The rule of law action group seeks to assist IBA members, both individual and member organisations, to be active voices in supporting the rule of law within their home communities. This is in accordance with the IBA Council's Resolution of September 2005, 'The Rule of Law' which states as follows:

> An independent, impartial judiciary; the presumption of innocence; the right to a fair and public trial without undue delay; a rational and proportionate approach to punishment; a strong and independent legal profession; strict protection of confidential communications between lawyer and client; equality of all before the law; these are all fundamental principles of the rule of law. Accordingly, arbitrary arrests; secret trials; indefinite detention without trial; cruel or degrading treatment or punishment; intimidation or corruption in the electoral process; are all unacceptable.[173]

Finally, the task force on illicit financial flows seeks to analyse how illicit financial transactions impact upon human rights and create poverty. It concentrates upon the proceeds of tax evasion and how these can affect the enforce-

[170] The IBA annual conference was held in Dublin from 30th September to the 5th October 2012.
[171] The IBA website with links to Codes of Conduct is available at:
<www.ibanet.org/documents_on_the_regulation_of_the_legal_profession.aspx > Accessed 31/7/2012
[172] For more information, see the IBA's website dedicated to its Financial Action Task Force at:
<www.ibanet.org/LPD/Task_Force_on_the_Financial_Crisis.aspx> Accessed 31/7/2012
[173] The Resolution may be accessed as a pdf document entitled 'Rule of Law Resolution – adopted by the IBA Council in September 2006', available at:
<www.ibanet.org/PPID/Constituent/Rule_of_Law_Action_Group/Overview.aspx > Accessed 31/7/2012

ment of socio-economic and cultural rights.

The International Bar Association's General Principles for the Legal Profession

In September 2006 the IBA adopted its General Principles for the Legal Profession, which are aimed at establishing a generally accepted framework to form the basis of codes of conduct to be adopted by lawyer regulation bodies internationally.[174] Where the IBA General Principles are accepted, they promote and further the ideals of the legal profession. However, they do not replace or limit a lawyer's duty under other relevant national laws or rules of conduct, and they do not serve as criteria for the imposition of disciplinary measures. The General Principles require the maintenance of lawyer independence so that clients can be given unbiased advice.[175] A client must be given advice based upon a lawyer's unbiased professional judgement regarding the likelihood of success in his/her case, and the nature of any representations to be made on his/her behalf. Honesty, integrity and fairness must be maintained by lawyers towards the court, colleagues and all others with whom he/she might make contact upon a professional basis.[176] Conflicts of interest are to be avoided, unless permitted either by law, or the authorisation of the client.[177] Confidentiality and professional secrecy must be maintained by lawyers in relation to clients' affairs, both past and present, unless otherwise permitted or required either by law or a client's authorisation.[178]

A client's interests must always be treated as paramount by a lawyer, subject to his/her duties to the court and the interests of justice.[179] A lawyer must also honour undertakings given in the course of his/her professional practice.[180] The freedom of a client to choose a particular lawyer to represent him/her must be respected, and a lawyer should be free to either select or reject potential clients, unless prevented from so doing by either professional rules or law.[181] A lawyer must also account properly for clients' property, and for property which is held in trust on behalf of a third party, and must keep such property separately from his/her own property.[182] A lawyer must only accept work within his/her field of competence and such work is to be carried out in a timely manner.[183] Finally, a lawyer, though entitled to a reasonable fee for work done, must not generate unnecessary work.[184]

---

[174] The General Principles for the Legal Profession may be accessed as a pdf document, available at: <www.ibanet.org/About_the_IBA/IBA_resolutions.aspx> Accessed 31/7/2102

[175] IBA General Principles for the Legal Profession, Principle 1

[176] Ibid, Principle 2

[177] Ibid, Principle 3

[178] Ibid, Principle 4

[179] Ibid, Principle 5

[180] Ibid, Principle 6

[181] Ibid, Principle 7

[182] Ibid, Principle 8

[183] Ibid, Principle 9

[184] Ibid, Principle 10

Given its sheer size and wide international presence, the IBA is a formidable voice for the representation of the legal profession. It also has a significant regulatory impact, directly and indirectly, upon members of the legal profession across many jurisdictions. It impacts directly upon the conduct of lawyers not only by virtue of the adoption of its General Principles for the Legal Profession, but also due to the work of its various committees in shaping best practice in respect of issues such as the prevention of money laundering, international tax evasion, the funding of terrorism and the protection of human rights. It also impacts indirectly upon the regulation of the legal profession within individual states by means of its campaigning activities and lobbying of governments regarding the content of national legislation affecting the legal profession and the provision of legal services. The following section will consider the impact of the International Law Association upon the regulation of the legal profession.

2.9 The International Law Association

The International Law Association (ILA) was founded in Brussels in 1873. It is devoted to the study and development of both public and private international law, and the development of understanding and respect for international law.[185] Its International Committees hold biennial conferences, and it is through the work of the Committees that the association pursues its aims. The association enjoys consultative status as an international non-governmental organisation with several UN specialised agencies.

The Hague Principles on Ethical Standards for Counsel Appearing before International Courts and Tribunals

The Study Group of the ILA on Practice and Procedure of International Courts issued The Hague Principles on Ethical Standards for Counsel Appearing before International Courts and Tribunals in September 2010. The Hague Principles were established in order to give both the courts and counsel guidance for the resolution of ethical questions which may arise as a consequence of tensions which can occur between duties to a client on the one hand, and to the court on the other hand, and to contribute towards maintaining high standards of professional conduct for counsel appearing before international courts and tribunals. The Principles apply to all persons who appear before an international court or tribunal, or who provide legal advice to a party in proceedings before such a court or tribunal. Counsel should ensure compliance with both the Hague Principles and also any national ethical rules which may apply to him/her.

It is necessary for counsel to strike a balance between the Hague Principles and any relevant national code of conduct.[186] Counsel has a duty of loyalty to his/her client which is consistent with his/her duty to the international court or tribunal to assist in the fair administration of justice.[187] Counsel must remain

---

[185] Article 3.1 of the Constitution of the ILA, adopted at the 74th Conference, 2010. A link to the Constitution is available at <http://www.ila-hq.org/en/about_us/index.cfm> Accessed 12/7/2012

[186] The Hague Principles on Ethical Standards for Counsel Appearing before International Courts and Tribunals, Principle 2

[187] Ibid, Principle 2.1

independent in performing his/her duties, and ignore personal interests or pressures.[188] Counsel must also perform his/her duties with integrity, diligence, efficiency and in a fashion which avoids unnecessary expense or delay.[189] The confidential nature of information received in the course of litigation must be respected.[190] The Hague Principles govern relations with clients.[191] Counsel must be loyal in the exercise of professional responsibilities, and place the client's interests before his/her own or those of any other party.[192] A high standard of integrity must be maintained by counsel, who must also refrain from engaging in conduct he/she reasonably believes to be either criminal or fraudulent.[193] Nor should counsel allow another person to engage in such activity on his/her behalf.

Counsel must avoid conduct which is incompatible with the Hague Principles in general. Professionalism must be maintained by counsel, who must also display requisite skill in the course of performing duties, and ensure he/she has the necessary time and resources to perform those duties effectively.[194] Counsel must not disclose information divulged to him/her by a client whilst acting in a professional capacity, without prejudice to the rules of the international court or tribunal.

The Hague Principles also govern conflicts of interest.[195] They state that counsel may not represent two or more clients in the same proceedings where there is a reasonable chance of a conflict arising between their respective interests.[196] Nor may a new client be represented where a former client is party to the same or related proceedings, or where there is a material risk of a breach of confidentiality, unless the former client expressly authorises the counsel to represent the new client in question.[197] Also, an impermissible conflict regarding a counsel's personal interests will be deemed to exist where he/she has personal links to another party that may give rise to a reasonable risk of conflict of interest, or where he/she has a material, personal, professional or financial interest in the outcome of a matter. An impermissible conflict will also be deemed to exist where counsel has a reasonable expectation that he/she may be called as a witness of fact to give evidence in a matter or where he/she has served in a judicial capacity of the international court or tribunal within three years (or any such other period which may be specified by the court or tribunal in question).[198]

Counsel must adhere to the court or tribunal's rules of conduct, orders and directions, act in a fashion compatible with the fair conduct of proceedings and

---

[188] Ibid, Principle 2.2
[189] Ibid, Principle 2.3
[190] Ibid, Principle 2.4
[191] Ibid, Principle 3
[192] Ibid, Principle 3.1
[193] Ibid, Principle 3.2
[194] Ibid, Principle 3.3
[195] Ibid, Principle 4
[196] Ibid, Principle 4.1
[197] Ibid, Principle 4.2
[198] Ibid, Principle 4.3

address the court or tribunal respectfully.[199] Counsel must also be careful with regard to personal contact with the judiciary, officers and staff of the international court or tribunal, especially where a case is pending.[200] Any such contact must not compromise the exercise of an independent judicial function.

Finally, counsel must present evidence in a fair and reasonable way, and refrain from presenting or relying upon evidence that he/she either knows or has reason to believe is false or misleading.[201] When presenting evidence, counsel must also comply with the procedural rules of the international court or tribunal.[202] Counsel must treat other counsel, witnesses, third parties and officers of the court or tribunal with courtesy and respect.[203] He/she must also strive to cooperate effectively with other counsel.[204] Nor should counsel communicate directly with an opposing party where counsel has been retained by the party, in the absence of that counsel's consent, or on foot of an order from the international court or tribunal.[205]

According to Kazazi, given the increasing number of international courts and tribunals which have been established in recent years, there has been a growing need for the establishment of a set of principles governing the ethical issues which may arise in such fora, and the ILA's Hague Principles have been most valuable in satisfying this need.[206] The aim of the Hague Principles are to assist in the promoting of, 'the fair administration of justice and in enhancing the independence and professionalism of counsel in international proceedings'.[207] Rather than providing a set of binding rules for international courts and tribunals, the Hague Principles are designed to guide these institutions in developing their own codes of conduct to be adhered to by counsel appearing therein.[208] They also provide a set of minimum standards for counsel appearing before international courts and tribunals, some of whom may not be members of national bar associations and who consequently may not be subject to a national code of professional conduct.[209]

2.10 The International Association of Lawyers

The International Association of Lawyers (IAL) was founded in 1927, and is concerned with the universal protection and defence of the human rights of

---

[199] Ibid, Principle 5

[200] Ibid, Principle 5.5

[201] Ibid, Principle 6.1

[202] Ibid, Principle 6.3

[203] Ibid, Principle 7.1

[204] Ibid, Principle 7.2

[205] Ibid, Principle 7.4

[206] M Kazazi, 'Commentary on the Hague Principles on Ethical Standards for Counsel Appearing Before the Courts and Tribunals' (2011) 10 *The Law and Practice of International Courts and Tribunals* 17

[207] Ibid, 23

[208] Ibid, 21

[209] Ibid, 22

lawyers.[210] The association also works to safeguard the right of lawyers to freely and independently practice their profession in the absence of hindrance, harassment or interference. The association's Commission for the Protection of the Legal Profession supports the application of the Basic Principles on the Role of Lawyers which were adopted by the 5th UN Congress on the Prevention of Crime and the Treatment of Offenders.[211] This asserts that lawyers must be free to perform their professional duties without hindrance, and that the independence of lawyers and their professional organisations must be protected within national frameworks of legislation.

The Turin Principles of Professional Conduct for the Legal Profession in the Twenty-first Century

In 2002, the IAL adopted the Turin Principles of Professional Conduct for the Legal Profession in the Twenty-first Century. These state that it is a lawyer's role to ensure the protection of everyone before the law, and that whilst lawyers have a right and duty to practise their profession, they must do so in a manner that promotes knowledge and application of the law, whilst also protecting the interests for which they are responsible. The role of lawyers must be recognised and respected both within society and by authorities, as it forms an essential element of the administration of justice. Lawyers must therefore strive to preserve this recognition by providing their services in a fair fashion, in accordance with the highest ethical standards and cultural norms. They must also be given access to their clients and to all necessary documents so that they can properly defend the interests entrusted to them.

Laurel Terry has identified a transformation in legal ethics scholarship which began towards the end of the twentieth century and has continued since.[212] This transformation has occurred as a result of global and comparative perspectives being brought to bear in shaping the nature and content of the global ethics debate.[213] She has argued that the IAL has been a key contributor to the international conversation about global legal ethics, and has cited the Turin Principles as an important product of that international dialogue.[214]

An Overview of General Principles and International Codes of Conduct for the Legal Profession

The Codes of Conduct and the Basic Principles which have been considered above offer a variety of perspectives upon the core issue of how lawyers ought to behave in the course of representing their clients and in their interactions with one another, both nationally and transnationally as well as internationally. These regulatory instruments vary in that they may be either binding or aspira-

---

[210] The International Association of Lawyers is also known as the Union Internationale des Avocats.

[211] See ch 2 § 2.5

[212] L Terry, 'US Legal Ethics: The Coming of Age of Global and Comparative Perspectives' (2005) 4 (1) *Washington University Global Studies Law Review* 463

[213] Ibid, 463

[214] Ibid, 512 – 514

tional. On the one hand, the IBA General Principles and the CCBE Code are binding upon all practitioners whose jurisdictions have adopted the instruments, and on the other hand, the UN Recommendations and both the Turin and Hague Principles offer a more aspirational vision of how the legal profession should conduct itself in modern democratic societies. The degree to which adherence to these instruments is enforceable also varies. Breaches of the CCBE Code and IBA Principles may give rise to disciplinary action on the part of national regulatory authorities, although they will not be directly enforced by either the CCBE or the IBA.[215] However, breaches of the UN Recommendations, the Turin or Hague Principles will not necessarily be enforced by national regulatory bodies, nor will they be pursued by the ILA or the IAL.

The nature of the activities to which the Codes and Principles apply also varies considerably; whereas the IBA General Principles and the CCBE Code of Conduct apply to lawyers' cross border and international activities, the ILA Hague Principles apply only to the activities of Counsel appearing before International Courts and Tribunals, and the UN Recommendations and the Turin Principles apply to all activities of legal professionals, at both a national and international level. Given the generality of much of the instruments there is little scope for direct conflict amongst their various provisions. The most notable point of difference arises in respect of contingency fees which the IBA General Principles state must be reasonable, whilst the CCBE Code of Conduct outlaws the making of a *pactum de quota litiz*. However, the general prohibition is qualified as it does not include fees which are charged in proportion to the value of a matter where the charging arrangement is part of a recognized fee scale, or is controlled by a competent authority with jurisdiction over the lawyer.[216] The instruments serve a variety of purposes beyond the resolution or avoidance of the double deontology dilemma. They also have a legitimating function in that they justify the lawyers' professional role in society and provide ideological justification for their existence as defenders of both the rule of law and the rights of individuals.[217] Finally, the instruments serve a political function in that they signify the existence of rules and regulations to govern the activities of legal professionals and are a useful demonstration of the self-regulation of the legal profession's activities on an international level. As such they may be used to justify the argument that state regulators need not involve themselves in the imposition of further regulatory standards pertaining to the international activities of lawyers. The following section will explore the impact of the process of globalization upon the regulation and practice of the legal profession.

---

[215] LSI, 'A Guide to Professional Conduct of Solicitors' Para 1.1. Proper conduct in relation to cross border conduct and practice outside of the Irish jurisdiction is governed by the provisions of both the CCBE Code of Conduct and the IBA general Principles.

[216] CCBE Code of Conduct Para 3.3.3 in A Boon & J Flood, 'The Globalization of Professional Ethics? The Significance of Lawyers' International Codes of Conduct' (1999) 2 (1) *Legal Ethics* 29, 37

[217] Ibid 43

2.11 The Impact of the Globalization Process

This chapter has illustrated that in order to understand how the legal profession in Ireland is regulated, it is necessary to look beyond the confines of our jurisdiction. It is also necessary to appreciate the influence of international forces in the form of the process of globalization. Globalization has been defined by Joseph Stiglitz as:

> [T]he closer integration of countries and peoples of the world which has been brought about by the enormous reduction of costs of transportation and communication, and the breaking down of artificial barriers to flows of goods, services, capital, knowledge and (to a lesser extent) people across borders. Globalization has been accomplished by the creation of the new institutions that have joined with existing ones to work across boarders.[218]

Mauro Guillén has defined globalization as 'a process leading to greater dependence and mutual awareness (reflexivity) among economic, political and social units in the world, and among actors in general'.[219] Andrew Boon and John Flood have offered a sophisticated description of the globalization concept as 'a process giving rise to fundamental changes in systems and goals of the modern state, [and which] provides a set of values which can be integrated with professional ethics.'[220]

Whilst many aspects of the process are broadly welcomed, Stiglitz has observed that the economic aspects of globalization have been more controversial. For instance, he has pointed to the effect in developing countries of policies of international institutions such as the IMF and the World Bank. The policies which were initially designed to stabilise the flow of capital both inwards and outwards have arguably served to stifle economic growth and hinder development.[221] Eleanor Fox has also observed the more toxic effects of globalization which offset its positive aspects, such as the flow of ideas and technology, the increase in economic welfare and opportunities and the surmounting of national borders.[222] She has noted:

> Relentless pressure from global competition in business to cut costs to be 'competitive' combined with the pressure of multinationals on governments to sweeten tax obligations, can tend to squeeze out things that we care about but for which we do not have the fighting power (or money) to pay.[223]

---

[218] J Stiglitz, *Globalization and its Discontents* (FN 81) 9

[219] M Guillén, 'Is Globalization Civilizing, Destructive or Feeble? A Critique of Five Key Debates in the Social Science Literature' (2001) 27 *Annual Review of Sociology* 235, 236

[220] A Boon & J Flood, 'The Globalization of Professional Ethics?' (FN 216) 52

[221] Ibid 10

[222] E Fox, 'Globalization and its Challenges for Law and Society' (1997 – 1998) 29 *Loyola University of Chicago Law Journal* 891

[223] Ibid 896

Fox has highlighted the role of the law school in training a new type of Renaissance lawyer who can effectively respond to the challenge and opportunity of globalization in the form of the new global economy, the shrinking nation state and the developing networks of global public policy.[224] Law school curricula should incorporate comparative and global perspectives and encourage intercultural exchanges at both student and staff level.[225] Law faculties should also foster multi-disciplinary programmes that combine sociology, economics, political science and law to enhance our understanding of the impact of globalization upon fairness and social cohesion.[226]

On a macro level, Boon and Flood's 'globalization' thesis considers the regulation of lawyers' behaviour from an international perspective.[227] Notwithstanding the growing 'Americanisation' of world cultures, the phenomenon of globalization involves processes of both homogenisation and fragmentation, whereby pressures are applied upon society which on the one hand tend to unify practices on a global scale, and on the other hand tend to fragment processes internationally and transnationally.[228] The financial markets illustrate the homogenisation process, whereby currency traders for instance, engage in non-stop global currency transactions, unfettered by limited business hours or local customs and practice. Facilitated by information technology, and not confined to specific geographic locations, currency traders are global inhabitants, whose activities are shaped by currency exchange rates as opposed to specific national loyalties. The process of fragmentation on the other hand is illustrated by the increased use of contracting out or outsourcing of activities by many firms, including law firms. Whilst Irish law firms have used legal process outsourcing to achieve efficiencies within their operations, Ireland has increasingly become a destination for international firms looking to outsource legal processing work. Northern Ireland has been particularly successful in this regard, with Allen & Overy, a London 'magic circle' firm succumbing to its attractions as a location for a support office in 2011, and the US-based, international law firm Axiom announcing plans in March 2012 to create over one hundred jobs in Belfast in a legal outsourcing venture.[229] This shift in organizational culture is primarily economically driven, as firms increasingly recognise the favourable cost implications of

---

[274] Ibid 904

[225] Ibid 904 – 905

[226] Ibid 905

[227] A Boon & J Flood, 'The Globalization of Professional Ethics?' (FN 216) 29

[228] Flood has described the process of Americanisation as the ever-increasing 'Coca-Cola world'. J Flood, 'The Cultures of Globalization: Professional Restructuring for the International Market', in Y Dezalay & D Sugarman (eds), *Professional Competition and Professional Power: Lawyers, Accountants and the Social Construction of Markets* (Routledge, 1995) 140. Flood's Chapter is available at: <http://ssrn.com/abstract=98046> Accessed 25/8/2012

[229] M Canning, 'Global legal firm Allen & Overy outsources to Belfast', *Belfast Telegraph* (Belfast, 4 February 2011) Available at: <http://www.belfasttelegraph.co.uk/business/business-news/global--legal-firm-allen-amp-overy-outsources-to-belfast-15073428.html>; M Canning, 'US legal firm to bring 100 posts to Northern Ireland', *Belfast Telegraph* (Belfast, 21 March 2012) Available at: <http://www.belfasttelegraph.co.uk/business/business-news/us-legal-firm-to-bring-100-posts-to-northern-ireland-16133947.html > Accessed 8/6/2012

outsourcing work, often to international locations. There are also the advantages and attractions of increased market access, whereby firms with an international presence are better placed to compete for business opportunities with a transnational or international aspect.

Large accounting firms have been more active than law firms in developing their presence internationally. Flood attributes the accountancy firms' relative success in this regard to their diversification from the auditing sector into the areas of management consultancy, and tax and corporate reconstruction.[230] Accountancy firms have also embraced the possibilities offered by MDPs more willingly than law firms, who in many jurisdictions have been prohibited by regulatory authorities from joining MDPs. Concerns regarding the impact of MDPs upon client confidentiality have been raised by some members of the legal profession, given that other professionals are not bound by such a duty in respect of their clients. Ian Forrester has noted:

> Conflicts of interest might often arise within MDPs between lawyers and accountants: for example, where an MDP was responsible for producing the financial accounts of a company in respect of whose sale its legal services were also required.[231]

Also, a conflict of interest may arise within an MDP between a legal practitioner's obligation to act in his/her client's best interest at all times on the one hand, and pressure which might be exerted by a practice manager to maximise the firm's profits on the other. The CCBE has raised concerns regarding the problems which MDPs may present with regard to many aspects of lawyers' professional conduct:

> The legal profession is a crucial and indispensable element in the administration of justice and in the protection available to citizens under the law.... CCBE consequently advises that there are over-riding reasons for not permitting forms of integrated co-operation between lawyers and non-lawyers with relevantly different professional duties and correspondingly different rules of conduct. In those countries where such forms of co-operation are nevertheless permitted, lawyer independence, client confidentiality and disciplinary supervision of conflicts-of-interests rules must be safeguarded.[232]

Flood has argued that law firms face fundamental problems in expanding globally, because by their very nature they are inhibited from expanding beyond a certain point as a result of the rules of professional conduct, such as those relating to the avoidance of conflicts of interest. These prevent law firms from adopting a transactional as opposed to a relational approach to business. Conflict of interest rules can limit a law firm's ability to expand, as the possibility of

---

[230] J Flood, 'The Cultures of Globalization' (FN 228) 156

[231] I Forrester, 'Where Law Meets Competition: Is Wouters Like a Cassis de Dijon or a Platypus?' (FN 32), citing Case C-309/99 *JCJ Wouters et al v Algemene Raad van de Nederlandse Orde van Advocaten* [2002] ECR I-1577, paras 102 – 103

[232] Ibid 5, citing the CCBE position on Integrated Forms of Co-operation, available at: <http://ccbe.org/UK/uk.htm> Accessed 28/8/2012

taking on a new client may be fettered if the firm has previously advised its adversary. There is also the fact that, with the exception of EU law, lawyers' education and training has traditionally focused upon national law and given the difference between national systems of law, this presents a considerable barrier to those wishing to practise either transnationally or internationally. The central question arising here is whether the rules governing the legal profession are sufficiently flexible to permit it to benefit from the opportunities for expansion which the developing global business culture offers, or whether it will prove too inflexible, and in consequence will lose ground and market share to other professionals who are willing to adapt in order to meet clients' needs in a growing global context. Flood warns:

> As long as lawyers are tied to particular conceptions of the role of law and operate within particular legal systems, others in the international financial field will compete aggressively and not feel bound by the ideological and cultural constraint lawyers impose on themselves... At bottom, the problem is the nature of law itself. Historically it has been grounded in diverse cultures and has rarely been deployed across them in the same manner as accounting or business principles. In many respects then, the forces of globalization are creating a tumultuous environment for a potentially endangered species.[233]

The ethical and ideological objections of many lawyers to MDPs appear to have impeded the profession from benefiting from the globalization process by adapting traditional practice structures to accommodate the needs of global clients. The following section examines the problem of corruption and the challenges it presents for the global regulation of the legal profession.

2.12 A Case Study: Global Anti-Corruption Instruments

The global nature of modern legal practice is aptly illustrated by the challenge the legal profession faces from money laundering and corruption. Lalountus et al have argued that whilst there is no evidence of a formal link between corruption and globalization, there is a positive correlation between the phenomena in countries which rank as having middle and higher incomes, as classified by the World Bank.[234] Their analysis of the corruption/globalization nexus indicates that, 'more discretion and regulations lead to a higher burden on business, provide incentives to move to the underground economy and also to more corruption'.[235]

The link between corruption and globalization arises due to many different factors. Where there are significant barriers to international trade, bribery of public officials will be contemplated more frequently, and in reducing such barriers, globalization reduces the likelihood of corrupt practices. Furthermore, the structural changes and institutional reforms which foster globalization are

---

[233] Ibid 161

[234] D Lalountas et al, 'Corruption, Globalization and Development: How Are These Three Phenomena Related?' (2011) 33 (4) *Journal of Policy Modelling* 636, § 1

[235] Ibid, § 2

those which reduce the scope for corruption; these are market liberalization, increased competition and transparency of transactions.[236]

Peter Andreas has sounded a note of caution in relation to the dearth of scholarship on 'illicit globalization', our understanding of which is prone to myths and misconceptions.[237] Andreas has observed that the same transformations in communication and finance which facilitate licit business transactions may just as readily be used to further illicit transactions.[238] Whilst acknowledging that trade liberalization negates the *raison* of much illicit trading which arises due to the desire to evade tariffs and import and export duties, Andreas has argued that the prevalence of illicit global commerce reflects that the process of globalization is limited and incomplete, rather than 'out of control'.[239] According to Andreas:

> In fact, some of today's illicit economic activities were only criminalised a few decades ago, including trade prohibitions on toxic waste, antiquities, endangered species, and money laundering.[240]

In considering the efficacy of the global anti-corruption instruments below, it is instructive to reflect upon Andreas' observation that counterproductive policy initiatives may emerge in the rush to 'do something' in response to flawed or incomplete narratives of illicit globalization.[241]

In 2010 the IBA joined forces with the Organisation for Economic Co-operation and Development (OECD) and the UN Office on Drugs and Crime (UNODC), to conduct a joint survey investigating the role which lawyers play in tackling corruption in international business transactions.[242] The survey also examined the impact of the international anti-corruption regulatory framework and related national legislation having extraterritorial effect upon the legal profession. The objectives of the survey were to establish the degree of risk awareness amongst lawyers regarding corruption, to examine their level of understanding regarding methods of risk mitigation and to look at the contribution which law firms, law societies and bar associations can effectively make in the global fight against corruption. The key international anti-corruption instruments which impinge upon European legal practitioners have been implemented by the UN, the OECD, the Council of Europe and the EU. These instruments have an indirect impact upon the international and transnational activities of lawyers.

---

[236] Ibid, § 2

[237] P Andreas, 'Illicit Globalization: Myths, Misconceptions and Historical Lessons' (2011) 126 *Political Science Quarterly* 403

[238] Ibid, 404

[239] Ibid, 405

[240] Ibid, 405

[241] Ibid, 423

[242] The IBA Survey 'Anti-Corruption Strategy for the Legal Profession: Risks and Threats of Corruption in the Legal Profession' (2010) is available at: <http://www.oecd.org/investment/briberyininternationalbusiness/46137847.pdf> Accessed 28/8/2012

UN Convention against Corruption

The General Assembly of the UN adopted its Convention against Corruption in 2003, and it came into force in 2005.[243] The Convention focuses upon the prevention of corruption, its criminalisation, the development of international co-operation to fight corruption and asset recovery where national wealth has been dissipated as a result of corruption. Article 16 of the UN Convention against Corruption states as follows:

> 16.1 Each party shall adopt such legislative and other measures as may be necessary to establish as a criminal offence, when committed intentionally, the promise, offering or giving to a foreign public official or an official of a public international organisation, direct or indirect, of an undue advantage, for the official himself or herself or another person or entity, in order that the official act or refrain from acting in the exercise of his or her official duties, in order to obtain or retain business or other undue advantage in relation to the conduct of international business.

> 16.2 Each party shall consider adopting such legislative and other measures as may be necessary to establish as a criminal offence, when committed intentionally, the solicitation or acceptance by a foreign public official or an official of a public international organisation, directly or indirectly, of an undue advantage, for the official himself or herself or another party or entity, in order that the official act or refrain from acting in the exercise of his or her official duties.

In accordance with Article 16 of the Convention, a lawyer who represents or advises a client in relation to an international business transaction must avoid acting as an intermediary in any such transaction involving bribery or corruption.

OECD Convention on Combating Bribery of Foreign Public Officials in International Business Transactions

The OECD Convention on Combating Bribery of Foreign Public Officials in International Business Transactions was ratified in 1997 and came into force in 1999.[244] It sets down legally binding standards which criminalise the bribery of foreign public officials in the course of international business transactions. The Convention establishes a three phase monitoring system for the prevention of bribery in international business transactions. Phase One assesses the strength of a country's anti-bribery legislation. Phase Two establishes the country's level of implementation and compliance with the legislation. Phase Three is concerned with enforcement of the Convention's provisions. The Convention establishes liability on the part of legal persons involved in the bribery of foreign

---

[243] The UN Convention against Corruption is available at:
<http://www.unodc.org/documents/treaties/UNCAC/Publications/Convention/08-50026_E.pdf> Accessed 6/8/2012

[244] The OECD Anti-Bribery Convention is available at:
<www.oecd.org/daf/briberyininternationalbusiness/anti-briberyconvention/38028044.pdf> Accessed 7/8/2012

public officials.[245]

Council of Europe Criminal Law Convention on Corruption and Civil Law Convention on Corruption

The Council of Europe has adopted two international anti-corruption instruments. The Criminal Law Convention on Corruption was adopted in 1998.[246] It requires parties to the Convention to adopt legislation and other measures to criminalise the active or passive bribery of domestic or foreign public officials, the bribery of domestic or foreign public assemblies and also of judges and officials of international courts. The Convention requires parties to criminalise money laundering of the proceeds of corruption offences. It also requires the criminalisation of the aiding or abetting of the above-mentioned offences, and promotes co-operation on an international level to outlaw and prevent corruption. The responsibility for monitoring the Convention's implementation lies with the Council of Europe's Group of States against Corruption (GRECO). GRECO was established in 1999 in order to monitor the compliance of the Council of Europe's member states with its anti-corruption standards.[247] It encourages compliance with the standards using a dynamic process of mutual evaluation and peer pressure. The Civil Law Convention on Corruption was adopted in 1999 and provides for effective remedies, including the payment of compensation to persons who have suffered damage due to acts of corruption.[248] It encourages international cooperation between parties to facilitate such compensation claims. The implementation of the Civil Law Convention on Corruption is also monitored by GRECO.

Whilst neither of the Council of Europe's anti-corruption conventions directly mention the legal profession, it is clear that lawyers may potentially be involved in the facilitation of asset transfers which are associated with bribery or corruption, and as such, they may be deemed to have participated in such corrupt activities in contravention of the Criminal Convention.[249] Colares has outlined a number of hypothetical scenarios which illustrate the challenge which global corruption presents for lawyers when advising commercial clients.[250] He has argued that where an in-house counsel may warn against the legitimacy of a proposed transaction on the basis that it potentially involves the payment of a bribe rather than a commission:

---

[245] OECD Convention on Combating Bribery of Foreign Public Officials in International Business Transactions, Art 2

[246] The Council of Europe Criminal Law Convention on Corruption is available at: <conventions.coe.int/Treaty/en/Treaties/html/173.htm> Accessed 26/8/2012

[247] Further information about GRECO and its role is available at: <www.coe.int/t/dghl/monitoring/greco/general/3.WhatisGRECO_en.asp> Accessed 7/8/2012

[248] The Council of Europe Civil Law Convention on Corruption is available at: <http://conventions.coe.int/Treaty/en/Treaties/Html/174.htm> Accessed 7/8/2012

[249] Council of Europe Criminal Law Convention on Corruption, Art 15

[250] J Colares, 'The Evolving Domestic and International Law Against Foreign Corruption: Some New and Old Dilemmas facing the International Lawyer' (2006), 5 (1) *Washington University Global Studies Law Review* 1, 23 –24

[T]he client may be strongly dissuaded from heading counsel's sound legal advice, and worse, the circumstances may cause the client to think counsel is too risk averse or merely trying to protect himself from liability. These perceptions can strain significantly the relationship between the client and his attorney'.[251]

Colares has argued that statutes and conventions aimed at preventing global corruption cannot be an effective substitute for a lawyer's reliance upon sound professional and ethical judgment when trying to reconcile responsibility towards a client on the one hand, and the need to uphold the spirit and letter of the law on the other hand.[252]

The Challenge of International Corruption for Lawyers

The IBA survey results revealed a worryingly low level of knowledge amongst the legal profession internationally regarding the international anti-corruption regulatory framework. Over 40% of respondents declared themselves to have no knowledge whatever about the global anti-corruption instruments, although these had binding effect in their jurisdictions. This widespread lack of knowledge regarding anti-corruption instruments indicates a similar level of ignorance regarding the potential liability of lawyers as intermediaries in international business transactions which involve bribery or corruption. The IBA survey concluded that there was a 'dangerous lack of awareness of the international anti-corruption instruments amongst legal professionals'.[253] This is notwithstanding the fact that a half of all respondents acknowledged that corruption was an issue in their own legal communities, and also for legal professionals in their neighbouring jurisdictions. The survey also found that bar associations, law societies and individual firms were not actively engaging their members on the problem of international bribery and corruption. There was a particular lack of engagement on the issue with regard to younger and less senior members of the legal profession. The survey recommends that an industry-wide programme of anti-corruption awareness should be initiated, and that individual firms should devise methods to increase awareness amongst their personnel of methods to combat international bribery and corruption.

International anti-corruption instruments impact upon the regulation of the legal profession on various levels, both direct and indirect. They illustrate how regulations which are primarily aimed at issues or sectors other than legal practice many nonetheless impact significantly upon it. As such, they aptly illustrate the interconnectedness of global regulatory instruments. These international anti-corruption instruments also illustrate that in order to develop a comprehensive understanding of lawyer regulation, both within Ireland, and also on an international level, one must look beyond the confines of specific regulations and legislation which directly apply to the legal profession, and recognise that a vast array of regulations, legislation and codes of conduct may effect lawyers' practice. Such regulatory influences are not confined to interna-

---

[251] Ibid, 24

[252] Ibid, 1 – 2

[253] IBA Survey 2010 (FN 242) 20

tional instruments. Domestic legislation and regulations may also reach beyond national boundaries to influence the nature of legal practice in foreign jurisdictions. Terry cites the Sarbanes Oxley Act 2002 in this regard.[254] Following its enactment, the Securities and Exchange Commission (SEC) proposed new rules setting out standards of professional conduct for attorneys who appeared before the SEC on behalf of issuers.[255] Initially, the proposed rule contained a very broad definition of the phrase "practising before the SEC", which would have encompassed a large number of foreign lawyers and law firms. The SEC received a large volume of responses from foreign lawyers and foreign bar associations, seeking amendment of the proposals and ultimately the proposed rule was altered to include fewer foreign lawyers.[256]

A further example of how one jurisdiction's regulatory framework may impact upon lawyer regulation abroad is to be found in the American Bar Association's (ABA) Model Rule of Professional Conduct 5.5 which concerns Multi-Jurisdictional Practice (MJP).[257] Internationally based regulators and commentators contributed to the debate within the ABA prior to its adoption of two recommendations concerning the regulation of practice of foreign lawyers within the US.[258] Following those discussions, the ABA Commission on Ethics 20/20 issued proposals for the modification of Model Rule of Professional Conduct 5.5, so that it would apply not only to US lawyers providing legal services in states other than that in which they are licensed to practice, but also to the provision of legal services by foreign lawyers within the US.[259] The proposed changes apply to

---

[254] L Terry, 'A "How To" Guide for Incorporating Global and Comparative Perspectives into the Required Professional Responsibility Course' (2007) 51 *St Louis University Law Journal* 1135, 1142

[255] Section 309 of the Sarbanes Oxley Act 2002 set down minimum standards of professional conduct for lawyers appearing and practising before the SEC. Section 307 of the Act requires the SEC to establish rules of professional conduct which oblige attorneys who have evidence of a material violation of either securities law, a breach of fiduciary duty or similar wrongdoing to report the matter to the company's chief legal officer or its chief executive officer, and if the chief legal officer or chief executive does not respond appropriately, the attorney must report the matter to the audit committee of the board of directors or other committee of the board of directors, where the directors are not in the employ of the issuer, or alternatively, the attorney may report the violation directly to the board of directors.

[256] The new rule may be found at 17 Code of Federal Regulations Part 205, Standards of Professional Conduct for Attorneys Appearing and Practising before the Commission in the Representation of an Issuer, available at: <www.law.justia.com/cfr/title17/17cfr205_main_02.html> Accessed 8/8/2012

[257] ABA Model Rules of Professional Conduct 5.5 (2007) A link to the 2007 Rules and also to the current version of the ABA Model Rules of Professional Conduct is available at: <http://www.americanbar.org/groups/professional_responsibility/publications/model_rules_of_professional_conduct.html> Accessed 26/8/2012. See also L Terry, 'A "How To" Guide' (FN 254) 1142 – 43

[258] ABA MJP Recommendation 8 reaffirmed ABA Model Foreign (Legal) Consultant Rule and ABA MJP Recommendation 9 established a Model Rule for Temporary Practice by Foreign Lawyers.

[259] The ABA Commission on Ethics 20/20 Recommendation for the modification of RPC Rule 5.5 (19th September 2011) is available at: <http://www.americanbar.org/content/dam/aba/administrative/ethics_2020/20110919_ethics_20_20_foreign_lawyers_and_model_rule _5_5_resolution_report.authcheckdam.pdf> Accessed 29/8/2012

foreign lawyers who wish to provide services on a temporary basis, and also to foreign in-house counsel. Their inclusion within the existing Rule 5.5 would establish the boundaries of their permitted areas of practice, and subject them to a regime of registration and discipline. Foreign lawyers wishing to provide services on a continuous basis within the US must comply with the Model Rules for the Licensing and Practice of Foreign Legal Consultants (FLCs) which provide for the licensing of foreign lawyers who are of good standing, and who have at least five years' professional experience in the state in which they are registered to practice. The permitted scope of practice of FLCs is strictly limited, and they may not advise or represent clients in relation to US law unless they have taken advice from a US qualified lawyer in the matter.

2.13 Concluding Remarks

This chapter has examined the diverse range of regulatory institutions and associations which impact upon the regulation of the legal profession at a transnational, international and global level. The many ways in which the institutions of the EU have impacted upon the practice of law in member states was examined as lawyers increasingly avail of their fundamental freedoms to either provide services or establish themselves throughout the Union. The EU's primary law was examined, along with the secondary legislation which applies to the legal services market in the form of Directives and Regulations. Also, the key rulings of the ECJ in relation to MDPs, the use of minimum fee schedules and the parameters of legal professional privilege as recognised by the ECJ was reviewed. This analysis of the EU's influence on the activities of the legal profession revealed a degree of tension between the efforts of the Commission to bring greater competitiveness to the market on the one hand, and the European Parliament's articulation of the view of lawyers' representative bodies to the effect that member states must retain a pivotal role in regulating their legal professions in light of individual, national, cultural traditions on the other hand.

The role of the Troika in shaping the regulation of the legal profession in Ireland was also explored in this chapter. The Troika's influence in this regard is most evident with the publication of the LSRB 2011, and although the final form of the legislation remains to be seen, it heralds the most fundamental reform of the legal profession since the foundation of the state. The impact of other international institutions including the Council of Europe, the UN and the WTO was also examined. These bodies impact in different ways upon the practice of lawyers internationally, and whilst they have not all produced binding forms of regulation, they nonetheless affect lawyers' practice given their normative impact upon national rules and codes of conduct. The chapter also looked at the effect of international professional associations of lawyers including the IBA, the CCBE, the ILA and the IAL in regulating lawyers' practice. These bodies affect the activities of lawyers in a variety of ways in many different practice contexts. Their examination reveals a highly complex international regulatory framework, an understanding of which must present considerable challenges to lawyers practising in the transnational or international arenas.

The impact of the globalization process upon lawyers' practice was also considered and it is clear that the profession faces opportunities and challenges, perhaps in equal measure, as a result of globalization. The process of globalization is transforming the needs and expectations of clients, and in so doing, it challenges the legal profession to devise novel globalized solutions to clients' problems which are increasingly rooted in a globalized context. The chapter concluded with an examination of anti-corruption instruments which although not explicitly directed at lawyers, frequently impact upon their work. This examination revealed the manner in which lawyers' practice may be influenced by a wide array of regulatory provisions beyond those which are primarily aimed at the legal profession. What has emerged from the above examination is a complex international regulatory framework for the legal profession which is constantly evolving due to the myriad of international institutions, associations and processes which impact upon the behaviour of lawyers, nationally, transnationally, internationally and globally. The following chapter will seek to identify shortcomings in the present system of lawyer regulation in Ireland, with a view to identifying whether the regulatory changes contained in the LSRB 2011 are necessary and sufficient to rectify the weaknesses in the present regulatory framework.

3

PROBLEMS WITH THE PRESENT REGULATORY FRAMEWORK FOR THE LEGAL PROFESSION IN IRELAND

3.0 Introduction

When considering the adequacy of the present regulatory framework governing the legal profession in Ireland the following issues should be considered:

(1) Why should the legal profession be regulated?

(2) Who should be responsible for its regulation?

(3) Which entities and activities should be regulated?

(4) When should regulation occur?

(5) Where should regulation occur?

(6) How should regulation occur?[1]

The first of these questions is the most fundamental, as the response to this query will affect the answer to the following five questions. The first question requires a regulator to consider the rationale behind the activity of regulation, and to articulate the objectives to be attained by means of the regulatory process. This is a beneficial exercise for both the regulator and the regulated community. The identification of the regulatory objectives provides a valuable point of reference for a regulator to assist in the task of applying the regulations. The process may also help to justify the regulator's approach to the application of rules in the event that this should be challenged or criticized by the regulated community. The regulated community can also more readily understand the regulator's application of the regulations in a given case, where the regulatory objectives have been clearly articulated and made known to the community. This chapter will commence with an examination of the regulatory objectives of the present regulatory framework, and it will compare these objectives with those which have been articulated in other jurisdictions. Economics has increasingly

---

[1] These six issues have recently been identified by Terry as providing a useful checklist against which to assess a regulatory framework for the legal profession. L Terry et al, 'Trends and Challenges in Lawyer Regulation: The Impact of Globalization and Technology' (2012) 80 (6) *Fordham Law Review* 2261, 2263

been used as a tool to examine regulation in a variety of contexts, and recently there has been a growing interest in the analysis of law and regulation from an economic perspective. Economics provides a valuable perspective from which to consider the relative merits of different forms of regulation. Whilst bodies such as The Competition Authority and The National Consumer Council have contributed to an increased understanding of law in the context of market choices, the traditional modes of thinking regarding the regulation of the legal profession have been resistant to change.[2] Therefore this chapter seeks to explore the question of why the legal profession should be regulated from an economic perspective.

The issue of who should regulate the lawyers has been the subject of much debate within the legal profession, in wider society, and also amongst politicians and economists. Much of this debate has focused on the issue of whether the legal profession should be its own primary regulator – whether it should it be self-regulating – or whether a co-regulatory model should be deployed, whereby outside agencies, often associated with the executive, legislative or judicial branches of the state should perform a regulatory function.

The question of which entities and what activities should be regulated is important, given that there has been an international movement towards regulating legal services as they are provided by firms, as opposed to regulating services which are provided by individuals. The question of whose activities should be regulated is also relevant, given that legal services are increasingly provided (in other jurisdictions) by paralegals such as conveyancers and legal executives, and also by MDPs, which include non-lawyers such as accountants or tax consultants. Regulation of legal services at the level of the firm rather than the individual practitioner has recently been adopted in England and Wales, where the Solicitors Regulation Authority (SRA) is responsible for regulating not only solicitors, but also the firms in which they work.[3] Neary has argued that the failure to regulate legal practice at firm level has given rise to ongoing unhappiness regarding the cost and effectiveness of legal services provision in Ireland, and also to an assumption amongst practitioners that the law firm entity operates outside the scope of regulation.[4]

> We believe the problem lies not with *how* the profession is regulated, but *what* exactly is being regulated? If the aim of regulation is to protect the public interest, and encourage a cost effective, innovative and consumer friendly legal profession, then there needs to be a shift in regulatory emphasis away from regulating the individual solicitor towards the regulation of the economic unit, the law firm.[5]

---

[2] A Devlin, 'Law and Economics' (2011) 46 *Irish Jurist* 166

[3] For a description of firm based regulation, see the SRA website: <http://www.sra.org.uk/sra/legal-services-act/faqs/02-terms-and-concepts/What-do-you-mean-by-firm-based-regulation.page> Accessed 8/9/2012

[4] A Neary & F O'Toole, *The Blueprint Report: A Review of the Legal Profession in Ireland and a Vision for Irish Law Firms* (Anne Neary Consultations, 2011) 140

[5] Ibid 140

The traditional approach to the timing of regulatory intervention in Ireland is typical to that which is adopted in many jurisdictions, whereby the majority of interventions occur *ex post*, following a complaint initiated by a client, colleague or a member of the judiciary. On occasion, however, disciplinary intervention may occur in Ireland upon foot of a random audit, carried out in accordance with the Solicitor Accounts Regulations.[6] In contrast to the predominantly *ex post* Irish approach, an *ex ante* model of intervention has been adopted in New South Wales (NSW). The NSW Legal Profession Act 2004 requires incorporated legal practices to develop appropriate management systems which address ten specific objectives, such as the avoidance of conflicts of interest and the establishment of appropriate costs disclosure and billing policies. This *ex ante* approach to regulatory intervention allows the Office of the Legal Services Commissioner (OLSC) to implement an 'education-towards-compliance' policy, which seeks to work in partnership with the legal profession to reduce the level of consumer complaints. This is in contrast to the adoption of a confrontational approach that may have the effect of provoking an equally confrontational or evasive response from the legal profession. The NSW approach has had considerable success, with a 67% reduction in the level of consumer complaints being received following the adoption of the proactive appropriate management system approach.[7]

Nowadays, regulators of the legal profession are confronted with the question of where regulation should occur. This question arises as a result of technological advances such as cloud computing, the development of modern business practices such as outsourcing and also the process of globalization. The latter has given rise to an increased emphasis upon international and transnational aspects of legal practice for many lawyers. Together, these developments prompt the question of whether a regulator which is geographically rooted in one jurisdiction can adequately oversee all aspects of the legal profession's activities. Terry has argued that there is a fundamental mismatch between the virtual practice world and the physically, defined regulatory world.[8] This chapter will consider this mismatch from an Irish perspective.

The chapter continues with an examination of the question of how the legal profession is currently regulated. A single regulatory approach is adopted in Ireland with regard to all lawyers and firms regardless of the nature of their individual areas of practice; in particular whether they provide services to corporate or private clients. Corporate clients tend to be repeat users of certain legal services, and they are often highly knowledgeable regarding the service being supplied. In contrast, private clients tend to use legal services on a 'once off' basis, and frequently lack knowledge regarding the service being provided. Whether a single regulatory approach should be applied to such a diverse range

---

[6] SI 204/84. In accordance with section 29 (1) & (2) of the Solicitors Accounts Regulations 1984, the Council of the LSI has, on it own motion, powers to inspect solicitors' accounts.

[7] C Parker et al, 'Regulating Law Firm Ethics Management: An Empirical Assessment of an Innovation in Regulation of the Legal Profession in New South Wales' (2010) 37 *Journal of Law and Society* 466,485, in L Terry et al, 'Trends and Challenges in Lawyer Regulation' (FN 1) 2679

[8] Ibid 2680 – 2681

of service providers is open to question.[9] Another issue to consider in the context of how regulation of the legal profession should occur concerns the relative merits of adopting a rules-based approach as opposed to focusing upon the attainment of specific outcomes through the use of a principled-based approach to regulation. The present system of regulation of the legal profession reflects aspects of both these approaches, with the main statutory provisions pertaining to the legal profession being primarily rules-based, and the codes of conduct governing the legal profession reflecting a more principles oriented approach. The question arises whether the correct balance of rules and principles exists in the current regulatory framework.

When considering the necessary characteristics of good regulation, the OECD's 2005 Report 'Guiding Principles for Regulatory Quality and Performance' is instructive. This report states that good regulation should fulfil the following criteria:

(i)   serve clearly identified policy goals, and be effective in achieving those goals;

(ii)   have a sound legal and empirical basis;

(iii) produce benefits and justify costs, considering the distribution of effects across society and taking economic, environmental and social effects into account;

(iv) minimise costs and market distortions;

(v)   promote innovation through market incentives and goal-based approaches;

(vi) be clear, simple, and practical for users;

(vii) be consistent with other regulations and policies; and

(viii) be compatible as far as possible with competition, trade and investment-facilitating principles at domestic and international levels.[10]

Whilst these characteristics have been selected as desirable for all types of regulation in general, and were not designed for exclusive application to the legal profession, they nonetheless serve as a valuable reference point to facilitate a critical analysis of the regulatory regime for the legal profession in Ireland today. This chapter will also consider the merits of the present system of regulating the legal profession in Ireland in light of the OECD criteria.

The chapter concludes by presenting the findings of a quantitative study of professional misconduct amongst Irish solicitors. Professional misconduct amongst lawyers presents similar problems for regulators globally, with a con-

---

[9] Flood has questioned the suitability of the provisions of the Legal Services Act 2007 for regulating Global Professional Service Firms.   J Flood, 'The Re-landscaping of the Legal Profession: Firms and Professional Re-regulation' [2010 – 2011] *Current Sociology* 11 – 12

[10] OECD 'Guiding Principles for Regulatory Quality and Performance' (OECD, 2005). Cited by L Terry et al, 'Adopting Regulatory Objectives for the Legal Profession' (2012) 80 (6) *Fordham Law Review* 2685, 2689

siderable degree of similarity emerging in the nature of offending patterns of behaviour across the jurisdictions.[11] One common theme of professional misconduct internationally is that there is often a financial aspect to the wrongdoing. This study seeks to identify the most common facets of professional misconduct amongst Irish solicitors and offers suggestions for further research to improve our understanding of this problem. It also seeks to examine whether the present regulatory response to the issue of professional misconduct can be improved.

3.1 The Rationale for Regulating the Legal Profession in Ireland

In order to make an informed judgment as to whether the regulatory regime for the legal profession in Ireland is fit for purpose, it is firstly necessary to identify the purpose or objectives of the regime. A good system of regulation would undoubtedly result in fewer complaints from consumers concerning substandard provision of services, or the levying of excessively high fees. But whilst the enhancement of consumer satisfaction and welfare is one important reason for the regulation of the legal profession, it is not the only one. The regulation of the legal profession is important to ensure the proper administration of justice and also to establish legal certainty, both of these objectives being for the benefit of wider society, and not simply for the benefit of an individual client.[12] Davies has observed that lawyers mediate and adjudicate regarding both entitlements and obligations, thereby contributing to the maintenance of networks of "governmentality".[13] This refers to the way that lawyers make an important contribution to the functioning of the state, and also facilitate the process of government. The participation of lawyers in the political process also contributes towards the maintenance of such networks.

The disproportionate number of lawyer legislators compared to non-lawyer legislators has been well documented internationally, with between 40 and 50% of US Congress members being lawyers over the course of the last two hundred years.[14] Eulau and Sprague have argued that lawyers' involvement in politics is more common than amongst non-lawyers because their frequent contacts with politically active people enables them to become easily integrated within the political community.[15] They have also argued that lawyers tend to belong to

---

[11] R Abel , *Lawyers in the Dock: Learning from Attorney Disciplinary Proceedings* (Oxford University Press, 2010); R Abel, *Lawyers on Trial: Understanding Ethical Misconduct* (Oxford University Press, 2011), N Doornbos & L De Groot-Van Leeuwen, 'Incorrigible Advocates' [2012] 15 (2) *Legal Ethics* 335, A Boon & A Whyte, 'Icarus Falls: The Coal Health Scandal' [2012] 15 (2) *Legal Ethics* 227; M Davies, 'Solicitors, Dishonesty and the Solicitors' Disciplinary Tribunal' (1999) 6 (2) *International Journal of the Legal Profession* 141

[12] The Competition Authority, 'Competition in Professional Services: Solicitors and Barristers' December 2006. 1

[13] M Davies, 'The Demise of Professional Self-Regulation? Evidence from the "ideal type" professions of medicine and law' (2010*) Professional Negligence* 5

[14] R Eakins, 'Lawyers in the Legislature: The Case of Ohio' (2006) 43 (4) *The Social Science Journal* 717

[15] H Eulau & J Sprague, *Lawyers in Politics: A Study of Professional Convergence* (Bobbs-Merrill, 1964)

politically active families, and that they are more likely to be involved in party politics. According to Meinhold and Hadley, '[t]he impact of legal training on the behaviour and attitudes of party political activists is considerable and reinforces the importance of lawyers in politics'.[16]

Paik et al have drawn attention to the bridge which lawyer politicians provide between organisations to which they are affiliated and the political community, and also to their valuable fundraising potential.[17] They have also argued that lawyers' networks, both formal, such as those arising as a result of involvement in law firms and professional representative associations, and informal networks which arise as a consequence of attendance at churches, synagogues or children's soccer games, serve as a foundation for building alliances in relation to public policy.[18]

The influence of lawyer-politicians has been examined by Halliday and Nelson, who have referred to the work of Heinz to show how the legal profession has been influential in drawing up Criminal Codes of Law, and how American state legislatures have delegated legislative drafting responsibilities to lawyers' representative associations, such as the Chicago and Illinois Bar Associations.[19] Heinz has argued that corporate clients exert a stronger influence than their private client counterparts over their lawyers. This influence is carried over into the political arena, and shapes the activities of corporate-lawyer-politicians. However, Heinz has also been critical of attributing a discernable political function to such corporate-lawyer-politicians, and has argued that there is a vacuum at the centre of the American legislative network space that is filled by neither non-lawyers nor lawyers.[20]

Thus, lawyers' regulation has a political dimension, their work being essential in maintaining the functioning of a modern, democratic state. A thorough exploration of the rationale behind the regulation of the legal profession will also assist in answering the other questions which this chapter seeks to answer, namely who should regulate the legal profession? What entities should be regulated? When should regulation occur? Where should regulation occur? And finally, how should the regulation of the legal profession occur?

Terry has argued that the articulation of regulatory objectives serves several functions.[21] It is helpful for both the regulators and the regulated community in deciding how regulations should be interpreted and applied in particular circumstances. The clear identification of the purpose to be served by a regulatory

---

[16] S Meinhold & C Hadley, 'Lawyers as Political Party Activists' (1995) 76 (2) *Social Science Quarterly* 364

[17] Paik et al, 'Political Lawyers: The Structure of a National Network' (2011) 36 (4) *Law and Social Inquiry* 892, 912

[18] Ibid 908. According to Paik et al, the politicians to the right of the spectrum have been much more successful in developing such networks than their counterparts on the left of the spectrum.

[19] T Halliday & R Nelson, 'Lawyers, Structure and Power: A Tribute to John Heinz' (2011) 36 (4) *Law and Social Inquiry* 885, 887

[20] Ibid 888, citing J Heinz, 'Lawyers' Professional and Political Networks Compared: Core and Periphery' (2011) 53 (2) *Arizona Law Review* 455, 482– 485

[21] Ibid 2687

regime assists the legal profession in negotiating with government and other bodies regarding how that regime impacts upon legal practice. It also facilitates public debate regarding legislative proposals and regulatory change.

Terry has drawn up a model set of regulatory objectives which she offers as a template to facilitate the debate about regulatory objectives, the adoption of which may be contemplated by a particular jurisdiction. These are as follows:

1. Protection of clients;

2. Protection of the public interest;

3. Promoting public understanding of the legal system and respect for the rule of law;

4. Supporting the rule of law and ensuring lawyer independence sufficient to allow for a robust rule-of-law culture;

5. Increasing access to justice (including clients' willingness and ability to access lawyers' services);

6. Promoting lawyers' compliance with professional principles (including competent and professional delivery of services);

7. Ensuring that lawyer regulation is consistent with principles of "good regulation"[22]

Whereas both Terry's and the OECD's regulatory objectives promote the idea of social justice, the OECD objectives differ from Terry's in that they explicitly promote the attainment of market liberalisation as a means of achieving enhanced consumer welfare and an equitable society. Given that the current interest in regulatory objectives has emerged in the wake of their inclusion in the UK's Legal Services Act (LSA) 2007, it is not surprising that they were not included in the Solicitors Act 1954. For reference, section 1 of the LSA 2007 states:

(1) In this Act a reference to "the regulatory objectives" is a reference to the objectives of-

(a) protecting and promoting the public interest;

(b) supporting the constitutional principle of the rule of law;

(c) improving access to justice;

(d) protecting and promoting the interests of consumers;

(e) promoting competition in the provision of services within subsection 2 [referring to authorized persons];

(f) encouraging an independent, strong, diverse and effective legal profession;

---

[22] L Terry, 'Adopting Regulatory Objectives for the Legal Profession' (2012) (FN 10) 2734

(g) increasing public understanding of the citizen's legal rights and duties;

(h) promoting and maintaining adherence to the professional principles.

By contrast, the long title of the 1954 Act more prosaically sets out its function as being 'to provide for the admission, enrolment and control of solicitors of the courts of justice and to provide for other matters connected with the matters aforesaid.' The 1954 Act does not explicitly refer to any of the issues which were contained in Terry's list of ideal regulatory objectives. Hogan has stated that the enactment of the 1954 Act, 'was the culmination of efforts extending over more than a decade by the Law Society to amend and update the law on the regulation (more precisely, the self-regulation) of the solicitors' profession.'[23] The 1954 Act confers self-regulatory status upon the profession by granting powers to the LSI to make regulations in relation to all matters covered by the Act, or to matters which are prescribed 'as being the subject of regulations'.[24] Thus insofar as there is any discernable objective in the 1954 Act, it might be described as the establishment of the self-regulation of the solicitors' profession upon a statutory basis.

The 1960 Act also omitted to identify regulatory objectives, its key purpose being the amendment and extension of the 1954 Act. As was seen in Chapter 1, it was primarily aimed at rectifying the constitutional flaws which emerged in the 1954 Act shortly after its enactment. The subsequent amending legislation has similarly failed to offer any further enlightenment with regard to the overall objectives of the statutory framework.[25] Again this was in keeping with legislative drafting practice of the day, with the identification of regulatory objectives generally not being articulated until post 2007.

The Economic Argument for the Regulation of the Legal Profession

From an economic perspective, the objective of regulation is the correction of market failures. In revealing these, economic analysis provides a means to identify policies aimed at the alleviation of such failures. In the context of the provision of legal services, two particular factors may be identified which contribute towards market failure, and as such, they may be used to justify regulatory intervention. These are information asymmetry and externalities.

Information Asymmetry

The provision of a legal service is, in economic terms a 'credence good', the quality of which is less discernable by a client than it is by its provider.[26] Not only is a client reliant upon the lawyer to supply him/her with a good quality service,

---

[23] D Hogan, 'The Society from Independence to 1960', in E Hall & D Hogan (eds), *The Law Society of Ireland (1852 – 2002)* (Four Courts Press, 2002) 86

[24] Solicitors Act 1954 § 5

[25] Solicitors (Amendment) Act 1994, Solicitors (Amendment) Act 2002, Civil Law (Miscellaneous Provisions) Act 2008 and Civil Law (Miscellaneous Provisions) Act 2011

[26] F Stephen & J Love, 'Regulation of the Legal Profession', *Encyclopaedia of Law and Economics* 989. Available at: <http://encyclo.findlaw.com/5860book.pdf> Accessed 12/9/2012

he/she must also rely upon the lawyer to identify the particular service which should be supplied in order to resolve an issue. The lawyer therefore performs two separate roles; firstly that of agency whereby the client's needs are identified, and secondly there is the service function whereby the identified service is supplied to the client. The lawyer's dual function in the circumstances gives rise to a moral hazard, as a result of the potential for oversupply of services, and this in turn creates the need for regulatory intervention, to protect the client from being exploited by the service provider.

A further problem which arises due to information asymmetry has been described by Akerlof as 'the lemons problem'.[27] This refers to the process of 'adverse selection' to which clients may resort when they are unable to judge the quality of a credence good on offer. In these circumstances, a client will be reluctant to pay a high price for the service, and will opt instead for a service provided at a lower cost. This adverse selection process gives rise to a general deterioration in the quality of services on offer, as eventually, there is no longer an effective market for high quality services.[28] Antonioni and Flynn have argued that the 'lemons' problem was responsible for exacerbating the credit crunch which occurred globally in the wake of the collapse of Lehman Brothers.[29] This was because lenders feared that borrowers were 'lemons', and this fear resulted in a drying up of credit. It is arguable that the 'lemons' phenomenon also resulted in the rapid shrinking of the professional indemnity insurance market for solicitors in Ireland which occurred in 2010 and 2011, when four leading insurers abandoned the market, and the Solicitors Mutual Indemnity Fund became insolvent.[30] The insurers experienced information asymmetry, and were unable to adequately identify good quality legal services providers from the 'lemons'. The potential for information asymmetry to arise is reduced in circumstances where the service user regularly purchases legal services, and by virtue of his experience, is better able to make an informed judgment regarding the quality of service being offered. This observation may be used to support the proposition that business and corporate clients require less regulatory protection than private clients.[31]

Various regulatory interventions may alleviate the market failure which arises due to information asymmetry. Spigelman has identified these as the requirement for lawyers to obtain certain educational qualifications, the enforcement of professional ethical obligations, the imposition of fiduciary duties, compulsory insurance and the use of mandatory or recommended fee scales.[32]

---

[27] G Akerlof, 'The Market for 'Lemons': Quality Uncertainty and the Market Mechanism' (1970) 84 (3) *Quarterly Journal of Economics* 488

[28] The term 'lemons' refers to used cars of inferior quality, which featured in Akerlof's original exposition of his theory.

[29] P Antonioni & S Flynn, *Economics for Dummies* (John Wiley & Sons Ltd, 2011) 333

[30] A Neary, 'Cause and Effect' (2011) 105 (7) LSG 33

[31] See ch 3 § 3.6.1 for a fuller discussion of the issue of whether regulation of the legal profession should be 'client specific'.

[32] J Spigelman, 'Are Lawyers Lemons? Competition Principles and Professional Regulation' 29th October 2002. (The 2002 Lawyers' Lecture, St James Ethics Centre) 15. Available at: <http://ssrn.com/abstract=1800450> Accessed 1/12/2011

Spigelman has suggested that the 'lemons' problem might be alleviated in Akerlof's original formulation of the phenomenon by the establishment of a trusted independent organisation to verify the quality of used cars. The award of a quality mark to legal service providers by an independent authority may serve a similar function in reducing market failure as a result of information asymmetry. Neary and Rowe have recently announced the introduction of a new quality risk-management standard for Irish solicitors, the award of which will assist practitioners in obtaining lower cost insurance cover.[33] Those who obtain the standard distinguish themselves in the market as 'non-lemons' who pose less risk to an insurer.

Externalities

Another cause of failure in the market for legal services arises due to the problem of externalities. These arise where the quality of service being provided affects others than the actual recipient of the service. For example; wider society may be deemed to have accrued a benefit from the establishment of legal certainty regarding the point of law at issue in a particular case, and also due to the proper administration of justice, in a case where the quality of legal service received was of a high standard. Both the establishment of legal certainty and the proper administration of justice are positive externalities associated with the provision of good quality legal services. Similarly, where the quality of service received by a client is of a poor quality, it is not only the individual client who suffers loss in the circumstances. Wider society also pays a price in terms of legal uncertainty and weaker administration of justice. Negative externalities also arise due to the failure to properly establish legal certainty on the relevant point of law, and also as a consequence of the failure to secure the proper administration of justice in the matter. Where a lawyer experiences a conflict of interest, this may also give rise to a negative externality.[34] Where a client receives a service the provision of which has given rise to positive externalities, he/she will be disinclined to pay for that element of the benefit which accrued to others as a result of the service performance, as a consumer is generally only willing to pay for a benefit which directly accrues to him/her.

The provision of high quality legal services constitutes a form of public good, because it gives rise to positive externalities. Such public goods will tend to be under produced in a free market, because producers are unable to exclude non-paying recipients from gaining benefits due to the service provision.[35] Regulation, by means of the implementation of fixed scale fees is one means of correcting the market failure which occurs due to positive externalities. Regulation may also be implemented to correct market failure which arises as a result of negative externalities. Such regulations might be aimed at ensuring that providers of legal

---

[33] K O Higgins, 'Neary and Rowe announce new 'Q Standard' (2012) 106 (7) LSG 10

[34] A Andreangeli, 'Between Public Interest and the Free Market: Would liberalisation of the legal profession bring benefits to the client – and to the Market?' (2008) 19 (6) *European Business Law Review* 1051, 1054

[35] R Van den Bergh, 'Towards Better Regulation of the Legal Professions in the European Union' (2008) Rotterdam Institute of Law and Economics. Working Paper Series (2008/07) 5. Available at: <http://ssrn.com/abstract=1113310> Accessed 1/9/2011

services are trained to a high standard, so that poor quality services are not provided in the first instance. Regulation to reduce the problem of negative externalities may also be effected via the imposition of civil liability in the tort of negligence, where the quality of legal service provided falls below the reasonable standard of care, and where the client has suffered harm as a consequence, or alternatively, where the provision of inadequate legal services gives rise to the imposition of a sanction by professional bodies such as the LSI, BCI, BPCT, BPCAB or the SDT. Apart from the problem of market failure, Van den Bergh has identified a further public interest based rationale for state intervention in the market for legal services as being the state's desire to achieve distributive justice. The imposition of price regulation by the setting of maximum price schedules can be adopted in order to secure access to legal services for those on a low income, and as such, they may help to vindicate constitutional rights.[36]

Economic analysis may also be applied to facilitate some useful insights into the effect of self-regulation on the market for legal services, which has been described as the ultimate form of regulatory capture.[37] This is the process where a regulated entity effectively hijacks the regulatory function of the regulator with the result that regulation occurs for that entity's own benefit rather than in the public interest. Where self-regulation occurs, there is also the potential for rent-seeking behaviour. A self-regulating legal profession can erect barriers to entry, to create a permanent under-supply of services, with a view to ensuring that members of the profession have a constant supply of work. A self-regulating legal profession may also adopt mandatory or recommended fee schedules as a means of ensuring high incomes for its members. Whilst cartels may be notoriously difficult to sustain when they have a large membership, the legal profession has a relatively small membership. The self-regulating legal profession appears to display some cartel-like features, in that it can generate economic rents, and deploy entry barriers to maintain a level of income stability for its members.

The compact nature of the profession also allows it to efficiently lobby government in the event that the group's financial interests are challenged, because the benefits which can be accrued from joint lobbying endeavours significantly outweigh the cost associated with such efforts. This is in contrast with the position of consumers of legal services. They are a diverse group of individuals, and the costs involved in order for them to present a unified challenge to the rent-seeking behaviour of a self-regulating legal profession outweigh the expected benefits which might be achieved from such efforts.[38]

The amalgamation of The Competition Authority and The National Consumer Authority which is due to take place following the enactment of the Competition (Amendment) Bill 2011, will go some way towards alleviating the inequality of arms which currently exists between the legal profession on the one hand, and

---

[36] Ibid 6

[37] J Kay, 'The Forms of Regulation' in A Sheldon (ed), *Financial Regulation – or Over-regulation,* The Institute of Economic Affairs 33 (cited in R Van den Bergh, 'Towards Better Regulation') (FN 35) 6

[38] Ibid (FN 35) 7

consumers of its services on the other.[39] The following section looks at the question of who should be responsible for regulating the legal profession.

3.2 Who should be responsible for regulating the legal profession?

This section will consider the findings of a series of reports which have been commissioned by public authorities over the last two decades, and which have made findings regarding who should be responsible for the regulation of the legal profession in Ireland. Several of the reports have been critical of the current system of self-regulation, and the advantages and disadvantages of self-regulation will therefore also be considered. The section commences with a consideration of the recommendations of the Fair Trade Commission Report 1990 for changes to the regulation of the legal profession.

3.2.1 The Fair Trade Commission Report 1990

Barristers in Ireland are regulated by both the Honorable Society of Kings Inns (HSKI) and the Bar Council of Ireland. The Fair Trade Commission compiled a report on the legal profession for the Minister for Industry and Commerce in 1990.[40] This was critical of the HSKI's educational activities, and the manner in which it controls the entry of barristers into the profession. Holders of an approved law degree are eligible to apply for the Degree of Barrister-at-law. Those without an approved degree must obtain a Diploma in Legal Studies from the HSKI, and will then be eligible to apply for the Degree of Barrister-at-Law. The Commission was also critical of the requirement for students to attend commons on twenty occasions, presumably on the basis that the requirement served no discernable function in enhancing the legal skills of attendees. Concerns were also raised regarding the disciplinary powers of the HSKI, which the Commission argued were most probably unconstitutional, given the ruling of the Supreme Court in O'Farrell.[41] It may be implied from the O'Farrell ruling that it would be unconstitutional of the HSKI Benchers to disbar a barrister, because although O'Farrell concerned a solicitor, the essence of the ruling was that the disbarment of a legal professional was a judicial function. In the case of barristers who are called to the Bar by the Chief Justice of Ireland, the power to disbar ought to lie with the Supreme Court (contrary to solicitors, who are admitted to the profession by the President of the High Court and who accordingly may be disbarred only by the President of the High Court).

The Fair Trade Commission also expressed surprise at the role of the judiciary within the HSKI in matters relating to the barristers' profession. The Com-

---

[39] A Murtagh, 'Irish Competition Policy Under the EU/IMF Spotlight' [2012] Competition Law 62, 72. Citing Department of Jobs, Enterprise and Innovation, 'Competition (Amendment) Bill 2011, Regulatory Impact Analysis (September 2011). According to Murtagh, "The Bill's Regulatory Impact Analysis suggests that it will create a 'level playing field for all participants in the market, enhance consumer welfare and improve national competitiveness'".

[40] Fair Trade Commission Report of Study into Restrictive Practices in the Legal Profession (Dublin: Government of Ireland Stationery Office, 1990)

[41] Re O'Farrell and the Solicitors Act 1954 [1961] 95 ILTR 167

mission recommended that neither the Bar Council nor the HSKI should either disbar or disband a barrister:

> At this stage, it seems appropriate that the Commission should express its surprise at the involvement of the judiciary with the barristers' profession through the institution of Kings Inns. There seems no sound reason for any aspect of the profession of barrister to be influenced by the direct participation of the judiciary. Barristers are subject to the authority of the judges in their courts, judges can complain to the Bar Council about the behaviour of barristers, and no further involvement would appear to be warranted.... If Kings Inns were to retain any disciplinary function however, we consider the judiciary should play no part in that function, and that a lay presence might be introduced. Furthermore, the Commission considers that the association of the judiciary with the Kings Inns might be carefully re-examined in the light of the remaining functions of Kings Inns after account has been taken of our recommendations in the field of discipline and other matters.[42]

Complaints from fellow members of the Bar regarding a barrister's conduct are considered by the Bar Council's Professional Practices Committee, whilst complaints regarding a barrister's conduct from a member of the public, a solicitor or a client are considered by the Bar's Professional Conduct Tribunal. Until recently, there has been just one recorded case of a barrister having been disbarred due to professional misconduct by the HSKI in its entire 470-year history.[43] However, on the 11th of January 2012 history was made when the HSKI disbarred Patrick Russell, who was found guilty of "disgraceful acts of professional misconduct".[44] Following a complaint that he had acted unprofessionally insofar as he falsely informed the complainant that a named solicitor was acting on his behalf in a matter, caused the complainant to make a substantial payment to him in order to pursue an appeal and falsely told the complainant that his claim had been settled and a substantial sum in compensation was pending, the Supreme Court having made a ruling in his favour. By his conduct in this regard Mr Russell failed to 'uphold the standard set out in the Code of Conduct, and the dignity and high standing of the profession and their [sic] own standing as members of the profession', as required by The Code of Conduct of the Bar.[45] The Disciplinary Committee found that such wrongdoing also constituted a breach of the General Rules of the HSKI.[46] The Benchers, having considered the Disciplinary Committee's Report of the 7th October 2011, confirmed its findings and also endorsed the Disciplinary Committee's recommended sanction that Mr Russell should be disbarred.

---

[42] *Fair Trade Commission Report* (FN 40) paras 16.49 – 16.50

[43] See ch 1 § 1.1.4

[44] The HSKI Decision of Benchers to disbar Mr Patrick Russell barrister-at-law, 11th January 2012, may be accessed at
<http://www.kingsinns.ie/website/prospective_students/DisciplinaryDecisions2012.htm>
Accessed 8/10/2012

[45] BCI 'Code of Conduct of the Bar for the Bar of Ireland 25th July 2011', para 2.4

[46] General Rules of the HSKI, Rule 30 (1) (b) – (e)

More recently, the case of Alan Toal epitomises all that is lacking in the current system for regulating barristers' misconduct.[47] Following the finding of the BPCT that Toal, a former garda, had used threatening and aggressive behaviour towards a client, and had also accepted money directly from a client, his case is due to be completely reheard by the DC of the HSKI. The original complaint was made to the BCI in 2010, yet three years later, the complainant has yet to see a final resolution of the matter, notwithstanding the findings of the BPCT. The current barristers' disciplinary procedure, which involves the complete rehearing of the facts of a case by the DC undermines the role of the BPCT in the disciplinary process, and adds unnecessary delay to the disciplinary process, with resultant stress for all parties concerned. Given the secrecy surrounding the activities of the Benchers of the HSKI, it is not possible to identify the factors contributing to its failure to efficiently and effectively fulfil its role in the disciplinary process.

The Bar Council also plays a role in the education of barristers as evidenced by its Continuing Professional Development Programme and its link with the Law Library which it operates. Membership of the Law Library is compulsory for all practising barristers, a feature which was criticised by the Fair Trade Commission.[48] The Fair Trade Commission also criticised the patents of precedence system for its 'mysterious' connection with Government.[49] The granting of patents is at the discretion of the Government, and the system was recently criticised once again due to the unnecessary and artificial distinction it creates between junior and senior counsel:

> The Group [Special Group on Public Numbers and Expenditure Programmes] looked at the difference in the level of legal fees payable to junior and senior counsel. The Government at its discretion grants Patents of Precedence at the Bar on the recommendation of an Advisory Council consisting of the Chief Justice, the President of the High Court, the Attorney General and the Chairman of the Bar Council. The Group is of the view that the distinction is unnecessary and contributes to higher legal costs payable by the State. Other jurisdictions function adequately without this hierarchy of legal professionals. The Group notes that this practice applies across the entire legal industry but considers that the removal of this distinction is unlikely to have a significant negative impact on the legal system.[50]

To date, the recommendations of the Fair Trade Commission Report have been largely ignored, as have those of the Special Group on Public Service Numbers and Expenditure Programmes with regard to the patents of precedence

---

[47] N Tallant, 'Don's Brief in the Dock', *The Sunday World* (Dublin, 25th June 2012) 1. Available at: <http://www.sundayworld.com/top-stories/crime-desk/investigations/don-s-brief-in-the-dock> Accessed 29/7/2014

[48] *Fair Trade Commission Report* (FN 40) para 7.159.

[49] Ibid

[50] Department of Justice and Equality. *Report of the Special Group on Public Service Numbers and Expenditure Programmes Volume II:* 210. Available at: <http://www.djei.ie/publications/corporate/2009/volume2.pdf> Accessed 22/3/2012

isssue. However, the LSRB 2011 does herald the implementation of significant changes in the regulatory functions of the HSKI and whilst it will not abolish the patents of precedence system, it will introduce significant changes to the manner in which senior counsel are appointed.[51] The following section will consider the recommendations of the Legal Costs Working Group (LCWG) 2003 for the reform of the system for establishing legal costs.

3.2.2 Report of The Legal Costs Working Group 2003

In 2003, the LCWG published a report recommending that a Legal Costs Regulatory Body should be established 'to formulate guidelines setting out the amounts of legal costs that normally can be expected to be recovered in respect of particular types of proceedings or steps within proceedings.[52] This would have been a major departure from the status quo whereby the LSI and The BCI are primarily responsible for matters of costs. The LCWG recommended that costs should be proportionate to the time spent by a legal practitioner on a matter, the complexity of the proceedings and the court level involved in the case. This approach would introduce much needed transparency into the present system where such considerations are combined in the setting of a single instruction or brief fee. It was also recommended that the fees of Junior Counsel in a case should not be automatically levied at a rate of two thirds of that of the Senior Counsel in that case. The Legal Costs Regulatory Body would have responsibility for formulating guidelines for costs assessment in contentious matters, and would be endowed with all powers necessary for the regulation of such costs. Its duties and powers should include responsibility for the formulation and updating of cost recovery guidelines to facilitate billing and assessment. It would specify the maximum number of billing hours recoverable as party and party costs for certain proceedings or steps within proceedings.[53] The Legal Costs Regulatory Body would also be responsible for the regulation of procedures for costs assessment and for prescription of information to be given regarding costs, fees and disbursements by solicitors and barristers to those seeking or receiving legal services or costs estimates. It would also provide the public with information on the law and clients' entitlements concerning costs.[54] The LCWG also recommended that the appointment of an Appeals Adjudicator should be made, by means of a system of open competition, to be conducted by the Public Appointments Service.[55] The competition should be open to all suitably qualified persons, and should not be limited to members of the legal profession.

The LCWG also recommended that the Office of the Taxing Master should be replaced by a Legal Costs Assessment Office, the functions of which would be

---

[51] Ch 5 describes the provisions of the LSRB 2011 in detail.

[52] *Report of the Legal Costs Working Group* (Stationery Office, Dublin, 2003) para 5.2.2. The report is available at: <http://www.justice.ie/en/JELR/leglalcosts.pdf/Files/legalcosts.pdf> Accessed 18/9/2012

[53] Party and party costs are those which may be recovered by one party to proceedings from another party, generally the unsuccessful party pays the costs of the successful party. Liability for party and party costs is determined at the conclusion of proceedings.

[54] *Report of the Legal Costs Working Group* (FN 52) para 7.17

[55] Ibid, para 7.37

to operate a procedure for the assessment of costs, to provide support for the Legal Costs Regulatory Body and Appeals Adjudicators and to regularly provide information and data to the public on outcomes of assessments and appeals, by reference to the type of litigation or application involved, the value of the claim and other criteria, to be set down by the Legal Costs Regulatory Body.[56] Although the vast majority of the recommendations of the LCWG have not been implemented in the ten years since the publication of its Report, many of its recommendations are contained in the LSRB 2011 and should be implemented in the near future, in accordance with the terms of the Memorandum of Understanding which was agreed with the Troika.[57] The only recommendation of the LCWG which has been adopted is that concerning the fees of Junior Counsel which are no longer automatically levied at a rate which is two thirds of that of Senior Counsel. The following section will consider the extent to which the recommendations of the Competition Authority's Report of 2006 concerning competition in the provision of professional services by solicitors and barristers have been implemented.

3.2.3 The Competition Authority 'Competition in Professional Services – Solicitors and Barristers' (2006)

In December 2006, The Competition Authority published a comprehensive report on the Legal Services Sector in Ireland, entitled 'Competition in Professional Services: Solicitors and Barristers', which found that the legal profession required a considerable degree of reform. The Competition Authority found the profession to be 'permeated with unnecessary and disproportionate restrictions on competition', the removal of which were desirable to increase competition in the sector, for the benefit of consumers.[58] In common with the earlier Report of the LCWG of 2003, the Competition Authority's 2006 Report also recommended an end to the system whereby a Junior Counsel's fee was automatically levied at two thirds of that of the Senior Counsel in a case. The Competition Authority recommended that both the legal profession and the legal services market should be regulated by an independent Legal Services Commission. This would be an independent, transparent and accountable body which would encompass a more diverse range of stakeholders in the regulatory process than the current self-regulatory model. The Competition Authority was of the view that the establishment of such a body would be in accordance with the Government's principles of good regulation, and that its establishment was necessary in order to mitigate the risks associated with self-regulation. It referred in particular to the conflict of interest facing both the LSI and the BCI, which arose between their representative roles on behalf of their members, and their role in protecting consumers' interests. The report also recommended that the LSI and BCI

---

[56] Ibid, para 7.34

[57] Ch 2, § 2.3 considers the relevant sections of the Memorandum of Understanding which was agreed between the Irish Government and the Troika in return for the bailout funds.

[58] The Competition Authority Report stated that whilst solicitors were largely self-regulated by the LSI, with a small amount of oversight in some areas, barristers were totally self-regulated by the BCI. *Report on Legal Services: Solicitors and Barristers* (The Competition Authority, December 2006) 10.

should cease to set standards for providing legal education, as this power had historically been used by those bodies to 'facilitate monopolies'. The report stated:

> Independent regulation of the legal profession would be consistent with reform towards a greater transparency, accountability and consumer-focused regulation in other professions and sectors in Ireland (for example, financial services and the medical profession) and in the legal profession internationally.[59]

The Authority recommended that the Minister for Justice, Equality and Law Reform should establish the Legal Services Commission on or before June 2008, and envisaged that this would work in conjunction with the Legal Services Ombudsman.[60]

The recommendations in the Competition Authority Report met with a similar level of inaction as those contained in the LCWG Report of 2003, with the exception of the recommendation regarding Junior Counsel's fees.[61] Once more, many of the proposals, or variants of them, have been included in the LSRB 2011 which is examined in Chapter 5. The following section will consider the recommendations of the Committee of Public Accounts in 2011 regarding competition in the legal profession.

3.2.4 Committee of Public Accounts Third Interim Report on the Procurement of Legal Services by Public Bodies (January 2011)

In 2011 The Committee of Public Accounts published its third interim report on the Procurement of Legal Services by Public Bodies. Chapter 5 of the Report dealt with competitiveness in the legal profession.[62] The report criticised the present system of self-regulation of the legal profession, which was described as 'a significant problem'.[63] It noted that almost all other professions have split regulatory and representative bodies, and it also observed that England and Wales have recently ceased self-regulation of the legal profession. It also commented that the Bar lacks any form of statutory regulation whatever, and that the BCI was simply an association of undertakings. The Committee stated that the planned appointment of the Legal Services Ombudsman in accordance with the provisions of the Legal Services Ombudsman Act 2009 did not constitute the fundamental reform which it considered was necessary in the legal services market.[64] It was noted that the Ombudsman would not have the power to resolve

---

[59] Ibid 5

[60] The appointment of a Legal Services Ombudsman will not take place, as § 5 of the LSRB 2011 provides for the repeal of the Legal Services Ombudsman Act 2009. See ch 1, § 1.3.3.7 for a discussion of this Act.

[61] Also, the BCI has divested itself of much of its regulatory functions through the establishment of the independent BPCT and BPCAB. See ch 1, § 1.2.2.1 for a further description of these bodies.

[62] *Committee of Public Accounts Third Interim Report on the Procurement of Legal Services by Public Bodies* (Dáil Éireann, January 2011)

[63] Ibid, para 5.2

[64] See FN 60 *supra* regarding repeal of the Legal Services Ombudsman Act 2009.

consumer complaints, but could only refer these back to either the LSI or the BCI for further investigation by the self-regulatory bodies. The following section will examine the strengths and weaknesses of the present system of self-regulation of the legal profession.

3.2.5 Self-regulation of the legal profession

The concept of self-regulation epitomises the traditional notion of professionalism. Faulconbridge has noted that professionalism is a form of jurisdiction which confers both rewards and privileges upon members.[65] These are either symbolic, for example; the professional has access and proximity to the centres of established power or material, as evidenced by the earning potential of legal practitioners. Also, the profession as an entity is permitted to self-regulate, which in turn facilitates 'the creation of skill scarcity, [and] the exclusive authority over the application of certain knowledge and techniques'.[66]

Davies has argued that self-regulation supports the 'mythology of professionalism by disputing the capability of external organizations to regulate the complex activities of professionals. From this political perspective, professionalism is seen as a form of social contract, whereby in return for privileges which are commonly monopolistic in nature, the profession undertakes to ensure a level of expertise and to uphold a requisite standard of behaviour amongst its members. The arrangement prima facie has the benefit of shifting the cost of regulation to the profession itself, thereby sparing wider the society the expense. Davies offers the following description of the phenomenon:

> Self-regulation, broadly defined, can therefore be seen to underpin the professional status, offering an efficient, cost effective mechanism which seeks to address the disadvantageous position of the client or patient caused by information asymmetries.[67]

The term 'self-regulation' is used in different ways in different jurisdictions. Terry has disputed whether the legal profession in any jurisdiction is completely self-regulated as generally there is some degree of regulatory intervention from either the judicial, legislative or executive branch of government.[68] In the US, the legal profession describes itself as self-regulated, and justifies the use of the term on the basis that it is regulated by the judicial rather than the executive or legislative branch of the Government. Canada justifies the use of the term on the basis that law societies are the primary regulators of the profession, but the law societies' authority is derived from legislative measures, and as such, the Canadian model would not meet the US criteria for a self-regulated profession. Ireland's self-regulatory system for the solicitors' profession is similar to that in Canada, with the LSI's regulatory power being derived from statute. Yet the LSI

---

[65] J Faulconbridge et al, 'Global Law Firms: Globalization and Organizational Spaces of Cross-Border Legal Work' (2008) 28 (3) *Northwestern Journal of International Law and Business* 455, 471, in M Davies, 'The Demise of professional self-regulation? Evidence from the "ideal type" of professions of medicine and law' (2010) *Professional Negligence* 4.

[66] Ibid 4

[67] Ibid

[68] L Terry, ' Trends and Challenges in Lawyer Regulation' (FN 1) 2669

rejects its description as a self-regulatory body, and argues that the present regime is more accurately described as 'co-regulatory'.[69] However, the self-regulatory system for barristers is more akin to the US model, as the judiciary, through their role in the HSKI, play a primary role in the regulatory system. Regardless of the precise definition of self-regulation which is adopted, the principle has traditionally been a cornerstone of the legal profession's self-identity.[70] The concept is also closely related to that of the independence of the legal profession, which is included in many international and national codes of conduct, and other regulatory instruments.[71] The last decade has seen the emergence of a global debate regarding self-regulation and whether it is an appropriate system to be applied to the legal profession. In several jurisdictions there has been a growing shift towards co-regulatory systems.[72]

Van den Bergh has stated that one advantage of self-regulation is that professionals are more committed to rules aimed at ensuring high standards within a profession where those rules have been adopted by the profession itself rather than by statute.[73] However, there is no available research to support such a proposition, and a perusal of the SDT's annual report suggests that breaches of professional codes of conduct and common law rules are, if anything, more frequent than breaches of statutory obligations.[74]

The expanding nature of the legal profession has presented ever-increasing challenges to the traditional method of self-regulation. Historically, a small, compacted group of professionals existed, in which peer pressure and informal regulatory influences were, by and large, sufficient to secure compliance with behavioural norms within the 'gentleman's club' which was the nineteenth century legal profession in England and Ireland.[75] However, as the legal profession expanded in the modern era, the ability of such informal regulatory mechanisms to achieve compliance with accepted norms diminished. As Abel observed:

---

[69] LSI, 'Legal Services Regulation Bill 2011: Submission to the Minister for Justice, Equality and Defence' February 2012. 21. Interview with Ken Murphy, Director General, LSI (Dublin, 13th Sept 2013). In challenging what it describes as 'the myth of self-regulation', the LSI points to the involvement of various external authorities in the regulation of solicitors. These include the President of the High Court, the SDT, the IA and lay members of the CCRC.

[70] The ideal of self-regulation is included in the CCBE Core Principles: (j). See ch 2 § 2.7

[71] The ideal of the independence of the legal profession is included in the CCBE Core Principles: (a) (Ch 2 § 2.7); IBA General Principles 1 (Ch 2, § 2.8); The Legal Services Act 20007 § 1 (1) (f) (England and Wales); Terry's model regulatory objectives for the legal profession, as contained in L Terry, 'Adopting Regulatory Objectives for the Legal Profession' (FN 10) 2734.

[72] For example, the UK has seen the introduction of a co-regulatory model with the establishment of the Legal Services Board which oversees the regulators of separate branches of the legal profession.

[73] R Van den Bergh, 'Towards Better Regulation' (FN 35) 7

[74] Solicitors Disciplinary Tribunal Annual Reports from 2003 – 2010 are available at: <http://distrib.ie/reports.htm> Accessed 20/9/2012>. The precedence of breaches of undertakings in cases of misconduct is notable, and this is an area of practice which is not governed by statutory provisions; breach of an undertaking constitutes 'unprofessional conduct' (LSI 'Guide to Professional Conduct of Solicitors', para 7.3).

[75] M Stacey, *Regulating British Medicine: the General Medical Council* (Wiley, 1992) in R Van den Bergh, 'Towards Better Regulation' (FN 35) 6

Modern professions suffer worsening crises of self-regulation. (Prominent examples include the police, accountants, and the clergy.) The legal profession's shameless defence of restrictive practices undermined its altruistic pretensions to solicitude for clients. As professions expand and diversify (in background and practice), peers, seniors, and judges are less likely to observe or correct misconduct. One-off consumers lack information about lawyers' reputations; third-party lawyers claim that the same division of labour that makes lay clients dependent on professional expertise also mandates peer review. Clients respond by insisting that regulators enjoy the same independence from lawyers that lawyers demand from the state ... Instead of demonstrating professionalism by setting standards above those of the market or state, lawyers did the least they could get away with. Like a confirmed alcoholic, the profession constantly vowed to reform, raising client expectations and thence the number of complaints, overburdening the system, and initiating a new cycle of rising backlog and frustration.[76]

The emergence of the Troika on the Irish political and economic landscape has heralded the beginning of a new era for professional governance in Ireland, and it also appears to have inflicted a fatal blow to the self-regulating ideology of the legal profession.[77] The new challenge to professionalism is driven primarily by fiscal policy; in particular the desire to obtain cost savings. The adoption of a neo-liberal philosophy centring upon ideas of consumer choice has been another influential factor in challenging the self-regulatory status quo. Finally, there has been the desire upon the part of the government to protect the public from the worst excesses of professional monopolistic excesses. From this perspective, the legal profession in Ireland is undergoing a reformation which has some parallels with the reform of the English legal profession which took place during the Thatcherite era. Prime Minister Thatcher considered the Law Society and the Bar Council to be "little more than powerful lobby groups".[78]

Abel has described Thatcher as "a true believer in the market", which she endowed with "moral force".[79] In his view, Thatcher "identified free societies with free markets".[80] Neoliberalism assumes that free market economics may be applied to markets for professional services, including legal services, in just the same way as it may be applied to the market for other goods and services. The lack of corporate alternatives in Ireland to the traditional partnership model accords with the mutual monitoring of colleagues which is synonymous with self-regulation. Where a partner risks losing personal assets in the event of his/her partner's professional failure, there is a strong incentive to implement mutual monitoring systems. However, the potential for such mutual monitoring

---

[76] R Abel, *English Lawyers between Market and State: The Politics of Professionalism* (Oxford University Press, 2003) 488 – 490

[77] See ch 2 § 2.3 for a full discussion of the impact of the Troika upon the regulation of the legal profession. See also Appendix 1 for background.

[78] M Davies, 'The Demise of professional self-regulation?' (FN 65) 6

[79] R Abel, *English Lawyers* (FN 76) 26

[80] Ibid 27

is largely absent in the case of sole practitioners who form a large proportion of Irish legal service providers. Nor is there an opportunity to exercise self-regulation via whistle-blowing in the context of the sole practitioner. The Irish legal profession has faced unprecedented difficulties in recent times, as evidenced by the turmoil in the PII market. The widespread level of professional failure which gave rise to the increased level of PII claims suggests that the current self-regulatory system is not fit for purpose, and presents a powerful threat to the profession's traditional autonomy.

Dingwall and Fenn have located self-regulation within the social institution of trust, whereby the social contract between the legal profession and wider society alleviates the problem of moral hazard caused by information asymmetry.[81] Dingwall and Fenn have maintained that both economic and public interest based analyses of the professions fail to recognise the place of 'professionalization' in maintaining trust and confidence in the workings of the market in a modern complex society. Professionalization may be defined as 'the process by which producers of special services [seek] to constitute *and control* a market for their expertise ... professionalization also appears as a collective process of upward social mobility'.[82]

Whilst Dingwall and Fenn's model of a self-regulated group of professionals is somewhat benign, they do caution that where the professional group breaches the trust of wider society and abuses its position, its privileges should be withdrawn. The question arises whether a systemic failure of the Irish legal profession has occurred in recent times, and if so whether as Dingwall and Fenn have asserted, privileges should be withdrawn as a consequence. Authority for the view that such a failure occurred may be found in the view of the Master of the High Court:

> The Master of the High Court Edmund Honohan yesterday ramped up his criticism of solicitors telling lies in court. Mr Honohan has said that "economy with the truth" by solicitors under oath could stop people getting justice in courts ... especially those in debt who represent themselves against banks and other creditors because they can't afford legal representation.... "My comments about solicitors telling the truth was part of an overall analysis of whether the court should accept the evidence of a solicitor as reliable. My view is that the oath has become debased to such an extent that it shouldn't."[83]

Further evidence of a systemic failure within the profession is also found in the recent insolvency of the SMDF after it experienced loss ratios of up to

---

[81] R Dingwall & P Fenn, 'A Respectable Profession? Sociological and Economic Perspectives on the Regulation of Professional Services' (1987) 7 *International Review of Law and Economics* 51-64, in M Davies, 'The Demise of professional self-regulation?' (FN 65) 5.

[82] M Larson, *The Rise of Professionalism: A Sociological Analysis* (University of California Press, 1977) xvi-xvii, in R Dingwall & P Fenn, 'A Respectable Profession?' Ibid 53

[83] J Riely, 'Unrepentant Honohan Ups Criticism of Solicitors', *Independent.ie,* 27th November 2011. Available at: <http://www.independent.ie/national-news/unrepentant-honohan-ups-criticism-of-solicitors-2946944.html> Accessed 1/10/2012

1,100% in 2008/2009.[84] In the face of such evidence, the continuing self-regulation of the profession appears to be fundamentally uninsurable. Ogus has observed that the ability of self-regulating agencies to formulate rules, to interpret those rules and to adjudicate in relation to their enforcement represents a fundamental breach of the separation of powers.[85] Both the LSI and the BCI formulate and interpret rules, and also adjudicate regarding their enforcement, and aptly illustrate Ogus' proposition concerning a breach of the separation of powers. In Shinnick's view:

> The dual role of the Law Society of representing their members and in policing these same members should be abolished due to an inherent conflict of interest, which is not in the public interest. One solution to this is to allow the Law Society to represent their members and introduce a fully independent body (or regulator) responsible for admission, policing solicitors and investigating complaints.[86]

Shinnick's comments might equally have been made with respect to the Barristers' profession, where the BCI and the HSKI together perform both representative and regulatory functions. Shinnick has outlined the merits of a regulatory reform agenda for the Irish legal profession which would improve both economic performance in Ireland and also consumer welfare; increasing the quality of governance and also improving levels of efficiency and effectiveness in the public sector.[87] However, he also argues that any reform agenda should be the subject of public debate and that specific proposals for reform should be subjected to a regulatory impact analysis consisting of both a cost/benefit analysis and a cost-effectiveness analysis. Yet within the current Irish climate, it appears that time is of the essence as far as the implementation of the Troika's reform agenda is concerned, as evidenced by the Irish Government's commitment to have implemented reforms in the legal services sector by the third quarter of 2011.[88] At the time of writing, the results of a regulatory impact analysis on the proposed reforms contained in the LSRB 2011 have not yet been published. The following section will consider the questions of whether individual lawyers or legal firms should be regulated and also, which activities of lawyers should be regulated?

3.3 What entities and activities should be regulated?

A fundamental issue for regulators is deciding what exactly should be regulated. The traditional approach has been to regulate individual practitioners as opposed to regulating legal work, with the LSI regulating solicitors and the BCI,

---

[84] A Neary & F O'Toole, *The Blueprint Report* (FN 4) 131

[85] A Ogus, 'Rethinking Regulation' (1995) 15 (1) *Oxford Journal of Legal Studies* 97, 99

[86] E Shinnick, 'Aspects of Regulatory Reform in the Irish Solicitor Profession: Review and Evaluation' (2003) 2 *Quarterly Economic Commentary*: Special Article; Economic and Social Research Institute 12

[87] Ibid 11

[88] Memorandum of Understanding on Specific Economic Policy Conditionality 27. Available at: <http://www.imf.org/external/np/loi/2010/irl/120310.pdf> Accessed 20/9/2012

BPCT and BPCAB and HSKI regulating barristers. Whilst this approach has the virtue of simplicity, it leaves open the possibility that sub-optimal practice may go undetected. There are also the questions of whether and how lay litigants should be regulated, as they are increasingly responsible for providing legal services albeit to themselves, and as such, they present particular challenges to the legal system, and especially for the proper administration of justice.[89] This section will also consider both the regulation of legal services by lay litigants, and the provision of legal services by unqualified persons.

3.3.1 Regulation of legal firms

Neary has argued that the failure of the Irish legal regulatory system to focus on firms as opposed to individuals has led to a situation where practice and risk management issues have been routinely excluded from the regulatory process.[90] For instance, the SDT can only impose sanctions on individual solicitors rather than on firms. Similarly, the LSI's Guide to Professional Conduct focuses exclusively upon the behaviour of the individual solicitor rather than addressing the regulation of the law firm itself, which is the single economic unit, in terms of the provision of legal services. The regulatory focus upon individual practitioners has given rise to a number of assumptions which have contributed to substandard practice:

  • that the law firm entity operates outside the scope of regulation

  • that law firm management disciplines are subsidiary to and of lesser importance than the rules of professional conduct

  • that managing a practice is a matter for solicitors to carry out as they see fit

  • there is no need for practice management or quality standards because the perception is that one solicitor's practice management techniques are as good as the next solicitor's

  • that solicitors acquire the knowledge and expertise to manage law firms from their own experiences rather than from the training they receive and therefore the skills needed to run an efficient law firm can be picked up without formal training.[91]

Neary has argued that the introduction of a Practice Management Framework is 'the missing link' in the present system of regulation of the legal profession in Ireland.[92] In order to effectively manage and supervise a firm's provision of services, such a framework would encompass all its 'procedures, processes, policies and methods'.[93] This would facilitate the attainment of business efficiency, risk management and the effective supervision of personnel and practice.

---

[89] The terms self-litigant and litigant in person are also used to refer to lay litigants.

[90] A Neary and F O'Toole, *The Blueprint Report* (FN 4) 140

[91] Ibid 140

[92] Ibid 142

[93] Ibid 141

Neary has further argued that firms should be obliged to produce evidence of compliance with their management responsibilities. The regulatory approach which has been adopted in NSW, and which requires firms to introduce 'appropriate management systems' is instructive in this regard.[94] There is evidence that the NSW approach resulted in a considerable reduction in complaints against incorporated legal practices. Such firms were obliged to carry out a self-assessment procedure to judge their own compliance with ten objectives of an appropriate management system, which covered aspects including competent work practices, effective and timely communications, prompt delivery and review of legal services and prompt resolution of document and file transfers. The implementation of the self-assessment system led to a two-thirds reduction in the level of complaints against incorporated legal practices.[95]

3.3.2 Lay litigants

Historically in Ireland there has been considerable overlap between the activities of lawyers on the one hand and the provision of legal services on the other. However, recently, there has been a shift in the pattern of legal services provision. As Terry has stated, '[t]he legal profession is no longer the only game in town'.[96] This is evidenced by a growing number of lay litigants, a trend driven primarily by the increasingly prohibitive cost of legal services, and also arguably by a growing disillusionment with legal services providers. The regulation of lay litigants is a matter for individual judges, who vary considerably in their approach to the task, and also with regard to the degree of latitude they are willing to extend to such individuals.

In 2010 the President of the High Court, Nicholas Kearns, issued a Practice Directive concerning lay litigants, a measure which reflects the increasing role they play, and also the challenge which they present to traditional court practice.[97] The purpose of the Directive is to assist lay litigants in understanding the nature and purpose of applications made in the course of proceedings, and to facilitate them in preparing adequately for such proceedings. The Directive also provides for notice to be given to a lay litigant in relation to applications which would not normally require such notice to be given in the event that the matter was being dealt with by a qualified legal professional. In this way, the Directive is designed to facilitate the proper and efficient administration of justice.

The Master of the High Court Edmund Honohan recently addressed the issue of the increasing numbers of lay litigants appearing in Irish Courts, having previously engaged in a public exchange of correspondence with Ken Murphy, the Director General of the LSI.[98] Mr Murphy took issue with Mr Honohan's

---

[94] The New South Wales Legal Profession Act 2004, §§ 140 and 168

[95] C Parker et al, 'Regulating Law Firm Ethics Management, An Empirical Assessment of an Innovation in the Regulation of the Legal Profession in New South Wales' (2010) 37 (3) *Journal of Law and Society* 466, 485

[96] L Terry, 'Trends and Challenges in Lawyer Regulation' (FN 1) 2677

[97] High Court Practice Directive 54, 'Proceedings involving a litigant in person', 26th July 2010

[98] J Kelly, 'Unrepentant Honohan Ups Criticism of Solicitors', *Independent.ie*, 27th November 2011. Available at: <http://www.independent.ie/national-news/unrepentant-honohan-ups-criticisms-of-solicitors-2946944.html> Accessed: 30/9/2012

observation that of all people who swore affidavits, solicitors were the group most frequently found to have only 'a nodding acquaintance with the truth'.[99] Mr Honohan noted that 'economy with the truth' by solicitors under oath could stop people getting justice in the court – especially those who represent themselves against banks and other creditors, because they can't afford legal representation'. Mr Honohan further commented:

> You can understand that anywhere there is a fast track approach ... it is difficult for a lay person to understand where, or what he should say or do.... Now the number of lay litigants without representation has skyrocketed because they can't afford lawyers. The question is do they get a fair hearing?[100]

A similar trend of increasing numbers of lay litigants is apparent in cases coming before the Commercial Court. Justice Peter Kelly recently noted that whilst the phenomenon of lay litigants was unheard of in the Commercial Court up until last year, they are now becoming a regular feature in the court's proceedings.[101] Justice Kelly attributed this to the 'massive destruction of wealth', which resulted in the fact that '[v]ery decent people's lives are ruined'.[102] The ranks of lay litigants have recently been swelled by the Quinn family, which is engaged in complex litigation with the Irish Banking Resolution Corporation (IBRC):

> The Quinn family said yesterday that they had been forced to drop their legal team for financial reasons – because of recent court orders obtained by the IBRC, which saw their bank accounts frozen and receivers appointed over their worldwide assets. They will now represent themselves as lay litigants in their actions, which could result in Sean Quinn senior being sent to jail.[103]

Bell has stated that lay litigants represent a significant part of today's judicial landscape.[104] However, their appearance presents a challenge to the adversarial system, which relies upon the participation of professionals to identify relevant issues, to effectively present facts and to both understand and argue the law.[105] Judges dealing with lay litigants often face considerable dilemmas in how and when to intervene, in order to further the proper administration of justice without compromise to their neutrality. Judges are therefore at the front line in

---

[99] Ibid

[100] Ibid

[101] C Coulter, 'Court sees human misery after Celtic Tiger demise', irishtimes.com, 9th Apr 2012. Available at: <http://www.irishtimes.com/newspaper/ireland/2012/0409/ 1224314548021_pf.html> Accessed 30/9/2012

[102] Ibid

[103] D McDonald, 'Bank denies Quinn family phones', *Independent.ie,* 1st Sept 2012. Available at: <http://www.inependent.ie/national-news/bank-denies-tapping-quinn-family-phones-3216527.html > Accessed 8/10/2012

[104] E Bell, 'Judges, Fairness and Litigants in Person' [2010] *Judicial Studies Institute Journal* 1 – 45, 42

[105] Ibid 43

the regulation of lay litigants, and they have little in the way of formal guidance to assist them in negotiating this difficult terrain. Ultimately, reasonable minds may differ as to the assistance which a lay litigant should be given. The proper scope of the court's responsibility to a lay litigant is necessarily an expression of judicial discretion, and cannot be fully described by a specific formula.[106]

3.3.3 Unqualified Persons

The provision of legal services by either non-qualified practitioners, or by those whose names do not appear either on the roll of solicitors, or who have not been called to the bar, may result in the imposition of stiff penalties. The legal profession is assisted in preserving its monopoly for the provision of legal services by the Solicitors Acts 1954 to 2011. It is an offence for an unqualified person to provide legal services, such as the drawing up of documents.[107] Where an unqualified person acts as a solicitor, he may face a penalty upon conviction of up to two years' imprisonment, a fine of up to £10,000 or both. If the offence occurs 'in relation to a court of justice', it will constitute contempt of court, and may be dealt with accordingly by the trial judge.[108] No offence will be deemed to have occurred where the drawing up of the document was not done for gain.[109] The judiciary has an inherent jurisdiction in the courts to ensure that only those whose names appear on the roll of solicitors or who have been called to the bar will be granted a right of audience. In *Re Burke* the Supreme Court rejected the applicant's appeal against the decision of the President of the High Court to reject his application to have his name reinstated to the roll of solicitors, noting that he had been guilty of repeated acts of dishonesty, and also that 'even after his ultimate removal from the roll, he held himself out as being a solicitor'.[110]

3.3.4 The Regulation of Providers of Information about the Quality of Legal Services – Rate-Your-Solicitor.com

Until January 2012, consumers of legal services were able to access a website entitled Rate-Your-Solicitor.com, which was established by an organisation called Victims of the Legal Profession Society (VLPS). The site contained feedback from clients about the quality of the legal services which they received from legal professionals in Ireland, both solicitors and barristers. However, following litigation by Mr Damien Tansey against the website, Mr Justice Michael Peart ordered that the site be closed down, on the grounds that it contained defamatory material.[111] An order was granted prohibiting the publication or further publication of the defamatory material complained of, and an injunction was granted requiring the removal from the internet of the defamatory material concerning Mr Tansey, and which restrained the defendants from publishing

---

[106] Ibid 44-45

[107] The Solicitors Act 1954 § 58

[108] The Solicitors Act 1954 § 55 (3)

[109] The Solicitors Act 1954 § 58 (3)

[110] *In the matter of Frank Burke and Lorna Burke carrying on Practice as Frank Burke & Company & in the matter of the Solicitors Acts 1954 – 1994* [2001] IESC 13 (9th February 2001) SC, Keane CJ

[111] *Tansey v Gill and Others* [2012] IEHC 42

any further defamatory material concerning him. A mandatory interlocutory injunction terminating the operation of the website was granted, and a further mandatory injunction directed the defendants to deliver up to the plaintiff the names and addresses of all persons involved in the publication of the defamatory material concerning him.

Whilst it is undoubtedly the case that such websites have the potential to display information which is untrue regarding legal practitioners, they also arguably provide a unique and valuable source of information for consumers regarding the quality of legal services they may expect to receive from individual service providers; information which is not available from any other source. The complete shut down of the site was, in the circumstances, an over-reaction. Flood has considered the question of whether a similar website which deals with English lawyers entitled 'Solicitors from Hell' is defamatory:

> Whatever one thinks of [the] website, it serves a need. It demonstrates clearly that people need an outlet to express their feelings and concerns about how they are treated. Instead of attacking Solicitors from Hell the Law Society should be doing something about those complaints. It should be preventing a need for a website like Solicitors from Hell.[112]

3.4 When should regulation of the legal profession occur?

The current system of regulation of the legal profession in Ireland reflects a largely *ex post* approach, whereby intervention follows the occurrence of a regulatory breach. Whilst there are some elements of the system which reflect an *ex ante* approach; for instance, the requirement to comply with a level of continuing professional development, and also the random audits of accounts which firms periodically undergo, *ex ante* intervention is presently an exception to the general rule.[113] This *ex post* emphasis is similar to the approach towards the timing of regulatory intervention in many other jurisdictions.[114] However, the success of the NSW innovation in introducing appropriate management systems for incorporated law practices has resulted in a growing interest in *ex ante* regulatory intervention.

Ex ante models of regulation have the advantage of preventing regulatory breaches from occurring in the first instance, thereby reducing the level of damage and distress suffered by clients as a consequence of such breaches. The findings of the investigation of professional misconduct which are presented below, suggest that past patterns of practitioner misconduct may provide a useful tool for predicting the occurrence of future misconduct. The results of the investigation raise the possibility of *ex ante* regulatory intervention being target-

---

[112] John Flood's blog, available at: <http://www.johnflood.blogspot.ie/2011/07/is-solicitors-from-hell-criminal.html> Accessed 30/9/2012

[113] In accordance with section 66 (10) Solicitors Act 1954, as inserted by section 76 Solicitors (Amendment) Act 1994, an authorized person from the LSI may attend a solicitor's practice to police the proper operation of the Solicitors Accounts Regulations by that solicitor.

[114] For instance, in the US, the ABA Model Rules for Lawyer Disciplinary Enforcement R (1) (2002) state that it will be grounds for discipline for a lawyer to breach or attempt to breach State Rules of Professional Conduct.

ed at the cohort of practitioners who pose the highest risk of future misconduct. The adoption of such an *ex ante* approach to regulation is arguably in the public interest, and also in that of the profession, given that it raises the prospect of enhancing consumer protection by preventing the occurrence of regulatory breaches, thereby maintaining higher standards of professional practice with consequential benefit to the standing of the legal profession.

3.5 Where should regulation of the legal profession occur?

Given the ever-increasing cross-border character of legal services, and the effect of the process of globalization on the legal profession, lawyer regulators more frequently face dilemmas regarding where legal service provision has taken place, and which particular activities fall within their jurisdiction. Terry has observed that as a result of these challenges, the legal profession is experiencing a 'Copernican Revolution'.[115] The regulators of the Irish legal profession are largely confined, both in their activities and authority, to the geographic location comprised of the national territory of Ireland. However, practitioners increasingly take advantage of virtual technology in the course of their practice. For instance; a lawyer may communicate with a client via email or mobile phone from outside Ireland, and the client may be unaware that the lawyer is not still in Ireland. As a consequence of the mismatch between the geographically bound regulatory framework on the one hand, and the virtual practice world on the other, there is scope for a considerable degree of uncertainty regarding the application and efficiency of the traditional regulatory structure. Terry has argued that the development of cross-border practice has considerably outpaced the development of theories regarding how such practice should be regulated.[116]

Issues may arise concerning the use of cloud technology in the event that a legal firm's data is stored outside Ireland. Caution is required when using this emergent form of technology to ensure that data is both securely stored and retrievable. A further challenge to the traditional regulatory system is presented by the emergence of on-line legal services which enable clients to take a DIY approach to resolving their legal issues at a much reduced price than that attached to the provision of services by legal professionals. Neary has identified several such internet sites, including that which has been provided by Linklaters for its clients, entitled 'Blue Flag Service'. There is also 'Complete Case' which provides a low cost divorce facility in the US and 'Google Scholar' which gives the general public access to a wide range of legal resources.[117] Neary has outlined several options for law firms of the future which will present particular challenges for the traditional geographically based regulatory system. She suggests that future firms may choose to:

---

[115] L Terry, 'Trends and Challenges in Lawyer Regulation' (FN 1) 2680

[116] L Terry, 'A Case Study of the Hybrid Model for Facilitating Cross Border Legal Practice: The Agreement between the American Bar Association and the Brussels Bars' [1998] 21 (4) *Fordham Law Review* 1382, 1384

[117] These websites may be accessed at: <http://www.blueflag.com>, <http://completecase.com> and <http://googlescholar.com>. Accessed 23/9/2012. See A Neary and F O'Toole, *The Blueprint Report* (FN 4) 167 –168

• Establish a virtual presence in addition to their physical office

• Dispense with a physical office, where networks of fee earners operate from home. The firm may retain a meeting space to meet with clients, but there is no centralised physical office

• Run their entire business as a virtual office

• Provide a legal product such as template legal documents and dispense with legal advises or contact with consumers.[118]

Irish regulators can prepare themselves for meeting challenges posed by virtual legal offices by keeping informed of developments in other jurisdictions regarding such trends, given that the trend for legal services provision via the internet is growing rapidly. This phenomenon is in accordance with the vision of the legal futurist Richard Susskind, who has predicted a radical shift in the nature of legal practice as a result of internet based technological advances.[119] Susskind has predicted that lawyers of the future will change the nature of their service provision to meet a growing demand from clients for advice about how to avoid future legal problems rather than for advice in relation to problems which have already arisen. According to Susskind at present, 'hardly a lawyer or law firm on the planet has chosen to develop methods, tools, techniques or systems to help their clients review, identify, quantify and control the legal risks they face'. Susskind has asserted that this lacuna will be filled in the future.[120] The following section will consider the question of how the legal profession should be regulated.

3.6 How should regulation of the legal profession occur?

There are two issues which must be considered by regulators when considering how they should regulate the legal profession. Firstly they must decide whether the same regulatory regime should apply to all service users regardless of their level of sophistication. Secondly, regulators must identify whether a system based either upon rules, or upon standards or principles is most appropriate for the regulation of the legal profession, or alternatively whether a hybrid system is most appropriate to fulfil the regulatory function.[121]

3.6.1 Should regulation of the legal profession be client specific?

The wisdom of Ireland's current unified approach to the regulation of legal services providers, regardless of their clients' level of sophistication, may be challenged from an economic perspective, given that the factors giving rise to

---

[118] Ibid 200

[119] M Neil, 'Prophet Richard Susskind Predicts the Future of Law; Internet is Key' 17th Feb 2009. Available at: <http://www.abajournal.com/news/article/prophet_richard_susskind_predicts _the_future_of_law/> Accessed 23/9/2012

[120] D Cassens Weiss, 'Futurist Says Lawyers Will Become Legal Risk Consultants', 14th Nov 2008. Available at: <http://www.abajournal.com/news/article/futurist_says_lawyers_will _become_legal_risk_consultants/> Accessed 23/9/2012

[121] Terry has identified these issues as pertinent to the question of how the legal profession should be regulated. L Terry, 'Trends and Challenges in Lawyer Regulation' (FN 1) 2681, 2263

information asymmetries and hence market failure, are largely confined to private clients who are once-off or occasional service users. Hadfield has been highly critical of the failure of the American legal profession to respond to the needs of corporate clients for the provision of legal services from non-lawyers in the form of MDPs.[122] She has also criticised the failure of regulators to respond to the demand from the corporate sector for the provision of commercial legal services from non-lawyers. Her criticisms might equally be applied to today's Irish legal services market, which also prohibits MDPs and other innovative forms of service providers. Hadfield has argued that '[t]ruly innovative lawyering for the new [global] economy ... needs a far less restrictive and myopic regulatory model'.[123] She has identified the regulatory dominance of the ABA as a key cause in the development of the inefficient American legal services market, and parallels can readily be drawn in that regard with the self-regulatory powers which are enjoyed in Ireland by the LSI, the BCI and the HSKI. These organisations have used their regulatory dominance to perpetuate the unified regulatory approach to the provision of services to both private and corporate clients. This 'one size fits all' regulatory policy gives rise to inefficiency in service provision, as a consequence of the failure to respond to the specific needs of the client.

Support for such a targeted approach to regulatory protection which is dependent upon a client's degree of sophistication is to be found in the European Commission's Communication to other European Institutions entitled 'Professional Services: The Scope for More Reform'.[124] The Commission was of the view that individual consumers of legal services required more carefully targeted regulatory protection when using legal services than businesses and the public sector, which required a much more limited, if any, degree of regulatory protection. This is due to the fact that businesses and the public sector are capable of making a more informed choice about the nature of the legal service they require. The Commission stated that this dichotomy of regulatory needs should be a key consideration when reviewing existing forms of regulation.

3.6.2 Should regulation of the legal profession be rules-based, principles-based or should a hybrid system of rules and principles be deployed?

Another aspect of the question of how the legal profession in Ireland should be regulated concerns the issue of whether a regulatory system should focus upon either rules or upon principles or standards. The Irish system of regulation of the legal profession primarily adopts a rules-based approach, although it does display some aspects of a principles based approach, as evidenced by the contents of the BCI's Code of Conduct, the LSI's Guide to Professional Conduct and also by international regulatory codes which apply to Irish lawyers, such as the IBA's General Principles for the Legal Profession.[125] The remainder of the regula-

---

[122] G Hadfield, 'Legal Barriers to Innovation: The Growing Economic Cost of Professional Control over Corporate Legal Markets' [2008] *Stanford Law Review* (6) 1689, 1728

[123] Ibid 1732

[124] EU Commission. Communication from the Commission to the Council, the European Parliament, the European Economic and Social Committee and the Committee of the Regions 'Professional Services – Scope for More Reform' (5th Nov 2005) COM (2005) 405 para 30

[125] Descriptions of the LSI's Guide to Professional Conduct and the BCI's Code of Conduct may

tory framework as contained in both statutes and subordinate regulations adopts a rules-based approach.

Arjoon has identified the relative advantages and disadvantages of rules and principles-based approaches to regulation.[126] Rules-based systems require compliance with specific procedural requirements, demand compliance in all circumstances and are associated with bureaucratic types of organisations. They tend to represent minimal ethical standards, and emphasize the use of an analytical approach towards compliance. They also tend to follow the letter of the law, to promote blind obedience, to be fear driven and they tend to require constant monitoring.

By contrast, principles-based approaches to regulation emphasize 'doing the right thing' by appropriate methods and they tend to guide appropriate behaviour by accentuating objectives rather than processes. Principles-based approaches are likely to be used in organisations with robustly functioning social controls, and they emphasize communication and abiding by the spirit, as opposed to the letter of the law. They focus on prevention rather than detection, tend to be values-driven and are able to deal with issues in grey areas, rather than addressing only black and white cases.

The shortcomings of rules-based regulatory approaches have been well documented. As Schauer has noted, '[r]ules doom decision making to mediocrity by mandating the inaccessibility of excellence'.[127] According to Black the failure of rules to control discretion is well recognized and, 'the limitations of rules as a regulatory technique have been pointed out in the literature on enforcement and compliance'. [128]

Yet Daly has illustrated how there are also limitations in principles or standards-based systems of regulation.[129] She has documented how during the twentieth century the ABA moved from a standards-based model, The Canons of Legal Conduct, which was adopted in 1908 to a rules based system, The Model Rules of Professional Conduct, adopted in 1983. Daly has argued that The Canons of Legal Conduct were more suitable for the regulation of a small fraternity of legal professionals, rather than the heterogeneous body of practitioners which is found in today's legal community. In Daly's view; '[t]he legal profession's embrace of rules and jettison of standards was partly a response to the need of large law firms for a clearer, more direct set of professional norms that reduced the permissible range of a lawyer's ethical discretion'.[130] The US transition from a standards-based to a rules-based approach was prompted by the findings of the

---

be found in ch 1, §§ 1.3.4.1 – 1.3.4.2. There is a description of the IBA's General Principles for the Legal Profession in ch 2 § 2.8

[126] S Arjoon, 'Striking a Balance Between Rules and Principles-based Approaches for Effective Governance: A Risks-based Approach' (2006) 68 (1) *Journal of Business Ethics* 53, 58

[127] F Schauer, 'Formalism' (1988) 97 *Yale Law Journal* 509, 539, in J Black, *Rules and Regulators* (Clarendon Press, 1997) 5

[128] J Black, *Rules and Regulators* Ibid 5

[129] C Daly, 'The Dichotomy Between Standards and Rules: A New Way of Understanding the Differences in Perceptions of Lawyer Codes of Conduct by US and Foreign Lawyers' (1999) 32 *Vanderbilt Journal of Transnational Law* 1117

[130] Ibid 1132

ABA Clark Commission Study which was published in 1970, and which described the state of lawyer discipline at the time as 'a scandalous situation'.[131]

Daly has asserted that the prominent place which professional responsibility occupies is due to the current rules-based focus within the US legal tradition, and this is not replicated in other parts of the world.[132] She has pointed to a lack of emphasis at undergraduate level upon professional responsibility and legal ethics as a reason for these differing approaches towards the rules-standards dichotomy. However, the Irish regulatory environment provides little support for Daly's thesis in this regard, given that although it primarily adopts a rules-based approach, there is little, if any, emphasis on teaching the rules of professional ethics at undergraduate level. Also, Rose has argued that the choice between standards or rules-based regulatory frameworks depends upon whether the regulated community consists of either acquaintances or strangers; standards may suffice to regulate the former, whereas rules are necessary to regulate the latter.[133] From this perspective, whilst European jurisdictions remained relatively unexplored by foreign lawyers, standards based regulatory models were fit for purpose, but as greater numbers of foreign lawyers begin to penetrate the EU legal services market with more frequency, the need for a more rules-based system has emerged.[134]

The challenge for regulators is to identify the correct balance between rules and standards which should be incorporated into a regulatory framework, and the optimum balance will depend upon both the size and the level of diversity within the regulated community. Regulators of the legal profession in Ireland, when contemplating this issue, might usefully consider the evidence which has emerged concerning the impact of regulatory interventions within a more general organizational context in recent years. Arjoon has argued that an excessive reliance upon compliance with rules can impede good corporate governance by creating a culture of legal absolutism.[135] According to Arjoon, ethical 'organizational DNA' (ODNA) is a critical force that drives compliance with legal and regulatory requirements. The concept of ODNA refers to those core characteristics of an organisation which shape its structure and functioning.

Arjoon has proposed that a risk-based analysis is the best means of identifying the optimal balance between rules and principles in a given regulatory framework. He cites the implementation of the Sarbanes-Oxley Act 2002 in response to corporate scandals such as those which occurred at WorldCom and Enron, as an example of a rules-based intervention which, in an effort to completely eradicate business risk, introduced excessive new business costs and reduced competitiveness. The Sarbanes-Oxley Act also ironically 'provided a

---

[131] Ibid 1135. Citing 'The ABA Special Commission on Evaluation of Disciplinary Enforcement, Problems and Recommendations' (ABA, 1970) 5 – 6

[132] Ibid 1145

[133] Ibid 1153. Citing C Rose, 'Crystals and Mud in Property Law' (1988) 40 *Stanford Law Review* 577 – 610, 601 – 605

[134] For example, the rules-based CCBE Code of Conduct adopted in 1998, which is described in ch 2, § 2.7

[135] S Arjoon, 'Striking a Balance' (FN 126) 53

bonanza for accountants and auditors – the very professions thought to be at fault in the original scandal'.[136] These observations serve to support the notion that a balance between rules and principles in regulatory frameworks may avoid some of the problems associated with the over-reliance upon rules alone to regulate complex activities and organisations.

3.7 Application of the OECD General Principles for Regulatory Quality and Performance to the Regulation of the Legal Profession in Ireland

The OECD General Principles for Regulatory Quality and Performance provide a useful analytical instrument with which to assess the quality of the present system for the regulation of the legal profession in Ireland. Given that the Principal Act saw the fulfilment of the efforts of the solicitors' profession to secure self-regulation, the current system has been effective in achieving that particular goal, and as such, it fulfils the requirement of the first OECD principle, which is the identification and attainment of clear policy goals.[137] The BCI and HSKI have been equally as effective as the LSI in achieving the policy goal of self-regulation.

However, the policy goal of self-regulation has no sound legal or empirical basis as required by the second OECD principle. This view is supported by the economic analysis of self-regulation, which reveals the various forms of market failure associated with self-regulation, including rent-seeking behaviour, barriers to entry, undersupply of services, artificially high price maintenance and cartel-like behaviour. The present regulatory system's costs in terms of economic and social effects would appear to considerably outweigh its benefits, as illustrated by the above economic analysis.[138] Problems of excessive costs and poor service provision have reached a critical level in the legal profession, as evidenced by rocketing insurance costs and rapidly growing numbers of lay litigants. It is clear that the third OECD principle which requires that the regulatory system should produce benefits and justify costs from an economic and social perspective is not met by the present system. Also, the present system appears to maximise costs and market distortions in direct contradiction to the fourth OECED principle, which requires these to be at the minimum level possible. The present regulatory framework for the solicitors' profession which was established almost sixty years ago fails to promote innovation through market incentives, and the regulatory framework for the barristers' profession being entirely steeped in history and tradition, also signally fails in this regard. Law by its very nature is shaped by precedent and does not lend itself to innovation, as required

---

[136] Ibid 79. Arjoon also cited Blitz's example of business inspection regimes which are focused upon those firms which are deemed most likely to breach the law. J Blitz, 'Attack by Blair on US-Style Red Tape', *Financial Times,* 27th May 2005, 1 – 3

[137] The General Principles for Regulatory Quality and Performance are listed at ch 3 § 3.0.

[138] See ch 3 § 3.1 for the economic argument for the regulation of the legal profession, and ch 3 § 3.2.5 for an economic analysis of self-regulation.

by the fifth OECD principle. The HSKI motto *nolumus mutari* aptly reflects the mindset of the barristers' profession with regard to modernisation and change.[139]

The present regulatory framework is also extremely complex, as evidenced by the labyrinthine set of rules and regulations described in Chapters 1 and 2, and it does not meet with the requirements of the sixth OECD principle that it should be clear and simple. Whilst there is some degree of consistency within the regulatory framework, there is also the potential for double deontology as far as the international regulations are concerned, and in this regard the current framework lacks consistency with other regulations, as demanded by the seventh OECD principle.

The final OECD requirement for a regulatory system to be compatible with competitive trade and investment-facilitating principles is not met by the current framework, as was illustrated by the economic analysis of the present system, and widespread reform is necessary in order to establish a competitive market for legal services in Ireland. The following section presents a case study which investigates professional misconduct amongst Irish solicitors.

3.8 A Case Study: An Investigation of Professional Misconduct amongst Irish Solicitors

In order to better understand the shortcomings of the present Irish system for regulating the legal profession, this section focuses upon the problem of lawyers' misconduct and the challenge which it presents for regulators. This issue was explored by means of a small quantitative study of professional misconduct amongst Irish solicitors which sought to identify its most common facets. The research was limited to the solicitors' branch of the legal profession because there is an absence of publicly available information regarding the outcome of barristers' disciplinary hearings conducted by either the BCI, BPCT, BPCAB or the HSKI.[140] As has been noted above, professional misconduct amongst lawyers presents similar problems for regulators globally, with a financial aspect to the misconduct being a predominant theme.[141] An examination of one hundred professional misconduct cases which were heard by the Solicitors' Disciplinary Tribunal (SDT) and reported in the *Law Society Gazette* (LSG) between January 2008 and May 2010 revealed that many of these cases concerned not only financial wrongdoing of some sort, but they also related to a

---

[139] 'We will not change' or 'We will not be changed'.

[140] The BCI provides limited composite information regarding the number and general nature of complaints which are upheld by the Barristers Professional Conduct Tribunal (BPCT) in the BPCT Annual Report. More serious cases of misconduct are referred by the BPCT or BPCAB to the Benchers' Disciplinary Committee at HSKI. In accordance with Rule 37 (3) of the General Rules of the Society (HSKI), all adverse findings where a barrister is either disbarred or suspended shall be published either on a website maintained by the Society (www.kingsinns.ie) or in another suitable publication. However, such published findings are very uncommon, with details of just one such case being made public in the last fifteen months. See HSKI Decision of Benchers to Disbar Mr Patrick Russell, 11th Jan 2012. Available at: <http://kingsinns.ie/ website/prospective_stuents/DisciplinaryDecisions2012.htm> Accessed 15/8/2013

[141] See ch 3 § 3.8.1 for details of professional misconduct patterns in other jurisdictions.

property matter and involved either dishonesty or breach of an undertaking (BOU).[142]

The use of statistically based technology to predict the occurrence of property based crime and offences against the person has recently proved highly effective in Memphis, and it was hoped that the findings of this quantitative investigation of solicitors' professional misconduct might provide some evidence to support the view that a statistical analysis of patterns of misconduct may be used to identify that cohort of professionals which is most likely to engage in future professional misconduct.[143] Unfortunately, this study did not bear fruit in the form of a useful predictive tool in relation to future misconduct, but its findings support the view that the existing regulatory framework fails to adequately address the problem of professional misconduct and that the LSRB 2011 should be further amended to more effectively respond to this problem.

3.8.1 Lawyers' misconduct: comparing perspectives

The following section presents a brief overview of the research on the professional misconduct of lawyers in the USA, England and Wales.

(i) The United States of America

Having conducted extensive research into the issue of lawyers' misconduct in the USA, Abel has identified three major problems which commonly result in attorney discipline proceedings as being client neglect, manipulation of fees and the excessive zeal of a lawyer on a client's behalf.[144] An examination of the disciplinary cases which belong to the first two of these categories reveals that a financial element is a common factor in many instances of lawyers' offending behaviour. Shapiro has argued that in order to understand the nature of white collar crime, a researcher must firstly gain an insight into both the distribution of structural opportunities for trust abuse and also the conditions under which individual or organizational fiduciaries either seize or ignore such opportunities.[145] She identified the modus operandi of white-collar criminals as being 'the violation and manipulation of the norms of trust – disclosure, disinterestedness and role competence'.[146] The Celtic Tiger years in Ireland presented a particularly rich hunting ground in terms of structural opportunities for the abuse of trust by legal practitioners. The Irish legal profession's monopolization of the market for conveyancing services is pertinent in this regard.

Abel has argued that the boundaries of the legal monopoly should be severely reduced as one means of addressing the perennial problem of lawyers' mis-

---

[142] Rule 59 of the Solicitors Disciplinary Rules 2003 provides for the publication of The Tribunal's orders and case summaries.

[143] IBM Press Release, 'Memphis Police Department Reduces Crime Rates with IBM Predictive Analysis Software', 21st July 2010. Available at: <http://www-03.ibm.com/press/us/en/pressrelease/32169.wss> Accessed 3/4/2013

[144] R Abel, *Lawyers in the Dock* (FN 11) vii

[145] S Shapiro, 'Collaring The Crime, not the Criminal: Reconsidering the Concept of White-Collar Crime' 55 (3) *American Sociological Review* 346

[146] Ibid 350.

conduct.[147] Other measures which he has advocated include making available a second opinion to clients from an independent lawyer regarding the merits of the proposed course of action which is advocated by a client's lawyer and also as to the reasonableness of the likely costs of such a course of action.[148] He has also suggested that sole practitioners should be prohibited from practising, and that all lawyers should be obliged to practice in larger partnership structures which would facilitate and encourage the oversight by colleagues of an individual lawyer's practice, especially in circumstances where a partner bears financial responsibility for his/her partner's professional failures.[149]

Acts of dishonesty and breaches of undertakings share the common feature of being 'betrayals of trust'. Abel has located trust at the epicentre of the lawyer-client relationship and its betrayal or violation as the ultimate challenge for lawyers' disciplinary bodies.[150] It is in part as a result of the unique place of trust within lawyer and client relations that the need arises for effective regulatory structures. Rhode and Woolley have argued that:

> [R]egulation fails when it does not effectively deter or remedy breaches of lawyers' obligations to clients and to the legal system. In the market for legal service, a common imperfection involves many consumers' inability to make accurate assessments about the services they receive, either before or after purchase.[151]

Where clients lack the requisite skills to assess the quality of legal services they receive, they must rely upon the good offices of the service provider to deliver services of a reasonable quality. However, Rhode and Woolley have argued that a failure to meet this standard may not become apparent for a long time after the receipt of poor quality legal services, and even sophisticated clients such as corporate or other repeat users of legal services may not be able to correctly assess the quality of services received.[152] The lack of consumer knowledge regarding service quality and other imperfections in the legal services market give rise to the need for external oversight focused upon the requirements of 'public protection rather than [professional] public image'.[153] The inability of clients to assess the quality of legal services they receive exposes a weakness in the regulatory process in many jurisdictions. Many disciplinary systems rely primarily upon clients to bring forward complaints regarding lawyers as a first step in the investigative process. However, where clients lack

---

[147] R Abel, *Lawyers in the Dock* (FN 11) 515 – 516

[148] Ibid 514 – 515

[149] Ibid 525. The beneficial effect of the oversight of legal practitioners resulting from such a move would be severely diluted if partnerships were permitted to become incorporated, and to function as entities with limited liability. See ch 5 § 5.3.3 for details of a proposed amendment of the LSRB 2011 to this effect.

[150] R Abel, *Lawyers in the Dock* (FN 11) 1 – 59.

[151] D Rhode and A Woolley, 'Globalization and the Legal Profession: Comparative Perspectives on Lawyer Regulation: An Agenda for Reform in the United States and Canada' (2012) 80 *Fordham Law Review* 2761, 2763.

[152] Ibid 2763

[153] Ibid 2762

the skills to identify poor professional performance, this *ex post* approach to professional discipline fails from the outset. Even where clients are dissatisfied with the quality of legal services received from a lawyer, the vast majority do not proceed to make a formal complaint.[154] The almost entirely reactive nature of lawyers' disciplinary systems has been identified by Abel as a 'fatal flaw' as a result of which; 'the dark shadow of uncorrected misconduct totally overshadows the few who are caught'.[155]

Ineffective Assistance of Council

In Ireland, barristers enjoy immunity from suit on the basis that to impose a duty of care may conflict with the duty the barrister owes to the court, and also, that the imposition of such a duty would be contrary to public policy.[156] According to Holohan and Curran, there is no seminal case in Ireland on barristers' negligence.[157] However, they have expressed the view that the Bar may in future lose their immunity from suit for advocacy work, having already lost their immunity in respect of preparatory and case management activities.[158]

In considering what changes, if any, should be made to the current position in this regard, the American system which permits a claim based on the concept of ineffective assistance of counsel might be usefully considered.

This concept was first recognised in *Strickland v Washington*.[159] In *Strickland*, the Court held that the right to counsel implied "a right to adequate and effective" representation.[160] This right to the assistance of counsel is constitutional in nature.[161] *Strickland* established a two-part test for evaluating counsel's assistance. Firstly, the defendant must show that counsel's performance was deficient in accordance with an objective standard of reasonableness, and secondly, it must be established that the deficiency prejudiced the defendant's rights.[162] In formulating this test, the court referred to the ABA Standards for

---

[154] R Abel, *Lawyers in the Dock* (FN 11) 499. In England only 2% of dissatisfied clients made a complaint about their lawyer's service provision. The BPCT Annual Report 2007/2008 stated that of 58 complaint forms issued in the course 2007 only 18 resulted in a formal complaint being made.

[155] Ibid 499

[156] B Holohan & D Curran, *Lawyers' Professional Negligence and Insurance* (Thomson Reuters (Professional) Ireland Ltd, 2012) 613; *McMahon v Ireland* [1998] ILRM 610; *W v Ireland* [1997] 2 IR 141

[157] B Holohan & D Curran, *Lawyers' Professional Negligence* (FN 156) 615

[158] *Behan v McGinley* [2008] IEHC 18

[159] 466 US 668 (1984)

[160] Ibid at 686.

[161] The Sixth Amendment to the US Constitution states that:

> In all criminal proceedings, the accused shall enjoy the right to a speedy and public trial, by an impartial jury of the state and district wherein the crime shall have been committed, which district shall have been previously ascertained by law, and to be informed of the nature and cause of the accusation, to be confronted with the witnesses against him, to have compulsory process for obtaining witnesses in his favour, and to have the assistance of Counsel for his defence.

[162] J Marceau, 'Embracing a New Era of Ineffective Assistance of Counsel' [2012] 14 (5) *Journal of Constitutional Law* 1166

Criminal Justice.[163] Rigg has argued that there has been an evolution in the courts' approach to the issue of ineffective assistance of counsel since the original ruling in *Strickland v Washington* in 1984.[164] Currently, the ABA Standards for Criminal Justice are now used not simply as mere guidelines, but as an evaluative tool in judging the efficacy of counsel's assistance.[165]

Whilst in the US, the parameters of ineffective assistance of counsel claims are limited to criminal proceedings, there is no reason in theory why such a claim should not also be available in the context of civil proceedings. In the absence of robust disciplinary machinery for the Irish Bar, the possibility of such a claim for injured clients would do much to focus the attention of barristers upon the duty of care which is owed to clients and the need to provide care of the requisite standard.

(ii) England and Wales

Davies' research into the nature and frequency of dishonest behaviour amongst solicitors in England provides a useful point of comparison for this research.[166] Whilst the investigation of professional misconduct in this chapter focuses upon the findings of the Irish SDT, Davies has focused upon the findings of the English SDT and attempted to identify the nature of the link, if any, between professional misconduct and dishonesty. In Davies' opinion, the SDT findings constitute an important source of information for academic research which has previously been ignored, but which has the potential to be most informative regarding the nature of solicitor dishonesty. He looked at 270 cases which were randomly selected from all those considered by the SDT between 1994 and 1996 as the basis for his research. He found that in 37% of the cases the Tribunal either expressly or impliedly found that there had been dishonesty on the part of the Respondent solicitor.

Davies has observed an inconsistent approach on the part of the SDT in classifying misconduct as dishonest, and also with regard to the penalty that is imposed in those cases which were deemed to involve dishonesty. He has noted that the Tribunal appeared to apply the definition of dishonesty as established in *R v Ghosh*.[167] The *Ghosh* test for dishonesty is as follows:

> Dishonesty arises were what was done was dishonest according to the ordinary standards of reasonable and honest people and that the accused realised that what he or she was doing was dishonest according to those standards.[168]

In seeking to apply this test, first, the Tribunal asked whether the conduct complained of was dishonest when considered in relation to the standards of

---

[163] R Rigg, 'The T-Rex Without Teeth: Evolving *Strickland v Washington* and the Test for Ineffective Asssistance of Counsel' (2007) 35 *Pepperdine Law Review* 77

[164] Ibid 104

[165] For the ABA Standards for Criminal Justice see <www.american.bar.org/groups/criminal _justice/standards.html> Accessed 4/9/2013

[166] M Davies, 'Solicitors' Dishonesty' (FN 11) 141 – 174

[167] *R v Ghosh* [1982] QB 1053 (CA)

[168] Ibid

reasonable and honest people, and if so, it then proceeded to ask whether the Respondent solicitor realised that his conduct would be so considered by such reasonable and honest people. However, Davies has identified some inconsistency on the Tribunal's part in applying the second part of the test, and suggested that instead of asking whether the solicitor realised that reasonable and honest people would have considered the behaviour to be dishonest, he suggested that the Tribunal often appeared to ask whether other solicitors would classify the behaviour as dishonest. Davies has concluded that the Tribunal tended to adopt a subjective approach in identifying dishonesty, and that it was not willing to give precedent value to its previous decisions. Whilst this may have allowed the Tribunal a degree of flexibility in making findings it also gave rise to a level of inconsistency in its decision making.

Dishonesty refers to behaviour which is fraudulent or deceptive. In Ireland, the term is defined in statute within the Criminal Justice (Theft and Fraud Offences) Act (CJA) 2001 as meaning 'without a claim of right made in good faith'.[169] The CJA 2001 also defines deception as the creation or reinforcement of a false impression as to law, value, intention or other state of mind, the prevention of another person from acquiring information that would affect their judgement of a transaction or the failure to correct a false impression which the deceiver previously created or reinforced, or knows to be influencing another person to whom he/she stands in a fiduciary or confidential relationship.[170] In English law dishonesty is undefined by statute and acquires its meaning from the common law. It is a matter for a jury to decide whether the two-part test as set out in *Ghosh* has been met.[171]

In seeking to investigate patterns of solicitors' misconduct, this study adopted a broad categorisation of 'dishonesty and BOU'. The inclusion within one category of instances of dishonesty and breaches of undertakings encompasses some acts or omissions which meet neither the statutory definition of dishonesty contained in either the CJA 2001 or the common law definition established in *Ghosh*. This was an expedient decision given that many of the BOUs concerned might well have involved an element of dishonesty. However, the lack of detail in the Tribunal summaries prevented a more precise categorisation being made in this regard.

Although Davies found elements of dishonesty in 37% of all cases which were investigated by the Tribunal, in only 2.5% of these cases were the solicitors concerned convicted of a criminal offence in relation to the subject matter of the complaint prior to the Tribunal hearing. Davies' research revealed that the field of conveyancing appears to be the most problematic as far as dishonesty is concerned. He identified three main areas of conveyancing practice which gave rise to dishonesty; the misuse of clients' funds to support a practice in financial difficulty, the theft of clients' funds for a solicitor's own purposes and mortgage fraud. There was a considerable overlap in all three aspects of dishonest practice within the context of conveyancing work.

---

[169] CJA 2001 § 2 (1)

[170] CJA 2001 § 2 (2)

[171] *R v Feely* [1973] 1 QB 530

Another area of particular vulnerability to solicitors' dishonesty identified by Davies was that of probate and trust work. He pointed to the potential for "drip stealing" here, which refers to the systematic siphoning off of small amounts of funds from the estates of deceased persons which may never be detected. There is also the possibility of claiming unearned fees over successive years which will gradually erode estate funds. Davies noted that sole practitioners are significantly over-represented in cases involving dishonesty. Whereas they constitute less than 10% of all solicitors, 42% of cases involving dishonesty concerned sole practitioners.[172] Davies' analysis suggested that a solicitor who is most likely to be involved in dishonesty will be a sole practitioner who is aged over forty, and who has been in practice for more than ten years.[173] He also drew attention to "sham" partnerships and those where there is insufficient oversight of solicitors' work by partner colleagues. Problems also arose due to inadequate monitoring by external entities such as the firm's accountant and the Investigation Accountant of the Law Society. The reluctance of solicitors to report errant colleagues at an early stage can also ultimately result in a finding of dishonesty against a practitioner. Pressure on solicitors to meet billing targets and the desire to obtain advancement within a firm were also identified as contributory factors.

Furthermore, there may be pressure upon employees within a firm, and a failure of internal monitoring procedures, which can result in dishonest practice. Davies was concerned that the reticence of lawyers to report suspicions regarding their colleagues may mask a much greater problem of misconduct within the profession. He suggested that the shortfall in the Solicitors Indemnity Fund (SIF) in 1997 of over £450 million focused attention upon the need to insure against future professional negligence and to identify solicitors at greater risk of dishonesty. Davies noted that only 2% of Respondents before the SDT were acquitted, and stated that this is not in accordance with a thorough and impartial prosecution process. He suggested that many solicitors whose conduct merits disciplinary scrutiny due to dishonesty and other matters are not being brought before the Tribunal, which is further evidence of a failure to detect professional misconduct by the present regulatory framework.

3.8.2 A Study of Professional Misconduct amongst Solicitors in Ireland: Finance, Property and Dishonesty

In view of the unique role which lawyers play in society, the need to maintain trust in the profession given its exclusive rights and privileges and the present system of self-regulation, it is incumbent upon the profession to ensure that it employs robust methods to deal with lawyers' misconduct. In the course of this research, the cases which appeared before the SDT were regularly reviewed, and it was observed that common patterns of misbehaviour were occurring. This brief study sought to gain a greater understanding of the nature of

---

[172] M Davies, 'Solicitors' Dishonesty' (FN 11). Davies' observations with regard to sole practitioners suggest a valuable future direction for this research in endeavouring to develop a predictive model for future professional misconduct amongst solicitors.

[173] Ibid. Davies' findings regarding levels of dishonesty are in accordance with those of Skordaki and Willis who examined the nature of claims against the Law Society's Compensation Fund. E Skordaki E & C Willis, *Defaults by Solicitors,* Research Study No 4 (London, The Law Society).

solicitors' misbehaviour, and the adequacy of the profession's response to the problem.

This study of solicitors' misconduct had the following three aims:

1. To investigate whether there is a link between a finding of professional misconduct in a case before the SDT and the presence of a financial, dishonesty/BOU or property element in the case.

2. To investigate the extent to which the misconduct of solicitors who are struck off involves the three elements of finance, dishonesty/BOU and property.

3. To establish whether a solicitor's past disciplinary history may be used to predict his/her future offending behaviour. In particular to explore the whether a past history of professional misconduct involving the three elements of finance, dishonesty/BOU and property is indicative of a solicitor who is more likely than his/her colleagues to be struck off in the future.

The methodology which was adopted for the investigation is described in Appendix 2.

(i) Summary of Results

As regards a potential link between a finding of professional misconduct in a case before the SDT and the presence of a financial, dishonesty/BOU or property element in the case, my research showed that 74% of cases concerned financial misconduct, 51% concerned dishonesty/BOU matters and 45% concerned a property matter. It was also established that 34% of cases of misconduct reflected all three factors in that they concerned finance, dishonesty/BOU and also concerned a property matter. Of those cases which concerned dishonesty/BOU, 78% concerned a financial matter, and 72% concerned a property matter. A total of 67% of these dishonesty/BOU cases concerned both a financial and a property matter.

The one hundred cases examined in the course of this investigation involved seventy-two solicitors, with some solicitors having multiple findings of misconduct made against them in the course of the sample period. As regards the extent to which the misconduct of solicitors who are struck off involves the three elements of finance, dishonesty/BOU and property, twenty-four of the solicitors (or pairs of solicitors involved in the same disciplinary hearing) were found guilty of misconduct involving all the elements of finance, dishonesty/BOU and property, with the remaining forty-eight being found guilty of offences which did not involve all three factors. 33.3% of cases involving all three elements resulted in a strike off, whereas 14% of cases which did not involve all three elements resulted in a strike off.

Finally, as regards the issue of whether a solicitor's past disciplinary history may be used to predict his/her future offending behaviour, an examination of the disciplinary records dating back to 2004 of the seventy-two solicitors (or pairs of solicitors involved in the same disciplinary hearing) who featured in the database revealed that nineteen had a past history of professional misconduct *prior* to a future strike off. Analysis revealed that where a practitioner had past history of misconduct involving all three elements of finance, dishonesty/BOU and property, this was not predictive of a future strike off.[174] 10.5% of misconduct cases in the study, where the solicitor concerned had a past history of offences involving all three elements, resulted in a strike off. However, 23.6% of the cases in the study where there was no such previous history resulted in a strike off. Whilst many of the cases of professional misconduct which resulted in the solicitor concerned being struck off did involve elements of finance, dishonesty/BOU and property, the misconduct giving rise to the strike off only emerged at the time of the SDT hearing resulting in the strike off, and was not known to the SDT as a result of a previous hearing. A comprehensive discussion and analysis of the results of the investigation is available in Appendix 2.

(ii) Interpreting this study's findings

I undertook this research into professional misconduct amongst Irish solicitors, to establish the frequency of cases involving finance, dishonesty/BOU and property. The creation of the database was a valuable tool for examining how these factors interacted with each other. Statistical analysis which was carried out facilitated a detailed examination of patterns of misconduct in order to identify aspects of legal practice which are particularly problematic as far as professional misconduct is concerned. The database which was developed could be extended to provide more detailed information about professional misconduct amongst solicitors. It could be expanded to include a greater number of cases. The frequency of misconduct amongst sole practitioners could be investigated, as could the frequency of misconduct involving the area of wills and probate. A distinction could also be made within the database between misconduct concerning relatively minor financial breaches such as the failure to promptly file annual accounts and more serious financial misconduct involving large sums of money, and this would facilitate a more sophisticated analysis of solicitors' misconduct patterns. Whilst the database in its current form was not suitable for use as a predictive tool to identify practitioners likely to engage in future serious professional misconduct it is possible that a larger, more detailed database might be more productive in this regard.

The potential for *ex ante* regulation of the legal profession has not been adequately exploited. However, given the success of the Australian innovation in introducing *ex ante* regulation of Incorporated Legal Practices (ILPs) which led to a sharp fall in client complaints regarding the quality of legal services which they received, this regulatory strategy deserves further scrutiny.[175] According to Rhode and Woolley:

> [One] justification for sanctions based on lawyers' personal conduct is that personal misconduct is predictive of future professional conduct. This rationale is most plausible when the actions closely relate to the lawyer's

---

[174] Appendix 2, Table 3

[175] L Terry, 'Trends and Challenges in Lawyer Regulation (FN 1) 2263; S Mark & G Cowdroy, 'Incorporated Legal Practices – A New Era in the Provision of Legal Services in the State of New South Wales' [2004] 22 (4) *Penn State International Law Review* 671

legal practice, or arise from opportunities afforded by the lawyer's practice.[176]

Crime prevention programmes using predictive techniques are currently being developed to predict the occurrence of future crimes. These prevention tools are becoming ever more popular in the 'fight against crime'. The ability to predict future offending patterns relies upon the development of much larger and more sophisticated databases than that which formed the basis of this small study. However, the underlying approach is essentially the same. Predictive analysis is a method of risk assessment which uses technology to calculate the chance of a future event occurring. Early trials of a crime prevention system using the method has shown promise in the USA, and the system known as CRUSH (Criminal Reduction Utilising Statistical History) is currently undergoing trials in Britain.[177] The software has been developed by IBM, who has reportedly invested over $11 billion in the project since 2006. Critics of the system have argued that it represents an abuse of human rights by targeting potential offenders who are innocent until 'predicted' guilty.[178] However, advocates of the system suggest that it permits efficient targeting of limited police resources to areas where they are most likely to detect offenders. The database which was formed in the course of this study has the potential to be further developed for use as a predictive tool for the identification of those solicitors who are most likely to engage in future professional misconduct. Finally, the research findings have prompted some suggestions for amendments of the LSRB 2011.[179]

3.9 Concluding Remarks

This chapter has examined the strengths and weaknesses of the present regulatory framework governing the legal profession in Ireland today, and has identified a series of failures which collectively render the present system entirely unfit for purpose. It is clear that widespread reform is needed if the legal profession is going to meet the needs of potential users of legal services in Ireland today. Failure to introduce a radical programme of reform may well have negative consequences for the rule of law, as increasing numbers of citizens continue to turn away from the legal profession as a viable channel for dispute resolution, and choose instead to resolve their issues without recourse to professional legal advice and assistance.[100] This chapter focused on Terry's analytic

---

[176] D Rhode and A Woolley, 'Globalization and the Legal Profession' (FN 151) 2779

[177] T Thompson, 'Software that can predict violent crime to help police', *The Observer*, 25th July 2010; IBM Press Release, Memphis Police Department Reduces Crime Rates with IBM Predictive Analysis Software', 21st July 2010. Available at: <http://www-03.ibm.com/press/us/en/pressrelease/32169.wss> Accessed 3/4/2013

[178] Ibid

[179] See ch 5 § 5.7 for a discussion of suggested amendments to the LSRB 2011 following the findings of this study of professional misconduct amongst Irish solicitors.

[180] M Wallace TD recently confessed to using the threat of a hired hitman in order to settle a business dispute regarding a debt, after having firstly considered using "the legal process". Mr Wallace dismissed the legal option for resolving the issue as it was too expensive, too slow and ineffective. <http://www.irishtimes.com/newspaper/2012/1006/breaking14.html> Accessed

framework, which poses a series of questions about regulatory regimes pertaining to the legal profession, as follows:

- Why should the legal profession be regulated?
- Who regulates the legal profession?
- Where does lawyer regulation take place?
- When does lawyer regulation occur?
- How are lawyers regulated?

The present regulatory framework lacks a discernable, explicit rationale, beyond the questionable fulfilment of self-serving, self-regulatory ambitions, and the legal profession has shown itself to be admirable in the command of its brief as far as justifying self-regulation is concerned. Its main argument for justification of the status quo appeared to be that self-regulation was in the public interest, not just in that of the profession. However, the rhetoric has worn thin in the face of the harsh economic climate which Ireland is still experiencing today. Self-regulation is no substitute for clearly articulated regulatory objectives such as those which are found in the UK Legal Services Act 2007, which begin with the protection of the public interest, and conclude with the promotion and maintenance of professional principles.[181] The economic argument for the regulation of the legal profession provides a further impetus for regulatory change in Ireland, insofar as it reveals a catalogue of regulatory failings which typify the self-regulatory model. In the course of the last two decades, a series of reports, commencing with the Fair Trade Commission in 1990 and culminating with that of the Committee of Public Accounts in 2011 have faithfully documented and reiterated the fundamental failures of the current system of regulating the legal professions in Ireland today. Further systemic regulatory failure is revealed by the failure of the present system to regulate firms rather than individual legal practitioners. This state of affairs is hopelessly inadequate, and creates a dangerous environment whereby a dysfunctional firm may evade detection by the authorities until such time as a critical mass of misconduct finally results in a toxic firm appearing on the regulatory radar. The growing community of lay litigants presents an increasingly potent challenge to the regulatory *status quo*. The rise of the lay litigant, more than any other factor, most potently illustrates the abject failure of the regulation of the Irish legal profession. Irish lawyers are in danger of becoming the preserve of an ever-diminishing elite cohort of society. Public disillusionment with the legal profession was expressed on a daily basis within the forum which was provided by The Victims of the Legal Profession on its website, RateYourSolicitor.com. Whilst

---

7/10/2012. See M Hosier, 'The Legal Profession in Troikaland: Before and After the Irish Bailout' 2 – 11. Extracted in Appendix 1. Available at. <http.///ssrn.com/abstract=2262083> Accessed 1/7/2013. The growing numbers of lay litigants also reflects a rejection of traditional legal services providers.

[181] Ch 3 § 3.1 contains a discussion of regulatory objectives, including those contained in the UK's Legal Services Act 2007.

defamation cannot be excused on any level, the closing of a valuable forum for public debate on the basis of one, possibly defamatory event is arguably, an overreaction. Furthermore, the present regulatory system is entrenched in responding to regulatory breaches after the event, as opposed to intervening prior to the occurrence of misconduct or regulatory failing.

Modern statistical modelling techniques offer the possibility of regulatory intervention prior to the *actus reus* of regulatory breach, and also for the identification of those members of a community who are most likely to engage in wrongdoing. There have been promising developments in this field in the US. The Memphis Police Department, working with Professor Richard Janiskowski, have used IBM SPSS software to predict the locations of criminal activity. This approach has resulted in a considerable saving in policing costs, alongside improvements in crime prevention.[182] The present Irish regulatory system does not directly address the issue of regulating virtual legal service provision, and is ill equipped to address potential problems presented by the growing use of technology, which will increasingly be a common feature in the provision of legal services in future.

The current Irish regulatory framework fails to distinguish between the needs of individual clients and organisations, even though their level of sophistication as far as judging the nature and quality of legal services is concerned is markedly different. This is contrary to the recommendations of the European Commission, and arguably prevents the emergence of innovative solutions to the needs of business and corporate clients. The balance in the present regulatory system favours the use of rules over principles as regulatory instruments, and whilst rules undoubtedly have an important place in a reformed system of regulation, the clear articulation of regulatory objectives and guiding principles would be useful for both regulators and the regulated community in applying the regulations to foster best practice. Finally, the present regulatory framework largely fails to comply with the OECD Guiding Principles for Regulatory Quality and Performance which provides a clear warning signal that the present system of regulating the legal profession in Ireland requires comprehensive reform. The chapter concluded with an investigation into the nature of professional misconduct amongst solicitors, the results of which emphasize the need to develop a robust regulatory response to such behaviour, in the interest of both the public and profession. The following chapter will examine the manner in which the legal profession is regulated in other jurisdictions, including Northern Ireland, England and Wales, Australia, Greece and Portugal. The consideration of the latter two jurisdictions provides an opportunity to identify common themes in terms of the Troika's intervention programmes which are applied to 'bailed out' nations within the EU. The comparative study in Chapter 4 will also help to identify amendments which should be made to the LSRB 2011, in order to ensure that following its enactment, Ireland will have a regulatory regime for its

---

[182] Nucleus Research Inc, 2010. 'IBM Business Analytics SPSS: Memphis Police Department. Available at: <http://www-01.ibm.com/software/sucess/cssdb.nsf/CS/SSAO8DJ5CL?OpenDocument8Site=default&cty=en_us> Accessed 8/10/2012

legal profession which is fit for purpose and which serves the interests of the public rather than those of the profession itself.

4

INTERNATIONAL COMPARISONS

4.0 Introduction

This chapter seeks to explore the manner in which the legal profession is regulated in jurisdictions outside Ireland. It begins by looking at the regulatory regime which currently pertains in the jurisdiction of our nearest neighbour, Northern Ireland, and then moves on to consider the regulatory framework in England and Wales. The Bain Report of 2006 recommended the retention of the self-regulatory system in Northern Ireland.[1] This recommendation contrasts with the conclusions of the Clementi Report which, having considered the advantages and disadvantages of the self-regulatory system in England and Wales and examined possible alternatives, concluded that self-regulation of the legal profession should be replaced by the establishment of a Legal Services Board (LSB), to oversee the activities of 'front line' regulators such as The Bar Council and the Law Society.[2] The regulation of the legal services market in Australia is also worthy of examination, given that it has adopted an innovative approach which has been influential in other jurisdictions, especially with regard the deregulation of business structures authorised to provide legal services.

Given Ireland's current 'bailed out' status, the chapter proceeds to focus on the regulation of the legal profession in other bailed-out EU states, namely Greece and Portugal. Like Ireland, these countries have agreed with the Troika to implement programmes of fiscal and structural reforms in return for the receipt of bailout funds, and together with Ireland they present an opportunity to examine the *modus operandi* of the Troika in its interaction with EU member states who are facing extreme financial difficulties. This examination of the regulatory regimes pertaining in Greece and Portugal also reveals the extent to which the Troika has sought to achieve a far reaching liberalisation of the European legal services market in return for bailout funds.

This chapter also examines the responses of the international bodies representing the legal profession to the Troika interventions and their impact upon

---

[1] G Bain, *Legal Services in Northern Ireland: Complaints, Regulation, Competition* (2006). Available at: <http://www.dfpni.gov.uk/legal_services.pdf> Accessed 25/2/2013

[2] D Clementi, *Report of the Review of the Regulatory Framework for Legal Services in England and Wales* (Dec 2004). Available at: <http://www.legal-services-review.org.uk/content/report/index.htm> Accessed 25/2/2013

affected parties. It is hoped that this comparative approach to the study of regulatory regimes for legal services will facilitate a thorough analysis of the LSRB 2011 and the identification of amendments which might be made to it, in order to ensure that following its enactment, Ireland will have a legal services market which meets the needs of the public through the provision of high quality legal services at an affordable cost. However, the comparisons herein will also reveal the Troika's role as a *de facto* regulator of the legal profession, and the extent to which in recent times it has been the prime mover for the liberalisation of the legal services sector within Europe.

4.1 The Regulation of the Legal Profession in Northern Ireland

4.1.1 Overview of the Regulatory Framework

Given their common ancestry and their geographical proximity, it is not surprising that the regulation of the legal profession in Northern Ireland and Ireland should have many common features. The legal profession in Northern Ireland is comprised of both barristers and solicitors. Similarly to the position in Ireland, barristers provide specialist advice and courtroom advocacy. In general, they do not provide services directly to the public, but accept instructions from solicitors on a client's behalf. However, as is the case in Ireland, the Bar provides a direct access service for certain organisations which it considers capable of instructing a barrister in relation to a non-contentious matter. The solicitors' branch of the profession provides legal advice and assistance directly to the public, with the majority of practitioners operating through High Street firms. They often provide a complete legal service to clients on matters including conveyancing, debt collection, wills and probate services.

Solicitors

Like its counterpart in Ireland, the Law Society of Northern Ireland (The Law Society) is responsible for both the representation and regulation of solicitors. The self-regulatory powers and duties of The Law Society are statutory-based, in accordance with the provisions of the Solicitors (Northern Ireland) Order 1976.[3]

The Law Society performs its regulatory functions through the working of the Client Complaints Committee which consists of members of The Council of the Law Society, solicitor members and lay members, the latter of whom are in

---

[3] As amended on 16th July 2009 by the Solicitors (Northern Ireland) (Amendment) Order 1989. The 1976 Order sets out the conditions to be met by solicitors in respect of qualification and admission. It also sets out the Law Society's responsibilities with regard to the issuance of practice certificates. The Order confers regulatory powers on the Society in relation to professional practice, conduct, discipline and the handling of clients' funds. It also provides the Society with the power to monitor the keeping of accounts by its members, and sets out obligations on the part of the Law Society to maintain a compensation fund and of solicitors to carry PII. The rules relating to the remuneratrion of solicitors are also included in the Order. A complete list of all the Orders which have been made by the Law Society in accordance with its statutory powers may be found on its website, The Law Society of Northern Ireland. Available at: <http://www.lawsoc-ni-org/role-of-the-law-society/regulation/regulations-by-category/> Accessed 8/2/2013

the minority. The Law Society is subject to the supervisory jurisdiction of the Lord Chief Justice of Northern Ireland. There is lay participation in the regulatory system, as evidenced by both the Lay Observer and the lay persons who participate in the Solicitors Disciplinary Tribunal (SDT). The Lay Observer is a unique feature of the regulatory framework in Northern Ireland, having no counterpart in Ireland, England and Wales, or in any of the other jurisdictions considered in this chapter. The Lay Observer does not have investigative powers, but may only examine the manner in which complaints are handled. He/she may refer a complaint to the Law Society's Professional Conduct Committee for assessment, and may also refer a complaint to the SDT where this is considered to be appropriate. The Lay Observer reviews the handling of particular cases of complaint by the Law Society, without actually adjudicating directly in relation to cases, and he/she may also make recommendations to reform the complaints handling procedure. Like its counterpart in Ireland, the Northern Ireland SDT is independent from the Law Society, and adjudicates upon more serious instances of alleged misconduct such as the breach of an undertaking or the breach of the rules which govern conflicts of interest. Findings of the SDT are not generally made public. However, serious matters may be reported upon in the Law Society's monthly magazine *The Writ*, and may also be reported upon in the Law Society's Annual Report.

Barristers

Presently, there are approximately 580 practising barristers in Northern Ireland. As in Ireland, they are categorised in terms of their seniority, with about 13% of members of the Bar being designated Queen's counsel, with the remainder being junior counsel. Junior counsel are members of the Outer Bar and Queen's counsel (QCs) are members of the Inner Bar, the latter supposedly being of a higher standard professionally.[4] As is the case in Ireland, all barristers operate from the Law Library.[5] Barristers unlike solicitors, have rights of audience in both the High Court and superior Courts, although solicitors who have undergone a course of specialist training may advocate on behalf of clients in the High Court. Barristers are excluded from the provision of conveyancing services and the administration of estates, and they do not generally have access to clients' funds.[6] Like its Irish counterpart, the General Council of the Bar of Northern Ireland ('The Bar Council') is a non-statutory, private body which is responsible along with the Benchers of the Inn of Court of Northern Ireland (The Inn), for the maintenance of standards, honour and the independence of the Bar, and also for the promotion, presentation and improvement of the provision of

---

[4] The Bar Library of Northern Ireland. <http://www.barlibrary.com/about-us/the-legal-profession-in-ni/> Accessed 9/2/2013

[5] Barristers in Northern Ireland do not operate a system of Chambers as in England and Wales. Both the Bar Council and the Inn of Court of Northern Ireland operate from the Bar Library in Northern Ireland, which is a private institution to which all practicing members of the Bar are joined. It provides information and technical services, along with accommodation and office support for Northern Ireland's barristers.

[6] G Bain, *Legal Services in Northern Ireland* (FN 1) Ch 2 para 2.36

services by barristers.[7] The Bar Council also has a representative role on behalf of the Bar. Its regulatory functions include overseeing matters relating to professional etiquette, the organisation and working conditions of the Bar and remuneration of barristers. The Bar Council makes its own bye-laws, and is responsible for the appointment of a Professional Conduct Committee to investigate matters relating to members' conduct. Committees may also be established in relation to other matters as and when this is deemed to be desirable by the Bar Council, and functions and powers may be delegated to such Committees where necessary by the Bar Council.

The Executive Council of the Bar is responsible for many matters which were formally part of the remit of the Benchers of the Inn, such as the financial and business administration of the Bar. It is also responsible for establishing the qualifications which are necessary for admission to the Bar, and for the appointment of members of the Disciplinary Committee which hears cases referred from the Professional Conduct Committee. Whilst the Education Committee of the Executive Council considers Memorials from prospective students at the Inn who are seeking admission to the degree of barrister-at-law, and for making recommendations on these to the Benchers, it is the latter who have the ultimate decision-making powers in relation to such applications.

The Benchers are a group of members of the Inn of Court of Northern Ireland which includes members of the Supreme Court Judiciary, the Attorney General, the Solicitor General and other senior members of the Bar, and they play a similar role in the regulation of the legal profession in both Northern Ireland and Ireland.[8] As is the case in Ireland, the Northern Ireland Benchers are responsible for the admission of student members to the Inn, and for calling them to the Bar. They also appoint a Disciplinary Appeals Committee to hear appeals from the Disciplinary Committee of the Executive Council of the Inn of Court. The Benchers have the power to either suspend or disbar a barrister from practice upon a recommendation from the Disciplinary Committee or the Disciplinary Appeals Committee of the Inn. Hearings of the Disciplinary Committee are in public and where there are findings of serious misconduct, these are published on a notice board in the Bar Library, and also in the Great Hall of the Royal Courts of Justice. There is no independent oversight of the regulation of the Bar in Northern Ireland, and the Lay Observer plays no role in relation to the regulation of the Bar.

As is the case in Ireland, barristers are only permitted to practice as sole practitioners, with partnerships between groups of two or more barristers, or between barristers and solicitors, being prohibited. External ownership of solicitors' practices is also forbidden.

---

[7] The General Council of the Bar of Northern Ireland. <http://www.barlibrary.com/about-us/the-general-council-of-the-bar-of-northern-ireland/> Accessed 9/2/2013

[8] The Inn was established in 1926, prior to which time the Lord Chief Justice had the power to call members to the Bar in Northern Ireland. The Inn consists of both the Benchers and the Bar Council, and it is governed by the Benchers. It operates in accordance with its Constitution and Bye Laws which were adopted in 1983 at a General Meeting of the Inn.

4.1.2 Recommendations for Reform

The Legal Services Review Group was established by the government in 2005, under the auspices of its Chairman Professor Bain in order to examine the regulation of the legal profession in Northern Ireland, and to report and make recommendations for reform. Its Report entitled 'Legal Services in Northern Ireland: Complaints, Regulation, Competition' was published in 2006, following the earlier publication of the 'Clementi Review of Legal Services in England and Wales', and the government's subsequent White Paper.[9] The key objectives of the Bain Review were as follows:

• To achieve a new regulatory framework appropriate to the particular needs of Northern Ireland consumers.

• To ensure that competition and choice are available to consumers from the legal profession in Northern Ireland.[10]

Whilst the Report endorses the principles and objectives of the regulation of legal services as set out in the Clementi Review, it does not accept all of its recommendations as appropriate for adoption in Northern Ireland, primarily on the basis that the jurisdiction of Northern Ireland is much smaller than that of England and Wales, and the legal community is also of a much smaller order.

The Bain Report identified the key purpose of regulating the legal profession as being to ensure that its members are suitably qualified and that they observe appropriate ethical standards.[11] However, the failure here to refer to the need for regulation to further the administration of justice is regrettable. The Report endorsed the objectives and principles of the regulation of legal services as identified in the Clementi Report, those objectives being the maintenance of the rule of law, the facilitation of access to justice, the protection and promotion of consumers' interests, the promotion of competition in the legal services market, the encouragement of a strong, confident and effective legal profession and the promotion of public understanding of the legal rights of citizens.[12] Clementi also identified four legal principles which should be upheld by the regulatory framework governing the provision of legal services. These are as follows:

• The maintenance of the independence of the legal profession.

• The requirement to uphold high standards of integrity in the legal profession.

---

[9] D Clementi, *Report of the Review of the Regulatory Framework for Legal Services in England and Wales* (Dec 2004). Available at <http://www.legal-services-review.org.uk/content/report/index.htm> Accessed 28/2/2013

[10] G Bain, *Legal Services in Northern Ireland* (2006) (FN 1) Ch 8 para 8.2

[11] Ibid Ch 3 para 3.2. This view is in accordance with that which was expressed in the Consultation Document which was issued by the Legal Services Review Group of the Department of Finance and Personnel. The Review Group was responsible for recommending to the Minister of Finance and Personnel how the legal profession in Northern Ireland should be regulated, and also for the publication of the Bain Report *Legal Services in Northern Ireland: Complaints, Regulation and Competition.*

[12] Ibid Ch 3 para 3.4

• The requirement to uphold a lawyer's duty to act in a client's best inter-ests, subject to the overriding duty to the court and the interests of justice.

• The maintenance of client confidentiality in accordance with the rules of professional conduct.[13]

In the course of the consultative process which preceded the publication of the Bain Report, the Law Society, which retains a dual regulatory and repre-sentative function, strongly defended the continuance of the self-regulatory model in Northern Ireland on the grounds that it protected the independence of the legal profession from state interference. This was particularly important in Northern Ireland given the historical context of 'The Troubles':

> [T]here are circumstances of legal practice in Northern Ireland which are unique. These, combined with a continued context in which manifest sensitivities exist about the accountability and independence of state bodies and Government influence over the administration of justice ... are all factors which should be taken into account.[14]

Whilst The Troubles have undoubtedly impacted upon the administration of justice in Northern Ireland, it is unclear from the Bain Report how this fact serves to support the preservation of the self-regulatory model. The Report concluded that an oversight regulatory body such as the Legal Services Board (LSB) as proposed by Clementi for the legal profession in England and Wales was not appropriate in the Northern Ireland context. This was because there was no evidence of a history of regulatory failure in Northern Ireland, nor did it have an existing overly complex regulatory structure, and the cost of establishing such an oversight body was not proportionate to any benefit it may bring for consum-ers of legal services in Northern Ireland.[15] However, the Report failed to present evidence to support its view that there has not been regulatory failure in North-ern Ireland, and the classic problems associated with self-regulation undoubted-ly impact negatively upon the legal services market in Northern Ireland as in other jurisdictions.[16] Instead, the Bain Report concluded that a more effective regulatory regime would be achieved in Northern Ireland by the establishment of an independent Legal Services Oversight Commissioner (LSOC) who would oversee the general regulation and complaints handling processes of both

---

[13] Ibid Ch 3 para 3.6

[14] Ibid Ch 3 para 3.17. 'The Troubles' refers to a period of approximately 40 years of civil disorder (or war) in Northern Ireland caused by ethnic conflict. Northern Ireland society was, and remains, deeply divided upon political, cultural and religious grounds between the largely Protestant, loyalist and unionist citizens who have allegiance to the British crown on the one hand, and Catholic nationalists who generally aspire towards the unification of Ireland on the other. A Civil Rights Movement initiated in the 1960s by nationalists in response to historical discriminatory practices against Catholics, led to a violent response from both state authorities and members of the unionist community. The signing of the Belfast (Good Friday) Agreement in 1998 brought an end to the worst excesses of the Troubles, but not before the loss of 3,500 lives, with a further 50,000 people being seriously injured.

[15] Ibid Ch 3 para 3.30

[16] For a discussion of the problems associated with self-regulation, see ch 3 § 3.2.5.

branches of the profession. It recommended an increased involvement of lay practitioners in the regulatory structure, especially with regard to complaints handling. It was also noted that the Lord Chief Justice's involvement in the regulation of the legal profession may not meet with the requirements of openness and transparency, and that a purely advisory role for him/her in future may be more appropriate.[17]

The Report concluded that the formal separation of regulatory and representative functions within the Law Society and Bar Council was not necessary given that these two roles may 'inform' one another in a small jurisdiction, and that in such a context their formal separation may be problematic.[18] Instead, it recommended that the regulatory and representative functions of the professional bodies should only be separated in respect of complaints handling. Whilst there may be some merit to the argument that the regulatory and representative roles might inform one another in a small jurisdiction, any such benefit may be outweighed by the conflict of interest which arises when the responsibility for both functions lies with one body.

With regard to the handling of client complaints, and having examined the manner in which client complaints are dealt with in England, Wales, Scotland and Ireland, and the submissions of the various stakeholders who took part in consultations with the Review Committee, the Bain Report made the following recommendations regarding the handling of complaints concerning members of the legal profession:[19]

> • The legal profession should have responsibility for the handling of complaints, subject to some provisios, including that lay persons should form the majority on complaint committees, which should also be chaired by lay persons.
>
> • Members of the Council of the Law Society should not be allowed to continue to be involved in the investigation of complaints against solicitors.
>
> • The SDT should have a lay majority whilst continuing to be chaired by a legal professional.
>
> • A new Disciplinary Committee of the Bar should be established, which has a lay majority and is chaired by a legal professional, the function of the Committee being to deal with complaints of serious misconduct and for other conduct related complaints.

---

[17] Ibid Ch 3 para 3.35

[18] Ibid Ch 3 para 3.35

[19] Prior to the Bain Report in 2006 there was no requirement for a complainant to bring a complaint to the attention of a particular solicitor's firm as a first step in the initiation of a formal complaint procedure. Nor did the Client Complaints Committee of the Law Society have the authority to award compensation to a client where they had suffered loss or damage as a consequence of solicitor misconduct.

• Lay persons who participate in complaints committees should be appointed following public advertisement of the positions and a public recruitment process, to be overseen by the LSOC. [20]

• All solicitors' firms should establish their own complaints investigation procedure, details of which should be made available to clients and prospective clients.

• Complaints which are upheld should be eligible for compensation up to the value of £3,500 for both service and conduct related complaints. A similar level of compensation should be made available in relation to a complaint which is upheld and which involves professional negligence.[21]

• Where appropriate, a complainant should be given access to expert opinion about the merits, specifically the value and nature of any case they may wish to pursue against the legal practitioner at fault.

The recommendations of the Bain Report are in accordance with the size of the Northern Ireland jurisdiction and represent more of a refinement of the existing regulatory framework rather than a radical departure from it. Essentially, the Report recommended a fine-tuning of the regulatory *status quo*. In supporting the maintenance of the traditional self-regulatory model, the Report sets its face against a large body of academic literature which has documented its drawbacks.[22] The Report proposed that 'revised' oversight arrangements should be implemented, with the establishment of the new office of LSOC.[23] The LSOC would be able to audit individual complaint files, set targets and monitor performance of the complaints-related duties of the professional bodies. Where the professional bodies fail in their duties, the LSOC would have the power to issue appropriate penalties. The LSOC would have the responsibility for selecting lay representatives from an available pool to hear specific cases. He/she would also have the power to offer advice on other regulatory functions of the professional bodies and to refer cases to the Government where such advice is not acted upon. The LSOC would have broad consultative powers in respect of relevant stakeholders regarding appropriate regulatory mechanisms, and should have the necessary staff and resources to support his/her work, in order to ensure consumers of legal services in Northern Ireland receive sufficient protection.

The office of the LSOC should be supported by a levy that applies firstly to all legal practitioners and secondly to those practitioners against whom adverse regulatory findings are made. The appointment of the LSOC should be in accordance with the normal public servant recruitment procedures. The establishment of the office of LSOC constitutes the key innovative reform advocated by the Bain Report. However, the office's lack of investigative and remedial

---

[20] Such appointments should be in accordance with the 'Nolan Principles'. See ch 4 § 4.2 for more details regarding the Nolan Principles.

[21] The monetary limits outlined above should be subject to ongoing review by the LSOC, who should make recommendations for changes where appropriate.

[22] See ch 3 § 3.2.5 for a discussion of self-regulation.

[23] G Bain, *Legal Services in Northern Ireland* (2006) (FN 1) Ch 5 para 5.32

powers in relation to individual client complaints illustrates its inherent weakness, and its establishment will do little to fortify the existing regulatory framework.

The conservative tone of the Bain Report was also apparent in its opposition to the introduction of ABSs and its recommendation that the prohibition on barristers forming associations in the form of partnerships should continue. Unsurprisingly, it also opposed the establishment of LDPs and MDPs, and recommended that the prohibition on external ownership of law firms should remain. With regard to the establishment of an independent conveyancing profession, the Report argued that in the Northern Ireland context, this would be prohibitive, given the small size of the jurisdiction. It thus concluded that the restriction on licensed conveyancing in Northern Ireland should remain. Once again, no convincing argument was offered in the Report as to why the small size of the jurisdiction in Northern Ireland justifies the removal of consumer choice with regard to the provision of conveyancing services. It also recommended that the traditional division of labour between solicitors and barristers in matters of litigation should remain. However, the Report stated that it was reasonable for individuals and organisations to have direct access to the Bar in relation to both contentious and non-contentious matters, and it recommended that further consideration should be given to this issue by the Bar. It also supported the proposition that suitably trained solicitor-advocates should be given rights of audience in higher courts in a manner equivalent to the position pertaining in England, Wales and Scotland.[24] Finally, the Report urged that further consideration should be given to the manner in which a barrister in employment is currently prevented from presenting a case on behalf of his employer.

Concluding Remarks

Whilst endorsing the Clementi recommendations as appropriate in an English and Welsh context, and welcoming those proposals on a philosophical level, the Bain Report asserted that the regulatory reform programme as proposed by Clementi was not suitable for Northern Ireland, which differs from England and Wales on many levels including size, nature, the structure of its legal profession and regulatory history.[25] It was argued that the present legal system in Northern Ireland facilitates a healthy degree of competition and consumer choice which should be safeguarded. According to Bain, the reforms which he proposed have placed the consumer at the heart of the system, and put him/her in as good, if not better a position as consumers elsewhere in the UK and Ireland.[26] However, no evidence was offered to support this optimistic view of the changes to the regulatory framework, or to justify the assertion in relation to the strong position of consumers of legal services in Northern Ireland. The pace of regulatory reform in Northern Ireland following the publication of the Bain Report has been slow. Proposals for reform will be contained in the Legal Complaints and Regulation Bill which has yet to be published. It is understood that the Finance

---

[24] This reform would require the amendment of the Judiciature (Northern Ireland) Act 1978.

[25] G Bain, *Legal Services in Northern Ireland* (2006) (FN 1) Ch 8 para 8.5

[26] Ibid Ch 8 para 8.7

and Personnel Department will consult on the draft Bill prior to bringing it before the Northern Ireland Legislative Assembly later this year.[27]

4.2 The Regulation of the Legal Profession in England and Wales

The Clementi Report was commissioned in 2003 by the Secretary of State for Constitutional Affairs, as a result of concerns about the regulatory framework which applied to the legal services market in England and Wales at the start of the twenty-first century.[28] It was perceived to be outdated, inflexible, over-complex and lacking accountability and transparency.[29] There were concerns about the effect of entrenched restrictive practices upon the competitiveness of the market for legal services and also the level of client complaints about the quality of services.[30] There was also a concern about the efficacy of the mechanisms for dealing with consumer complaints, in particular the self-regulatory process whereby complaints against legal professionals were dealt with by the legal profession itself. According to the consumer magazine 'Which?', up to one third of clients considered that they had received poor service from their lawyer.[31] Furthermore, there was perceived to be a lack of efficiency in the regulatory system.[32] Finally, there was a concern that the present system unduly restricted the types of business structures in which legal professionals could operate.[33] The Report gave rise to the most far reaching reform of the legal profession ever seen in England and Wales or arguably, globally.[34]

4.2.1 Aims of the Clementi Review

The aims of the Clementi Review were as follows:

---

[27] Email from the Northern Ireland Legislative Assembly Committee for Finance and Personnel to the author, 4th Mar 2013. The Committee for Finance and Personnel of the Northern Ireland Legislative Assembly was briefed on proposals for the Legal Complaints and Regulation Bill by officials from the Department of Finance and Personnel in April 2013. The Department of Finance and Personnel met on 18th September 2013, and it is understood that it was briefed by departmental officials on proposals in relation to the Bill. (Email from Phil Pateman, Assistant Assembly Clerk, Committee for Finance and Personnel, Northern Ireland Legislative Assembly, to the author, 11th September 2013.) It is unclear why the Bill has made such slow progress in the Northern Ireland Legislative Assembly.

[28] D Clementi, *Report* (Dec 2004) (FN 2)

[29] Ibid, Foreword, para 3 (1)

[30] J Flood, 'Will There Be Fallout from Clementi? The Repercussions for the Legal Profession After the Legal Services Act 2007' (2012) *Michigan State Law Review* 537, 541. Available at: <http://ssrn.com/abstract=1128398> Accessed 25/2/2013. Citing The Office of Fair Trading, *Competition in Professions: A Report by the Director General of Fair Trading* (2001) Available at: <http://www.oft.gov.uk/shared_oft/reports/professional_bodies/oft328.pdf> Accessed 1/3/2013

[31] Ibid, citing 'Which? Wants Law Regulation', at 'Which?' 21st Mar 2005. Available at: <http://www.which.co.uk/about-which/press/press-releases/campaign-press-relaeases/consumer-market/2005/03/which-wants-law-regulation> Accessed 1/3/2013

[32] D Clementi, *Report* (FN 2) Foreword, para 3 (ii)

[33] Ibid, Foreword, para 3 (iii).

[34] J Flood, 'Will There Be Fallout from Clementi?' (FN 30) 538

• To identify a means of providing high quality legal services at a cost within the reach of all members of society.

• To identify the core principles which should be protected in any codes of conduct which may be adopted by the legal profession.

• To identify what type of regulatory framework is most appropriate for providers of legal services in England and Wales.

• To identify the most appropriate means of responding to clients' complaints.

• To decide whether the establishment of ABSs should be permitted.

4.2.2 Recommendations

The Provision of High Quality Legal Services

In order to ensure the provision of high quality legal services, the Clementi Report advocated a move away from regulating the activities of individual lawyers towards regulating the activities of particular firms. This shift becomes very apparent in the regulatory mechanisms which were recommended for new business structures, where the regulatory focus is less on individuals than upon practice management systems.[35]

Regulatory Objectives

The objectives which should be met by the regulation of legal services in England and Wales were identified by Clementi as follows:

(i) maintaining the rule of law

(ii) ensuring access to justice

(iii) protecting and promoting consumer services

(iv) promoting competition

(v) encouraging a strong, confident and effective legal profession

(vi) promoting public understanding of citizens' legal rights.[36]

Core Principles of Professional Codes of Conduct

Clementi identified the core principles which should be protected in any professional codes of conduct which are adopted by the legal profession. These are independence, integrity, a duty to act in the best interests of the client and the maintenance of client confidentiality.[37]

---

[35] D Clementi, *Report* (FN 2) Foreword para 12

[36] Ibid Ch A para 7

[37] Ibid Ch A para 15

*An Appropriate Regulatory Framework for Providers of Legal Services
in England and Wales*

Clementi also considered the issue of what type of regulatory framework is
most appropriate for practitioner bodies that provide legal services in England
and Wales. These include the Law Society, the Bar Council, the Institute of Legal
Executives, the Chartered Institute of Patent Agents and the Institute of Trade
Mark Attorneys. Clementi considered two main options in that regard; Model A
which involved removing all the regulatory functions from front-line bodies such
as the Law Society and the Bar Council, and vesting it in a Legal Services Authority, and Model B, which allows the responsibility for regulatory functions to
remain with the practitioner bodies, subject to oversight by a Legal Services
Board (LSB). One particular variant of Model B, Model B+, requires the separation of regulatory and representative functions in the front-line bodies, and it is
this model which Clementi identified as most appropriate for the jurisdiction of
England and Wales, given that it builds upon the strength of the existing system
and is comparable with international law and practice. This model vests overall
regulatory power in the LSB, which in turn delegates regulatory functions to the
front-line regulators where they are deemed competent, and also where they
have split their regulatory and representative functions.

Responding to Consumer Complaints

With regard to the handling of consumer complaints, the Clementi Report
recommended the establishment of a single, independent body to respond to
complaints in relation to any of the front-line legal service providers, namely an
Office for Legal Complaints (OLC).[38] This body would be part of the LSB framework. Clementi also recommended that disciplinary matters should be the
responsibility of the front-line bodies, given that their existing disciplinary
systems work reasonably well.[39] It was envisaged that the LSB would have
oversight powers with respect to the OLC as far as systemic and policy issues are
concerned, but would not be involved with the investigation or adjudication of
individual complaints. With regard to the LSB, Clementi recommended that it
should be governed by a Board with a part-time Chairman, Chief Executive and
a further twelve to sixteen members.[40] Its Chairman, Chief Executive and a
majority of the Board members should, in the interests of independence, be lay
persons. Appointments to the LSB should be made in accordance with the Nolan
Principles.[41]

---

[38] Ibid Ch C para 88

[39] Ibid Ch C para 89

[40] Ibid Ch D para 42

[41] The UK Nolan Committee on Standards in Public Life was established in 1994, following
widespread concern about ethical standards in public life. The independent committee promotes adherence by all public officials and public bodies to the seven 'Nolan Principles'. These
are selflessness, integrity, objectivity, accountability, openness, honesty and leadership. The
principle of objectivity requires *inter alia* that the making of public appointments should be on
the basis of merit. The Seven Principles are available at: <http://www.public-standards.gov.uk/
about-us/what-we-do/the-seven-principles/> Accessed 3/3/2013

The Establishment of ABSs

The final issue which the Clementi Report addressed was the possibility of permitting legal services to be provided by ABSs such as LDPs or MDPs.[42] Both entities provide for the clear separation of functions and responsibilities between those who own a practice and those who manage it.[43] The Report's recommendation to permit the introduction of LDPs represented a shift in regulatory focus from the level of the individual practitioner to the level of the economic unit, the firm.[44] Of primary concern to the regulator is the question of who runs a LDP or MDP, and how he/she does so. This concern recognises the business reality that where the quality of legal services is concerned, the competence of senior management is critical, as is the quality of management systems which may be employed by service providers.[45] With regard to MDPs, Clementi observed that whilst high profile financial scandals such as the 'Enron' and 'Worldcom' cases have reduced corporate interest in the establishment of large scale MDPs on a global scale, there are considerable potential benefits associated with them for small to medium size professional service providers who wish to attract clients with inter-related professional needs.[46] The Report suggested that ABSs should be advanced firstly by means of permitting LDPs to be formed, and then by identifying the regulatory consequences of these before moving on to permit the establishment of MDPs which would also require greater cooperation between the various professions.[47]

4.2.3 The Implementation of the Clementi Recommendations: The Legal Services Act 2007

The years following the publication of the Clementi Report saw the implementation of many of its core recommendations including the splitting of the regulatory and representative functions of legal practitioner bodies and the establishment of the LSB in accordance with Clementi's Model B+. The Legal Services Act (LSA) 2007 was the key statutory means for implementing the Clementi recommendations and for facilitating the liberalisation of the legal services market in England and Wales. The Act which contains 214 sections and 24 schedules saw the implementation of the most significant reform of the legal services sector for over a century. The key provisions were as follows:

> • It sets out the Act's regulatory objectives and expands those objectives which were identified by Clementi to also include the protection and promotion of the public interest, the promotion and maintenance of adher-

---

[42] LDPs are legal practices which allow lawyers from different professional bodies, for example solicitors and barristers to work together in order to provide services to clients. LDPs allow non-lawyers such as accountants to assume a managerial role in a business whilst not actually providing professional services to the public. MDPs allow lawyers and other non-lawyer professionals to provide both legal and other professional services directly to the public.

[43] D Clementi, *Report* (FN 2) Ch F paras 9 & 10.

[44] Ibid Ch F para 71

[45] Ibid

[46] Ibid Ch F para 86

[47] Ibid Ch F paras 98 – 100

ence to professional principles and the promotion of a legal system which is not just strong, diverse and effective, but which is also independent.[48]

• It provides for the establishment of the LSB and specifies its role in relation to the regulation of legal services, education and training.[49]

• It sets out in detail which legal services constitute reserved activities, to be provided only by legal practitioners, and specifies the regulatory arrangements pertaining to such activities.[50]

• It provides for the regulation of approved regulatory bodies and the separation of the regulatory and representative functions of the front-line practitioner bodies.[51]

• It provides for the establishment of ABSs and in particular, for LDPs as recommended in the Clementi Report, and sets out the mechanisms for licensing and regulation of such practitioners.[52]

• It provides for the establishment of the OLC as recommended by Clementi.[53]

The LSB was created in January 2009, and received its full regulatory powers one year later in January 2010. It has a staff of less than 30 and a budget of less than £5 million.[54] Possibly its most important challenges relate to its role in the development of a regulatory framework to facilitate and regulate ABSs in the legal services market. The new ABS regime which was established in accordance with the LSA 2007 came into force in June 2012.

The process for the establishment of an ABS involves an application to be made by one of the approved regulators to become a 'licensing authority' (LA) of an ABS. LSB approval of an LA is dependent upon the prospective ABS meeting detailed requirements with regard to both its structure and ownership. The LSB clearly sets out the responsibilities of the LA with regard to the regulation of the ABS, and invests it with appropriate powers to carry out its role in that regard, such as the power to impose financial penalties and also enforcement powers. Currently both the Solicitors Regulation Authority (SRA) and the Council for Licensed Conveyancers (CLC) have both been granted LA status. ABS approval will only be granted by a LA where those who hold a material interest have been approved. This includes those who hold 10% or more of shares or voting rights in the company, and those who exert significant influence over management. The LA must also be satisfied that the proposed ABS does not compromise the regulatory objectives set out in section 1 of the LSA 2007. Prior to giving approv-

---

[48] LSA2007 § 1 (1) (a) – (h)

[49] LSA 2007 Part 2 §§ 2 – 11

[50] LSA 2007 Part 3 §§ 12 – 26

[51] LSA 2007 Part 4 §§ 27 – 70

[52] LSA 2007 Part 5 §§ 71 – 111

[53] LSA 2007 Parts 6 & 7 §§ 112 – 196

[54] C Kenny, Chief Executive, LSB: Speech, 'Changes, Trends and ABSs in England and Wales' (Conference: Regulatory Reform for a 21st Century Legal Profession. 6th July 2012. Dublin)

al to an ABS, the relevant licensing authority will also make an overall organisational evaluation, and examine its funding and business models, with a view to satisfying itself that suitable individuals are involved, and that proper management systems are in place. All ABSs must appoint a Head of Legal Practice (HOLP) who has a duty to take all reasonable steps to ensure there is compliance with the relevant rules, managerial duties and professional principles. A Head of Finance and Administration (HOFA) must also be appointed, and he/she has a duty to ensure that all reasonable steps are taken to comply with accounts rules, and that failures in this regard are notified to the relevant authority.

The new rules facilitating the establishment of ABSs have seen the emergence of new business models, such as franchises, retail legal services providers and fixed fee service providers.[55] By the end of July 2012, just eight ABS licences had been issued. The LSB has adopted an outcomes focused approach to regulation of ABSs which focuses on the risks posed by either a particular subject area of legal practice or a particular firm, with an accordingly lighter touch regulatory approach being used for lower risk entities. The LSB enjoys real independence from the Ministry of Justice as the Minister lacks the power for direct intervention in its operation.

4.2.4 Departing from Clementi: The Introduction of ABSs

The LSA 2007 did not follow Clementi's recommendations regarding the introduction of ABSs via a two-phased procedure, and instead it adopted a 'big bang' approach, which paved the way for the introduction of all ABSs.[56] In order to put all multi-professional firms on a level playing field, under the new rules, existing LDPs must convert to ABSs in accordance with SRA rules.[57]

As mentioned above, the liberalisation of the regulation of business structures authorised to provide legal services has led to the emergence of innovative forms of service providers. England and Wales has seen the establishment of the first franchise of legal firms, Quality Solicitors, who seek to combine high brand recognition via the introduction of 'legal access points' in High Street locations such as newsagents, thereby creating the 'Specsavers' of the legal world.[58] At the other end of the market, Mischcon de Reya is becoming an ABS in order to develop a new venture which offers high net worth individuals or families with assets of over £50 million access to non-legal advisors in relation to private bank relationship management, tax planning and concierge services.[59] There has also

---

[55] Examples of these new ABSs include Quality Solicitors, Co-operative Legal Services and Riverview Law.

[56] J Flood, 'Will There Be Fallout from Clementi?' (FN 30) 548.

[57] Ibid 555

[58] Ibid 555. Further information about Quality Solicitors is available at: <www.qualitysolicitors.com>. Steve Richards, Chairman of Quality Solicitors stated that the firm had a "vision of creating the Specsavers of the legal world". 'Quality Solicitors Hits the Big Time as PE Investor Buys Majority Stake', *Legal Futures*, 20th Oct 2011. Available at: <http://www.legalfutures.co.uk/legal-services-act/market-monitor/quality-solicitors-hits-the-big-time-as-pe-investor-buys-majorty-stake> Accessed 3/1/2013

[59] Ibid 556. Citing S Ring, 'Mischcon to go Beyond Legal with New High-Net Private Client Business' Legal Week (24th February 2012). Available at: <http://www.legalweek.com/legalweek/news/2154441/mishcons-legal-net-private-client-business> Accessed 1/3/2013

been the emergence of legal conglomerates, such as the Parabis Group, which offers a wide range of services including consultancy, risk assessment, and medical and accident claims expertise. It has approximately one thousand legal staff, including four hundred lawyers and six hundred paralegals. A £130 million stake in Parabis was recently sold to a private equity fund, subject to SRA approval.[60]

The LSA 2007 ABS provisions have also seen the entry to the legal services market of supermarkets such as the Co-op. Co-Operative Legal Services (CLS) has plans to expand exponentially to a staff of over 3000 legal professionals over the next five years.[61] CLS offers combinations of services such as 'life planning', which includes probate, conveyancing and personal injury services in consumer friendly packages. AA Legal Services and Halifax Legal Express are further examples of household names which have been diversifying into the legal services markets in recent times.[62] Other emergent business models have adopted an on-line approach to the delivery of legal services, for either individual consumers or businesses, for instance Legal365.com, Rocket Lawyer and Legal Zoom.[63] The LSA 2007 has also created the potential for the trading in law firms' stock on the stock exchange. This phenomenon firstly emerged in Australia which saw the initial public offering of shares in Slater and Gordon in 2007. Slater and Gordon recently entered the UK market, having purchased Russell, Jones & Walker, a major English personal injury firm.[64]

It is clear that the English experience post LSA 2007 provides a valuable point of comparison for Irish legal service regulators when contemplating the desirability and possible impact of many aspects of regulatory reform, notwithstanding the difference in size and scale between the two jurisdictions. In particular the English experience with regard to the introduction of ABSs provides food for thought in the Irish context about the future shape of the legal services market, especially if Ireland wishes to fully participate in the rapidly developing global market for legal services, and to avail of all the opportunities arising due to technological advances.

---

[60] Ibid 556. For further information, see <http://www.parabisgroup.co.uk/services>. Accessed 1/3/2013

[61] Ibid 557. For more information, see <http://www.co-operative.coop/finacialcare>. Accessed 1/3/2013

[62] Ibid 557. Citing AA Services, available at: <http://www.theaa.com/legal-services/legal-documents.html>, and HALIFAX, available at: <http://wwwhalifaxlegalexpress.co.uk/halifax>. Accessed 2/3/2013

[63] Ibid 558. Citing *Legal365*, available at: <http://www.legal365.com/about>; D Fisher, 'Google Jumps into Online-Law Business with Rocket Lawyer', *Forbes* (11th Aug 2011), available at: <http://www.forbes.com/sites/danielfisher/2011/08/11/google-jumps-into-online-law-business-with-rocket-lawyer/>. Accessed 2/3/2013

[64] Ibid 558. Citing C Parker, 'Peering over the Ethical Precipice: Incorporation, Listing and Ethical Responsibilities of Law Firms' (2008), University of Melbourne Legal Studies Paper No 339, 2008

Concluding Remarks

Stephen has argued that the enactment of the LSA 2007 would introduce a regime of competitive regulation amongst legal service providers.[65] The Act provides for the regulation of economic units rather than individual practitioners, and the nature of these economic units is likely to vary in accordance with the different types of legal and other professionals who constitute the ABSs. According to Stephen:

> This is likely to lead to differences in the front-line regulators licensing ABSs in different markets but also ABS [sic] operating in the same market being regulated by different front-line regulators. What emerges is likely to be competitive regulation based on the legal services market rather than the individual professional and subject to a minimum standard set by the LSB.[66]

Whereas competitive regulation has the benefit of protecting consumers against the peril of super-normal profit-making by service suppliers, the particular competitive regulatory framework established by the LSA 2007 is cumbersome, and may lack efficiency as a result.[67] The LSB acts as an overseeing regulator for ten different regulatory authorities, including the Solicitors Regulatory Authority (SRA), the Bar Standards Board (BSB), the Institute of Legal Executives Professional Standards Ltd, The Intellectual Property Regulation Board (IPRB) and the Association of Chartered Certified Accountants (ACCA).[68] Several of these bodies are authorised to approve practitioners to offer the same type of legal service, for instance; both the SRA and the ACCA may authorise the provision of probate services. Service providers may choose the regulator who imposes the least onerous burden upon them in terms of requisite standards to be met by the service provider, in order to receive authorisation to operate in the probate market. According to Stephen, it is this competition amongst regulators that mitigates against the imposition of super-normal costs by service providers.

Boon has argued that the most fundamental impact of the LSA 2007 has been on the ideology of professionalism, and he has outlined two possibilities for the profession following its implementation:

> On the one hand, competition and a more explicit focus will reinvigorate legal professionalism. Therefore the LSA may allow lawyers to reconstruct as a liberal profession (Flood, 2010), or operate as a corrective to professional failings (Maute, 2010), or foster a new version built on a responsive form of regulation (Parker, 1999; Webb, 2004). On the other hand, the purpose of the LSA is to compromise or destroy professionalism, at least

---

[65] F Stephen, 'Regulation of Legal Profession or Regulation of Markets for Legal Services: Potential Implications of the Legal Services Act 2007' (2008) 19 (6) *European Business Law Review* 1129, 1139

[66] Ibid 1139

[67] Ibid 1134

[68] Further information on LSB activities is available on its website: <http://www.legalservicesboard.org.uk/can_we_help/approved_regulators/index.htm> Accessed 19/8/2013

as a mechanism of occupational control. Therefore the LSA represents the interests of the state and private capital in controlling professional work (Friedson, 1998), or a process of competition or concentration and rationalisation reflecting political faith in market mechanisms and a rhetorical assault on justice as a public good (Sommerlad, 2010) or, according to Lord Neuberger, Master of the Rolls, a threat to the rule of law from "consumer fundamentalism" (Legal Futures, 2010a). The reality may be between these extremes, but assuming it survives, the LSA will redefine legal professionalism.[69]

Given the recent introduction of ABSs in England and Wales, it is too early to assess the impact of the LSA 2007 on either the legal services market or the legal professions. However, the Act has clearly resulted in greater choice for consumers in terms of service providers. Flood has argued that the Act has brought about a shift, "from [traditional] "professionalism to deskilling and proletarianization in the legal profession not unlike that which existed in the nineteenth century".[70] However, Flood has also observed that the profession has been impacted upon not only by the enactment of the LSA 2007, but also by the 'changing postmodern condition' which is profoundly influencing "traditional notions of careers, with temporary arrangements replacing life time commitments and a growing corporate reliance upon the services of inhouse lawyers as sources of knowledge, skill and competence".[71] Whilst it may be difficult to separate the precise effect of the enactment of the LSA 2007 from other social and economic influences upon the legal profession in a rapidly changing technological era, the Act has facilitated the legal profession's participation in the process of change. Whilst many of the changes which have occurred as a result of the Act have undoubtedly been painful, the profession may well reap the benefits of its flexibility in future, in maintaining a pre-eminent place on the legal landscape.

4.3 The Regulation of the Legal Profession in Australia

Australia is a federation consisting of six states and eight territories which obtained independence from Britain in 1901. Each state and territory has traditionally been responsible for the regulation of the legal profession within its own jurisdiction.[72] However, the difficulties associated with multiple separate regulatory frameworks for legal professionals began to become more apparent in recent years, as practitioners found themselves unable to practice in jurisdictions outside the one in which the were registered to practice, without first obtaining a practising certificate for the second jurisdiction. These state- and territory-specific requirements created considerable inefficiencies for practition-

---

[69] A Boon, 'Professionalism under the Legal Services Act 2007' (2010) 17(3) *International Journal of the Legal Profession* 195, 200

[70] J Flood, 'Will There Be Fallout From Clementi? (FN 30) 4

[71] Ibid 7

[72] Office of the Legal Services Commissioner, 'Regulation of the Legal Profession in Australia'. Available at: <http://www.olsc.nsw.gov.au/olsc/olsc_education/lsc_lawregulate.html> Accessed 21/8/2013

ers wishing to practice across the various state and territorial jurisdictions.[73] There were also problems for practitioners due to the variable levels of consumer protection in the different states and territories. Another factor which contributed to the momentum for national reform was a growing desire for more competition and for a more open market in professional services. There was also an increasing awareness of new opportunities in the international legal services market as a result of globalization, which highlighted the need for Australia to initiate significant reform if it was going to fully partake of these new opportunities.

At the beginning of the twenty-first century, the Attorneys General of the Territories along with the Attorney General of the Commonwealth sponsored a National Legal Profession Model Laws Project, whereby the various jurisdictions, with the assistance of the Law Council of Australia (LCA) collaborated to produce a Model Bill aimed at facilitating a national market in legal services and a national system of legal practice. This entailed both the harmonisation of standards and the attainment of legislative uniformity in some regulatory areas.[74] In 2008, it became clear that the Legal Professions Acts 2008 which was based upon the Model Bill was insufficient to sustain a national market for legal services in Australia, or to allow Australia to take part in the international services market. The Council of the Australian Government (COAG) is the primary intergovernmental forum in Australia. It is comprised of the Prime Minister, State and Territory Premiers, Chief Ministers and the President of the Australian Local Government Association.[75] In 2010 it was decided by the COAG that the establishment of a clear and efficient national system of regulation of the legal professions would form a part of the Council's micro-economic reform agenda. Accordingly, a taskforce was established to prepare a draft of appropriate uniform legislation. The taskforce recommended that a simpler national regulatory framework should be developed with a view to achieving national uniformity. The establishment of two new national bodies, the National Legal Services Board (NLSB) and the National Legal Services Ombudsman were proposed, which would regulate the profession alongside the Supreme Courts and the existing disciplinary tribunals.

The NLSB is responsible for setting professional rules, monitoring admission to the profession and the licensing of professionals. The Ombudsman is

---

[73] Office of Legal Services Commissioner, 'Mobility Between Jurisdictions'. Available at: <http://wwwo.lsc.nsw.gov.au/olsc/olsc_education/lsc_lawregulate/lsc_mobility.html#inter> Accessed 21/8/2013. In accordance with the Mutual Recognition Act of 1992 (Cth), legal practitioners wishing to practice as 'interstate lawyers' must apply to have their name entered upon the second state's Roll of Legal Practitioners and obtain a practising certificate for that jurisdiction. In 1998 an interstate practicing certificate regime was established which enabled legal practitioners from participating jurisdictions to practice in other jurisdictions without obtaining a second practicing certificate.

[74] G Ferguson (The Law Council of Australia), Speech at ABA Annual Meeting International Bar Leaders Roundtable Panel, 'National Legal Reform in Australia: An Overview', 6th Aug 2010. A link to the speech is available at: <www.lawcouncil.asn.au/lawcouncil/index/php/library/speeches/law-council-presidents/11-library/200-glenn-ferguson-2010> Accessed 1/9/2013

[75] Further information about the COAG is available at: <http://www.coag.gov.au> Accessed 27/8/2013

responsible for receiving and investigating complaints and for monitoring compliance auditing. The functions of these new national bodies will be carried out by existing regulatory entities which may delegate powers where appropriate. It was also proposed by the taskforce that the Standing Committee of Attorneys-General (SCAG) would be responsible for recommending appointments to the Board, for giving policy directions to it and for setting its rules. This new regulatory framework would bring considerable benefits for the profession, as admission in one Superior Court would lead to automatic recognition in all other Superior Courts in Australia, and it would also permit the creation of both a single Australian practice certificate and of one uniform and publicly accessible Australian Legal Profession Register. There will be a reduction in the regulatory burden faced by the Australian legal profession, as the need for the duplication of regulatory requirements will be removed for multi-jurisdictional practices, and the option of maintaining one single trust account is made available for such practices. There will also be a simplification of the requirements to be met by multi-jurisdictional practitioners in relation to professional indemnity insurance.

Although the LCA voiced concerns in relation to some aspects of the reform agenda, in particular; about the composition and manner of appointment of the NLSB and also about the powers of the SCAG which, it was argued, would serve to undermine the independence of the legal profession and to damage the separation of powers, the LCA has essentially welcomed the national reform agenda. Whilst the Model Bill has not yet entered into force, discussions are ongoing between relevant stakeholders regarding the Draft Rules for the National Legal Profession which are being co-ordinated by the COAG. The COAG is currently promoting a series of deregulatory reforms which include proposals concerning the legal profession. These are aimed at establishing uniform laws to apply in all Australian jurisdictions, regardless of the origin of a holder's practice certificate.[76]

4.3.1 Amendment of the Legal Profession National Laws

A series of amendments to the Legal Profession National Laws (LPNL) have been agreed since December 2010. Firstly, the manner in which the members of the NLSB will be appointed has been amended. The Council of Chief Justices will not be represented or involved in the Board. Instead, the Attorneys General and Lords Chief Justice of participating jurisdictions will each appoint three members to the Board. The Chair of the Board will be appointed with the agreement of both the LCA and the Australian Bar Association (ABA).[77] The requirements to be met in order for liability to attach to the principal of a legal practice in relation to a breach of the National Law or National Rules by that practice

---

[76] Further information is available at: <http://www.federalfinancialrelations.gov.au/content/other_related_agreements/current/legal_profession_reform_Jul_12.pdf> Accessed 16/2/2013

[77] COAG National Legal Profession Reforms 'Report on Key Issues and Amendments made to the National Law since December 2010'. Available at: <http://www.lawlink.nsw.gov.au/Lawlink/Corporate/ll_corporate.nsf/vwFiles/NLPR_Report_key_amendments_LegalProfesssionNationalLaw_since_Dec2010.doc/$file/NLPR_Report_key_amendments_LegalProfessionNationalLaw_since_Dec2010.doc> Accessed 16/2/2013

have been amended. Such liability will only attach where the principal either knowingly authorised or permitted the breach, or where he/she was, or ought reasonably have been, in a position to influence the actions of the practice with respect to the breach, and where the principal in either of these circumstances failed to take reasonable steps to prevent the breach. With regard to costs disclosure reforms, the Board will have the authority to make rules providing appropriate guidance to practitioners as to how to comply with such requirements. It will also have the authority to amend the threshold amount of legal costs above which the disclosure requirements must be met, and it has been agreed that the LPNL should increase the threshold of such costs from AU $750 to $1,500. The rules relating to PII cover have been amended to ensure that PII providers are notified of a legal practice's intent to change the jurisdiction in which it holds cover as soon as possible, and prior to a specified date (to be agreed) in the legislation. This is to enable PII providers to adequately plan for the flow of such multi-jurisdictional legal practices in and out of their schemes.[78]

The LPNL have also been amended to remove the power of the National Legal Services Commissioner to require either party to a costs dispute to lodge all or part of the disputed sum with that office. Finally, the LPNL have been amended to ensure that local representatives of the National Legal Services Commissioner are independent statutory bodies or office holders rather than professional legal associations. Such independent local representatives may then choose to delegate complaints handling functions to professional legal associations who will be subject to independent oversight. The requirement for an independent statutory body to be responsible for complaints handling does not extend to compliance functions, which will continue to be the responsibility of legal professional associations such as Law Societies and Bar Associations.[79]

4.3.2 New South Wales: An Innovative Approach to the Regulation of the Legal Profession

New South Wales (NSW) has been at the frontier of the regulation of legal services in Australia, particularly in relation to the introduction of ABSs. Whilst solicitor corporations have been permitted as early as 1990, legislation allowing for the establishment of MDPs was firstly enacted in 1994.[80] However, the initial rules required that a solicitor should be the major shareholder in the MDP, and that he/she should retain over one half of the net income of the firm.[81] These restrictions have since been abolished on the grounds that they were anticompetitive.[82] Since 2001, legal service providers in NSW are permitted to in-

---

[78] Ibid 2

[79] Ibid 3. Compliance functions include trust account oversight, external intervention and compliance auditing.

[80] Legal Profession (Solicitor Corporations) Amendment Act 1990 (An act to amend the Legal Profession Act 1987 to provide for the formation and regulation of corporations that carry on business as solicitors); Revised Professional Conduct and Practice Rules 1994 (Solicitors Rules 1994), Rule 40.

[81] Ibid. Solicitors Rules 1994, Rules 40.1.1 & 40.1.6.

[82] The Council of the Law Society in NSW repealed Rule 40 in 1999.

corporate as companies and to enlist with the Australian Securities and Investments Commission.[83] Presently there are approximately 1,300 Incorporated Legal Practices (ILPs) in NSW, the majority being in urban population centres. Each ILP must appoint a Legal Practice Director who is an Australian legal practitioner with a full practice certificate. In addition to his/her normal professional obligations, the Legal Practitioner Director must ensure the implementation and maintenance of appropriate management systems in the ILP and must report professional misconduct on the part of any director or legal practitioner in the ILP.

The Office of the Legal Services Commissioner (OLSC) in NSW has collaborated with the legal profession in NSW to identify the best means of ensuring the adoption of appropriate management systems in ILPs. A self-assessment process has been introduced, the aim of which is to illustrate a practice's compliance with ten specific objectives as follows:

1. To avoid work practices that may give rise to negligence.

2. To ensure effective and timely communication systems are in place.

3. To avoid delay and ensure the timely delivery of legal services.

4. To facilitate the timely delivery of document transfers.

5. To ensure that appropriate practices apply to billing, terminating retainers and cost disclosure.

6. To introduce procedures for the avoidance of conflicts of interest.

7. To ensure that best practice is observed for the management of documents.

8. To introduce a system to monitor the issuance of and compliance with undertakings.

9. To ensure the proper supervision of staff and practice.

10. To ensure compliance with trust account regulations.[84]

There are indications that the introduction of the self-assessment system has resulted in a significant reduction in client complaint rates in relation to firms which have elected to incorporate in NSW.[85] Research indicates that the self-assessment regime has had a considerable impact upon client complaint rates,

---

[83] Legal Profession Amendment (Incorporated Legal Practices) Act 2000. Incorporated law firms are currently governed by The Legal Profession Act 2004, §§ 134 – 164 and The Legal Profession Regulations 2005, Regs 41 – 43.

[84] The 'Ten Commandments' or Ten Objectives of a Sound Legal Practice have been enunciated by Mark and Cowdroy. S Mark & G Cowdroy, 'Incorporated Legal Practices – A New Era in the Provision of Legal Services in the State of New South Wales' (2004) 22 (4) *Penn State International Law Review* 671, 690

[85] C Parker et al, 'Regulating Law Firm Ethics Management: An Empirical Assessment of an Innovation of the Legal Profession in NSW' (September 2010) 37 (3) *Journal of Law and Society* 466, 493.

with the average complaint rate following the introduction of self-assessment being just one third of the rate prior to its introduction. It has been argued by Parker, et al that this reduction is a result of learning and changes within legal practices which are prompted by the process of self-assessment.[86]

Concluding Remarks

Whilst it would not be prudent to attempt to draw exact parallels between the Australian experience of MDPs and their possible introduction in other smaller, non-federal jurisdictions such as Ireland, the Australian example nonetheless provides some valuable information regarding the possible impact of such a liberalising measure. For instance, there is no evidence to support the view that such market liberalisation measures are detrimental to clients' interests, and given that the Australian experience in this area dates back almost twenty years, it arguably obviates the necessity for further delay and long term research prior to the liberalisation of business structures for the provision of legal services in Ireland. Ireland may also look to the English experience of ABSs if further reassurance is needed in respect of their invigorating effect upon the legal services market. Finally, the NSW self-assessment system may serve as an ethical framework for Irish law firms who could similarly benefit from the process of reflection and change at an organisational level which is fostered by the self-assessment system.

4.4 The Regulation of the Legal Profession in Greece

Greece has a long and distinguished legal history, the modern profession being comprised of notaries, mortgage registrars and lawyers.[87] Notaries are responsible for drafting documents including contracts, wills and memoranda of agreement. They are unsalaried public officials, who are appointed following a public competition, and their activities are governed by the Notaries Code.[88] They are organised and represented by the professional Association of Notaries. Mortgage registrars are also unsalaried public officials who are responsible for keeping registers of real estate mortgages, foreclosures and deeds of conveyance. They are also responsible for maintaining registers of court acts and other matters relating to real estate. Mortgage registrars have formed professional associations, and their appointment is also on foot of a system of public competition. Finally, lawyers in Greece are organised in 65 local bar associations, each of

---

[86] Ibid 493

[87] The Greek legal profession also includes judges, prosecutors, court clerks and bailiffs. These professionals are subject to the Organisation of the Courts Code. Judicial and prosecutorial appointments are for life. Court clerks also receive permanent appointments with their activities being governed by the Civil Service Code. Bailiffs are responsible for the service of summons and the preparation of court documentation. They are also governed by the Civil Service Code. Given that the roles of these professionals are confined exclusively to the administration of justice, and that they do not provide legal services directly to the public in return for a fee payment, the regulatory frameworks which govern their activities will not be considered further here.

[88] Information about the Greek legal system is available at:
<http://ec.europa.eu/civiljustice/legal_prof/legal_prof_gre_en.htm> Accessed 20/2/2013

which belongs to the territorial jurisdiction of a court of first instance. Having been initially admitted to a court of first instance, a lawyer may subsequently practice in the courts of appeal, and the supreme court, depending on his/her level of experience. Lawyers are bound by the Lawyers Code, which governs such matters as disciplinary procedures, fees and promotion within the profession. The Greek legal profession does not distinguish between barristers and solicitors. However, a distinction is made between attorneys and lawyers. Whilst on the one hand attorneys deal with international affairs, real estate, inheritance, contracts and other work that requires a legal representative, lawyers on the other hand represent clients in the courtroom.[89]

In order to register with one of the Bar Associations, one must either hold a law degree from a Greek University, or an equivalent qualification from a recognised foreign university. A period of probationary training of eighteen months must be completed by trainee lawyers under the supervision of either a qualified lawyer or the Legal Council of State.[90] Trainee lawyers must also pass the Bar Exam upon completion of their training period, prior to being admitted to the profession as fully qualified lawyers. The Greek profession does not restrict entry numbers to the profession, and all candidates who are successful in the Bar Exam are admitted. Greek lawyers have the exclusive right to give legal advice, and to represent clients in courts, or before judicial or administrative authorities, special committees and disciplinary boards.[91] They are also charged with both the legal and moral duty to safeguard the social, civil and political rights of people in accordance with the Constitution and international law. Legislative Decree No 3020 of 8th January 1954 contains the Lawyers' Code which governs the profession, in conjunction with the Lawyers' Code of Conduct and the rules of the Bars. They must behave honestly, decently and in a manner in keeping with their special position in the modern constitutional Greek state. According to the President of the Athens Bar Association, Giannis Adanopoulos, the profession's compliance with the rules of professional ethics is 'strictly supervised' by the Disciplinary Councils of the local Bar.[92] However, the Greek legal system is beset by extensive delays which have the effect of making an 'Odyssey' of what ought to be a simple interaction with either the justice system or public service authorities.[93] This leads to the *de facto* denial of justice in many cases. There are also problems due to the poor condition of court buildings, insufficient court secretarial staff, a lack of associated court services and the wide dispersal of the judiciary across the state.[94] Other difficulties for the profession have arisen due

---

[89] Bridgewest, 'Lawyer in Greece', available at: <http://www.bridgewest.eu/article/lawyer-in-greece> Accessed 20/2/2013

[90] G Adanopoulos, 'The Legal Profession in Greece', 9th January 2012, available at: <http://greeklawdigest.gr/topics/legal-profession-in-greece/item/125-the-legal-profession-in-greece> Accessed 20/2/2013. There is also the option for trainee lawyers to be supervised by the Courts for one Semester (Law no 3910 of 8th February 2011, Art 33).

[91] Ibid

[92] Ibid

[93] Ibid

[94] Ibid

to the high number of qualified practitioners, with Athens alone having 21,000 legal professionals. As a result, many lawyers cannot gain court experience.

4.4.1 The Troika in Greece

In recent years, Greece has experienced a period of unprecedented economic difficulty, which saw the Government lose grip of the country's finances, a situation which necessitated a series of Troika bailouts commencing in 2010. According to the IMF, the programme which was adopted to address the country's economic crisis focused upon restoring fiscal stability, boosting external competitiveness and safeguarding the stability of the financial sector. The programme aimed to lower the fiscal deficit to less than 3% of GDP by 2014 and to restore debt sustainability.[95]

On 2nd of May 2010, the Troika approved a €100 billion bailout for Greece following fears that its financial difficulties would result in a debt default. Not withstanding the implementation of a programme of austerity, the country's financial difficulties continued, and on 21st July 2011 a total of €109 billion was earmarked for a second Greek bailout, to be provided by the European Financial Stability Facility. The country's ongoing problems led to a 50% write off for Greece's debt being agreed by Eurozone leaders in October 2011. In February 2012 further harsh austerity measures were introduced in order to ensure the receipt of the second bailout from the Troika, which was increased in total value from €109 billion to €130 billion, in order to meet the totality of Greece's financial needs. Greece's economic difficulties have led to social and political unrest as the country faces high unemployment and as falling wages afflict many of its citizens. It is arguable that Greece has yet to reap the benefits which theoretically should accompany implementation of the widespread programme of liberalisation and deregulation of large sectors of the economy, which has affected everyone from truck drivers and taxi drivers, to pharmacists, accountants and lawyers.

4.4.2 The Impact of the Troika upon the Greek Legal Profession

In order to establish whether the Troika programme of liberalisation which was imposed upon Ireland was unique, or whether in fact other bailed-out nations have been the subject of similar reforming agendas, it is instructive to look at Greece's regulatory framework post-bailout. A comparison of the Troika's influence upon the regulation of the Greek, Irish and Portuguese legal professions will reveal whether Ireland has been the subject of a pioneering experiment on the Troika's part, or whether it has in fact succumbed to a broader movement for innovation and liberalisation in professional regulation.

As a result of the Troika's intervention in Greece, as well as embarking upon a programme of economic and fiscal reforms, Greece also committed itself to the implementation of a series of measures aimed at the liberalisation of the legal profession. The Memorandum of Economic and Financial Policies which accompanied Greece's Letter of Intent to the IMF in August 2010 stated:

---

[95] IMF, 'IMF Executive Board Approves €30 Billion Stand-By Arrangement for Greece', Press Release No 10/187, 9th May 2010. Available at: <http://www.imf.org.external/np/sec/pr/2010/pr10187.htm> Accessed 22/2/2013

22. Efforts are underway to increase competition and achieve a rebound in growth:

Restricted Professions. Pervasive restrictions to entry in a number of important professions impose high costs on the economy. As a first step, the government will remove barriers in the legal, pharmacy, notary, architecture, engineering and auditing professions. This will include reducing licensing requirements, geographic restrictions, and regulated tariffs.[96]

Further commitments were given in the Memoranda which accompanied a Greek Letter of Intent to the IMF in December 2010:

Structural Reform Policies.

21. Deregulation of restricted professions, and the wider service sector will be complete soon. The government will prepare legislation, taking into account the opinion of the competition authority, to remove restrictions to competition, business and trade in restricted professions and comply with the European Union's services directive. The legislation, to be adopted by the end – February 2011 will focus on high economic impact professions (including lawyers, notaries, engineers, architects, auditors, pharmacists and other high economic impact services as appropriate).[97]

... To Strengthen Competition in Open Markets

Restricted Professions

Government proposes legislation to remove restrictions to competition, business and trade in restricted professions including:

– the legal profession, to remove unnecessary restrictions on fixed minimum tariffs, the effective ban on advertising, territorial restrictions on where lawyers can practice.[98]

These structural reforms encompass all aspects of the regulation of the legal profession with the exception of conduct and disciplinary matters, the emphasis being upon changes which will reduce costs to service users, and remove internal barriers to the free movement of lawyers. The removal of barriers to entry to the

[96] Memorandum of Economic and Financial Policies accompanying the Letter of Intent of 6th Aug 2010 from George Papaconstantinou (Minister of Finance) and George Provopoulos (Governor of the Bank of Greece) to Dominque Strauss-Kahn (Managing Director of the IMF). Available at: <http://www.imf.org/external/np/loi/2010/grc/080610.pdf >Accessed 6/3/2013

[97] Memorandum of Economic and Financial Policies accompanying the Letter of Intent of 8th Dec 2010 from George Papaconstantinou (Minister of Finance) and George Provopoulos (Governor of the Bank of Greece) to Dominque Strauss-Kahn (Managing Director of the IMF), para 21, 5. Available at: <http://www.imf.org/external/np/loi/2010/grc/120810.pdf> Accessed 6/3/2013

[98] Memorandum on Specific Economic Policy Conditionality accompanying the Letter of Intent of 8th Dec 2010 from George Papaconstantinou (Minister of Finance) and George Provopoulos (Governor of the Bank of Greece) to Dominque Strauss-Kahn (Managing Director of the IMF), 40. Available at: <http://www.imf.org/external/np/loi/2010/grc/120810.pdf> Accessed 6/3/2013

profession is also of key significance for the Troika in increasing competition in the legal services market.

4.4.3 Progress on the Implementation of the Legal Regulation Reforms

In June 2012, the Greek Government enacted legislation to liberalise the 'closed professions' and to implement the programme of structural reforms, in accordance with its agreement with the Troika.[99] The reforms focus on the following areas:

- Entry to the legal profession
- The removal of restrictions on advertising
- The removal of geographical barriers to practice
- The lowering or removal of minimum tariffs.

Entry

In its Report of December 2012 on Greece's progress on implementation of its economic reform programme, the European Commission noted the progress of the Greek authorities in creating greater access to the legal profession.[100]

Advertising

Progress has also been made in identifying unnecessary prohibitions on commercial communications (advertising) and to ensure that rules governing such communications are proportionate and in the public interest.[101] Also, in accordance with its obligations as set out in the Memoranda of Understanding, the Government has requested written contributions from the legal professions on the conditions which govern access to the professions.

Geographical Restrictions on Practice within Greece

Geographic restrictions which used to apply to the exercise of the legal profession have been abolished, so that all lawyers may freely provide services anywhere within the Greek jurisdiction without encountering any legal obstacles, and they are no longer restricted to the provision of services within the region of the Bar Association with which they are registered.

Minimum Fee Tariffs

A Ministerial Decision which prescribed a high minimum value for a notary's pro rata fee has been repealed and replaced by a Ministerial Decision establishing a significantly lower minimum transaction value.[102]

---

[99] Law 4038/2012

[100] European Commission, 'Task force for Greece: Quarterly Report. December 2012', para 9.5, 31. Available at: <http://ec.europa.eu/commission_2010-2014//president/pdf/qr3_en.pdf> Accessed 8/3/2013

[101] Ibid 41

[102] Helenic National Reform Programme 2012 – 2015, 41. Available at: <http://ec.europa.eu/europ2020/pdf/nd/nrp/2012_greece_en.pdf> Accessed 8/3/2013

Further Reforms

• A programme to assess the justification and proportionality of rules which reserve certain professional activities to those with particular professional qualifications has been established .[103]

• Several interim studies looking at methods of increasing competition and reducing prices for regulated professional services have been carried out, and further studies are ongoing.[104]

• A programme aimed at removing the exclusive rights of certain professionals to provide particular services and which also seeks to remove unjustifiable, exclusive rights for the provision of certain services, either jointly or in partnership, has been established.

According to the most recent Troika Review in Greece, much work remains to be done on implementing regulatory reform of the legal profession.[105] There have been delays in the removal of entry restrictions, minimum service fees and the mandatory use of services, which were scheduled for completion in November and December 2012, but which are now instead due to be addressed during the course of 2013.[106] Further reforms to be implemented in the course of the next eighteen months include:

• The adoption of a new Code for Lawyers to provide for 'the research of mortgage books and land registry'

• The completion of a study of the twenty largest professions to examine the extent to which they have been liberalised, including with regard to new entrants and price changes.[107]

4.4.4 The Response of the Greek Legal Profession to the Troika Reforms

According to Adanopoulos, the effect of these structural reforms has been that fees for legal services must now be freely negotiated with clients, without reference to any fixed minimum thresholds. Legal services now attract the imposition of VAT so that lawyers are treated by the tax regime in the same manner as any other 'freelancer or merchant'.[108] Greece's provisional lawyers are particularly concerned about the impact of the removal of the geographical restrictions on practice. Nikolaos Pagidas, the head of the Bar Association in Syros has argued that lawyers are struggling to survive because, 'with the memo-

---

[103] Ibid 41

[104] Ibid 41

[105] IMF, 'Greece: Fourth Review Under the Extended Arrangement Under the Extended Fund Facility, and Request for Waivers of Applicability and Modification of Performance Criterion-Staff Report; Staff Statement; Press Release; and Statement by the Executive Director for Greece', July 2013 (Report No 13/241). Available at: <http://www.imf.org/external/pubs/ft/scr/2013/cr13241.pdf> Accessed 29/8/2013

[106] Ibid 56. 'Greece: Implementation of Structural Reforms'.

[107] Ibid 58. 'Greece: Selected Structural Reforms Ahead, 2013-14'.

[108] G Adanopoulos, 'The Legal Profession in Greece' (FN 90)

randum, with regulations that do not exist anywhere else in Europe, the government is harming lawyers'.[109] According to Tzotzadini:

> The [financial crimes] squad is raiding the offices of bar associations preparing protest action, in a bid to cow them, but it leaves alone those who never pay taxes... It's obvious they have chosen to blacken the image of the whole profession to serve their communication needs.[110]

Although the Greek bar associations may well be experiencing pressures from the authorities, given the similarity of the Troika's reforms in Greece, Portugal and Ireland, there is little merit to the proposition that the Greek Memorandum of Understanding has resulted in regulations which do not exist elsewhere in Europe. The following section will consider the regulation of the legal profession in yet another bailed-out country, Portugal, which will illustrate that the Greek legal profession is not presently being subject to a reform agenda without parallel internationally.

4.5 The Regulation of the Legal Profession in Portugal

The legal profession in Portugal consists of lawyers, legal agents, enforcement agents, notaries and registrars.[111] In Portugal only lawyers may represent clients in legal matters or provide legal advice for a fee.[112] All lawyers must be registered with their professional association which is the Portuguese Bar Association (PBA).[113] Lawyers are servants of both justice and the law, and they play a key role in the administration of justice. In representing their clients, they must abide by the rules of professional ethics which require the maintenance of independence and objectivity in the course of their activities, whilst also complying with their legal duties and those which arise from custom, practice and tradition.

Legal Agents (LAs) are a class of Portuguese legal professional who provide services for a fee. They must be members of their professional association, the Association of Legal Agents and must practice in accordance with the duties of their profession. In the event that a lawyer is not available in a judicial district, a legal agent may represent a client before a court. A LA may also make a court

---

[109] A Tzotzadini, 'Greek Lawyers Unhappy about New Measures', Greek Reporter.com, 14th Sept 2010. Available at: <http://greece.greekreporter.com/2010/09/14/provincial-lawyers-face-new-tough-measures/> Accessed 20/2/2013

[110] Ibid

[111] Legal professionals such as judges, public prosecutors, justices of the peace and legal officials also belong to the Portuguese legal profession. However, they will not be given further consideration here as they do not provide legal services directly to the public in return for payment of a fee.

[112] Further information about the Portuguese legal profession is available at: <http://ec.europa.eu/civiljustice/legalprof/legal_prof_pr_en.htm> Accessed 21/2/2013

[113] The following categories of lawyers do not need to be registered with the PBA:

- lawyers who are public officials
- lawyers who are in employment and who may provide legal advice to their employer
- teaching staff in law faculties who may provide legal opinions

appearance on behalf of a client provided that no point of law is involved. Portuguese Enforcement Agents (EAs) are also subject to the rules of practice which apply to LAs. Upon the application of a creditor an EA is responsible for the execution of court orders, and they also act as process servers. Under judicial direction they attend to the service of documents, notices and publications. Portuguese notaries are lawyers whose written documents may be relied upon by the public. They have a dual function in so far as they are both public officials responsible for the authentication and storage of official documentation, and are also independent and impartial professionals who provide legal services to the public for payment of a fee. Their practice is licensed by the Office of the Minister for Justice. The use of notarised documents is sometimes mandatory, for instance; where an act must be undertaken by public deed. Portuguese registrars are responsible for the maintenance of public registers including those relating to births, deaths, marriage, adoption, paternity and the establishment of companies. Matters relating to real property, motor vehicles, ships and aircraft are also recorded in registers by registrars. The registrar is responsible for checking and ensuring compliance with the relevant law as far as matters of registration are concerned. Registrars have exclusive competence in matters of compulsory registration.

On 4th May 2011, following in the footsteps of Greece and Ireland, Portugal had recourse to a €78 billion bailout from the Troika, a deal which was negotiated by its caretaker government, under the leadership of the caretaker Prime Minister Jose Socrates. In return for the bailout funds, Portugal committed to a series of austerity measures aimed at reducing its budget deficit from 9.1% in 2011 to 3% by 2013.[114] On 5th May 2011, Dominique Strauss-Kahn, Managing Director of the IMF welcomed the Portuguese economic programme to be implemented in return for the bailout funds, which he described as being built upon three strong measures:

> • A set of pro-growth measures aimed at making the country competitive again and creating jobs ...

> • A set of ambitious fiscal measures needed to reduce the public debt and deficit ...

> • A set of measures aimed at ensuring the stability of Portugal's financial sector.[115]

The Memorandum of Economic and Financial Policies which was attached to Portugal's Letter of Intent of 17th May 2011 to the IMF set out Portugal's commitment to reform the regulated professions as follows:

---

[114] G Tremlett, 'Portugal settles terms of €78 billion bailout with EU and IMF', *The Guardian*, 4th May 2011. Available at: <http://www.guardian.co.uk/business/2011/may/04/portugal-78bn-bailout-lmf> Accessed 21/2/2013

[115] D Strauss-Kahn, Statement on Portugal by IMF Managing Director Dominique Strauss-Kahn and European Commissioner for Economic and Monetary Affairs Olli Rehn (Press Release No 11/162), 5th May 2011, <http://www.imf.org/external/np/sec/pr/2011/pr11162.htm> Accessed 21/2/2013

We will take bold steps to address excessive profits and reduce the scope for rent-seeking behaviour.... We will review and reduce the number of regulated professions (by end-September 2011 for professions not regulated by Parliament and by end-Mar 2012 for all others); eliminate the restrictions on the use of advertising in regulated professions (end-Sept 2011); improve the recognition framework on professional qualifications, ease the requirements related to the establishment of foreign service providers in Portugal; and reduce the number of requirements to which cross-border service providers are subject (end-Dec 2011).[116]

The Memorandum also contained further commitments by Portugal to revise and strengthen its competition law regime, and to establish a new Court to deal with competition matters. It also agreed to implement a widespread series of reforms to its judicial sector to improve efficiency, reduce the backlog in cases and to establish an alternative dispute resolution regime to assist in the reduction of the backlog.[117] In its Memorandum of Understanding on Specific Economic Policy Conditionality accompanying its Letter of Intent of 17th May 2011 Portugal also undertook to improve the functioning of the regulated professions sector, including lawyers and notaries, by carrying out a comprehensive review of the requirements which govern the exercise of such activities, with a view to eliminating those which are not both justified and proportionate. Although the review was to be completed by the end of 2011, this timetable was revised in December 2012, when the Government stated that there would be a "second phase" investigation of the review of regulated professions to eliminate unjustified requirements by the middle of 2013.[118]

To date, and not unlike Ireland, Portugal has not achieved the reform of regulated professions to which it committed in its Memoranda of Understanding, although significant progress is being made. According to The European Commission, more decisive action must be taken by the authorities in order to liberalise access to the regulated professions.[119] However, the Commission has noted that many of the amendments which are needed to secure the full implementation of the Services Directive and to liberalise regulated professions are almost complete.[120] Following the sixth review of Portugal's implementation of its programme of reforms, the Commission estimated that approximately one-

---

[116] Memorandum of Economic and Financial Policies accompanying the Letter of Intent from Fernando Teixeira dos Santos (Minister of State and Finance) and Carlos Silva da Costa (Governor of the Banco de Portugal) to Dominque Strauss-Kahn (Managing Director of the IMF), 17th May 2011, para 41, 16. Available at: <http://www.imf.org/external/np/loi/2011/prt/051711.pdf> Accessed 22/2/2010

[117] Ibid, paras 43 – 48, 16 – 17

[118] Ibid. Memorandum of Understanding on Specific Economic Policy Conditionality, paras 5.28 – 5.34. 61 – 62; IMF 'Portugal: Letter of Intent. Memorandum of Economic and Financial Policies, and Technical Memorandum of Understanding', 19th Dec 2012.

[119] European Commission, 'Commission Staff Working Document: Assessment of the 2012 National Reform Programme and Stability Programme for Portugal', 8. Available at: <http://ec.europa.eu/europe2020/pdf/nd/swd2012_protugal_en.pdf> Accessed 7/3/2013

[120] Ibid 8. The Services Directive. Directive 2006/123/EC of 12th December 2006 on services in the internal market.

third of amendments which are necessary in order for Portugal to fully comply with the Services Directive were still pending.[121]

The Portuguese Government commenced a second phase of its review of regulated professions in 2013 which seeks to remove entry barriers to regulated professions which are no longer justified and appropriate.[122] According to the IMF's latest review of Portugal, a new legal framework to improve the functioning of regulated professions, including lawyers and notaries, has recently been published. This states that the professional bodies' statutes are being amended, with the removal of unjustified entry restrictions, and the facilitation of mobility in accordance with EU directives in the area of free movement of professionals.[123]

4.6 The Response of International Lawyers' Bodies to the Troika's intervention in the Regulation of the Legal Profession in Bailed-Out Countries

It is clear that one part of the price paid by bailed-out European states, in return for their bailout funds, was a commitment to liberalise their regulated professions, including the legal profession. A pattern has emerged in the Memoranda of Understanding which were agreed by Greece, Ireland and Portugal with the Troika, as far as the opening up of what were deemed to be 'sheltered sectors' of these economies.[124] The reality is that, "[e]xternal supra-national agencies are telling governments how to regulate their professions".[125] Professions and the rule of law are seen as key to helping countries raise their economic standards, especially if they want to participate in global markets. According to Flood, the blueprint for the 'liberalisation' revolution has been the changes which were introduced to the UK legal services market following the Clementi review, a key example of which is the introduction of ABSs. The changes which the bailout countries have agreed to implement will facilitate the adoption of new forms of practice structures, introducing greater choice and flexibility in the manner in which legal services are delivered. The Troika programme also aims to remove entry barriers to the legal profession, and to secure the removal of barriers to freedom to provide services within the European Union. The liberalisation programme, if fully implemented, is supposed to reduce the cost of legal

---

[121] European Commission, 'The Economic Adjustment Programme for Portugal: Sixth Review – Autumn 2012'. European Economy. Occasional Papers 124 December 2012, 14. Available at: <http://peprobe.org/peprobe-library/document/5500/2012-12-21_The_Economic _Adjustment_Programme_for_Portugal_6th_Review.pdf> Accessed 8/3/2013

[122] Ibid, para 70, 27.

[123] IMF, 'Portugal: Seventh Review Under the Extended Arrangement and Request for Modification of End-June Performance Criteria. Staff Report; Press Release on the Executive Board Discussion', and Statement by the Executive Director for Portugal (Report No 13/160), June 2013, para 31. Available at: <http://www.imf.org/external/pubs/ft/scr/2013/cr13160.pdf> Accessed 26/8/2013

[124] J Flood, 'When the Troika comes to the Rescue', *Iberian Lawyer*, 9th July 2012. Available at: <http://www.iberianlawyer.com/panorama/3622-when-the-troika-come-to-the-rescue> Accessed 20/2/2013

[125] Ibid

services for consumers and businesses alike, thereby contributing to the attainment of greater efficiency and competitiveness in the economies of bailed-out member states, whilst also supporting the rule of law by facilitating easier, more affordable access to the justice system for citizens. However, it is too soon to judge the impact of the reforms, as they have yet to be fully implemented in any of the three bailed-out jurisdictions considered herein.

The regulatory reform of the legal professions which has swept across Europe on foot of the Troika's intervention has provoked a storm of opposition on the part of legal professionals throughout Europe. This groundswell of opposition is illustrated most aptly by the letter of the 21st December 2011 from the CCBE and the ABA to Christine Lagarde, Managing Director of the IMF.[126] With regard to the proposed reforms of the legal profession and the legal services market in Greece, Ireland and Portugal, they wrote as follows:

> We write to you on behalf of the Council of Bars and Law Societies of Europe (CCBE) and the American Bar Association (ABA) to convey our growing concern about disturbing trends affecting the independence of the legal profession. An independent legal profession is a critical component of a well-functioning judiciary and is the keystone of a democratic society based on the rule of law. Pressure to undermine the independence of the legal profession is not only a matter of concern to lawyers and judges, but to people everywhere as this independence is critical to the fair and equal protection of human rights, the development of healthy economies, and the facilitation of political stability ... The proposed reforms are plainly inconsistent with the Core Principles of the Legal Profession – as reflected in the CCBE Charter of Core Principles and as adopted by the ABA House of Delegates in 2006 – that commits the legal profession to "An independent legal profession without which there is no rule of law or freedom for the people". ... We believe that independent regulation, conceptually, must be seen as a logical and natural consequence of the independence of the profession.... We are concerned that all these developments will lead to an erosion of the administration of justice. They will not only affect the structure of the legal profession and the lawyer's role in society, but most importantly will be to the detriment of all people who need a lawyer.[127]

The letter concluded with an appeal to Ms Lagarde, given her previous role as a partner in a multi-national law firm, to pass on the representative bodies' concerns to the Troika.

In its reply of 3rd February 2012 to the CCBE and the ABA, the IMF acknowledged the important place of the rule of law in establishing a positive business and investment environment, and asserted that the IMF programmes for loan recipients were designed to underpin the rule of law by encouraging the devel-

---

[126] Letter from Geroges-Albert Dal (CCBE President) and William T (Bill) Robinson III (ABA President) to Christine Lagarde, Managing Director of the IMF, 21st Dec 2011. Available at: <http://www.ccbe.eu/fileadmin/user_upload/NTCdocument/CCBE_and_ABA_letter_1_1325 686329.pdf> Accessed 7/3/2013

[127] Ibid 1 – 3

opment of strong, independent institutions 'including the judiciary and the legal profession'.[128] The IMF also stated that the Irish government had agreed to amend the LSRB 2011 in response to the profession's concerns regarding the independence of the LSRA from executive interference, and attached a letter from the Department of Justice and Equality to the IMF confirming the nature of the proposed reforms to the Bill, which are aimed at ensuring the new regulatory authority will have both actual and perceived independence from the executive branch of the government.[129]

The IMF correspondence with the regulatory bodies aptly illustrates the sensitivities which have been exposed by the far-reaching programmes of fiscal and sectoral reforms demanded by the Troika in return for the Greek, Irish and Portuguese bailouts. It would appear that the Troika has used the economic crisis as an opportunity to further its long-established agenda for liberalisation and deregulation of professional services in the European Union.[130] This view is supported by the similarity of the core reforms which were sought in the three bailed-out European Union member states, and which are indicative of the underlying liberalising agenda supporting the Troika's reform programmes. It is notable that the academic community has not generally supported the position of the representative bodies in their argument with the Troika regarding the reform of legal services. Scott has noted that the government appointment of regulators for the legal profession is common practice internationally, for example a similar system for such appointment is used in England, Wales and Australia.[131] He has also observed that the legal profession is dependent upon the state as the main purchaser of legal services, for instance; in relation to the criminal justice system. The question arises as to whether this relationship may not serve to compromise the independence of the legal profession just as much as the government appointment of the profession's regulator might also serve to undermine it?

Flood has argued that the liberalisation agenda, if adopted, may bring rewards for the 'PI(I)GS' countries (Portugal, Ireland, Italy, Greece and Spain) as they will be able to actively participate in a global market for legal services if they persevere with their deregulation programmes.[132] He argues that the Troika is challenging longstanding processes of 'professional closure' which serve to

---

[128] Letter from Sean Hagan (General Council of the Legal Department of the IMF) to the CCBE and ABA, of 3rd February 2012. Available at:
<http://www.lawlibrary.ie/documents/views_events/IMFResponseToCCBEABALetter030220 12.pdf> Accessed 7/3/2013

[129] Letter from Richard Fallon, Principal Officer, Civil Law Reform Division, Department of Justice and Equality to Sean Hagan, IMF. 31st January 2012. Attached to the letter from IMF to CCBE and ABA, 3rd February 2012 (FN 128).

[130] The EU project for liberalisation of the professions in member states was described in ch 2 §§ 2.1 – 2.2.

[131] Letter from Colin Scott to *Irish Times*, 12th December 2011. Available at:
<http://www.irishtimes.com/newspaper/letters/2011/1209/1224308/986/6.html> Accessed 2/3/2013

[132] J Flood, Blog, 'PI(I)GS Might Fly!', 6th January 2012. John Flood's Random Academic Thoughts (RATS). Available at: <http://johnflood.blogspot.ie/2012/01/piigs-might-fly.html> Accessed 23/2/2013

exclude many individuals who lack the requisite 'social capital' from the ranks of the legal profession.[133] In Flood's opinion, the Troika is demanding 'proper regulation and accountability which lawyers have [thus far] avoided'.[134]

4.7 To What Extent Have the Troika Reforms Been Implemented?

An examination of the most recent Troika reviews for Ireland, Greece and Portugal reveals that the legal profession has been somewhat intransigent in the face of the Troika's pressures to reform.

According to the most recent Troika review, Ireland has committed to the reform of its legal services insofar as, "[o]nce the relevant legislation has been enacted, the authorities will take the appropriate measures to establish the LSRA in an expedited fashion".[135] This commitment falls somewhat short of the government's commitment in 2010 to the effect that by the end of the third quarter of 2011 the Government would introduce legislative changes to remove restrictions to trade and competition in sheltered sectors, including the legal profession.[136] The most recent commitment does not tie the Government to any particular timetable for the enactment of legislation, which is probably prudent given the pace of progress of the LSRB 2011 through the legislature thus far.

In Greece, the Troika has fared little better in achieving its liberalisation goals in the market for legal services, notwithstanding the removal of geographical restrictions upon lawyers within Greece. The majority of the Troika reforms remain unimplemented. In its most recent Technical Memorandum of Understanding, the Greek Government indicated that the following restrictions were to be eliminated by legislation, by the end of July 2013 by means of changes to Lawyers' Codes and also by Presidential Decree:

(i) ease the re-entry into the legal professions

(ii) repeal age limit to take the Bar examinations

(iii) abolish total bans on commercial communications

(iv) provide for licenses of unlimited duration

(v) remove the reference to 'exclusivity' for lawyers for the research of books of mortgage and land registry

(vi) clarify that lawyers' fees are freely determined through a written agreement between lawyers and clients (in cases where there is no written agreement for court appearances, reference fees still apply)

---

[133] Ibid

[134] Ibid

[135] IMF, 'Ireland: Tenth Review under the Extended Arrangement', Country Report No 13/163. Attachment IV. Memorandum of Understanding on Specific Economic Policy Conditionality (European Commission). Actions for the Thirteenth Review (actions to be completed by end of Q4-2013), para 61. Available at: <www.imf.org/external/pubs/cat/longres.aspx?sk=40686.0> Accessed 29/8/2013

[136] The Memorandum of Understanding on Specific Economic Policy Conditionality, attached to Ireland's Letter of Intent to the IMF, 31st October 2010. Available at: <http://www.imf.org/external/np.loi/2010/irl/120310.pdf> Accessed 29/1/2013

(vii)   eliminate any kind of minimum wages for salaried lawyers working in the private sector

(viii) de-link contributions paid by lawyers from lawyer's [sic] reference amounts for contracts and eliminates [sic] those reference amounts, and

(ix)   set a system of prepaid fixed/contract sums for each procedural act or court appearance by a lawyer, which is not linked to a specific 'reference amount'.[137]

It is unclear at the time of writing whether these targets have been met.[138] However, the above list of reforms indicates that the pace of reform in the Greek legal sector remains painfully slow.

Like its bailed-out counterparts, the Portuguese legal profession has yet to yield to the Troika's demands for liberalisation. According to its latest Memorandum of Understanding:

> A new legal framework aimed at improving the functioning of the regulated professions (such as accountants, lawyers, notaries) for which regulation involves a professional body was recently published. The professional bodies' statutes are being amended accordingly for approval by Parliament, including by eliminating unjustified restrictions to activity and further improving the conditions for mobility of professions in line with EU Directives in the area of free movement of professions.[139]

Once again, although there is some movement in the direction of the Troika liberalisation agenda, it has yet to be fully implemented.

It is evident that the legal professions in Ireland, Greece and Portugal are presently in a state of transition. They are all being subject to the same liberalisation experiment in the Troika's laboratory, and the outcome is as yet unknown. The concluding section of this chapter seeks to identify the best regulatory practices in the jurisdictions which have been considered herein, the extent to which these have influenced the LSRB 2011 and whether the Bill should be further amended to reflect best practice internationally.

4.8 Concluding Remarks

This chapter has examined the manner in which other jurisdictions regulate their legal professions and the provision of legal services, in order to inform a view as to what changes if any should be made to the LSRB 2011 prior to its enactment. It has looked at the choices that have been made in that regard by our nearest neighbour Northern Ireland, which following the publication of the Bain Report, has opted to preserve the key elements of its traditional system of self-regulating the legal profession. The retention of self-regulation in Northern

---

[137] IMF, 'Greece: Technical Memorandum of Understanding', 17th July 2013. Attached to the 'Fourth Review' (FN 105).

[138] The fifth Troika Review for Greece (as per the extended arrangement, under the extended fund facility), the results of which are due to be published in October 2013, may clarify the position in this regard.

[139] IMF, 'Portugal: Seventh Review' (FN 123), para 31

Ireland on foot of the Bain recommendations is regrettable for its citizens, and also for the administration of justice therein. The problems associated with self-regulation have been the subject of considerable academic research.[140] Bain's justification for the preservation of self-regulation on the grounds that Northern Ireland is a small jurisdiction lacks conviction, having no basis in evidence, either academic or empirical. It must be concluded that there is nothing within Northern Ireland's legal regulatory framework, either in its present form, or following the implementation of Bain's recommendations, which might usefully influence amendment of the LSRB 2011.

The far-reaching reforms which were introduced in England and Wales following the Clementi Review have provided a thought-provoking example upon which to reflect as Ireland contemplates the finer details of the Bill. The regulatory framework in England and Wales has been revolutionised in recent years following the publication of the Clementi Review and the enactment of the LSA 2007. At a time of regulatory transition in Ireland, the Clementi Report has been most valuable in setting out the various regulatory options available, and in identifying their strengths and weaknesses. In the Irish context this has facilitated the debate about which regulatory model is most suited to the needs of our jurisdiction. Whereas the British Government opted for Clementi's Model B+, which required the separation of the regulatory and representative functions of front-line bodies, and the oversight of those regulatory bodies by the LSB, this model would not be appropriate in Ireland, given the smaller size of our jurisdiction and our legal profession.[141] England and Wales has a much more diverse range of legal professionals than Ireland, with eight different types of practitioner, including legal executives, licensed conveyancers, patent attorneys and notaries. Given the diversity of their associated regulatory bodies, it is prudent to have an oversight body such as the LSB to oversee their operation. Ireland, on the other hand has only two branches to its legal profession, and in the circumstances, the costs associated with the establishment of an oversight regulator would be excessive. Clementi's Model A format, which entails the removal of regulatory powers from front-line bodies such as the LSI and the BCI and divesting them in an independent body, forms the basis of the regulatory framework in the LSRB 2011. Also, the introduction of ABSs in England and Wales in accordance with the LSA 2007 offers an example of the opportunities and challenges which might accompany this particular innovation.

The English experience of ABSs most probably influenced the Minister for Justice to include provision for them in the LSRB 2011, and he may also have been persuaded of their merits by the Australian ABS experience. The latter experience also provides us with valuable insights into the effect of deregulating the types of business structures which can be adopted by legal practices, and affords a glimpse of what the future may hold for Ireland if it should follow suit. There is no evidence to suggest that the introduction of MDPs and incorporated legal practices in Australia has been associated with a decline in professional legal standards. On the contrary, given that the self-assessment method for

---

[140] For a discussion of self-regulation, see ch 3 § 3.2.5.

[141] The alternative regulatory models identified by Clementi are discussed in ch 4 § 4.2.2.

practice management systems in incorporated legal practices has resulted in a decline in the level of client complaints, the LSRB 2011 might usefully be amended to provide for the introduction of a similar self-assessment system for legal practices in Ireland.[142]

The regulation of the legal profession in Greece and Portugal, and the changes which are currently being experienced in our fellow bailed-out members of the European Union illustrate the common thread which has united the Troika reform programmes with regard to 'sheltered professions' such as the legal profession. It would appear that a central theme of the Troika's intervention is to increase competition in the professional services sector through removal of artificial restrictions to trade, including barriers to entry to the professions, minimum fee schedules and prohibitions on advertising. It is not yet possible to judge the efficacy of the Troika's efforts in this regard given that the bailed-out member states are still in the process of implementing the requisite changes. The chapter also considered the response of the international representatives of the legal profession to the Troika reforms. This illustrated the depth of hostility to the reforms, and was characterised by a staunch defence of the regulatory *status quo* in the affected jurisdictions, and the interpretation of the reform programme as a direct attack upon both the independence of the legal profession and the rule of law.

A perusal of Troika reform programmes for the regulation of the legal professions in Greece and Portugal indicates that these jurisdictions are being subjected to a similar liberalisation regime as that which is being imposed upon the legal profession in Ireland. These reforms are aimed at increasing competition within the professions, enhancing consumer choice and reducing the cost of legal services. The similarity of the Troika reform packages which have been considered above does not accord with the recent statement of the IMF Managing Director who observed, "[i]f there is one thing that we learned from the crisis is [sic] that it cannot be a one-size-fits-all policy mix. It's very peculiar to each set of circumstances, it's very particular to the state of development the countries are in".[143] Contrary to Ms Lagarde's assertion, if there is one thing which can be learned from the comparison of the Troika structural reforms in Greece, Portugal and Ireland it is that a one-size-fits-all policy mix has indeed been imposed upon these legal professions.

Whereas Greece, Portugal and Ireland have not yet completed the implementation of their reform agendas, it is too early to assess whether the Troika programme has been effective in achieving its goals. The LSRB 2011 is the mechanism for the implementation of the Troika reforms in Ireland, and provided it is not radically weakened by subsequent amendment prior to its enactment, it promises, in due course to revolutionise the legal services market in Ireland. The following chapter will examine the provisions of the LSRB 2011 and the response of the key stakeholders to its publication. It will also consider the

---

[142] For a further discussion of this suggested amendment to the LSRB 2011, see ch 5 § 5.7.

[143] IMF, 'Transcript of a Press Roundtable with IMF Managing Director Christine Lagarde', 1st August 2013. Available at: <www.imf.org/external/np/tr/2013/tr080113a.htm> Accessed 30/8/2013

stakeholders' proposed amendments to the Bill and make further suggestions as to how it may be improved.

5

THE LEGAL SERVICES REGULATION BILL 2011

5.0 Introduction

This chapter focuses upon the Legal Services Regulation Bill 2011, and the response of the Irish legal profession to its publication. It commences with a consideration of the reasons for the Bill's publication, with particular emphasis upon the structural reforms which the Irish Government agreed to implement in return for receipt of the bailout funds from the Troika. The Memorandum of Understanding which accompanied Ireland's Letter of Intent to the Troika in December 2010, committed Ireland to the implementation of the outstanding recommendations of the Competition Authority Report on Legal Services 2006 and the Legal Cost Working Group 2003.[1] The LSRB 2011 is considered here in the context of those recommendations. The provisions of the Bill are described in detail and the key changes to the existing system of regulation are identified. The publication of the Bill in October 2011 gave rise to a considerable controversy within the legal profession. This chapter examines the responses of both the legal profession and other key stakeholders to the Bill's publication. Finally, the probable amendments which may be made to the Bill are considered and suggestions for further amendments are also made.

The LSRB 2011 will introduce the most fundamental reform of the legal profession since the foundation of the state. With the establishment of the Legal Services Regulation Authority (LSRA), it will replace the traditional self-regulatory system with an independent system of regulation, a reform which will benefit the profession and the consumer of legal services alike. The establishment of the Legal Practitioners' Disciplinary Tribunal (LPDT), which is also to be welcomed will provide a forum for the independent investigation of clients' complaints. Finally, the Office of the Legal Costs Adjudicator will bring greater transparency to the issue of legal costs, which is most desirable from the perspective of legal services users. A list of proposed amendments has recently been published, following the Committee Stage of the Bill's passage, many of which

---

[1] *Report on Legal Services: Solicitors and Barristers* (The Competition Authority, December 2006); *Report of the Legal Costs Working Group* (Stationery Office, Dublin, 2003). The report is available at: <http://www.justice.ie/en/JELR/leglalcosts.pdf/Files/legalcosts.pdf > Accessed 18/9/2012; The Memorandum of Understanding between the Troika and Ireland may be accessed at: IMF Ireland: Letter of Intent, Memorandum of Economic and Financial Policies, and Technical Memorandum of Understanding 3rd Dec 2010. Available at: <http://www.imf.org/external/np/loi/2010/irl/120310.pdf> Accessed 14/6/2012

would considerably reduce the Minister for Justice's involvement with the LSRA and its functioning. Some of the proposed amendments replace the Minister's role with a form of judicial oversight, whilst others replace it with oversight either by the Minister for Public Expenditure and Reform or an Oireachtas Committee.[2] However, given that the final form of the Bill is not known at the time of writing, it is not possible to comment categorically upon it, or to fully assess its impact on the present regulatory system.

5.1 Background to the Publication of the Legal Services Regulation Bill 2011

In return for the bailout funds which Ireland requested from the Troika in December 2010, Ireland not only committed to reform of its financial and banking sectors, it also undertook to remove 'structural impediments' to Ireland's competitiveness and its prospects for employment creation.[3] The Memorandum of Understanding on Specific Economic Policy Conditionality which was attached to the IMF/EU Letters of Intent outlined the structural reforms to be implemented by the end of the third quarter of 2011:

> Government will introduce legislative changes to remove restrictions to trade and competition in sheltered sections including:
>
>> — the legal profession, establishing an independent regulator for the profession and implementing the recommendations of the Legal Costs Working Group and outstanding Competition Authority recommendations to reduce legal costs.[4]

The LSRB 2011 is the Government's chosen mechanism for meeting the state's obligations concerning the legal profession as contained in the aforementioned Memorandum of Understanding and the Government's National Recovery Plan, both of which identified the provision of legal services as a sheltered sector in need of radical reform.[5] The National Recovery Plan committed the Government to a programme of fiscal consolidation measures, by means of a series of budgets until 2014, which will consistently cut spending and increase tax revenue. It also set out a strategy for competitiveness, growth and employment, in which cost competitiveness will be improved, "by a series of specific measures in the waste, energy, transport, telecommunications, professional

---

[2] Dáil Éireann, Legal Services Regulation Bill 2011. Committee Amendments, 13th July 2013. Available at: <www.oireachtas.ie/viewdoc.asp?fn=/documents/bills28/bills/2011/5811/b5811d-dscn.pdf> Accessed 1/8/2013

[3] The Memorandum of Understanding on Specific Economic Policy Conditionality, attached to Ireland's Letter of Intent to the IMF, 3rd December 2010. Available at: <http://www.imf.org/external/np.loi/2010/irl/120310.pdf> Accessed 29/1/2013

[4] Ibid 27

[5] The National Recovery Plan 2011 – 2014 was a part of the Irish Government's strategy for putting the nation's finances on a stable footing, according to the Letter of Intent, 3rd December 2010, para 3 (FN 1). The National Recovery Plan 2011 – 2014 is available at: <http://www.budget.gov.ie/The%20National%20Recovery%20Plan%202011-2014.pdf > Accessed 29/1/2013

services and public administration sectors".[6] The specific commitments in relation to professional services in the Plan are as follows:

• Competition in the professions will be promoted and overseen by an independent figure, reporting regularly to Government

• Provide for a more structured approach to mediation in the legal system and promote further use of Alternative Dispute Resolution taking account of recommendations of the Law Reform Commission in its Final Report 2010 on the subject

• A package of measures to reduce legal costs will be implemented including

— increased use of tendering by the State

— prioritizing publication and enactment of the Legal Costs Bill

— additional proposals for legislation to reduce legal costs, drawing on the recommendations of the Legal Costs Working Group and the Competition Authority

— provide for increased use of arbitration and mediation[7]

The Programme for Government 2011 – 2016 also contains several commitments in relation to the legal services sector which have come to fruition in the LSRB 2011:

We will establish independent regulation of the legal professions to improve access and competition, make legal costs more transparent and ensure adequate procedures for addressing consumer complaints.[8]

The Programme for Government 2011 – 2016 contains a further commitment to spread the Government's requirements for legal services amongst a wider pool of service providers:

We intend to end the heavy dependence on a very limited pool of extremely expensive private solicitors' firms providing legal services to the State and agencies, look at ways to require agencies to seek legal advice from the CSSO [Chief State Solicitors Office] and not from the private sector in order to save costs, and ensure that legal work at the bar for the State is spread more equitably rather than confined to a very limited pool as at

---

[6] Ibid 29

[7] Ibid 33. The Legal Costs Bill referred to in the The National Recovery Plan 2011 – 2014 was neither published nor enacted.

[8] 'Programme for Government 2011 – 2016' (Government for National Recovery 2011 – 2016: Law Reform, Courts and Judiciary), 51. Available at: <http:www.socialjustice/sites/defaut/ files/file/Government%20Docs%20etc/2011-13-06%20-%20Programme%20for %20Government%202011-2016.pdf> Accessed 29/1/2013

present. We will progress the Statute Law Review Project in order to en-hance public accessibility to the statute book.[9]

The Minister for Justice, Equality and Defence, Alan Shatter, has endeav-oured to trace the origins of the Bill not only to the Memorandum of Under-standing, and other statements of Government policy as identified above, but also to the current climate which is characterized by a 'change imperative'.[10] He has pointed to processes of change, both incremental and radical, which are taking place in many sectors of society, the combined effect of which create a unique environment nowadays, unlike any previous era, particularly in relation to the challenges that these processes present to the legal professions. Minister Shatter argued that there has been a blurring of inter-professional boundaries as a result of the emergence of new technologies and new kinds of knowledge.[11] This has given rise to struggles between professions such as lawyers, accountants and investment bankers for jurisdictional control over emerging fields of service provision. Other manifestations of change include the emergence of global financial difficulties and Irish economic problems which have combined to create unique challenges for Irish businesses.[12] It is within this context of radical change that the Government has undertaken to overhaul the regulation of the legal profession and the provision of legal services, with a view to establishing a dynamic and modern profession, capable of meeting the demands of the legal services market in the twenty-first century.

The legal services sector has traditionally been sheltered, as a result of self-regulation, the profession's allegiance to traditional practice models and a lack of transparency with regard to costs. The Memorandum of Understanding, the Legal Costs Working Group, The Competition Authority and the Programme for Government all identify the sheltered nature of the legal services market as problematic.[13] A sheltered legal services market leads not only to artificially high costs for businesses, but it also arguably threatens the rule of law, as private

---

[9] Ibid ('Government for National Recovery 2011 – 2016: We Will Overhaul the Way Politics and Government Work', 21.)

[10] A Shatter, Minister for Justice, Equality and Defence, Speech, 'Regulation, Representation and the Future of the Legal Profession', 14th April 2012. Legal Services Regulation Bill 2011 Law Society Annual Conference. Available at: <http://www.justice.ie/en/JELR/Pages/SP12000102> Accessed 7/1/2013

[11] Ibid. Citing M Sako, 'Global Strategies in the Legal Services Marketplace: Institutional Impacts on Value Chain Dynamics' (July 2009). Available at: <http://www.sbs.ox.ac.uk/research/people/Documents/Mari%20Sako//Global%20Strategies %20by%20LPO%20paper%20June2010.pdf> Accessed 29/1/2013

[12] For a thorough exposition of the myriad forces of change which are impacting upon the legal profession and the legal services market, see R Susskind, *Tomorrow's Lawyers: An Introduction to Your Future* (Oxford University Press, 2013).

[13] The Memorandum of Understanding 3rd December 2010 (FN 3), 27; *Report of the Legal Costs Working Group* (FN 1) Executive Summary 11 – 25. The report is available at: <http://www.justice.ie/en/JELR/leglalcosts.pdf/Files/legalcosts.pdf> Accessed 18/9/2012; *Report on Legal Services: Solicitors and Barristers* (FN 1), Executive Summary i – xviii; 'Programme for Government 2011 – 2016' (FN 8), 51.

consumers become increasingly unable to access legal services at an affordable price. A key test for the Bill will therefore be whether it succeeds in increasing consumer choice for both business and private individuals, and whether it makes legal services available in a more competitive costs environment.

Viewed in this light, it is unsurprising that the primary aim of the LSRB 2011 is to expose the legal sector to more competition. Murtagh has rightly argued that the Troika Agreement 'identifies competition policy as an essential tool to assist Ireland's economic recovery'.[14] This approach is evident from the inclusion of the Competition Authority's recommendations from its 2006 Report on the Legal Professions within the Memorandum of Understanding; the recommendations to be implemented, along with other wide-ranging financial and structural reforms, in return for the bailout funds. Whereas the Competition Authority found itself languishing during the deepening financial crisis in Ireland as the Government failed to engage positively with it, the arrival of the Troika has seen its star once more in the ascendant, in recognition of its potential as an instrument to rectify systemic weaknesses in sheltered sectors, such as legal services, pharmacy and medical services.[15] As Murtagh has observed, 'the [Competition] Authority's relationship with the Troika appears to have given it a renewed sense of purpose and reinvigoration'.[16] However, given that the LSRB 2011 has yet to be enacted, and may face significant amendment prior to its enactment, it is not yet possible to assess the Troika's effectiveness as an agent for change in the market for legal services. The following section will provide a detailed description of the provisions of the LSRB 2011.

5.2 The Provisions of the Legal Services Regulation Bill 2011

Contrary to the Government's declared intention to reduce the number of state bodies, the LSRB 2011 provides for the establishment of five new regulatory bodies, which are:

- The Legal Services Regulatory Authority (LSRA),

- The Legal Practitioners Disciplinary Tribunal (LPDT)

- The Office of The Legal Costs Adjudicator (the OLCA)

- The Complaints Committee of the LSRA

- The Advisory Committee on the Grants of Patents of Precedence.[17]

These new regulatory bodies are illustrated in Diagram 4, to follow.

---

[14] A Murtagh, 'Irish Competition Policy under the EU/IMF Spotlight' [2012] *Competition Law* 62 – 76, 62

[15] Ibid 66. The Government's failure to engage actively with the Competition Authority in the past is illustrated by its lack of progress in implementing the recommendations of the *Report on Legal Services* (FN 1).

[16] Ibid 68

[17] Department of Public Expenditure and Reform, 'Rationalistation of State Agencies', available at: <reformplan.per.gov.ie/appendix-ii-rationalsation-of-state-agencies/> Accessed 3/8/2013

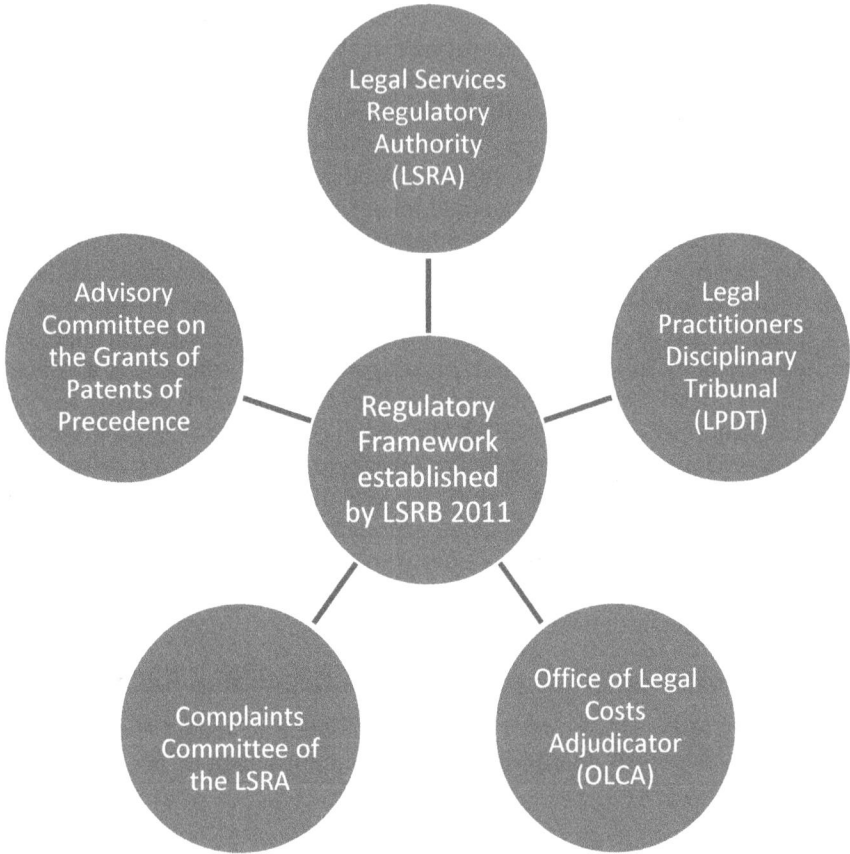

Diagram 4. Five new regulatory bodies to be established following the enactment of the Legal Services Regulation Bill 2011

The Bill sets out the regulatory objectives of the new LSRA, as follows:

The Authority shall, in performing its functions of the regulation of the provision of legal services under this Act, have regard to the objectives of –

(a) protecting and promoting the public interest,

(b) supporting the proper and effective administration of justice,

(c) protecting and promoting the interests of consumers relating to the provision of legal services,

(d) promoting competition in the provision of legal services in the State,

(e) encouraging an independent, strong and effective legal profession, and

(f) promoting and maintaining adherence to the professional principles specified in subsection (5) [These professional principles require legal practitioners to act with independence and integrity, to act in the best interests of their clients and to maintain proper standards of work. Legal practitioners must also comply with their duties to courts, and, subject to professional obligations and those arising as officers of the court, they must maintain client confidentiality.][18]

There is a considerable degree of overlap between the regulatory objectives of the LSRA and Terry's list of suggested objectives, which is commendable, particularly given the tight time constraints facing the drafters of the Bill. Section 9 of the Bill which includes both the protection and promotion of the public interest extends the parameters of Terry's ideal list of objectives which refers only to the protection of the public interest. It therefore adopts a more positive, proactive approach towards the public interest, as opposed to considering it only when it comes under attack. Both sets of objectives also promote adherence to professional principles, and encourage or support lawyer independence. The LSRB 2011 has adopted a similarly proactive approach towards consumers' interests, by expressly promoting both their protection and promotion.[19] This is in contrast to Terry, whose ideal objectives include only the protection of clients' interests.

Whereas the LSRB 2011 refers to the protection and promotion of the interests of *consumers* of legal services, Terry's ideal objectives include increasing *clients'* access to justice. Whilst both of these objectives have a similar effect as regards users of legal services, there is an interesting difference in emphasis in their use of language. The choice of 'consumer' rather than 'client' in the Bill arguably constitutes an inherent challenge to lawyers' professionalism. If a lawyer is perceived as just another service provider, there is little justification for maintaining reserved areas of practice. However, where there exists a unique bond of trust and confidence between lawyer and client, and where a lawyer always acts in the best interests of his/her client, then there is a justification of professional status. This higher standard pertaining to the legal practitioner is explicitly included in the LSRB 2011, and may be contrasted with the lesser onus upon the 'ordinary' service provider as contained in Sale of Goods and Supply of Services Act 1980.[20] There is a danger that lawyers' professional status may be

---

[18] LSRB 2011 § 9 (4)

[19] Ibid

[20] The Sale of Goods and Supply of Services Act 1980 § 39 (b) requires the service provider to act with due skill, care and diligence when providing services, which is arguably a less onerous requirement than the obligation in the LSRB § 9 (5) (ii), which requires that a legal practitioner *shall* act in a client's best interests.

mortally injured in the event that legal services are relegated to business transactions, and where clients are replaced by consumers. For instance, whilst it may
be difficult to justify the denial of *consumer* choice which is a consequence of
reserved areas of practice, it is easier to justify this as a *client* protection measure
that safeguards high quality service provision. The consumer emphasis in the
Bill is also evident in its overt promotion of competition in the provision of legal
services, which is notable by its absence from Terry's ideal list of objectives.

Parts 2, 3 and 4 of the Bill concern the LSRA, whose function is to regulate
the provision of services by legal practitioners, and to ensure the maintenance
and improvement of standards in the provision of legal services.[21] The majority
of its members will be lay persons.[22] Its remit includes the review and regulation
of the following:

- Procedures for admission to the legal profession

- The availability and quality of education and training of legal professionals

- The specification of rules relating to professional indemnity insurance.[23]

The Authority is authorised to publish Codes of Practice for the legal profession, and to approve such codes as may be prepared by legal professional bodies,
subject to Ministerial approval.[24] It is also authorised to appoint Inspectors with
powers to enter the place of business of a legal practitioner for the purpose of
examining documents, and to obtain access to details of bank accounts opened
by legal practitioners.[25] The Authority is also responsible for the preparation of a
report to the Minister for Justice regarding the possible unification of the professions of solicitors and barristers.[26] It will oversee the regulation and supervision of accounts held by legal practitioners, and is responsible for matters
concerning the protection of clients. It may make regulations requiring legal
practitioners to maintain professional indemnity insurance, and may specify
minimum levels of insurance which must be maintained by practitioners, and
also the maximum excess amount which shall apply, either by reference to a
specific type of claim, or to a specified class of legal practitioner.[27] The Authority
may also set out the terms and conditions upon which a legal practitioner can
seek to limit civil liability to a client in respect of the provision of professional
services.[28] With the consent of the Minister, the Authority may make regulations
regarding the advertising of legal services.[29] These may refer to the manner of

---

[21] LSRB 2011 § 9
[22] LSRB 2011 § 8 (4) (a)
[23] LSRB 2011 § 9 (2)
[24] LSRB 2011 §§ 18 (1) (a), (b) (2) (b)
[25] LSRB 2011 § 28 (1),(2) (a), (c)
[26] LSRB 2011 § 30 (1) (b)
[27] LSRB 2011 § 43 (1), (4), (5)
[28] LSRB 2011 § 44
[29] LSRB 2011 § 123

publication and the form, content and size of an advertisement.[30]

Part 5 of the Bill concerns complaints and disciplinary hearings in respect of legal practitioners. The Authority is authorised to receive and investigate complaints from any person who has concerns about an act or omission of a legal practitioner which may constitute misconduct.[31] It may also act upon its own initiative as far as such investigations are concerned.[32] The investigation of complaints of professional misconduct is to be undertaken by a Complaints Committee, to be appointed by the Authority, and consisting of a majority of lay persons.[33] Where the Complaints Committee determines that there has been misconduct of other than a minor nature, it shall recommend to the Authority that the case be referred to the LPDT for the holding of an inquiry.[34]

LPDT members will be appointed by the Government, upon nomination by the Minister for Justice, and the majority of its members will be lay persons.[35] Only the Authority may make an application for the holding of an inquiry by the Tribunal, and the Authority, or a person appointed by it will present the evidence grounding the contention of misconduct.[36] The LPDT may also make regulations governing the making of applications and proceedings of the Tribunal, and it will have powers, rights and privileges equivalent to those vested in the High Court regarding the enforcement of witness attendance and compelling the production of, and discovery under oath of documents.[37] Where the LPDT finds there has been misconduct on the part of a legal practitioner it has various powers which range from the issuance of a reprimand, warning or caution, to the making of a direction either that the errant practitioner should rectify, at his own expense, any deficiency arising on foot of the legal services the provision of which gave rise to the finding of misconduct, or that he/she should transfer the relevant documents to another legal practitioner, with the consent of the client, subject to the Tribunal's terms and conditions.[38] The LPDT may also refer its recommendations concerning serious findings of misconduct to the High Court in the following circumstances:

• Where it is of the opinion that a legal practitioner should pay a sum of money either to the Authority or the complainant.

• Where it wishes to place restrictions regarding the type of work in which a legal practitioner may engage.

• Where it seeks to suspend a practitioner for a specified period.

• Where it wishes to see a solicitor struck off or a barrister disbarred.

---

[30] LSRB 2011 § 123 (2) (b)

[31] LSRB 2011 § 46, misconduct being extensively defined in LSRB 2011 § 45

[32] LSRB 2011 § 47

[33] LSRB 2011 §§ 49 and 50 (1)

[34] LSRB 2011 § 51 (7)

[35] LSRB 2011 § 53 (1)

[36] LSRB 2011 § 55

[37] LSRB 2011 § 56

[38] LSRB 2011 § 59

• Where it seeks the revocation of the grant of a patent.[39]

The LPDT's decisions may be appealed to the High Court.[40] Finally, Part 6 of the Bill provides for the imposition of a levy on both the Bar Council and the Law Society to cover the expenses of the Authority and the Tribunal.

The Bill also seeks to introduce significant reforms to bring greater transparency to the area of legal costs. The current Office of the Taxing Master will be replaced by the Office of the Legal Costs Adjudicator (OLCA). The determinations of Legal Costs Adjudicators (LCAs), with reasons for the outcomes of their adjudications, will be published to allow for greater transparency and public awareness regarding legal costs.[41] The Chief LCA must prepare a strategic three year plan setting out the objectives, outputs and strategies of the OLCA, having regard to the need to ensure the most effective and strategic use of resources.[42] He/she must also prepare annual business plans indicating the planned activities of LCAs in the forthcoming year and annual reports setting out the activities undertaken in the preceding year.[43]

The Bill prohibits charging by legal practitioners on a percentage basis of damages payable to clients in contentious matters, except in relation to either a debt recovery or a liquidated demand. It is also prohibits the setting of a Junior Counsel's costs as a fixed percentage of those to be paid to a Senior Counsel.[44] Legal practitioners must provide clients with a notice upon receipt of instructions which comprehensively sets out information relating to costs and the basis on which they are likely to be calculated.[45] Where a matter may involve litigation, the notice must set out the likely or actual associated costs which may be incurred at each stage of litigation, the financial consequences for the client in the event of withdrawal from litigation, and the likely costs which the client will face in respect of the costs of other parties if the litigation is not successful.[46] The client must also be given an undertaking that he/she will be informed in the event that the legal practitioner becomes aware of any matter which may give rise to a material increase in the legal costs which are likely to be incurred.[47] The information to be given to clients includes the amount of costs to be incurred, including the amount of VAT, the need to engage witnesses and an undertaking not to engage them except where a client has given explicit approval for this, and where the likely costs have been established and made known to the client. Clients should also be informed regarding the probability of increased costs, recoverable costs which may arise and the circumstances which may lead to him/her having to pay the costs of another party. They must also be given a

---

[39] LSRB 2011 §§ 60 and 114 (2)

[40] LSRB 2011 §§ 61 – 63

[41] LSRB 2011 § 82

[42] LSRB 2011 § 84

[43] LSRB 2011 §§ 84 – 45

[44] LSRB 2011 § 89

[45] LSRB 2011

[46] LSRB 2011 § 90 (1) (a) and Schedule 1

[47] LSRB 2011 § 90 (g)

'cooling off' period during which they may reflect upon the proposed course of legal action before being committed to same. Legal practitioners may make agreements with clients regarding the amount and manner of the payment of legal costs that may arise, and if such an agreement is made, the costs arising may not be amenable to adjudication by the LCA, although the LCA may refer the matter to the High Court.[48]

Upon completion of the provision of legal services, the client must be provided with a bill of costs consisting of a summary of the legal services rendered, an itemised statement of amounts in respect of fees and disbursements, the amount of damages or other money recovered by, or payable to the client, in respect of services provided and the amount of any legal costs recovered on the client's behalf from either another party or an insurer.[49] If the Bill is enacted in its current form, in view of the definition of a 'legal practitioner' which includes both solicitors and barristers, a bill of costs will include any fee note which is prepared by a barrister.[50] It therefore appears that the traditional method of claiming barristers' fees as disbursements incurred by solicitors will be significantly altered, with solicitors no longer assuming responsibility for the payment of barristers' fees. The present requirement for solicitors to issue 'section 68 letters' to clients will be superseded by their new obligations in the Bill to provide comprehensive information to clients in relation to the costs which are likely to be incurred for the provision of legal services.[51]

Where a person is subject to pay the costs or a part thereof of another party by order of a court, tribunal or other body, having attempted to agree the bill of costs, he may apply to the Chief LCA for adjudication on any item claimed on that bill of costs.[52] A person who receives a bill of costs from a legal practitioner and considers that an item on the bill is not properly chargeable may also make such an application.[53] A legal practitioner may also apply to the Chief LCA where a client has failed to pay a bill of costs 30 days after its receipt.[54] Upon determination of an application, a LCA will either confirm a charge as fair and reasonable, or substitute an amount for the services rendered which is fair and reasonable in the circumstances.[55] Where the LCA determines that the aggregate amount of costs to be paid is less than 15% lower than the aggregate amount contained in the bill of costs, the party chargeable to those costs shall pay the costs of the adjudication, and where the aggregate amount is 15% or over, the

---

[48] LSRB 2011 § 91. Where such an agreement contains all the relevant information required under section 90 (2) of the Bill there is no need to provide a separate notice to the client in that regard.

[49] LSRB 2011 § 92

[50] LSRB 2011 §§ 2, 80

[51] LSRB 2011 § 90 (2). In accordance with section 68 of the Solicitors (Amendment) Act 1994, upon receipt of a client's instructions, a solicitor must provide a client with written information regarding the charges which will arise, or an estimate of same, for the provision of legal services by either that solicitor or his firm.

[52] LSRB 2011 § 94 (1) (2)

[53] LSRB 2011 § 94 (4)

[54] LSRB 2011 § 94 (5)

[55] LSRB 2011 § 97 (2), (3)

legal practitioner will be responsible for the costs of the adjudication.[56] Parties to an application to the LCA may appeal a determination either to the court which heard the proceedings to which the costs relate in the case of party and party costs, or to the High Court in other cases.[57]

Parties to the adjudication process may challenge either a full bill or any item on it, provided they have tried to resolve their differences prior to seeking adjudication.[58] Applications for adjudication must be made before six months has elapsed either from the date of issuance of the bill or the date of its payment, whichever date expires first. This is a considerable reduction from the present expiry limit for applications for the taxing of legal costs which is twelve months. An adjudicator must be able to verify that legal work billed for was actually done and that claimed disbursements were made.[59] He/she must also be able to establish the nature and extent of work that is billed for, and the identity of the legal practitioner who carried out the work. The adjudication process will not be in public, which also constitutes a significant departure from the current taxing regime.

Last but not least, Part 11 of the Bill concerns patents of precedence. The grant of patents of precedence is extended to solicitors who may adopt the title of 'Senior Counsel'.[60] There will be greater transparency in the process of granting patents which will be overseen by the newly formed Advisory Committee on the grant of Patents of Precedence.[61] This will consider applications in accordance with published criteria, including the degree of competence and probity of a legal practitioner, his/her capacity for advocacy, specialist litigation or specialist knowledge and suitability of character and temperament.[62]

It is clear that the LSRB 2011 heralds a fundamental change in the regulation of the legal profession and the provision of legal services, and if enacted, will give substantive effect to the Government's commitments as follows:

- To establish independent regulation of the sector

- To improve access to the market and competition within it

- To introduce greater transparency to legal costs

- To make available effective procedures to deal with consumers' complaints.[63]

The following section will examine the responses of key stakeholders within the legal profession to the publication of the Bill.

---

[56] LSRB 2011 § 98

[57] LSRB 2011 § 100

[58] LSRB 2011 § 94

[59] LSRB 2011 § 95

[60] LSRB 2011 § 109

[61] LSRB 2011 § 111

[62] LSRB 2011 § 112 (2)

[63] Legal Services Regulation Bill 2011. Explanatory Memorandum, 1

5.3 The Response of the Legal Profession to the publication of the LSRB 2011

Following the publication of the LSRB 2011, both the solicitors' and barristers' branches of the profession denounced it, declaring that it heralded an unprecedented attack on the independence of the legal profession and the rule of law. The Minister for Justice retorted that the legal profession had briefed against the state in the course of their campaigning against the Bill. The following sections will examine the responses of the profession's representative bodies to the regulatory changes contained in the Bill, and the Minister's reply to their criticisms.

5.3.1 The Bar Council

Since its publication in October 2011, the Barristers' profession has remained steadfast in it opposition to the LSRB 2011. The Bar Council was particularly disappointed that there was "extremely limited consultation" on the Minister for Justice's part, and a lack of meaningful discussion in relation to the proposed reforms.[64] It also noted that the proposed changes do not accord with the Competition Authority's 2006 recommendations, which supported the establishment of an independent statutory body – The Legal Services Commission – that was to have responsibility for the regulation of both solicitors and barristers. The Legal Services Commission would have delegated many regulatory functions to either the existing regulatory bodies, the LSI and the BCI, or to new self-regulatory bodies. In the Bar Council's opinion, the LSRB 2011 provisions regarding the establishment of the LSRA go far beyond what was required to comply with the Competition Authority's recommendations. The BCI also criticised the Bill's provisions concerning the LSRA on the grounds that it lacks sufficient independence from Executive or Ministerial control, and its establishment amounts to a system of direct state regulation of the legal profession, as opposed to the Competition Authority's preferred model of an oversight regulator. The BCI argued that an independent legal profession is an essential element of a democratic society which respects the rule of law. However, the LSRA's alleged lack of independence would not be compatible with the maintenance of such an independent legal profession, and given that over 50% of court cases concern a dispute involving the state, the consequences of the absence of such independence for the proper administration of justice is a matter of serious concern.[65] If the Bill is implemented in its current form, the independence of the LSRA would be further undermined by the manner in which the Government would be able to appoint LSRA members, determine the terms and conditions of their employment and also determine the duration of their tenure.[66] Its inde-

---

[64] The Bar Council of Ireland, 'Initial submission on the LSRB 2011' Executive Summary 7. Available at: <http://www.lawlibrary.ie/documents/memberdocs/ BarCouncilInitialSubmissionDecember2011.pdf> Accessed 29/1/2013

[65] Ibid, para 24.

[66] The proposed amendments to the LSRB 2011 which were recently published following the Committee Stage of the Bill's passage address many of the BCI's concerns in relation to the Authority. Dáil Éireann, Legal Services Regulation Bill 2011 Committee Amendments (FN 2). See ch 5 § 5.6 for a discussion of the proposed amendments to the Bill.

pendence would also be compromised by the provisions of the Bill which permit the Government to remove a member of the Authority where it considers this to be necessary for the effective performance of its functions.[67] The BCI has compared the lack of involvement of the professional bodies in the appointment of LSRA members with the method used to appoint members of the Medical Council, the Pharmaceutical Society of Ireland, the Dental Council and the Veterinary Council. In those cases, the relevant Minister does not have the power to veto a significant proportion of Council appointments which are made by the relevant professional bodies.

The BCI also argued that the direct regulatory model contained in the LSRB 2011, whereby a regulatory body which lacks independence from Government assumes direct regulatory responsibility over the legal profession lacks any parallel in other common law jurisdictions or EU states, and does not constitute "independent oversight regulation", as per the Competition Authority's recommendations, particularly with regard to the level of Government interference in the affairs of the LSRA, as envisaged by the Bill.[68]

Further concerns were raised by the BCI relating to what it considers to be the excessive costs attached to the establishment of the five new regulatory bodies proposed by the Bill, which it describes as an "enormous and unnecessary superstructure".[69] Such a superstructure is at variance with the Government's stated objective to facilitate a process of rationalisation, including the reduction or abolition of quangos.[70] The BCI noted that the failure to carry out a RIA or to consult with stakeholders prior to the publication of the Bill was not in accordance with best regulatory practice.[71] As far as the Bill's disciplinary measures are concerned, the BCI criticised the complete exclusion of the professional bodies from considering cases of even trivial wrongdoing, and the limited nature of the professional bodies' involvement in the proposed LPDT. It also alluded to a lack of independence on the part of both the LSRA Complaints Committee and the LPDT, given the system for Government appointment of members of those bodies. It argued that, 'in effect the Minister appoints the investigator together with the judge and jury in all disciplinary matters and will exercise near total control over the disciplinary practice with the presence of the professions reduced to a spectre'.[72] The BCI was also dissatisfied with the lay majority that is proposed for these bodies which in its opinion does not accord with the system in any other statutorily regulated profession. The BCI took particular issue with the inspectorate powers in section 27 of the Bill which allow for entrance without a warrant to the place of a barrister's business, including his/her home, to the

---

[67] The Bar Council of Ireland, 'Initial Submission' (FN 64), para 24

[68] Ibid, para 25

[69] Ibid, para 26. These bodies are the LSRA, the Complaints Committee of the LSRA, LPDT, the Office of the LCA and the Advisory Committee on the Grants of Patents of Precedence.

[70] Ibid, para 27; Department of Public Expenditure and Reform 'Rationalisation of State Agencies' (FN 17)

[71] Ibid, para 28. The Competition Authority also failed to carry out a RIA in its 2006 Report. *Report on Legal Services* (FN 1).

[72] Ibid, para 36

lack of any appeal against a finding of misconduct by the Complaints Committee, and the inclusion within the definition of misconduct of the issuance of an excessive bill of costs.[73]

With regard to the proposed introduction of new business structures, including MDPs and barristers' partnerships, the BCI once more criticised the lack of consultation about the desirability of such innovations prior to the Bill's publication.[74] It also criticised the proposals relating to the public consultation process for the Bill on the grounds that they are limited, ineffective and that they 'bizarrely' require a process of public consultation, to include the professional bodies only where the LSRA deems it to be appropriate.[75] The BCI asserted that that the new business structures will undermine two core values of the present Bar, namely its integrity and independence, on the basis that ethical problems will arise as a result of duties owed to partners or employers which will destabilise and dilute existing clear, ethical frameworks.[76] Similarly, proposals to allow employed barristers to provide in-house legal advice have been criticised as they apparently would undermine a barrister's primary duty to the court, thus damaging the integrity and independence of the delivery of legal services.[77]

The BCI is of the view that the proposed new business structures are likely to diminish competition in the delivery of legal services, and it pointed to the Competition Authority's opinion that MDPs might result in a reduced supply and quality of advocacy services.[78] However, any possible diminution in this regard is more than offset by the proposals to permit solicitors to provide advocacy services to clients, a measure which would serve to increase client choice with regard to advocacy provision. The BCI also argued that there is no prohibition in the Bill on non-legal members or employees of MDPs providing legal services or advice in the course of employment.[79] In the BCI's opinion, the Bill also fails to provide adequate guiding principles concerning the rules and responsibilities of regulatory bodies to investigate complaints of misconduct in relation to the provision of services by multiple professionals who are employed in a MDP.[80]

By contrast, the BCI broadly endorsed the Bill's provisions concerning legal costs and noted that many of these have already been enacted by the BCI, such as the prohibition of the two-thirds Junior Counsel fee rule, and the necessity to give fee estimates.[81] It noted that hearings of the LCA will be held in private, unlike the hearings of the present Taxing Master which are heard in public, and it has questioned whether there is, in fact, any good reason for this less trans-

---

[73] Ibid, para 37

[74] Ibid, para 30

[75] Ibid, paras 39, 40; LSRB 2011 § 75

[76] Ibid, para 40

[77] Ibid, para 40

[78] Ibid, para 41

[79] Ibid, para 42

[80] Ibid, para 42

[81] Ibid, para 43; LSRB 2011 §§ 89, 90. The two-thirds rule automatically set a Junior Counsel's fee at a rate which was two-thirds of that of the Senior Counsel in a case.

parent approach. It also queried the rationale of the provision which appears to prevent the Chief LCA from publishing information concerning the identity of legal representatives in family law and 'in camera' hearings.[82]. Finally, the BCI alluded to the conflict of interest which would arise for barristers in employment in the event that they should be allowed to represent their employer in court. This conflict of interest would arise as a result of the duty owed to the court and also to the employer.[83] Whilst such a conflict may indeed arise, it is not such that a competent professional could not resolve it by giving priority in every such instance to the higher duty owed to the court.

In its submission to the Joint Committee on Justice, Defence and Equality on the Bill on 21st March 2012, the BCI reiterated the concerns which were raised in its initial submission and summarised them before the Committee.[84] Whilst it supported the empowerment of the Authority to receive and investigate complaints, and to conduct research on a wide variety of matters concerning the legal profession, including the merits or otherwise of increasing direct access to barristers, the introduction of appropriate business structures for the provision of legal services and the establishment of an independent conveyancing profession, the BCI also referred to the amendments to the Bill that it wished to see adopted which were as follows:

> • There should be an independent system of regulation for the legal profession, to conform with the model endorsed by the Competition Authority Report of 2006, and which would be similar to the regulatory model which was introduced in England and Wales in 2007, on foot of the Clementi Report in 2004.[85] The BCI argued that such a regulatory system would be more efficient, less costly and would preserve the independence of the legal profession, in the public interest.

> • The BCI sought the removal of the provisions in the Bill relating to the terms and conditions of members' appointment to the LSRA in section 8, and their replacement with provisions similar to those which govern appointments to the Medical Council as per the Medical Practitioners Act of 2007.

> • The BCI proposed that the LSRA should function as an oversight regulator with extensive functions and powers to oversee the regulatory activi-

---

[82] LSRB 2011 § 82

[83] Ibid, para 53. By contrast, in England and Wales, in some limited circumstances employed barristers may have rights of audience and may appear in court on behalf of their employers. See 'Guidance for Employed Barristers', paras 3.2 – 3.8 (Professional Standards Committee, Professional Conduct and Complaints Committee and Employed Barristers Committee of the Bar Council, December 2003).

[84] Oireachtas Joint Committee on Justice, Defence and Equality, 'Legal Services Regulation Bill 2011', Discussion. Available at: <http://debates.oireachtas.ie/JVJ/2012/03/21/0004.asp> Accessed 6/9/2012

[85] D Clementi, *Report of the Review of Regulatory Framework for Legal Services in England and Wales* (December 2004). Available at: <http://webarchive.nationalrachives.gov.uk/t/http://www.legal.services-review.org.uk/content/report/index.htm> Accessed 29/1/2013

ties of the BCI and the LSI.[86] This would lead to removal of the Minister for Justice's involvement in activities such as the approval and amendment of codes of practice for the legal profession.

• The BCI argued for the deletion of sections 9, 16, 17 and 18 of the Bill, stating that they should be replaced by the insertion of provisions to make the LSRA responsible for oversight functions in respect of the BCI and the LSI, with the exception of matters relating to discipline and costs.[87]

• The BCI proposed that the LSRA should have the power to require the BCI and the LSI to remove unnecessary barriers to legal practitioners who wish to switch between the solicitors' and barristers' branches of the profession and to regulate the advertising policies of both branches of the profession.

• The BCI requested the deletion of section 69 of the Bill which provides for the imposition of a levy on both branches of the legal profession to cover the costs of the LSRA.[88]

• The BCI supported the amendment of the Bill so that reports commissioned in accordance with its terms are made available to the Houses of the Oireachtas rather than to the Minister for Justice.

At the Oireachtas Joint Committee on Justice, Defence and Equality on 21st March 2012, Mr Guillicuddy discussed the LSRB 2011 on behalf of the Junior members of the BCI. He recommended that provisions for the use of videolinks for court hearings should be included in the Bill along with reform of the current court listing systems and the introduction of new procedures to ensure that gardai do not have to wait all day at court for cases to be heard. He also recommended amendment of the LSRB 2011 to allow for the use of arbitration and mediation in order to reduce pressure on the courts, and expressed the hope that the BCI may establish a centre to facilitate such an innovation.

The Compecon Report

In March 2012, the Bar Council commissioned a RIA for the LSRB 2011 in the form of a Report from Compecon.[89] This examined the economic impact of the proposed regulatory regime to be implemented by the LSRA, and did not include an assessment of other regulatory changes contained in the Bill such as the changes relating to direct access to barristers. The report commenced with

---

[86] Bar Council of Ireland, 'Submission of the Bar Council of Ireland to the Oireachtas Committee on Justice, Defence and Equality on the LSRB 2011', paras 21 – 23.

[87] Ibid, para 23

[88] Ibid, para 81

[89] Compecon – Competition Economics, *An Economic Analysis of the Government's Proposed Regulatory Regime for the Legal Profession in Ireland.* Final Report. 3rd Mar 2012. Available at: <http://www.lawlibrary.ie/documents/news_events/BarCouncilRegulatoryImpact Assessment03032012.pdf> Accessed 29/1/2013. Compecon is an economic consulting firm which specializes in the application of economic analysis to competition policy issues, industry regulation and the economics and regulation of public utilities. The Compecon website is available at: <www.compecon.ie> Accessed 7/8/2013

the observation that the establishment of the LSRA goes far beyond the recommendations of the Competition Authority which recommended the establishment of an 'oversight' model of regulation, thereby maintaining some of the advantages of self-regulation whilst protecting against the possible abuses associated with it. As previously noted, the Competition Authority Model had indeed favoured an oversight regulator which would entail the establishment of a new state agency, the Legal Services Commission, to oversee the activities of the existing regulatory bodies, the BCI and the LSI.

The Compecon report asserted that no evidence has been produced to show that such an independent regulatory regime is necessary, that its establishment would lead to lower prices, or that its possible benefits would outweigh the associated costs.[90] On the contrary, the Report offered the view that the establishment of the LSRA will lead to an increase in the cost of legal services. It estimated that the average annual cost of regulation for each barrister will increase from €58 per year to almost €1,000 (for solicitors, the increase will be from €1,353 under the present system to almost €2,000).[91] In addition to these annual increases in regulatory costs, the establishment of the LSRA would lead to a once-off transition cost of approximately €6 million, which would also have to be borne by the legal profession.[92] The Report argued that such costs will be passed on to private sector clients rather than being partly absorbed by the state, the largest purchaser of legal services, which will use its buying power to avoid an increase in service costs arising from the establishment of the LSRA. It was also asserted that the increased costs of regulation will hasten the flow of barristers from the profession as a result of the growing financial pressures they are experiencing, thus leading to a reduced choice of service providers for consumers.[93] However, this analysis fails to take account of the fact that other measures in the Bill, such as the proposed new practice structures, including barristers' partnerships and MDPs are likely to provide more opportunities for barristers, as will the proposal to allow barristers to represent their employers and to provide services directly to the public in non-contentious matters. The Report also failed to acknowledge that there would be an increased level of efficiency in the performance of legal regulatory functions and a greater economy of scale when the presently separate regulatory functions of the two branches of the profession are combined. Inefficiencies in the present regulatory system arise due to the fact the complaints regarding solicitors may be made either to the LSI, the Solicitors' Disciplinary Tribunal or both these bodies. Those who are dissatisfied with the LSI's handling of a matter can refer it to an independent

---

[90] Ibid 5

[91] Ibid 7, Table 2. The difference in the present cost of regulating the two branches of the profession arise because barristers do not handle clients' money, and as such, their activities are less likely to constitute misconduct.

[92] Ibid 7

[93] Ibid 9. Both solicitors and barristers are feeling the effects of the recession, which is causing increasing numbers to leave the profession in search of new employment. See D McDonald, 'Barristers 'struggling to survive' as 180 quit in a year', *Independent.ie,* 11th Mar 2013. Available at: <www.independent.ie/irish-news/barristers-struggling-to-survive-as-180-quit-in-a-year-29121339.html> Accessed 7/8/2013

adjudicator who is appointed by the Minister for Justice. The Report instead claimed that efficiencies and economies of scale will be reduced because regulatory and non-regulatory functions of the existing bodies will be separated. A balanced cost-benefit analysis should have included a consideration of all these factors. The Compecon Report stated:

> The failure to carry out a RIA prior to the publication of the Bill suggests that its introduction was not based upon principles of good regulation. To conduct the RIA after the Bill's publication raises the possibility that the RIA is merely an *ex post* justification, rather than an objective analysis of the proposed regulation.[94]

The Compecon Report noted that regulatory regimes involve two types of implementation costs; those associated with setting up the regulatory agency and those incurred by the regulated community as a result of compliance. The 'hidden' nature of the compliance costs, which are greater than the set-up costs gives rise to excessive levels of regulation in society. Six principles which may be applied in order to evaluate regulatory proposals were set out in the Government's White Paper 'Regulating Better'.[95] These are: necessity, effectiveness, proportionality, transparency, accountability and consistency. The Compecon Report asserted that the Bill fails to meet several of these requirements. It argued that a departure from the self-regulatory model was not necessary, as although such systems have the potential to be abused, they are not necessarily exposed to such abuse. To abandon such a system on principle results in the loss of an opportunity to reduce legal costs due to the lower cost of information acquisition for the regulator in self-regulatory models. This is illustrated in Northern Ireland, where the Bain Report, having acknowledged the potential for abuse in self-regulatory systems, asserted that such abuse had not in fact occurred in Northern Ireland.[96] The Report also noted that complexities associated with the market for legal services mean that greater competition through an increased number of lawyers does not necessarily lead to a reduction of legal costs, but may in fact increase them.[97] Neither the Minister for Justice nor the Competition Authority has presented an argument to show why a change in the regulatory structure of the Irish legal profession would lead to lower prices; as such, the proposals in the Bill fail to satisfy the effectiveness principle. Nor do the benefits associated with the proposed regulatory changes demonstrably outweigh their costs. Whilst increased competitiveness for manufacturing firms

---

[94] Ibid 33

[95] Department of the Taoiseach, 'Regulating Better. A Government White Paper setting out six principles of Better Regulation' (2001). Available at: <http://www.taoiseach.gov.ie/eng/Publications/Publications_Archive/Publications2011/Regulating_Better_Government_White_Paper.pdf> Accessed 29/1/2013

[96] G Bain, *Legal Services in Northern Ireland: Complaints, Regulation, Competition* (2006) Legal Services Review Group. Para 3.32. Available at: <http://www.lawlibrary.ie/documents/memberdocs/Bainreport.pdf> Accessed 29/1/2013. According to Compecon, self-regulation of the legal profession is also working successfully in Scotland. Ibid, para 3.32.

[97] O Shy, 'The Economics of Network Industries' (Cambridge University Press, 2001), ch 11. Cited in the Compecon Report, *An Economic Analysis* (FN 89), para 4.2

may be achieved by removing restrictions on price competition, in the legal services market the entire abolition of the present regulatory system is not necessary to achieve this.

When analysing the direct costs of the Bill's new regulatory regime, the Compecon Report adopted a working assumption that the present self-regulatory system functions effectively. However, it presented no evidence to support this assumption, and the annual cost of €58 per barrister for regulatory matters belies the fact that the present system is not fit for purpose, notwith-standing the voluntary regulatory functions which Bar Council members per-form. There is also the fact that the new regulatory framework will, for the first time, provide a means of rooting out historic, archaic practices within the legal profession which have traditionally served to maintain legal costs at an artificial-ly high level.[98] The Report calculated that the total direct costs associated with the regulatory regime in the Bill may be as much as €20 – €24 million more than that of the present model. In addition, the indirect costs are likely to exceed direct costs. The Compecon Report pointed to increased compliance costs which will arise for barristers who handle clients' money following the introduction of the Bill, as a consequence of the requirement to obtain an accountant's certifi-cate to show that a practitioner is compliant with the Bill's requirements.[99] This may amount to €1.1 million if all barristers choose to handle clients' money. However, this requirement will only arise for barristers who provide services directly to the public, and this eventuality will enable their clients to secure an efficiently provided service, and reduced overall costs, as they will have avoided a solicitor's fee which would have inevitably arisen had the barrister not been able to provide direct services.

Increased legal costs may also arise for practitioners if the Authority avails of its powers in the Bill to increase minimum levels of PII.[100] If PII costs were to rise by €100 per practitioner this would lead to an increase of €1 million in costs for the profession as a whole. However, the Compecon Report failed to identify the associated benefit which would be achieved if such a measure was imple-mented. There is less likely to be a need for clients to resort to litigation in order to make good their losses, if practitioners are adequately covered by their own PII. The Report also offered the view that the mechanism for allocating the cost of the LSRA between the professions creates a disproportionate burden for barristers.[101] It was asserted that the degree of Ministerial involvement in regula-tory operations would adversely affect the legal profession's independence and also that of the regulator. However, the Select Committee on Justice, Defence and Equality has recently agreed a series of amendments to the Bill in order to

---

[98] For instance, the monopoly for the provision of conveyancing services and the maintenance of the artificial division of labour between the two branches of the profession.

[99] Compecon Report, *An Economic Analysis* (FN 89), para 4.4. LSRB 2011 § 38

[100] Ibid, para 4.4. LSRB 2011 § 43

[101] Ibid, para 4.6. In accordance with the Bill, practitioners will equally share the burden of the proportion of costs which relate to non-complaint related activities, whilst the LSI and BCI will each pay 10% of complaints associated costs, and split the remaining 80% of this element in proportion to the number of complaints upheld against each branch of the profession.

protect the independence of the profession and its regulator from Ministerial involvement.[102]

The Report analysed the costs associated with the introduction of an over-sight regulator, such as the Legal Services Commission as envisaged by the Competition Report, and found that these would be considerably less than the costs associated with the establishment of the LSRA as provided for in the Bill.[103] It argued that the costs to be imposed on practitioners will force many from the profession as they will be unable to sustain the extra expense. However, this argument fails to take account of the larger number of employment opportuni-ties which may arise for practitioners due to greater flexibility in permissible business structures, and the possibility for barristers to provide services directly to clients and to represent their employers. These innovative opportunities are more likely to appeal to younger members of the profession, the cohort suffering most acutely in the current financial climate.

The Compecon Report was critical of the Competition Authority Report and its conclusions on the grounds that its recommendations followed from a form-based analysis of the self-regulation model which presently applies to the legal profession, whereas in view of the Compecon authors, an effects-based approach would have been most suited for such an analysis. The criticism of the Competi-tion Authority's form-based analysis is warranted, and its study would have benefited from the inclusion of an analysis of the effects of the self-regulatory system as opposed to focusing exclusively upon its form. However, the Com-pecon Report presented a somewhat one-sided analysis of the proposed regula-tory changes in the LSRB 2011, focusing specifically upon those aspects of the changes which have been subjected to criticism by the BCI. Whilst it is to be expected that the Report's authors might wish to support the agenda of its commissioning body, the Report appears to lack balance as a result, and conse-quently will do little to promote the position of the BCI in the debate regarding the Bill.

The BCI's main criticisms of the LSRB 2011 relate to its potentially damaging impact upon the independence of the legal profession, which, it argues, is an essential element in a democratic society wishing to uphold the rule of law. There is undoubtedly some merit in the BCI's criticisms in this regard, and many of the proposed amendments to the Bill which have recently been agreed by the Bill's Select Committee would rectify the defects which have been identified by the BCI, especially in relation to the independence of the LSRA.[104] However, the BCI's criticisms in relation to the cost of the LPDT have less merit, as to date the barristers' profession has arguably failed to engage fully with the problem of professional misconduct, or to invest sufficiently in robust and transparent procedures to deal with it. The Government's ongoing failure to publish a RIA for the Bill has rightly been criticised by the BCI, and until this is addressed it is difficult to counter the BCI's argument that the Bill will introduce 'an enormous and unnecessary regulatory superstructure', which is at odds with the current

[102] See ch 5 § 5.4 for a further discussion of the recent amendments to the Bill.
[103] Compecon Report, *An Economic Analysis* (FN 89), para 4.5
[104] Dáil Éireann. Legal Services Regulation Bill 2011. Committee Amendments (FN 2).

programme of rationalisation of public bodies which the government professes to pursue. Finally, whilst the BCI has been generally positive in its response to the new legal costs regime contained in the Bill, its reaction to the proposed new business structures has been less than welcoming. It may be argued that MDPs have more to offer the less well established members of the Bar, and the BCI's opposition to them would appear to reflect the views, and also to protect the interests, of a more established and successful sector of the profession. The following section will consider the response of the HSKI to the publication of the LSRB 2011.

5.3.2 The Honorable Society of Kings Inns

The HSKI appeared before the Oireachtas Joint Committee on Justice, Defence and Equality on 21st March 2012, to discuss the LSRB 2011. In outlining the key functions of the HSKI for the Committee, Mr Conor Maguire, Chairman of the Council of the HSKI, identified its role in admitting people to the qualification of barrister, thereby permitting them to be called to the Bar, and the provision of a professional education course for such persons. He also briefly alluded to the disciplinary function it exercises over barristers. The HSKI recommended that the provisions of the Bill which refer to the constitution of the LSRA should be amended to permit the HSKI to nominate two people to the Authority.[105] In its view, this would allegedly serve to properly represent the interests of professional legal education on the Authority, and to provide it with valuable assistance in relation to such matters. It also argued that the Bill should be amended to reflect the fact the it is the HSKI and not the Bar Council which is responsible for the content of the education course which must be completed prior to being called to the Bar, for setting admission standards policies, and for making arrangements relating to the course.[106] Even though the HSKI is responsible for establishing the criteria for accrediting foreign legal practitioners and for making the rules governing the movement of persons between both branches of the legal profession, according to the HSKI, the Bill does not reflect these facts.

The HSKI also identified a logical flaw in the Bill as first published in that it requires the Authority within twelve months of its establishment to provide a comprehensive report on the current legal education and training systems for legal professionals.[107] On the other hand, the Bill requires the Authority, within two years of its establishment to report on the possible unification of both branches of the profession.[108] The HSKI has argued that the education report should follow, not precede, the unification report, given that the structure and content of professional legal education is dependent upon the nature of the relationship between the two branches of the legal profession. This is a most sensible observation and the Bill should be amended accordingly.

The HSKI has been much more measured than the BCI in its public com-

---

[105] LSRB 2011 § 8 (4)

[106] LSRB 2011 § 9 (2) (a) (i) and (ii)

[107] LSRB 2011 § 30 (1)

[108] LSRB 2011 § 30 (4)

ments on the content of the LSRB 2011. This is most probably due to the fact that the senior judiciary are members of the HSKI, and in light of the Doctrine of Separation of Powers, it would not be appropriate for this cohort of the HSKI to be openly critical of the actions of either the executive or legislative branches of government. However, given the radical impact which the Bill, if enacted in its current form, would have in removing both the disciplinary powers and the monopolistic position of the HSKI as a provider of professional education for barristers, it might be expected that the members of the HSKI are making their opposition to the Bill felt in more private circles.

5.3.3 *The Law Society of Ireland*

Similarly to the BCI, the LSI did not welcome the initial publication of the LSRB 2011. In November 2011 its proposed new regulatory model was criticised by the former President of the LSI John Costello, on the grounds that it 'is unknown in any democracy and threatens the independence of the legal profession, which is the hallmark of any free society'.[109] The LSI is concerned that the Bill will potentially undermine the independence of the legal profession, with the Minister for Justice having ultimate power over the workings of the LSRA. The LSI has argued that the effect of the Bill as initially published would be to damage citizens' rights to receive advice free from improper state influence, which is a state of affairs not in accordance with the workings of a modern democratic and free society. It is also concerned that the Bill as it currently stands poses a threat not just to the independence of the legal profession, but also to the independence of its regulator. In defending the LSI's regulatory track record, its current President Donal Binchy cited the Society's handling of the SMDF crisis as illustrative of its abilities to effectively regulate the profession, and argued that it was as a consequence of its voluntary committee system that 'an awful lot' of attention was given to the issue, which enabled the LSI to 'move these matters along very quickly'.[110]

The LSI nevertheless, welcomed many elements of the LSRB 2011, including the modernisation of the costs system by means of the introduction of the Office of the Legal Costs Adjudicator and the extension of the patents of precedence system to include solicitors. It elected to largely accept the Bill's provisions relating to the adjudication of clients' complaints, and the establishment of an independent body to consider these. However, it considers that significant amendment to the Bill is necessary as follows:

> • Powers facilitating Government control of the LSRA and also of the legal profession as a consequence, should be removed from the Bill in order to ensure that the independence of both the legal profession and its regulator are maintained.

---

[109] 'Not Even Zimbabwe Has a Model Like This' (November 2011) 105 (9) LSG 12 – 13

[110] 'Changing of the Guard' (December 2011) 105 (10) LSG 26 – 29, 28. The SMDF crisis arose as a result of the Fund's inability to meet its obligations in respect of its insureds, who were those solicitors unable to obtain PII cover in the general market. The fund became insolvent in May 2011. Given the difficulties associated with the SMDF, it is an unlikely choice for the LSI President to cite as an example of the LSI's regulatory efficacy.

• There should be an ongoing role for the legal profession in the handling of complaints against it, as is, allegedly, the practice in other democratic states.[111]

• Ministerial powers to prepare, publish and modify codes of practice for the profession and also to develop policy on legal service provision should be removed from the Bill.

• Perceived threats to the principles of legal professional privilege and client confidentiality which arise in the Bill, as a consequence of the inspection powers of the LSRA must be addressed.[112]

• Appointments to the LSRA should be made by the President of the High Court, in order to preserve the separation of powers, following selection by the Public Appointments Service.[113]

• The LSI requested the removal from the Bill of the Ministerial powers to prepare, publish and modify codes of practice for the legal profession and also to develop policy on legal service provision.

• The LSI's regulatory powers in relation to the compensation fund, regulation of practice, inspections and PII matters should be retained, with provision being made for oversight of these functions by the LSRA.

• The LSI's existing oversight powers in relation to the advertising of legal services by solicitors should be preserved, along with fair procedures relating to the investigation of client complaints and consumer rights.

• Provisions in the Bill relating to legal partnerships and direct access to barristers should be contained in separate legislation and subject to separate, thorough, review processes prior to enactment.

• The LSI has also sought the outright removal of proposals for the introduction of MDPs, and the inclusion of provisions allowing for government approval for the introduction of limited liability partnerships, companies and corporations consisting of individual legal professionals.[114]

In response to the LSI's concerns, Alan Shatter assured it that at the Committee Stage, its concerns will be addressed.[115]

---

[111] Ch 4, § 4.1 describes the self-regulatory system in Northern Ireland, and § 4.2 describes the co-regulatory system in England and Wales, whereby the profession's regulatory bodies have responsibility for dealing with client complaints, whilst their activities in that regard are overseen by the Legal Services Board.

[112] LSRB 2011 §§ 15, 17

[113] However, the involvement of the judiciary in such a role arguably compromises the independence of the legal profession in a similar manner to that caused by the involvement of the Minister for Justice.

[114] The Minister has indicated that he is willing to consider further amendment of the Bill to include provision for limited liability partnerships. A Shatter, 'Regulation, Representation and the Future of the Legal Profession', Law Society Annual Conference, 14th April 2012. Available at: <www.justice.ie/en/JELR/Pages/SP12000102> Accessed 10/8/2013

[115] M McDermot, 'Debating Change in Castlemartyr' (May 2012) 106 (4) LSG 12

The LSI framed much of its criticisms of the LSRB 2011 with reference to the Competition Authority Report of 2006, the implementation of which was called for by the Troika.[116] The LSI President for 2011, Donald Binchy argued the evidence in the Competition Authority's Report supported the view that the market for legal services in Ireland was highly competitive.[117] Binchy claimed that the Report's proposals if implemented, would threaten the independence of the legal profession by creating the possibility of political interference. He also argued that the LSI, as a *quid pro quo* for its regulatory role, maintains the compensation fund for clients who suffer loss due to solicitors' dishonesty. However, the LSRB 2011 would remove the LSI's regulatory function whilst leaving it with the responsibility for the compensation fund. This would be unfair to the profession in the event that the LSRA is not as effective or efficient as the LSI in performing its regulatory functions. Binchey argued that insurance companies may be reluctant to continue to insure the compensation fund in the event that the LSI loses control over the regulation of the profession.[118]

Binchy also rejected the description of the legal profession in the Memorandum of Understanding as a 'sheltered profession' given the downward pressure on legal fees which has been exerted since the onset of the financial crisis. He asserted that the Competition Authority's recommended regulatory model of an independent, oversight regulator was similar to that which was recommended by the Clementi Report in relation to the regulation of the legal profession in England, which Clementi referred to as the 'Model B+' option.[119] This allowed for regulatory oversight at practitioner level, which preserved regulatory rule-making at the level of practitioner, thereby increasing practitioners' commitment to the maintenance of high standards. The alternative model which Clementi identified, and which was referred to as 'Model A', involved the establishment of an independent regulatory body, such as the LSRA as envisaged in the LSRB 2011. This entails conferring all regulatory functions on one body which may potentially become an unwieldy, large organisation. The establishment of an oversight regulatory body also presents less transitional difficulties, as the majority of regulatory positions would remain within the traditional regulatory bodies, with either minimal or no loss of regulatory expertise as a result.

Furthermore, the LSI expressed concern that the LSRB would effectively empower the Minister for Justice, rather than the LSRA, to be the ultimate decision-maker regarding the regulation of the legal profession. The LSI compiled a comprehensive list of all the provisions of the Bill which confer Ministerial power, and which have the potential to undermine the independence of the legal profession. The key powers allow the Government to appoint and remove

---

[116] The Competition Authority, *Report on Legal Services* (FN 1); IMF, 'Memorandum of Understanding', 3rd December 2010 (FN 1)

[117] D Binchy, 'The Good, The Bad, The Ugly', Special Issue (Dec 2011) LSG 8

[118] It might also, however, be argued that insurance companies would be more willing to insure the compensation fund if the regulation of the legal profession becomes the responsibility of an independent body such as the LSRA.

[119] D Clementi, *Report of the Review of the Regulatory Framework for Legal Services in England and Wales* (December 2004). Chapter 2, paras 26 – 32 describe the relative merits of Models A, B and B+.

members of the Authority, and to determine the terms of office, remuneration and expenses of such members.[120] In accordance with the Bill, the Minister has the power to request the LSRA to approve professional codes of practice, and his/her consent is needed for the amendment, revocation or withdrawal of approval for any such code.[121] The Bill also gives the Minister power to approve, and make directions in relation to the LSRA's three year strategic plan.[122] The LSI stressed that its primary aim is to preserve the independence of the legal profession in order to safeguard its ability to fearlessly act on clients' behalf, to protect the independence of the judiciary and to uphold Ireland's reputation internationally.

At the Oireachtas Joint Committee on Justice, Defence and Equality discussion on the LSRB held on 21st March 2012, the LSI reiterated its criticisms as enunciated elsewhere and also noted its concern in relation to the likely increased cost of the proposed new regulatory authority and of other bodies including the LPDT. These costs, arguably will be passed on to clients, and will therefore have the effect of increasing legal costs rather than reducing them, thereby defeating a key aim of the new legislation. Finally, the LSI submitted that these increased costs may also cause many firms to cease trading in the present climate where they struggle for economic survival.

5.4 The Response of Other Stakeholders to Publication of the LSRB 2011

During the course of the Oireachtas Debate mentioned above, the Joint Committee on Justice, Defence and Equality also heard the views of various stakeholders regarding the Bill, including that of Noeline Blackwell, on behalf of the Free Legal Aid Centres (FLAC) and the Irish Human Rights Committee (IHRC) which made a written submission to the Committee.

5.4.1 Free Legal Aid Centres

On appearing before the Oireachtas Joint Committee on Justice, Defence and Equality to discuss the LSRB 2011, Noeline Blackwell, Director of FLAC brought a human rights perspective to the proposed Bill. As an organisation, FLAC relies upon the voluntary work of members of the legal profession, government funding and philanthropy in order to provide legal advice and information to over 24,000 people per year.[123]

FLAC recommended that the principles which inform the LSRA ought to include the maintenance of the honour and dignity of their profession by lawyers, and the upholding of fundamental freedoms. It proposed amendments to the Bill to ensure that the structure of the LSRA is not only independent, but that it is also perceived to be so. It also recommended amendment of the Bill to remove any perception of Government interference or overdependence on the legal

---

[120] LSRB 2011 §§ 8 (2) (11)

[121] LSRB 2011 § 18 (4)

[122] LSRB 2011 § 16

[123] FLAC, 'Submission on the Legal Services Bill' February 2012, 1. Available at: <http://www.flac.ie/download/pdf/20120220130320.pdf> Accessed 11/8/2013

profession. FLAC recognised that the Bill will bring greater transparency to the issue of costs. However, it argued that the Bill will do nothing to address the fact that excessive legal costs have prevented people from having access to justice, especially by means of litigation. FLAC was concerned that in its initial form, the Bill contained no provisions for protective cost orders or multi-party actions which, if included, would have facilitated greater access to justice in cases of public importance. FLAC also expressed the view that the proposed new business structures may serve to increase the cost of legal services for once off or occasional service users, and that provisions should also be included to permit the establishment of legal co-operative ventures.

In addition to the above suggested amendments, FLAC made some further recommendations in its written submissions to the Committee as follows:

> • The objectives of the LSRA should be expanded to include the protection and promotion of the fundamental human rights of access to justice and the rule of law.

> • The objective of 'encouraging an independent, strong and effective legal profession' should be extended to include the term 'diverse'.[124]

> • All the professional principles contained in the UN Basic Principles on the Role of Lawyers should be included in the Bill.[125]

> • The LSRA's functions should include the promotion of the understanding of law and the legal system, and awareness of legal services and their costs.

> • A working group including legal practitioners, legal costs accountants and other stakeholders should be established to identify why legal costs are so high, to propose means of reducing them and to facilitate greater access to affordable justice.

> • Given its concerns that the new business structures facilitated by the Bill may reduce choice for consumers of legal services who require an expert legal opinion, FLAC argued that no change should be made to the current arrangements until the Authority has established that the proposed new structures are in the interests of access to justice and of the general public, and there has been further public debate following the Authority's investigations in this regard.

> • Resources should be provided to identify means of increasing efficiency in both the administration of justice and the legal system.

> • A pre-complaint or investigation stage should be established so that where information regarding costs is needed, it can be received and a simple mechanism for determining minor complaints should be available.

---

[124] LSRB 2011 § 9 (4) (e)

[125] The UN Basic Principles on the Role of Lawyers adopted by the Eighth UN Congress on the Prevention of Crime and Treatment of Offenders, Havana, Cuba, 27th August to 7th September 1990. Available at: <http://www2.ohcr.org/english/law/lawyers.htm> Accessed 10/7/2012. The UN Basic Principles on the Role of Lawyers were discussed in ch 2 § 2.5.

• Information about the procedures to be used by the Legal Costs Adjudicator's Office and the procedures to be applied to resolve costs disputes should be widely and readily available.

• The outcome of all fee adjudications should be published with the obscuring of identities for *in camera* cases.

• The Legal Aid Budget ought to be sufficient to ensure that recipients should not have to wait more than two to four months to receive aid.

• The LSRA should conduct a national study to establish the level of unmet legal need in Ireland.[126]

5.4.2 The Irish Human Rights Commission

The IHRC presented its observations on the Bill to the Minister for Justice, Equality and Defence in February 2012. The Commission is responsible for reviewing the adequacy and effectiveness of law and practice in Ireland which relates to the protection of human rights.[127] It is also responsible for examining legislative proposals, forming an opinion on them and making recommendations to Government for measures aimed at strengthening and protecting human rights in Ireland. The Commission believes that robust, independent oversight of Government policies and private bodies is fundamental to the safeguarding and promotion of human rights in Ireland.

The Commission was of the view that one of the main human rights challenges arising from the Bill concerns the independence of the LSRA. The Commission stated that lawyers should not be directly regulated by Government, and that the independence of the legal profession is necessary to ensure the independence of the judiciary. It also noted that, "the freedom and independence of lawyers to act without fear or favour on behalf of their clients is one of the cornerstones of a properly functioning democratic state".[128] The Commission raised concerns regarding the manner of appointment to the LSRA, which essentially lies in the hands of the Minister for Justice, Equality and Defence. It expressed concern that the Ministerial powers contained in the Bill are not in accordance with international best practice for the establishment of independent state institutions.[129] The Commission also called for changes in the functioning

---

[126] FLAC Submission on the LSRB 2011 (FN 123)

[127] The IHRC was established in accordance with the Human Rights Commission Act (HRCA) 2000 § 4. Its functions *inter alia* are: to review the adequacy and effectiveness of Irish law in protecting human rights; to examine legislative proposals and report on their implications for human rights at the request of a Government Minister; to consult with other national or international bodies with knowledge or expertise regarding human rights as it sees fit; and to make recommendations upon its own volition or at the Government's request regarding measures to strengthen, protect and uphold human rights in Ireland (HRCA 2000 § 8 (a) – (d)).

[128] Irish Human Rights Commission, 'Observations on the Legal Services Regulation Bill 2011: February 2012', available at: <www.irhc.ie/publications/list/ihrc-observations-on-lsra-bill-2011/> Accessed 19/9/2013

[129] UN General Assembly Resolution 48/134 of 20th December 1993, 'The Paris Principles for the Independence of National Human Rights Institutions', available at: <www.2ohcr/english

of the LSRA, in particular with regard to its duty to report to the Minister and the need to obtain Ministerial consent in respect of its activities.[130] This should be altered so that the LSRA has a duty to submit reports to the Government, such reports being instigated at its own volition, rather than at the request of the Minister. It also recommended that safeguards should be included in the Bill to prevent the unnecessary compromising of solicitor-client confidentiality, and to ensure that any such breaches are minimal and directly proportional to the purpose of the investigation. It recommended that the Bill, along with the Civil Legal Aid Act 1995 and regulations made under it, should be reviewed and that any unnecessary exclusions for eligibility to Legal Aid should be removed. Finally, it recommended that following *O'Donoghue*, the Legal Aid Board should be adequately funded in order to avoid significant waiting lists for Aid.[131]

5.5 Minister Shatter's Response to Critics of the LSRB 2011

Mr Shatter took the opportunity to respond to criticisms of the LSRB 2011 at the LSI Annual Conference on 14th April 2012, and indicated the areas of the Bill in relation to which he was willing to contemplate amendment.[132] In particular, he undertook to review provisions which required Ministerial approval for the appointment of members of the LSRA and in relation to its functioning. The Minister declared that upon reflection, these provisions were unnecessary and that the Bill would be amended accordingly. However, he also defended the Bill's impact upon the independence of the profession by pointing to the provisions in section 9 (4) (e) of the Bill which require the LSRA to encourage an independent, strong and effective legal profession, and he noted that the LSRA will promote and maintain professional principles including the requirement that legal professionals shall act with independence and integrity.[133]

In a second speech given at the Conference on 'Regulatory Reform for a 21st Century Legal Profession' in Dublin, on 6th July 2012, the Minister responded to further criticisms of the Bill, focusing particularly upon objections to the introduction of MDPs. The Minister identified some of the possible benefits of MDPs, including the potential for a larger clientele for such practices, which may be achieved by linking up with the existing client bases of other professional services providers, such as accountants or insurance providers.[134] MDPs may also

---

/law/parisprinciples.htm> Accessed 1/2/2013

[130] LSRB 2011 § 18

[131] *O'Donoghue v The Legal Aid Board, the Minister for Justice, Equality and Law Reform, Ireland & the Attorney General* [2004] IEHC 413. The case concerned a delay of over two years between the making of an application for Legal Aid and the receipt of assistance from the Legal Aid Board, which constituted a breach of the applicant's constitutional entitlements.

[132] A Shatter, 'Speech on Legal Services Regulation Bill 2011', LSI Annual Conference, 14th April 2012. Available at: <http://www.merrionstreet.ie/index.php/2012/04/minister-alan-shatter-speech-on-legal-services-regulation-bill-2011-law-society-annual-conference/> Accessed 11/8/2013

[133] LSRB 2011 § 9 (5) (a) (i)

[134] A Shatter, Conference speech, 'Regulatory Reform for a 21st Century Legal Profession', 6th July 2012. Available at: <http://www.justice.ie/en/JELR/Pages/SP1200204> Accessed 7/1/2013

facilitate wider access to financial investment, liquidity or debt equity in order to enhance the viability of legal practices and to assist with business growth both nationally and internationally. The establishment of MDPs would also permit various professional service providers to spread the risks inherent in establishing and maintaining a viable practice. They would allow for greater operational flexibility within groups of professional practices, and would provide more attractive and plentiful service options for consumers by means of 'synergies' which would develop between both lawyers and non-legal service providers in areas including insurance, accounting and finance. MDPs would create new opportunities for legal professionals whose current outlooks are inhibited by the existing range of possible business structures. Minister Shatter argued strongly in favour of the introduction of MDPs as follows:

> What is being proposed is an alternative structure in which legal services can be provided using the innovative business techniques now in play, with greater competitiveness and in support of early economic national recovery.[135]

The Minister also pointed out that there will be a process of public consultation and evaluation prior to the introduction of new service delivery models and the outcome of this will shape the regulations and codes of practice which are subsequently introduced.[136] He emphasized that the Bill would not impede lawyers in the fulfilment of their duties as officers of the court, in safeguarding the proper administration of justice and ensuring that their clients receive a fair trial. Lawyers will continue to freely provide services to clients of their own choosing without suffering executive control or pressure. They will also continue to uphold the rights of clients in accordance with the Constitution and will be free to sue the state through both national and international courts, without fear of executive disapproval.

5.6 Amendments to the LSRB 2011

On the 13th July 2013 a list of seventy-five proposed amendments to Parts 1 and 2 of the LSRB 2011 was published by the Select Committee on Justice, Defence and Equality.[137] The first thirty-five of the amendments were considered by the Select Committee on the 17th July 2013.[138] Seventeen of these amendments were proposed by the Minister for Justice, and all of these were accepted by the Select Committee. The most notable of the Minister's amendments were as follows:

---

[135] Ibid 5

[136] LSRB 2011 § 75

[137] The Select Committee list of LSRB 2011 amendments is available at:
<http://www.oireachtas.ie/viewdoc.asp?fn=/documents/bills28/bills/2011/5811/b5811d-dscn.pdf> Accessed 14/8/2013

[138] Details of the Select Committee Debate of 17th July 2013 are available at:
<http://oireachtasdebates.ie/Debates%20Authoring/WebAttachments.nsf/%28$vLookupByConstructedKey/%29Committees~20130717~JUS/$File/Daily%20Book%20Unrevised.pdf?openelement> Accessed 11/8/2013

• The definition of 'lay person' should be altered to include solicitors and barristers who have not practised for a period of five years prior to their appointment by the LSRA.[139]

• The LPDT should not be empowered to include incidental, supplementary and consequential provisions in regulations or orders made by the LSRA.[140]

• LSRA members should be appointed by the Government following a resolution in favour by both Houses of the Oireachtas.[141]

• The diversity of the bodies which are responsible for the nomination of lay members of the LSRA should be increased, to allow the Citizens Information Board, the Consumers' Association and FLAC to participate in the nomination process.

Some of the proposed amendments which were not accepted by the Select Committee in July 2013 were as follows:

• The LSRA should consist of thirteen rather than eleven members.

• The Government should not have the power to remove a member of the LSRA where this appears to the Government to be necessary for the effective performance of the functions of the Authority.[142]

• The Government's role in the election of lay members of the LSRA should be transferred to the President of the High Court.[143]

• The professional principle requiring legal practitioners to act in a client's best interests should be subject to the proviso 'except where that conflicts with a paramount interest in the proper and effective administration of justice'.[144]

The following amendments were agreed by the Select Committee on Justice, Defence and Equality at the Committee Stage of the Bill's passage through the legislature:

• The Minister's powers over the LSRA's ability to appoint consultants and to make contracts will be removed.

• The Minister's power to appoint the Chief Executive of the LSRA will be removed, with the approval of that appointment to be the prerogative of the Minister for Public Expenditure and Reform.

---

[139] The previous definition in section 2 (1) of the Bill defined a lay person as a person who is not and never was a practising solicitor or barrister.

[140] Amendment of LSRB 2011 § 3 (1)

[141] Amendment of LSRB 2011 § 8 (2)

[142] Amendment of LSRB 2011 § 8 (12) (d)

[143] Amendment of LSRB 2011 § 8 (2)

[144] Amendment of LSRB 2011 § 9 (5) (a)

• The Minister's power to appoint members of the LSRA will be removed, with the LSRA itself to be responsible for such appointments, with the approval of the Minister for Public Expenditure and Reform.

• The Minister's power to prescribe fees to be paid to the LSRA for the performance of its functions and the provision of its services will be removed.

• There will be an informal mechanism for the resolution of clients' complaints by means of mediation or alternative forms of dispute resolution.

• The membership of the Complaints Committee will be increased from 16 to 27, in order to ensure that a backlog of complaints will not develop.

• The range of sanctions which the Complaints Committee can impose is increased, and it can now require a legal practitioner to pay up to €3,000 in compensation to a client for loss suffered as a consequence of the inadequate provision of services.

• Members of the LPDT will be appointed by the President of the High Court instead of the Government, upon the nomination of the Minister.

• Partners in MDPs will be jointly and severally liable in respect of their acts or omissions, those of other partners and those of the partnerships' employees.

• MDPs will have a managing legal practitioner with responsibility for the provision of legal services by the practice.

• MDPs shall have written procedures in place to which all partners and employees are subject in order to ensure legal services are provided in accordance with the relevant legislation.

• The LSRA shall engage in public consultation regarding the operation, monitoring and regulation of MDPs.

• The Chief LCA will maintain a publicly examinable register of determinations. He/she will also prepare guidelines for the benefit of anyone making an application to the Office setting out how the process works and what is required of the applicant.

A further list of amendments which are to be considered at the Report Stage of the Bill's passage was published on 11th July 2014.

5.7 Further Suggested Amendments to the LSRB 2011

Following the above consideration of the response of various stakeholders to the publication of the LSRB 2011, the discussion in Chapter 3 of the problems with the current regulation of the legal profession and the comparative perspectives from other jurisdictions in Chapter 4, further suggestions for the amendment of the LSRB 2011 may be made.

The suggestion from Noeline Blackwell from FLAC that the Bill should be amended to include provisions for both protective costs orders and multi-party actions should be acted upon as such amendments would go some way towards allowing greater access to justice for citizens who may lack resources to initiate litigation in the absence of such measures.[145] These amendments would also facilitate litigation in matters of public interest. FLAC has argued that hearings of the Legal Costs Adjudicators should be held in public, and it is proposed herein that the Bill should be amended accordingly in that regard.[146] The Bill should also be amended to incorporate the proposal from FLAC for the establishment of legal co-operatives.

Further amendment should take account of the view of The Fair Trade Commission Report of 1990 in relation to the patents of precedence system, the removal of which it concludes 'is unlikely to have a significant negative impact on the legal system'.[147] Accordingly, the Bill should include a provision which rather than extending the granting of patents of precedence to solicitors, brings this system to an end, thereby removing the archaic distinction between Junior and Senior Counsel which arguably contributes nothing whatever to the quality of legal services provided by barristers. The Bill would also benefit from an amendment to allow for the introduction of a system of regulatory self-assessment for legal practitioners, to be undertaken either by individual practitioners or legal practices, and which is similar to that which was introduced in New South Wales for ILPs. The introduction and monitoring of such a system could be overseen by the LSRA, and would contribute towards the establishment of codes of best practice at the level of individual practices. It would potentially enhance the quality of legal service provision and reduce the level of client complaints. There is no apparent reason why the demonstrable benefits which have flowed from the introduction of the self-assessment regime for ILPs in NSW cannot be replicated in Ireland if the system were to be adopted by other forms of legal practice business structures, including sole practitioners, partnerships and MDPs.

The LSRB 2011 should also be amended to take account of the increasing role which lay litigants play in today's Irish legal system.[148] The Bill provides an opportunity to put the rights of lay litigants, and the responsibilities of legal professionals with respect to them on a statutory basis. Such an amendment would aid the administration of justice in cases concerning lay litigants and would facilitate them in seeking access to justice. Legal professionals should be obliged to communicate clearly with lay litigants and to take all reasonable steps from the outset of a legal dispute to ensure that lay opponents are acquainted with the relevant law and legal principles which pertain in the matter at issue. In the event that provision is made in the Bill for the introduction of regulatory self-assessment procedures for legal professionals, these should include a protocol for communicating effectively with lay litigants. It would also be desirable to amend the Bill to explicitly acknowledge the right of a lay litigant to bring

---

[145] Protective costs orders allow a court to depart from the usual rule whereby 'costs follow the event' which results in a losing party paying the costs of the successful party, and which may have a chilling effect on public interest litigation.

[146] An exception to the amendment requiring disputed fee adjudications to be in public should be made where the dispute concerns an *in camera* case.

[147] *Fair Trade Commission Report of Study into Restrictive Practises in the Legal Profession* (Dublin: Government of Ireland Stationery Office, 1990), as discussed in ch 3 § 3.2.1

[148] The role of lay litigants in the Irish legal system is discussed in ch 3 § 3.3.2.

his/her own case before the Legal Practitioners Disciplinary Tribunal, and to confirm that the authority to bring such a case is not confined to either the LSRA or to persons appointed by the Authority.[149] The recent amendment to the Bill which alters the definition of 'lay person' is to be regretted, as this creates the possibility that the lay input to the LSRA will be 'hijacked' by former members of the legal profession, who will not bring the perspective of a non-legal practitioner to the working of the Authority.[150]

Following the investigation of solicitors' professional misconduct which was presented in Chapter 3, and in light of its findings, some further amendments of the Bill are desirable. This investigation of one hundred cases of professional misconduct was valuable in helping to develop an understanding of common patterns of offending behaviour. However, it is important to remember that the cases which are heard by the SDT, "represent the tip of the proverbial iceberg, the apex of a typical litigation pyramid, whose base is the "dark figure" of actual misconduct".[151] The disciplinary system's fundamental reliance upon clients to report misconduct is partly responsible for this, given that clients often lack the requisite skills to identify and respond to misconduct on the part of their lawyer or may even benefit from such misconduct. Lawyers, of course, may also complain about professional misconduct on their colleagues' part, but often they may hesitate to do so for many reasons including; 'indifference, complicity, material advantage, and a disinclination to encourage other lawyers to complain – perhaps about them'.[152]

In order to enhance our understanding of solicitors' professional misconduct in its 'pure' form, it would be most valuable to examine a random selection of solicitors' files for evidence of misconduct which has not been the subject of a complaint by either an individual client or a colleague. If such an examination was possible it would facilitate an entirely new understanding of this perennial problem and the possible identification of fresh solutions to address it.[153] Further amendment to the LSRB 2011 should be made so that the LSRA might explore the costs and benefits of such a research programme and report accordingly to the Oireachtas.

Abel has argued that a second opinion from an independent lawyer should be routinely available to clients regarding the merits of a course of action which is proposed by his/her lawyer and the reasonableness of its likely costs.[154] Whilst this proposal would introduce an added initial cost in the provision of legal

---

[149] LSRB 2011 § 55

[150] Amendment of LSRB 2011 § 2 (1). See ch 5 § 5.6, for further details in relation to this amendment.

[151] R Abel, *Lawyers on Trial: Understanding Ethical Misconduct* (Oxford University Press, 2011) 465

[152] Ibid 467

[153] This research programme would differ from audits which may occasionally be carried out into solicitors' practices by the LSI, as it would focus only upon researching the nature of offending patterns without the possibility of disciplinary procedures being initiated in cases where misconduct is identified (except in cases where criminality is involved). Such a research programme would certainly raise ethical issues particularly with regard to client confidentiality.

[154] R Abel, *Lawyers on Trial* (FN 151) 514 – 515

services, it would also increase the quality of legal service provision thereby possibly reducing the overall total cost of service delivery. The LSRA should therefore also be required to report to the Oireachtas upon the costs and benefits associated with this proposal. A further proposal which Abel made to alleviate the problem of lawyer misconduct was that sole practitioners should be outlawed with all lawyers being obliged to practice in larger partnership structures.[155] This reform would facilitate and encourage the oversight by colleagues of individual lawyers' practice especially in circumstances where partners bear mutual financial responsibility for one another's professional failures.[156] Whilst this proposal is the most controversial of Abel's suggestions, if implemented, it has the potential to greatly enhance the quality of legal service provision in Ireland.[157] The Bill should also be amended to require the LSRA to report to the Oireachtas on the costs and benefits of this proposal.

Finally, there is one desirable reform of the regulation of the legal profession in Ireland which cannot be achieved by means of an amendment of the LSRB 2011. This concerns the inability of a regulatory authority such as the LSI to strike practitioners from the register, as a result of the Supreme Court ruling in the *O'Farrell* case.[158] Indeed, given the ruling in *O'Farrell*, it is arguable that the recent decision of the Benchers of the HSKI to disbar Patrick Russell was unconstitutional.[159] A constitutional amendment is necessary to empower the appropriate regulatory authority, most probably the LPDT with the ability to either strike off or disbar practitioners who have been found guilty of either serious professional misconduct or criminal behaviour. The view of the Fair Trade Commission in 1990 with regard to the role of the Benchers in the disciplinary process is pertinent here.[160] Given that the decisions of the LPDT will be amenable to judicial review and also that an appeal of its decisions will lie to the High Court, it seems appropriate that the authority to either strike off a solicitor or to disbar a barrister should be the prerogative of the Tribunal. The central role of

---

[155] Ibid 525

[156] The beneficial effect of the oversight of legal practitioners resulting from such a move would be severely diluted if partnerships were permitted to become incorporated, and to function as entities with limited liability. Shatter has indicated that the LSRB 2011 will be amended to include this provision (see ch 5 § 5.3.3 for further discussion of this proposed amendment to the Bill).

[157] Sole practitioners feature in an excessive number of professional misconduct cases given their representation in the overall practitioner population. M Davies, 'Solicitors, Dishonesty and the Solicitors' Disciplinary Tribunal' (1999) 6 (2) *International Journal of the Legal Profession* 141 – 174; E Skordaki and C Willis, *Defaults by Solicitors,* Research Study No 4 (The Law Society, London).

[158] *Re O'Farrell and the Solicitors Act 1954* [1961] 95 ILTR 167. For a full discussion of the case, see ch 1 § 1.3.2.

[159] The Honorable Society of Kings Inns Decision of Benchers to disbar Patrick Russell, 11th January 2012. Available at: <http://www.kingsinns.ie/website/current_students/diplomas/pdfs/ Rule%2037(3)%20website%20notice/%2013/520Jan%202012.pdf> Accessed 12/3/2013. For a discussion of the Russell case, see ch 1 § 1.2.3.

[160] *Fair Trade Commission Report* (FN 147) The Commission expressed reservations about the constitutionality of the Benchers' role in the disciplining of barristers, and also with the general role of the judiciary in the regulation of the bar. For a discussion of this issue, see ch 3 § 3.2.1.

the judiciary in the administration of justice renders it singularly unsuitable for making decisions regarding which practitioners should be permitted to also play a role in that regard. As long as the judiciary continues to command the ultimate authority concerning who has the right to practice law, the Irish legal system is rendered open to the accusation that it operates as a type of cosy cartel, a situation which ill serves the needs of a modern, equitable and democratic state.

5.8 Concluding Remarks

This chapter has focused upon the publication of the LSRB 2011 and its role in fulfilling the State's commitment to the programme of reforms as set out in the Memoranda of Understanding which were agreed with the Troika in return for the receipt of the bailout funds. The Bill is also the mechanism whereby the Government will fulfil its commitments to reform the legal sector, as contained in both the National Recovery Plan 2011 – 2014 and the Programme for Government 2011 – 2016. The provisions of the LSRB 2011 were described in detail, and the reaction of the legal profession and other key stakeholders to its contents were considered. Given the considerable objections which were raised to the contents of the Bill by both the legal profession and other stakeholders, the Minister has indicated a willingness to make significant amendments which are aimed at underpinning not only the independence of the legal profession and its regulatory body, but also the perception of such independence. Whilst the final form of the Bill remains to be seen, it is hoped that these concessions and other amendments to be made in the coming days will go some way towards allaying the fears of the Bill's critics, and to ensuring fundamental reform of the legal services sector, for the benefit of both the legal profession and also of wider society.

The LSRB 2011 presents an opportunity for Ireland to revolutionise both the regulation of its legal profession and the provision of legal services in the state. Having considered the present system of regulating the legal profession in Ireland, identified its shortcomings, examined the proposed reforms as contained in the Bill and the responses of the legal profession to same both nationally and internationally, and having also looked at the manner in which the legal profession and the provision of legal services are regulated in various other jurisdictions, it may be concluded that the LSRB 2011 promises to deliver a great deal of what is necessary in order to allow the Irish legal profession to play a real and meaningful part in the modern, global, legal services market, and also to play a full and fair part in the administration of Irish justice. The process of globalization presents its share of opportunities and challenges for Ireland both nationally and internationally. Furthermore, the intervention of the Troika in Irish economic affairs which was necessitated by Ireland's monumental failure to exercise proper stewardship over our own financial affairs has presented our nation with an opportunity to sweep away traditional and outmoded methods of conducting our affairs on many levels, and the regulated professions have not been spared scrutiny in the course of this 'spring cleaning' exercise. Therefore this study identifies the dual processes of globalization and 'Troikisation' as positive, instrumental forces at play in shaping tomorrow's Irish legal services market. Whilst no rational commentator would welcome the necessity for

Ireland's bailout and the associated loss of sovereignty, the old adage that 'every cloud has a silver lining' would appear to hold true, even in these straitened circumstances, if Ireland is left a better place following on from the Troika programme of reforms, especially for our purposes, from the perspective of regulating the legal profession.

When considering the strengths and weaknesses of the LSRB 2011, it is pertinent to remember that the *status quo* with regard to the regulation of Ireland's legal profession is firmly rooted in the past; specifically in the period from the fifteenth to the mid twentieth century. This proposition may be justified, given that the Solicitors Act 1954 ordained the LSI with immense powers as the front line regulator of its members' professional activities, and also that the BCI and the HSKI have essentially remained as a law onto themselves in terms of regulating the practice of barristers over the course of the last several centuries. Whilst the two branches of the legal profession in Ireland have resisted regulatory change, albeit with varying degrees of conviction, the time has come for Irish citizens to ask ourselves whether we wish legal matters to be settled increasingly by lay litigants and non-lawyers, or whether we wish the administration of justice to largely remain the prerogative of legal professionals.[161] The proper administration of justice cannot be served in a society where ordinary citizens fundamentally lack trust in the legal profession, where they cannot be assured of receiving an identifiable service for an agreed price or where the costs of legal services are prohibitive for a large sector of society. The legal profession's neglect of its statutory obligations in accordance with section 68 of the Solicitors (Amendment) Act 1994, and the ongoing refusal of the Bar to provide advice directly to members of the public are both notable in that regard.[162] The question arises as to why 'the man/woman on the 'Dublin [omni]bus' may be deemed capable of giving informed consent to major surgery, and thereby acquiescing with a course of action to be undertaken in conjunction with a member of the Royal College of Surgeons which may have life-changing consequences, yet he/she is seemingly unable to instruct a member of the BCI in order to arrange matters of concern, arguably of less importance than the maintenance of his/her bodily integrity? There is no question that members of the BCI have superb advocacy skills, but given that they are unwilling to take instruction directly from members of the public generally, further convincing argument is required in order to justify this position.

Finally, whilst it is tempting to wish to see a speedy enactment of the LSRB 2011, given the extraordinary extent of the changes which it heralds for both the legal profession and consumers of legal services alike, it is essential that the Bill is subjected to thorough scrutiny and debate prior to its enactment. Its future progress through the Oireachtas will be closely monitored.

---

[161] The recourse to non-lawyers to settle disputes was graphically illustrated by Mick Wallace TD, and his threat to settle a dispute about a business debt with the assistance of a hit man. For further details, see ch 3 § 3.9.

[162] Section 68 of the Solicitors (Amendment) Act 1994 requires a solicitor to provide a client with particulars in writing concerning what charges will be incurred in the course of a retainer or an estimate of same, or alternatively, to give information on the basis upon which such charges will arise.

CONCLUSION

This study of the regulation of the legal profession in Ireland has revealed the present regulatory framework to be archaic, complex and unfit for the following purposes:

- Providing high quality legal services at a reasonable price
- Furthering the administration of justice
- Promoting and protecting the rule of law

Whereas the regulation of the solicitors' profession has changed little in the course of the last sixty years since the enactment of the Solicitors Act 1954, the regulation of the bar today is eerily similar to the regime of 1792, when the HSKI received its Royal Charter. Since then, it has remained faithful to its motto of *nolumus mutandi*. The international dimension of the regulatory regime is equally complex, and there is evidence to suggest that many lawyers are not adequately acquainted with their responsibilities, at least as far as the international anti-corruption regulatory framework is concerned.[1]

The present regulatory framework lacks a discernable rationale, beyond facilitation of the profession's self-regulatory agenda, adherence to which has served the interests of the profession rather than those of the public. An economic analysis of the current self-regulatory regime reveals the many failings which are associated with that model, and a series of reports which have been commissioned over the course of the last twenty years have also documented a catalogue of problems associated with self-regulation. The rise of the lay litigant further illustrates the problems inherent in the regulatory *status quo*. The present system largely responds only to regulatory breaches *ex post*, and is ill equipped to address the problem of breaches *ex ante*, thereby losing the opportunity to prevent the occurrence of breaches and to secure consequential benefits for the profession and clients alike. The present system also fails to distinguish between the differing needs of private and organisational clients, contrary to the recommendations of the European Commission. Nor does it comply with the OECD Guiding Principles for Regulatory Quality and Performance.[2]

---

[1] The IBA Survey, 'Anti-Corruption Strategy for the Legal Profession: Risks and Threats of Corruption in the Legal Profession' (2010 is available at: <http://www.oecd.org/investment/briberyininternatioanalbusiness/46137847.pdf> Accessed 28/8/2012

[2] EU Commission, Communication from the Commission to the Council, the European Parliament, the European Economic and Social Committee and the Committee of the Regions

A comparison between the Irish regulatory regime and those which pertain in other jurisdictions has been valuable in identifying what changes ought to be made to the current Irish framework. The English and Australian experience of ABSs suggests that the deregulation of business structures for legal practices brings new opportunities for both practitioners and clients. An examination of the regulation of the legal professions in Greece and Portugal reveals that these countries are in a process of transition, as they implement the programmes of structural reforms which were agreed with the Troika in return for their bailout funds. The legal professions in these countries are being subjected to the same experiment which the Troika is carrying out upon the Irish profession, the outcome of which is, as yet, unclear.

An examination of the provisions of the LSRB 2011 suggests that the Bill, if enacted, will go a considerable way towards rectifying many of the problems associated with the existing regulatory regime. The process of amending the Bill has not been concluded, and for now, a degree of caution must be observed regarding the form of the final legislation. Many of the published amendments would appear to address the criticisms of key stakeholders regarding the independence of the LSRA, and are aimed at removing the role of the Minister for Justice in the appointment and activities of the Authority. However, the dilution of the role of lay persons in the Authority which has been achieved through the alteration of the definition of lay person in the Bill is of concern, and suggests that the professions have succeeded in a degree of regulatory capture in this regard.[3]

The recommendations for further amendment of the Bill which are suggested based upon this research are as follows:

• To provide for the making of protective costs orders, the issuance of multi-party actions and the establishment of legal co-operatives.[4]

• To provide for the discontinuance of the patents of precedence system rather than its extension to include solicitors.[5]

'Professional Services – Scope for More Reform', 5th Sept 2005, COM (2005) 405 para 30; OECD, 'Guiding Principles for Regulatory Quality and Performance' (OECD, 2005). Cited by L Terry et al, 'Adopting Regulatory Objectives for the Legal Profession' (2012) 80 (6) *Fordham Law Review* 2685 – 3093, 2689

[3] The Select Committee list of LSRB 2011 amendments is available at: <http://www.oireachtas.ie/viewdoc.asp?fn=/documents/bills28/bills/2011/5811/b5811d-dscn .pdf> Accessed 14/8/2013. In section 2 (1) of the Bill, the definition of 'lay person' will be altered to include solicitors and barristers who have not practised for a period of five years prior to their appointment by the LSRA. This replaces the previous definition of a lay person in the Bill when first published as being a person who is not and never was a practising solicitor or barrister. The LSI has indicated that it did not seek amendment of the Bill in this regard. (Interview with Mr Ken Murphy, Director General, LSI, Blackhall Place, Dublin, 13th September 2013.)

[4] FLAC, 'Submission on the Legal Services Bill', February 2012, 1. Available at: <http://www.flac.ie/download/pdf/20120220130320.pdf> Accessed 11/8/2013

[5] LSRB 2011 Part 11

• To provide for the protection of the rights of lay litigants within the legal system, and to explicitly identify the responsibilities of legal professionals with regard to them.

• To provide for the conduct of a research project into the professional misconduct of legal practitioners. This should include the inspection of files which have not been the subject of a complaint from a client, a fellow legal professional or a member of the judiciary.

• To provide for the conduct of a research project into the desirability of establishing a two tier regulatory framework which is sensitive to the differing needs of the private and corporate sectors.

• To provide for the conduct of research into the desirability of making a second opinion routinely available to clients regarding the merits of the particular course of action which is proposed by a lawyer. The second opinion would include a cost-benefit analysis of the original lawyer's suggested course of conduct, a consideration of its reasonableness and the likely costs which its adoption would incur.[6]

• To provide for the conduct of research into the costs and benefits of prohibiting sole practitioners from practice, in order to facilitate and encourage the oversight of legal practitioners by their peers.[7]

• To provide for the introduction of appropriate business management systems.[8]

• To provide for the introduction of a cause of action arising from the ineffective assistance of counsel in both civil and criminal matters.

Following the enactment of the LSRB 2011, there should be a referendum in order to secure a constitutional amendment to empower the LPDT to strike off, or disbar, practitioners who have been found guilty of either serious professional misconduct or criminality.

This research supports the conclusion that the regulation of the legal profession in Ireland, and in other bailed-out nations, is undergoing a paradigm shift. National and self-regulatory mechanisms are being replaced by the imposition of 'liberalising' frameworks, which have been constructed by non-elected, international agencies, in the form of the Troika. A recent poll suggests that there is considerable public confusion about the bodies comprising the Troika:

> As Ireland edges closer to leaving the bailout, some residents still do not know who our benefactors were. A survey by Behaviour and Attitudes for The Sunday Times has found 4% of the population think Anglo Irish Bank was amongst the institutions funding Ireland's economic safety net. Asked to name the three members of the bailout Troika, only one in twenty

---

[6] R Abel, *Lawyers on Trial: Understanding Ethical Misconduct* (Oxford University Press, 2011) 514 – 515

[7] Ibid 525

[8] These would be similar to those which were introduced in New South Wales in accordance with The New South Wales Legal Profession Act 2004 §§ 140 & 168.

adults (5%) knew they were the International Monetary Fund, the European Central Bank and the European Union (*sic*). One in four respondents was able to name one of the institutions, but 60% could not name any. Some 6% thought NAMA was part of the Troika, another 8% thought The Allied Irish Bank was involved, and 7% answered Bank of Ireland'.[9]

The ignorance surrounding the Troika's identity is concerning, given its widespread influence in recent years upon the government of Ireland, and it contributes to a perception of democratic deficiency here and also, most probably, in other bailed-out states. The government might usefully consider doing more to promote public awareness of the positive changes for society which have flowed from the Troikaisation process. The process of globalization also offers new possibilities of growth for Ireland's legal services sector, and the implementation of the reforms contained in the LSRB 2011 will put Ireland in a stronger position to exploit such new opportunities.

One of the most concerning facts to emerge from this research is the manner in which the HSKI conducts itself insofar as it purports to 'regulate' the occurrence of professional misconduct in the barristers' branch of the legal profession. The evidence suggests a policy of 'non-regulation', the effect of which appears to positively undermine the efforts of the BPCT and the BPCAB to secure a satisfactory and timely conclusion of matters for complainants. The refusal of the HSKI to make available a copy of its General Rules to facilitate this research is disappointing, not least, given the contents of Rule 2 of the General Rules of the HSKI:

> (2) The main objects of the Society shall be:
>
> (i) the promotion and advancement of learning in the law[10]

In refusing to make its Rules available, the HSKI has hindered this research project, a stance which is in marked contrast to its stated object of the 'promotion and advancement of learning in the law'. The conclusion must be drawn that the HSKI, by virtue of both its conduct and its motto, continues to commit itself to arcane and secret practises which are singularly inappropriate in the functioning of a modern legal system in an open and democratic state. However, the approach of barristers to the modernisation of the regulatory framework has been in marked contrast to that of solicitors. Notwithstanding its initial reservations, the LSI has generally responded positively to the prospect of change.

As the author of the LSRB 2011, Deputy Shatter is set to make a historic contribution towards the attainment of a modern Irish democracy, if it is enacted. The Bill promises to bring much-needed openness and accountability to the regulation of what is, for now at least, one of the most influential professions.

---

[9] S O'Brien, 'Troika is IMF, ECB and, er, Anglo?', *The Sunday Times*, 30th June 2013
[10] General Rules of The Honorable Society of King's Inns (2009) Rule 2 (i). (This version of the Rules was most kindly provided to the author upon condition of anonymity.)

APPENDIX 1

THE ORIGINS OF IRELAND'S ECONOMIC CRISIS[1]

1.0 The Unholy Trinity Hypothesis

It is proposed herein that Ireland's economic demise was brought about by the combined activities of three groups of social actors – an Unholy Trinity consisting of bankers, property developers and lawyers. Lawyers have, to considerable effect, vociferously denied their role in the economic catastrophe which has engulfed Ireland. They have almost completely avoided concerted scrutiny in this regard in both the popular media and also the academic literature.[2] The argument in support of the 'Unholy Trinity Hypothesis' commences with the simple observation that lawyers have a monopoly in relation to the provision of conveyancing services in Ireland, and as such, they had a central role in every property transaction which occurred in Ireland throughout the notorious 'Celtic Tiger' years.[3] As every law student learns early in their legal studies, along with rights come responsibilities, and where rights are exclusive in a particular domain, so must the responsibilities be similarly exclusive. In order to understand the origins and development of Ireland's economic catastrophe it is necessary to consider the 'contributions' of each of these actors to the development of both the banking crisis and the property crash. Examining the role of these three groups of social actors reveals the interconnectedness of their activities and shows how their combined activities contributed to the 'lethal cocktail of events' which ultimately brought down the Celtic Tiger.[4] The case study of

---

[1] This is an extract from the author's paper entitled 'The Legal Profession in Troikaland: Before and After the Irish Bailout'. The paper was presented in May 2013 at the Law and Society Association (LSA) Annual Meeting, Boston, Massachusetts, USA, and is available at: <http://ssrn.com/abstract=2262083> Accessed 20/9/2013. The version presented as Appendix 1 is an abridged republication of the article as posted May 2013 and amended September 2013, and is current as of that date.

[2] G Doherty, 'No Shortage of Challenges' (May 2010) 104 (4) LSG. The LSI has been vociferous in rejecting any suggestion that the legal profession had any role whatever in the events which culminated in the banking crisis and subsequent Troika Bailout.

[3] The term 'Celtic Tiger' was firstly coined by the UK economist Kevin Gardiner in order to describe the economic boom in Ireland between 1995 and 2008. Finfacts Ireland, 'The UK Economist who coined the term "Celtic Tiger"'. Available at: <http://www.finfacts.com/celtictigereconomyIreland.htm> Accessed 14/3/2013

[4] A Neary & F O'Toole, *The Blueprint Report: A Review of the Legal Profession in Ireland and a Vision for Irish Law Firms* (Anne Neary Consulations, 2011) 8 – 9. Neary and O'Toole used

Michael Lynn below also illustrates the relationship between lawyers, property developers and bankers, and the devastating effect of their combined activities for Irish society.

1.1 Bankers

The development of the Irish banking crisis has been attributed by some to turbulence in the global financial markets in recent years as evidenced by the collapse of the Lehmann Brothers' Bank in 2008, the difficulties caused by the American sub-prime mortgage market and the demise of Iceland's economy. However, this 'global contamination theory' of Ireland's economic difficulties was not supported by a series of reports which were commissioned by the Irish Government in the wake of the banking crisis.[5] Whilst these reports acknowledge the role of international factors, they conclude that domestic factors were paramount in the development of the Irish economic collapse. As Regling and Watson have described it, the banking crisis arose as a consequence of, 'a plain vanilla property bubble, compounded by exceptional concentrations of lending for purposes related to property, and most notably commercial property'.[6] The growth in property-related lending resulted in a grave over-exposure to property loans in financial institutions in the years preceding the collapse. Whilst Kelly has acknowledged that 'the proximate cause of the boom and bust in Ireland is well known: construction', he has argued that the construction boom was fuelled by another boom, that in bank lending.[7] There was also a growing trend towards the adoption of neo-liberal policies, which facilitated the replacement of the 'old school', interventionist, paternalistic financial regulatory model with a 'growth-friendly', light touch approach which was supposedly more attractive to international financial capital.[8] There was a growing international call which found

---

the phrase 'a lethal cocktail of events' to refer to the series of events which culminated in the collapse of the Solicitors Mutual Defence Fund (SMDF), a leading provider of Professional Indemnity cover for solicitors in 2011, as a result of overexposure to conveyancing claims. The lethal cocktail of events included the certificate of title system, exposure to large volumes of commercial property transactions in the conveyancing market and a departure by banks from traditional lending criteria.

[5] K Regling & M Watson, *Preliminary Report on the Sources of Ireland's Banking Crisis* (Dublin: Government Publications Office, 2010), at <http://www.bankingenquiry.gov.ie/Preliminary%20Report%20into%20Ireland's%20Banking%20Crisis%2031/%20May%202010.pdf> Accessed 27/10/2012. P Honohan, *The Irish Banking Crisis: Regulatory and Financial Stability Policy 2003 – 2008: A Report to the Minister for Finance from the Governor of the Central Bank* (Dublin: Central Bank, May 2010), at <http://www.bankingenquiry.gov.ie/The%20Irish%20Banking%20Crisis%20Regulatory%20and%20Financial%20Stability%20Policy%202003-2008.pdf> Accessed 27/10/2012. P Nyberg, *Misjudging Risk: Causes of the Systemic Banking Crisis in Ireland: Report of the Commission of Investigation into the Banking Sector in Ireland* (Dublin 2011), at <http://www.bankingenquiry.gov.ie/Documents/Misjudging%20Risk%20-%20Causes%20of%20the%20Systemic%20Banking%20Crisis%20in%20Ireland.pdf> Accessed 27/10/2012

[6] Ibid; Regling & Watson 5 – 6

[7] M Kelly, 'The Irish Credit Bubble' (2009), UCD Centre for Economic Research Working Paper Series 2009 WP09/32 1

[8] G Taylor, 'Risk and Financial Armageddon in Ireland: The Politics of the Galway Tent' (2011) 82 (4) *The Political Quarterly Review* 596 – 597

favour in Ireland to alleviate the regulatory burden that resulted in a shift of responsibility for regulatory matters from the state to financial institutions. After all, so the theory went, risk modelling had improved, and the 'experts' in the financial sector could bring to bear their knowledge of innovative financial instruments to meet the challenges of international market conditions.[9] The end result of this political strategy was the complete abandonment of any effective regulatory oversight from the supposedly responsible authorities.[10] Honohan has summarised the problem as follows:

> By relying excessively on a regulatory philosophy emphasising process over outcomes, supervisory practice focused on verifying governance and risk management models rather than attempting an independent assessment of risk, whether on a line-by-line or whole-of-institution basis. This approach involved a degree of complacency about the likely performance of well-governed banks that proved unwarranted. It was not just a question of emphasising principles over rules, it was the degree of trust that well-governed banks could be relied upon to remain safe and sound.[11]

In seeking to identify the causes of the banking collapse, Honohan has also cited a deferential attitude on the part of the Financial Regulator towards the banks, the state's failure to properly resource banking supervision, a neglect of quantitative assessment measures with regard to regulatory strategy and a failure to accumulate sufficient capital in the face of increased property-related risks.[12] As Honohan has noted, there was a significant degree of 'regulatory capture' in the circumstances.[13]

The lack of any meaningful regulatory enforcement regime in the Irish financial sector during this period contributed to the development of a highly dysfunctional banking system. From the outset of his appointment in February 2006, the Chief Executive of the Financial Services Regulatory Authority Patrick Neary made it clear that he was an advocate of the light touch regulatory approach, and stated that, 'we will seek to implement the rules to the minimum extent necessary'.[14] As late as March 2008, Mr Neary was still promoting the 'collaborative' approach to regulation:

> [T]he development of the Irish financial services industry over the past twenty years has been a great success story.... [W]e believe in an open and collaborative style [of regulation] to help us respond to issues in the best

[9] Ibid 597

[10] Ireland adopted a hybrid financial regulatory authority comprising of both The Central Bank of Ireland the Financial Services Authority of Ireland (CBIFSA). This consisted of a monetary authority which was responsible for functions related to the European Central Bank and the Financial Services Regulatory Authority which was responsible for the regulation of financial and insurance services, and also for consumer protection.

[11] P Honohan, *The Irish Banking Crisis* (FN 5) 8

[11] Ibid 22

[12] Ibid 9 – 12

[13] Ibid 9

[14] The FSRA was subsequently referred to as the Financial Regulator.

interests of consumers and investors, while maintaining sound and profitable businesses and markets'.[15]

This statement was made less than six months before the state found it necessary to give the Bank Debt Guarantee in September 2008, and less than two weeks following this speech, the Anglo Irish Bank (Anglo) share price fell 18% over the course of one week, due to concerns over its exposure to the property sector.[16]

1.2 Property Developers

There were several factors which led to the development of Ireland's 'plain vanilla property bubble'. Regling and Watson have observed that there was a marked, three-fold concentration in the assets purchased with the loans made available by financial institutions during the Celtic Tiger years:

> It [the asset concentration] featured loans to the property sector in general; loans to commercial property specifically; and within this latter group, development loans to interests associated with a limited number of key developers of commercial property. In this respect Ireland stands out.[17]

At the height of the building boom, just twenty-five individuals controlled over 50% of all building land in North County Dublin, a dominance which enabled them to manipulate the market and force up prices.[18] The commercial property sector included not just properties to be used for commercial purposes. It also included newly constructed residential units built for rental purposes, and construction projects consisting of multiple units. In 2006 over 75% of loans at the Anglo Irish Bank (Anglo) were made available for property construction, with other institutions having similarly high exposures to the sector.[19] The growing exposure of financial institutions to the property market at a time of rapidly increasing property prices increased the risk of a property crash, a probability which was exacerbated by the increased availability of loan-to-value loans. These linked the sum loaned to the value of the asset being acquired rather than the borrower's ability to repay. This practice was not in accordance

---

[15] P Neary, 'IFSC 2.0 Conference – The Next Phase', 5th March 2008 UCD. The speech entitled 'Address by the Chief Executive to IFSC 2.0 Conference – The Next Phase' (5th March 2008) is available from the Speeches section on the Press Area Page of Central Bank Website. Available at: <http://centralbank.ie/press-area/speeches/Pages/default.aspx> Accessed 5/8/2014

[16] P Nyberg, *Misjudging Risk* (FN 5) 151

[17] K Regling & M Watson, *Preliminary Report* (FN 5) 31. In the Irish Nationwide Building Society's commercial loan book, 51% of borrowings were made available to just 25 individuals – its "top" customers. Houses of the Oireachtas Committee of Public Accounts (PAC), *Report on the Crisis in the Domestic Banking Sector: A Preliminary Analysis and a Framework for a Banking Enquiry* (July 2012) 40.

[18] F O'Toole, *Ship of Fools: How Stupidity and Corruption Sank the Celtic Tiger* (London: Faber & Faber), in B Clarke and N Hardiman, 'Crisis in the Irish Banking System' (2012) UCD Working Papers in Law, Criminology and Socio-Legal Studies. Research Paper No 2/2012 34. Available at: <http://ssrn.com/abstract=2008302> Accessed 26/10/2012

[19] K Regling & M Watson, *Preliminary Report* (FN 5) 32

with the prudent assessment of risks associated with future property price trends. The property boom saw an increase in the housing stock of 76.7% between 1991 and 2011, excluding replacement stock.[20] The neo-liberal agenda which favoured a light touch regulatory approach was not confined to the financial sector; the regulation of the property market also was shaped by a laissez-faire, non-interventionist philosophy. This marked a departure from social and affordable housing policies which had required property developers to allocate 20% of new stock for such purposes. The new regulatory regime permitted developers to take control of quality and standards through a system of self-certification.[21] The objective of balanced spatial development was abandoned, as tax relief for construction served to utterly undermine it.[22] The continual over-supply of housing proceeded until 2009, notwithstanding the fact that the 2006 census indicated that almost 250,000 housing units, excluding holiday properties were vacant. Almost another 250,000 were built before the end of 2009.[23]

The elite group of property developers who dominated Ireland's 'cement economy' in the early years of the twenty-first century were the *nouveau riche* who gained their wealth with remarkable speed.[24] There were persistent allegations of corruption associated with the planning process during these years which have been well documented as property developers lavished bribes upon local authority councillors in return for favourable land zoning decisions.[25] The Golden Circle of property developers was also closely associated with senior members of the Fianna Fáil government which dominated the Irish political landscape during this period, and along with politicians and bankers they frequented the 'Galway Tent', an annual hospitality suite established at the Galway Races.

One lasting consequence of this massive over-construction is the new phenomenon of 'ghost estates'; those housing estates consisting of ten or more units where at least 30% of units are either vacant or under construction.[26] Other consequences are a high housing vacancy rate and a steep decline in property prices with associated widespread problems of negative equity for mortgage holders. Ghost estates are at one end of a spectrum of 'unfinished estates' which consist of developments of two or more units where at least 10% of units are

[20] Central Statistics Office 2011 in R Kitchin et al, 'Unfinished Estates in Post Celtic Tiger Ireland', National Institute for Regional and Spatial Analysis. Working Paper Series No 67-2012 3

[21] R Kitchin et al, 'Unfinished Estates' (FN 20) 4. Referring to Part V Planning and Development Act 2000 (repealed in 2002)

[22] B Clarke & N Hardiman, 'Crisis in the Irish Banking System' (FN 18) 34

[23] R Kitchin et al, 'Unfinished Estates' (FN 20) 4, citing Department of Environment, Community and Local Government (DECLG) 2010 Housing Statistics. Available at: <http://www.environ.ie/en/Publications/StatisticsandRegularPublications/HousingStatistics>

[24] B Clarke & N Hardiman, 'Crisis in the Irish Banking System' (FN 18) 36

[25] The Moriarty Tribunal of Enquiry, *The Tribunal of Enquiry into Certain Planning Matters and Payments* (2012). Available at: <http://www.flood-tribunal.ie/asp/Reports.asp?objectid=310&Mode=0&RecordID=504> Accessed 12/11/2012

[26] R Kitchin et al, 'Unfinished Estates' (FN 20) 5

unoccupied.[27] Presently, there are 1770 unfinished estates in Ireland, 1100 of which are in a 'seriously problematic condition'.[28] Beyond the statistics the vast oversupply of housing units in Ireland has given rise to a tide of human misery as many citizens face difficulties on a daily basis caused by incomplete estates, with either poor or missing lighting, unfinished roads and pavements, dysfunctional sewerage systems and housing which does not comply with basic building and fire and safety regulations.[29] Antisocial behaviour such as vandalism and theft has occurred on the unfinished estates, and children use them as 'playgrounds'.[30] It is impossible for the social networks which characterise healthy communities to develop in such circumstances. Kitchin et al refer to unfinished and ghost estates as 'the new ruins of Ireland':

> Ruins have always been a feature of the Irish landscape, but their lack of antiquity and prior occupation coupled with the scale of the issue suggest that unfinished estates constitute a new type of ruin. The problem of unfinished estates is fittingly analogous to the severity of the financial crisis that exposed them.[31]

Kitchin et al have dismissed the Government response to the property crisis as being more neo-liberal policies which have only served to worsen the initial crisis. They identify three strands to the Government's response. Firstly, there was the establishment of the National Assets Management Agency (NAMA), a vehicle designed for recovering bad loans from the banks.[32] Secondly, the Social Housing Leasing Initiative was established. This is a scheme which rents properties from the private sector on long-term leases, usually for twenty years, to accommodate families on local authority housing lists.[33] However, at the expiry of the leases, the properties revert to the landlords or property developers. Site resolution plans are the third strand of the Government response to the housing crisis. These plans adopt a partnership approach to address the problem of unfinished estates, whereby local authorities, residents, estate management companies and other stakeholders such as the banks and property developers negotiate an action plan to remedy the problems in each estate on a case by case

---

[27] Ibid 5

[28] Department of Environment, Community and Local Government, *National Housing Development Survey Summary Report* (Nov 2012), 6, at <http://www.environ.ie/en/Publishing/DevelopmentandHousing/Housing/FileDownLoad,31621,en.pdf> Accessed 29/11/2012. (The Report does not use the term 'ghost estate' but instead refers to estates in a 'seriously problematic condition'.)

[29] The Priory Hall development in Dublin which was built by the bankrupt property developer Tom McFeely is a case in point. The development was a firetrap from which residents have been forcibly removed by Court Order. <http://www.irishtimes.com/newspaper/breaking/2012/1013//breaking3.html> Accessed 13/11/2012

[30] R Kitchin et al, 'Unfinished Estates' (FN 20) 10

[31] Ibid 15

[32] NAMA is an institution which was established to remove poorly performing property loans from Irish banks in order to enhance the overall credit rating of 'Ireland Inc'. <http://www.nama.ie> Accessed 18/3/2013

[33] In the Social Housing Leasing Initiative, rents are guaranteed by the local authorities to the landlords/property developers for the entire leasehold period regardless of occupancy.

basis. However, the Department of Environment, Community and Local Government (DECLG) fund of €5 million for the implementation of site resolution plans is utterly inadequate, given the scale of the problem, and reflects once more a light touch regulatory philosophy.

1.3 Lawyers

The Irish legal profession has undergone little in the way of meaningful reform over the last fifty years, and in its present regulatory state which is both archaic and complex, it is arguably unfit to contribute fully to the administration of justice in a modern democracy or to the preservation of the rule of law. Nor can the profession in its current state provide legal services of a quality which Irish society is reasonably entitled to expect.

When considering the legal profession in the context of the banking crisis and the property bubble, it is necessary to focus particularly upon the provision of conveyancing services for which the Irish legal profession has a monopoly. The profession's problems with regard to conveyancing arose in the context of increasingly easily available credit, and the Golden Circle who were determined to drive forward the 'cement economy' with the acquiescence of Government. Specific problems in Irish conveyancing began with the adoption of the two solicitor certificate of title system in place of the traditional system which involved the input of three solicitors.[34] Under the two solicitor system, the purchaser's solicitor provides an undertaking to the lending institution that the title to the property is good, and also that the relevant security will be registered appropriately. Financial institutions do not appoint their own solicitors, and instead they rely upon the purchaser's solicitor's professional indemnity in relation to these conveyances as a safeguard in the event that such mortgages are not actually registered, or that good title is not secured. The extension of the two solicitor certificate of title system from residential to commercial transactions resulted in an exponential growth in the exposure of both the Solicitors' Mutual Defence Fund (SMDF) and other Professional Indemnity Insurers to flawed conveyances because during the Celtic Tiger years solicitors who lacked the requisite skills frequently provided conveyancing services to the commercial sector without ensuring that appropriate safeguards were in place.

A particular problem arose regarding solicitors who gave undertakings in the course of commercial transactions to which they themselves were parties. This area of practice was ruthlessly exploited by dishonest solicitors with catastrophic effect for their clients, the legal profession, the property market, financial institutions and also wider society. The activities of one such dishonest solicitor, Mr Michael Lynn, will be considered below. A further compounding factor in the silently mounting difficulties for the legal profession was the practice increasingly adopted by financial institutions of making loans available to borrowers based upon the asset value securing the loan, rather than upon the borrowers' ability to

---

[34] Traditionally, three solicitors participated in the process of property transfers in Ireland; one who represented the interests of the purchaser, one who represented the interests of the seller, and another who represented the interests of the lending institution, which made available a mortgage, or other funds, to the purchaser.

repay. This trend also contributed to a scenario whereby lenders who became aware of defects in their securities sought compensation from solicitors on the basis that the latter were obliged to insure against losses resulting from defects in the registration of securities.

In 2009 over 70% of claims made against the Solicitors Mutual Defence Fund (SMDF) related to conveyancing.[35] It is not yet possible to quantify the extent of the losses accruing as a result of solicitors who lacked the requisite expertise dabbling in conveyancing, especially in the commercial sector. This is because damage or loss due the professional negligence in the form of flawed conveyancing is latent and may only become apparent years after the occurrence of the act or omission giving rise to the loss or damage. The Commercial Court is currently hearing a series of cases which are unprecedented in terms of both their number and value. A further difficulty in quantifying such losses arises because litigation concerning high value property transactions involving Irish lawyers and lenders is not confined to Ireland as many disputed properties are outside the jurisdiction, and some of the lawyers and property developers concerned have endeavoured to become 'bankruptcy tourists'.[36]

2.0 A Case Study: Michael Lynn

Michael Lynn was admitted to the roll of solicitors in 1994. After commencing practice with a Dublin firm, he established his own practice Capel Law in Dublin. However, Capel Law was closed down in October 2007 on foot of an application by the LSI to the President of the High Court. In September 2007 an employee at the firm Ms McAleenan became concerned that multiple undertakings relating to a number of properties had been given to several financial institutions, many of which had not been complied with, as no fixed charges were registered on the properties in relation to which the loans were made available and the undertakings given.[37] McAleenan also became aware that approximately €7 million received by Lynn from the Ulster Bank in these transactions had not been properly recorded in the company accounts. She informed the LSI of these issues and they entered the practice on 12th September 2007. It emerged that not only had multiple undertakings been given to several institutions relating to a number of properties, but that there had also been a failure to register first fixed charges over the relevant properties and that Lynn had benefited from these arrangements. It was also apparent that McAleenan's signature had been forged to facilitate these transactions.[38] On 22nd April 2008 The Solicitors Disciplinary Tribunal (SDT) heard two cases concerning Lynn in relation to

---

[35] SMDF Annual Report 2010, 6, at <http://www.smdf.ie/pubs/Solicitors_Report_Aug_2011
.pdf> Accessed 6/12/2012. In 2011 the SMDF became insolvent as a result of the excessive
level of conveyancing-related claims which it faced.

[36] 'O'Donnells fail to reverse ruling in UK bankruptcy', Irishtimes.com, 7th March 2013
<http://www.irishtimes.com/business/sectors/commercial-property-and-construction/
o-donnells-fail-to-reverse-ruling-on-uk-bankruptcy-1.1319321> Accessed 20/3/2013

[37] *McAleenan v AIG (Europe) Ltd* [2010] IEHC 128, Finlay Geoghan J, para 10

[38] Ibid, para 17

the issuance of the multiple undertakings and fined him €1 million in each case, to be paid to the LSI.[39]

In the first case, the Tribunal considered a series of allegations concerning the failure to honour multiple undertakings given by Lynn to several financial institutions and clients in relation to properties in Cluan Bui, Liscara, Carrick-on-Shannon.[40] In the second hearing, the Tribunal considered similar charges concerning land and property at Derrockstown, Dunshaughlin, Co Meath and also in relation to Lynn's own home, Glenlion House, Howth, Co Dublin.[41] The second hearing also considered twenty other serious regulatory breaches including attempting to mislead the LSI's investigating accountant, failing to maintain proper client files or books of account, causing large deficits to arise on clients' accounts, misappropriating clients' funds and failing to provide information sought by an authorized person conducting an investigation pursuant to the regulations. Lynn was found guilty of a total of 57 offences by the SDT. The Tribunal ruled that files be forwarded to the President of the High Court recommending that Lynn be struck off, and also to the DPP and the Fraud Squad for investigation. Lynn absented himself from the jurisdiction and ceased to cooperate with the LSI notwithstanding assurances by his legal representatives to the President of the High Court that he would fully cooperate with the investigation being conducted by the High Court.[42] However, the LSI made no application to the High Court during the course of the proceedings that Lynn's passport should be seized.

The extent of Lynn's mortgage frauds is estimated to be in the region of €80 million. However, the total value of his frauds are difficult to calculate precisely, as some of the financial institutions involved have been less than forthcoming in cooperating with the criminal investigations into Lynn's activities. Whilst no specific allegation of wrongdoing has been made in relation to any particular institution concerning loans to Lynn, their reluctance may be due to their having departed from good business practice and risk assessment policies in relation to his loans, or because of a breach of their fiduciary duties. It appears that some institutions were overly enthusiastic to make loans available to Lynn, possibly in an effort to increase their share of the speculative property market. The First Active Building Society was anxious to make extraordinary levels of borrowing available to Lynn to fund his property dealings, with €3.15 million being given in April 2004 (with no repayments whatsoever to be made for the first twelve months) and a further sum of €4.355 million being made available during the following 18 months (on an interest only repayment basis for the first twelve months).[43] Some of this funding was made available for the purchase of property

---

[39] *In the Matter of Michael Lynn, a solicitor formerly practicing under the style and title of Capel Law and in the matter of the Solicitors Acts 1954 – 2002* [7153/DT/15/08 and High Court Record no 2008 no 32SA; 7153/DT/16/08 and High Court Record no 2007 no 50SA]

[40] Case 7153/DT/15/08 and High Court Record no 2008 no 32SA concerned the following residential properties: 8,9,18,23 and 26 Cluan Bui, Liscara, Carrick-on-Shannon, Co Leitrim.

[41] Case 7153/DT/16/08 and High Court Record no 2007 no 50SA

[42] Ibid [7153/DT/16/08 and High Court Record no 2007 no 50SA], para 1

[43] 'Bank gave "payment holiday" on €3m loans', 6th January 2008, *Independent.ie*, <http://www.independent.ie/national-news/bank-gave-payment-holiday-on-3m-loans-

in Cluain Bui, Liscara, Carrick on Shannon, in relation to which Lynn also obtained mortgage funding from the Trustees Savings Bank (TSB). However, neither institution was able to lay claim to the properties as Lynn omitted to register their interests with the Land Registry and he further obstructed the financial institutions' efforts to register their interest in the properties by withdrawing leases and other relevant documentation from the Property Registration Authority.

It is doubtful whether either Lynn or any of the financial institutions which facilitated his property dealings would wish to obtain possession of any property in Cluain Bui today, as they most probably present a liability to an owner due to their dangerous condition.[44] Cluain Bui has the dubious distinction of being one of the worst planned estates in Ireland, and provides a stark example of what Kitchen et al identified as a 'new ruin'. Cluain Bui's one or two sole inhabitants live in conditions of advanced urban decay, reminiscent of a bombsite. Their situation reflects the human misery wrought by the combined ravages of the Celtic Tiger, and the worst excesses of the Unholy Trinity.

Having travelled extensively throughout Europe following his departure from Ireland, Lynn went to Brazil, where he resides with his family having recently been awarded a permanent family reunification visa. Until recently, he was concentrating upon his business and property interests in Brazil.[45] In a rare interview given to the media who located him in a Portuguese villa in January 2009 Lynn stated:

> I'm not going to be used as an example for what was recognized as an accepted form and practice of business by bankers, lawyers, accountants and auctioneers and I'm not going to be the poster boy who ends up in prison, to my cost.[46]

On the 29th August 2013 Lynn was arrested in Recife, Brazil, following an Irish request for his extradition. Although Ireland and Brazil do not have an extradition treaty, they recently entered into a bilateral agreement, which if invoked, would secure Lynn's return to Ireland where he faces thirty-three charges in relation to his debts of €80 million.[47]

Less than six months following the closure of Lynn's firm, the LSI and the Irish Banking Federation (IBF) appeared before the Oireachtas Joint Committee on Justice, Equality, Defence and Women's Rights to discuss the issue of Solici-

---

1258802.html> Accessed 4/12/2012

[44] M McDonagh, 'The worst-planned estates in Ireland?' Irishtimes.com, 21st April 2012 <http://www.irishtimes.com/newspaper/weekend/2012/0421/1224315001367.html> Accessed 17/11/2012

[45] M Sheehan, 'Lynn is taking the Mickey after bunking off to trainrobber haven', 7th October 2012, *Irish Independent*. <http://www.irishindependent.ie/opinion/analysis/lynn-is-taking-the-michael-after-bunking-off-to-trainrobber-haven-3251455.html> Accessed 30/10/2012. Mr Lynn has established a Real Estate Business in Fortaleza, Brazil, 'Golino Empreendimontos Imobiliarios' (Golino Venture Estates).

[46] Ibid

[47] *Irish Times*, 4th September 2013, 2

tors' Undertakings.[48] The testimony which was given before the Committee by some of contributors was remarkable given the events which were unfolding within the financial, property and legal sectors. Referring to the two solicitor certificate of title system, the LSI President James McGuill stated:

> The benefits of the two solicitor certificate of title system include reduced costs to borrowers as there are no third solicitor's legal fees to be paid. There are no additional costs to borrowers in the form of bank interest on bridging loans. There is no more duplication of title investigation work by a solicitor acting for the lending institution. There are fewer delays experienced by borrowers and their solicitors in arranging closings. There is a reduction in the administrative burden and cost to lenders of running their own in-house legal departments or panels of solicitors. Its longevity proves it has been successful ... There appears to be no desire on the part of any of the stakeholders in the conveyancing system to return to the 3-way conveyancing closing.[49]

McGuill also stated that the Law Society was in agreement with the establishment of a registration of undertakings system, and an electronic conveyancing system. The Director General of the Law Society, Ken Murphy, informed the Committee that:

> The Law Society [Compensation] fund is a matter of public record and contains approximately €33 million, as well as an additional €30 million in insurance. It is well funded. The amount of claims in recent years goes nowhere near challenging the size of the fund. In addition, every solicitor is obliged by the society to maintain professional indemnity insurance up to €2.5 million in respect of each case ... The Chief Executive of the AIB [Allied Irish Bank] spoke strongly in support of the undertakings and certificate of title system. I recall he stated it works in 99.99% of cases. I would state that in statistical terms it works well in an even greater number than 99.99%. Any response in terms of action or improvement of the system must be proportionate to the actual risk involved.[50]

Given that the LSI had been investigating the activities of Lynn, and other high profile cases of property fraud by solicitors in the previous six months before it gave evidence to the Committee, its confidence regarding the issuance of undertakings and the certificate of title system was surprising.[51]

---

[48] Joint Committee on Justice, Equality, Defence and Women's Rights 5th March 2008. 'Solicitors' Undertakings: Discussion with Law Society and Irish Banking Federation'. Available at: <http://debates.oireachtas.ie/JUJ/2008/03/05/00003.asp> Accessed 4/9/2012. The Oireachtas is the Lower House of the Irish Parliament (the Upper House is The Seanad).

[49] Ibid 4

[50] Ibid 13, 18.

[51] For example, Mr Thomas Byrne, solicitor was also found to have engaged in widespread illegality in respect of property matters around the same time that the SDT findings were made in relation to Mr Lynn. On 20th Feb 2008 the SDT found Mr Byrne guilty of multiple counts of fraud and breach of undertakings. He had obtained multiple mortgages on the same properties from various financial institutions. His total frauds were to the value of approximately €50 million. *In the matter of Thomas Byrne, a solicitor formerly practising under the style and*

What is most notable about the evidence given by these witnesses was their collective lack of concern regarding the dangers of the manner in which undertakings were being used at that time, and in particular; their use to obtain loans by solicitors in relation to property transactions to which they themselves were a party. It is arguable that the witnesses gravely underestimated the level of flawed mortgage transactions by value and misunderstood the magnitude of the difficulties which were unravelling in both the financial and legal sectors as a result of bad property loans. There was also the unfortunate fact that as a consequence of the Lynn and Byrne cases being *sub judicae*, neither the Committee nor the witnesses could directly address the serious issues arising from these cases, and the flaws in the conveyancing system which these lawyers had preyed upon. In the circumstances, it was inappropriate for the entire Committee hearing to be in public, as it was effectively fettered from cross-examining the witnesses on the most pertinent issues concerning the use of undertakings, and in particular their use by property-developer-lawyers in relation to transactions to which they themselves were a party, as evidenced by the Lynn and Byrne cases.

Contrary to the evidence of the Committee witnesses, it is argued herein that there were major flaws in the conveyancing system at the time of the Oireachtas hearing in March 2008. These included the adoption of the two solicitor certificate of title system; the absence of a register of undertakings; the absence of an e-conveyancing system; the inappropriate use of undertakings by solicitors in relation to commercial property transactions and those to which they themselves were party; the excessively low price of conveyancing services due to intense competition in the sector and the absence of an independent conveyancing profession. There was a failure to properly regulate the provision of conveyancing services by the legal profession. There was also overconfidence by the LSI concerning the risk posed by the use of undertakings and the conveyancing system generally, as evidenced by the LSI estimation that 99.99% of all mortgages by value were properly completed, and a refusal to countenance the idea that the use of undertakings was a problematic area of practice for the profession as a whole rather than being a problem only in relation to a handful of 'rogue' solicitors. It is ironic that the Oireachtas Committee should have heard the evidence concerning solicitors' undertakings on the same day that the Financial Regulator Patrick Neary was expressing confidence in the banking sector at a seminar being held nearby at University College Dublin.[52] These events occurred just two weeks before the spectacular collapse of Anglo's share price.

Lynn's activities as a property-developer-lawyer provide a unique insight into the activities of the Unholy Trinity in Ireland. As a lawyer, he was able to identify flaws in both the two solicitor conveyancing system and the system of undertakings, and to exploit those weaknesses in order to expand his own property portfolio. He also used his professional position as a lawyer to great effect when interacting with financial institutions in order to avail of zero or low interest loans to fund his rapidly expanding property portfolio. Like many of his

---

title of Thomas Byrne and Company, and in the matter of the Solicitors Acts 1954-2002 (6095/DT60/06, 6095/DT36/08 and High Court record no 2008 no 52SA)

[52] P Neary, Speech, IRFC Conference, UCD, 5th Mar 2008 (FN 15)

professional colleagues who have also been struck off the roll of solicitors in recent years, his professional misconduct concerned property-related financial fraud – the crime of choice for the white-collar legal professional in Ireland during the Celtic Tiger years.

3.0 Why was the Irish Bailout Necessary?

On 20th of March 2008, the Irish banking sector began to publicly display outward signs of what was to be an unprecedented collapse. The first evidence of this was the dramatic fall in the Anglo share price of over 18% in one week, as a direct result of its overexposure to the property sector.

On the 18th September 2008, the Government outlawed the short selling of financial stocks, and almost two weeks later on the 30th September 2008 it guaranteed all the liabilities of the seven major Irish banks to the value of €37.5 billion. The guarantee applied to all deposits including covered bonds, senior debt and dated subordinate debt of the major financial institutions. This move followed a run on deposits in Anglo. However, the blanket guarantee did little to stop the rapid decline in the banking sector, and on 14th December 2008 the Government found it necessary to recapitalize the domestic banks to the extent of €10 billion, followed by further support in the form of an investment one week later of €5.5 billion in preference shares in Anglo, AIB and BOI.

The new year brought no improvement in the financial situation and on 15th of January 2009 the Government moved to nationalize Anglo due to its weak financial position and "unacceptable practices". [53] It was reported that The Irish Life and Permanent Building Society had made funds available to Anglo in order to shore up its capital base prior to Financial Regulator inspections. It is unclear precisely what knowledge the Financial Regulator had regarding these inter-financial institution loans.[54] It has emerged that Anglo provided loans amounting to €1.1 billion to ten of its customers, 'The Maple Ten', and also to the Quinn family for the purpose of purchasing shares in the bank in an effort to shore up its share price. The Quinn family borrowed a total of €650 million, and the Maple Ten borrowed €45 million each.[55] It is understood that Sean Quinn lost a total of up to €2 billion as a result of his overall exposure to Anglo shares.[56] Further recapitalization of the banking sector was necessary in February 2009 with an investment of €7 billion being made in The Allied Irish Bank (AIB) and The Bank of Ireland (BOI) from the National Pension Reserve Fund. In an effort to stabilize the financial meltdown, on 7th April 2009 the Government announced plans to establish NAMA, with the aim of removing toxic property-

[53] Statement of the Financial Regulator 13th February 2009. RTE News. <http://www.rte.ie/news/2009/1213/financial.regulator.html> Accessed 4/11/2012

[54] Ibid

[55] D O'Donovan, '"Maple 10" developers are named in court', *Independent.ie*, 24th July 2012. <http://www.independent.ie/business/irish/maple-10-developers-are-named-in-court-3179000.html> Accessed 30/11/2012

[56] 'Quinn denies backdating loans to deprive Anglo of group's assets', Irishtimes.com, 24th Mar 2012. <http://www.irishtimes.com/newspaer/finance/2012/0324/1224313821680.html> Accessed 29/11/2012

related assets from the banks' books. Throughout 2009 the Government continued to pour taxpayers' money into the black hole which was once Ireland's banking sector but it seemed that this policy was unable to halt the catastrophic meltdown.[57] By the autumn of 2010 the deepening banking crisis was having an impact upon Irish bond yields, and Ireland found itself unable to borrow on the international financial markets at viable rates.[58] The situation had become untenable and the Government sought relief from the IMF, the ECB and the European Commission (The Troika) in the form of a €67.5 bailout on 28th November 2010.[59]

The Government's efforts to stabilise the banking sector resulted in 32.5% of GDP being allocated to it, but this funding and the accompanying nationalization programme was not sufficient to resolve the crisis in the failing banks, and the international markets lost faith in the country's ability to pay its debts. The average interest rate on the Troika bailout funds was 5.83%, and in return for the loan Ireland committed itself to a four year austerity programme. €35 billion of the bailout funds were allocated for further support of the beleaguered banking sector.

---

[57] P Nyberg, *Misjudging Risk* (FN 5) provides a useful timeline of events which occurred in the period before the Troika Bailout, including details of the capital funding which the Irish Government provided to the banking sector. (Nyberg, Appendix 3, 150 – 156)

[58] Bond yields had risen to over 7% on 10th October 2010 <http://www.irishtimes.com /newspaper/breaking/2010/1028/breaking15.html> Accessed 4/11/2012

[59] The total bailout package amounted to €113 billion: €67.5 billion from the Troika, €17.5 from the National Pension Reserve, €28 billion from the UK, Denmark and Sweden.

APPENDIX 2

INVESTIGATION INTO PROFESSIONAL MISCONDUCT AMONGST IRISH SOLICITORS: METHODOLOGY AND RESULTS

Methodology

One hundred cases which were heard consecutively by the SDT, the outcomes of which were published in the LSG between January 2008 and May 2010 were analysed to form a database. These were the most recent SDT cases the findings of which were available for analysis at the time of construction of the database. Each case was categorised in accordance with whether or not it concerned each of the three variables: finance, dishonesty/breach of undertaking (BOU) and property. Each case was given a three digit binary score reflecting the presence or absence of these variables. A database was formed to record the three digit binary scores allocated to each case as follows:

First digit = 1 where the case had a financial element

First digit = 0 where the case did not have a financial element

Second digit = 1 where the case had a dishonesty/BOU element

Second digit = 0 where the case did not have a dishonesty/BOU element

Third digit = 1 where the case had a property element

Third digit = 0 where the case did not have a property element.[1]

Whilst the classification of cases as to whether or not they concerned either financial or property matters was relatively straightforward, the categorisation with regard to dishonesty/BOU was more complex. A dishonest/BOU categorisation was only awarded to cases which displayed one of the following traits:

---

[1] To illustrate how the database was developed, consider a case which received a binary score of 100. The first digit 1 indicates that the case concerned a financial matter, the second digit 0 indicates that the case did not concern a matter of dishonesty/BOU and the third digit 0 indicates that the case did not concern a property matter.

(i)   Fraudulent misrepresentation; for example, a statement made with the aim of deceiving another person such as a client, a Revenue official, a Law Society investigator or other lawful authority.

(ii) Forgery; the creation of fake documentation with a view to concealing the truth of a matter from an investigatory body or other lawful authority.

(iii) Breach of undertaking; for instance to a client, a financial institution, another party or a court.[2]

The classification criteria were chosen to facilitate a statistical analysis of the selected traits of finance, dishonesty/BOU and property, and to show how they relate to findings of misconduct. The classification system which was adopted for this study was somewhat simplistic, and failed to distinguish between instances of financial misconduct which concerned nominal sums from those which concerned significant sums. A more refined classification system would yield significantly more information regarding the 'profile' of a solicitor who is likely to be found guilty of serious misconduct in future. Another useful refinement would be to distinguish between sole practitioners and other solicitors, to estab-lish whether the dominance of sole practitioners in misconduct cases in other jurisdictions is replicated in Ireland.[3] An investigation of a greater number of cases, using a more sophisticated classification system would contribute towards a deeper understanding of how matters of finance, dishonesty/BOU and proper-ty impinge upon the professional misconduct of solicitors.

To establish whether the solicitors involved in the professional misconduct cases used to form the database had a prior history of misconduct involving the three elements of finance, dishonesty/BOU and property, the records of each solicitor as contained on the LSI 'Solicitor Disciplinary Search' facility were examined. This facility contains details of the decisions in all the hearings of the SDT which appeared in the LSG from the 1st January 2004 onwards. The results of this examination were used to establish whether a past history of misconduct involving the three elements was a useful indicator to predict which solicitors were more likely to be struck off in future.

Results[4]

As regards a link between a finding of professional misconduct in a case before the SDT and the presence of a financial, dishonesty/BOU or property element in the case, analysis showed that 74% of cases concerned financial misconduct, 51% concerned dishonesty/BOU matters and 45% concerned a property matter. It was also established that 34% of cases of misconduct reflect-ed all three factors in that they concerned finance, dishonesty/BOU and also

---

[2] The necessity for repeated changes to the regulations relating to undertakings illustrates the problematic nature of this area of practice, and indicates that there may have been a failure on the part of the regulatory authorities to adequately supervise this area of practice.

[3] M Davies, 'Solicitors, Dishonesty and the Solicitors' Disciplinary Tribunal' (1999) 6 (2) *International Journal of the Legal Profession* 141 – 174

[4] This section gives further details of the study's results which were provided in ch 3 § 3.8.2

concerned a property matter. Of those cases which concerned dishonesty/BOU, 78% concerned a financial matter, and 72% concerned a property matter. A total of 67% of these dishonesty/BOU cases concerned both a financial and a property matter.

The existence of a relationship between the three factors of finance, dishonesty/BOU and property was measured using Minitab software to perform chi-square tests upon pairs of factors.[5] Whilst at a significance level of $\alpha = 0.05$ there is no evidence of a relationship between cases concerning finance and those with an element of dishonesty/BOU ($p = 0.303$) there is significant evidence of a relationship between cases concerning property and those having an element of dishonesty/BOU ($p = 0.000$), and cases concerning finance and those concerning property ($p = 0.002$).[6] The most significant relationship was between property and dishonesty/BOU. Thus where professional misconduct occurred, property based transactions were much more likely to concern dishonesty than those transactions which did not concern property. The significant relationship which was observed between both dishonesty/BOU and property factors reflects the fact that conveyancing was an area of legal practice which gave rise to a high level of serious misconduct on the part of solicitors. Conveyancing was a large part of the work of many solicitors during the Celtic Tiger years, and the findings here support Neary's proposition that many solicitors engaged in areas of conveyancing such as commercial transactions without having the requisite skills.[7]

The less significant relationship which was observed between financial and dishonesty factors also requires explanation. It is submitted that this finding reflects the fact that the majority of professional misconduct cases concern a financial matter and also involve a relatively minor breach of the accounting regulations, with only a small minority of such cases involving dishonesty on the part of the errant solicitor.

The one hundred cases examined in the course of this investigation involved seventy-two solicitors, with some solicitors having multiple findings of misconduct made against them in the course of the sample period. Twenty-four of the solicitors (or pairs of solicitors involved in the same disciplinary hearing) were found guilty of misconduct involving the elements of finance, dishonesty/BOU and property, with the remaining forty-eight being found guilty of offences which did not involve all three factors.

As regards the extent to which the misconduct of solicitors who are struck off involves the three elements of finance, dishonesty/BOU and property, 33% of cases in the study involving all three elements resulted in a strike off, whereas 14% of cases which did not involve all three elements resulted in a strike off.

An examination of the disciplinary records dating back to 2004 of the seventy-two solicitors (or pairs of solicitors involved in the same disciplinary hearing) who featured in the database revealed that nineteen had a past history of professional misconduct *prior* to any future strike off amongst this cohort of

---

[5] Table 1

[6] Here the null hypothesis is that there is no relationship between the variables.

[7] A Neary & F O'Toole, *The Blueprint Report: A Review of the Legal Profession in Ireland and a Vision for Irish Law Firms* (Anne Neary Consultations, 2011) 10

practitioners. With regard to whether a solicitor's past disciplinary history may be used to predict his/her future offending behaviour, analysis revealed that where a practitioner had past history of misconduct involving the three elements of finance, dishonesty/BOU and property, this was not predictive of a future strike off.[8] 10.5% of cases in the study where the solicitor had a past history of misconduct involving all three elements resulted in a strike off, whereas 23.6% of cases where there was no such past history resulted in a strike off. Whilst many of the cases of professional misconduct which resulted in the solicitor concerned being struck off did involve elements of finance, dishonesty/BOU and property, the misconduct giving rise to the strike off only emerged at the time of the SDT hearing resulting in the strike off, and was not known to the SDT as a result of a previous hearing.

Whilst analysis of the database provides some insight into the relationship between instances of professional misconduct and finance, dishonesty/BOU and property, it is not possible to draw general conclusions from the database given the small sample size used in its construction. A further difficulty for drawing general conclusions about solicitors' professional misconduct from the study arises as a consequence of the fact that the SDT may only have processed a small proportion of all actual instances of professional misconduct, with much offending behaviour possibly going undetected. If this is the case, the findings of the study will not be reflective of professional misconduct in general, and cannot be used as a basis for generalisations about the nature of solicitors' professional misconduct. If the present system of disciplinary regulation fails to detect a large proportion of misconduct, this would account for the weak predictive value of a past history of misconduct involving finance, dishonesty/BOU and property with regard to future strike offs. The study's findings regarding the predictive value of a past history of misconduct were also limited due to the fact that it was not possible to research the disciplinary history of the solicitors concerned prior to 2004 when the LSI firstly made this information publicly available.[9] At most, this study can offer a limited window of insight into complex and secretive behaviour patterns.

---

[8] Table 3

[9] Another possible explanation for the low predictive value of a past history of misconduct involving all three elements for a solicitor being struck off in the future is as follows. If a solicitor's past misconduct occurred prior to 2004, it would not be available for inclusion in the study, and therefore some instances of past misconduct by solicitors in the study, involving all three elements, which ought to have been included, were not, in fact, included. Access to any misconduct records for the solicitors included in the study, in the pre-2004 period, would enable correction of the results in this regard.

TABLE 1

STATISTICAL ANALYSIS OF RATES OF FINANCE, DISHONESTY/BOU AND PROPERTY IN ONE HUNDRED CASES OF SOLICITORS' PROFESSIONAL MISCONDUCT

1. Chi-square Test: Property/Dishonesty/BOU

	PROPERTY 0	PROPERTY 1	TOTAL
DISHONESTY/BOU 0	41 26.95 7.325	8 22.05 8.952	49
DISHONESTY/BOU 1	14 28.05 7.038	37 22.95 8.601	51
TOTAL	55	45	100

CHI-SQUARE = 31.916, **DF** = 1, **P-VALUE** = 0.000

2. Chi-square Test: Finance/Dishonesty/BOU

	FINANCE 0	FINANCE 1	TOTAL
DISHONESTY/BOU 0	15 12.74 0.401	34 36.26 0.141	49
DISHONESTY/BOU 1	11 13.26 0.385	40 37.74 0.135	51
TOTAL	26	74	100

CHI-SQUARE = 1.062, **DF** = 1, **P-VALUE** = 0.303

3. Chi-square Test: Finance/Property

	FINANCE 0	FINANCE 1	TOTAL
PROPERTY 0	21 14.30 3.139	34 40.70 1.103	55
PROPERTY 1	5 11.70 3.837	40 33.30 1.348	45
TOTAL	26	74	100

CHI-SQUARE = 9.427, **DF** = 1, **P-VALUE** = 0.002

TABLE 2

**INVESTIGATION OF SOLICITORS' PROFESSIONAL MISCONDUCT
DATA SHEET 2**

Sequential Case Number	Solicitors' Identification Code	Struck Off (Previous 111 – Y/N)	Score
35, 99	O2	N	000, 101
51, 53	V1	Y	000, 001
1	P1	N	000
76	E1	N	100
77	J2	SO 28/1/13 N	100
96	B2	N	100
13	X1	N	000
42	N2	SO 16/1/13 N	100
71	Y1	N	100
15	Y2	N	100
3	P2	N	110
74	O1	N	100
83	U2	SO 2009 N	010
80	R1	N	010
63	K2	N	001
86	L2	N	100
58	F2	Y	101
60	S3	N	100
97	B1	N	100
46, 70	I1	Y	000, 010
14	S2	N	100
37, 47, 59, 95	N3	Y	010, 010, 100
39	S1	N	101
66	P3	N	101
56	Q1	N	100
48	V2	N	100
25, 61, 68, 69	E2	Y	100, 100, 100, 100
54, 55	J1	N	000, 101
11, 12	B3	N	100
49	R2	N	000
43	A2	N	110
62	Q2	N	100
19	T2	N	000
98	H3	N	100
100	F3	SO 3/6/09 N	000
94	G1	N	100
			continued

90	V1	N	**110**
2, 92	X2	SO 14/6/10 N	**110, 100**
91	C2	N	**100**
21	T3	N	**010**
38	I2	N	**011**
57	M2	N	**110**
41	T1	N	**011**
44	N1	N	**010**
45	W2	SO 15/2/10 N	**000**
23, 89	R3	N	**000, 011**
17	M1	SO 12/10/09 N	**110**
64	D2	N	**100**
4,72,84,85	W1	N	**101, 010, 100, 100**
93	K1	N	**000**
75	O3	Y	**111**
81	D1	SO 16/6/08 N	**111**
27, 28, 29,30, 31, 32, 33	E3	SO 13/7/09 N	**111, 111, 111, 111, 111,111,111,**
8	L3	SO 1/3/10 Y	**111**
50	Z2	Y	**111**
36	L1	Y	**111**
16	A3	SO 12/10/09 N	**111**
65, 87, 88	M3	Y	**111, 111, 111**
52	D3	Y	**111**
6, 7	A1	Y	**111, 111**
10	F1	SO 14/12/09 N	**111**
82	K3	Y	**111**
20	U3	Y	**111**
5	G3	Y	**111**
26	I3	Y	**111**
24	C3	Y	**111**
78, 79	Q3	SO 23/5/08 N	**111, 111**
18	G2	Y	**111**
22	J3	SO 16/2/09 N	**111**
67	V3	SO 18/1/09 Y	**111**
73	H2	Y	**111**
9	Z1	Y	**111**
40	C1	Y	**111**
34	H1	Y	**111**

This data sheet records the randomised identification codes which were allotted to the seventy-two solicitors whose cases were involved in this quantitative analysis of professional misconduct.[10] The outcomes of the cases were published in the LSG between January 2008 and May 2010. The data sheet indicates whether a solicitor has been struck off by the High Court, whether he/she had a previous history of misconduct involving finance, dishonesty/BOU and property (a 111 offence) and the nature of the misconduct concerned in the cases before the SDT.

The probability of being struck off given that the misconduct case concerned a 111 offence is 8/24 = 33.3%. The probability of being struck off given that the misconduct did not concern a 111 offence is 7/50 =14%.

---

[10] Rand Corporation, *Million Random Digits* (The Free Press). Available at: http://www.rand .org/publications/classics/randomdigits. Last accessed 19/4/13. Appendix B of the Random Number Tables was used to randomly allocate identification codes to the seventy-two solicitors in the database.

TABLE 3

STATISTICAL ANALYSIS
THE PREDICTIVE VALUE OF A PAST HISTORY OF PROFESSIONAL MISCONDUCT IN RELATION TO A FUTURE STRIKE OFF

Solicitors with a past history of a '111' finding:

PREVIOUS '111' MISCONDUCT	SOLICITOR ID CODE
1	V1/03
2	F2/M3
3	I1/D3
4	N3
5	E2/C3
6	Z2
7	L1
8	K3
9	U3
10	G3
11	I3
12	G2
13	V3
14	H2
15	Z1
16	C1
17	H1
18	L3
19	A1

A total of 15 solicitors have been struck off from January 2008 until April 2013. Nineteen solicitors (or pairs of solicitors involved in one hearing) had a previous history of misconduct involving finance, dishonesty/BOU and property (a 111 finding). Two of these were struck off. Fifty-five solicitors (or pairs of solicitors involved in one hearing) had no previous history of misconduct involving a 111 finding. Thirteen of the fifty-five solicitors with no previous history of a 111 finding were struck off. The probability of being struck off given a past history of a 111 finding was 2/19 = 10.5%. The probability of being struck off given no past history of a 111 finding was 13/55 = 23.6%.

BIBLIOGRAPHY

Table of Statutes

Ireland

The Constitution of Ireland

Article 34
Article 37

Bills

Competition (Amendment) Bill 2011
Legal Services Regulation Bill 2011

Acts Pre 1922

1 Hen V c 8
10 Will III (1698) c 13 (Ir)
7 Geo II (1733) c 5 (Ir)
13 & 14 Geo III (1773) c 23 (Ir)
32 Geo III (1792) c 21 (Ir)
28 Hen VIII c 16
48 & 49 Vict (1885) c 20
2 Anne c 6 (Ir)
21 & 22 Geo III c 32
23 & 24 Geo III c 3
29 & 30 Vict (1866) c 84
40 & 41 Vict (1866) c 20
Judiciature (Ireland) Act 1877
Partnership Act 1890

Acts Post 1922

Civil Law (Miscellaneous Provisions) Act 2008
Courts (Supplemental Provisions) Act 1961
Criminal Justice Act 2001
Criminal Justice Act 2011
Legal Services Ombudsman Act 2009
National Assets Management Agency Act 2009
Sale of Goods and Supply of Services Act 1980
Solicitors Act 1954

Solicitors (Amendment) Act 1960
Solicitors (Amendment) Act 1994
Solicitors (Amendment) Act 2002
Solicitors (Amendment) Act 2008

Regulations

Financial Emergency Measures in the Public Interest (Reduction in Payments to State Solicitors) Regulations 2009 (SI 159/2009)
Solicitors Act 1954 (Apprenticeship and Education) Regulations 1955 (SI 217/1955)
Solicitors Act 1954 (Apprenticeship and Education) Regulations 1955 (SI 17/1968)
Solicitors (Accounting) Regulations 1984 (SI 204/84)
Solicitors (Accounting) Regulations (No 2) 1984 (SI 304/84)
Solicitors Acts, 1954 – 2002 (Professional Indemnity Insurance) Regulations 2002 (SI 617/2002)
Solicitors Acts, 1954 – 2008 (Professional Indemnity Insurance) (Amendment) Regulations 2009 (SI 384/2009)
Solicitors Acts, 1954 – 2008 (Professional Indemnity Insurance) (Amendment (No 2)) Regulations 2009 (SI 441/2009)
Solicitors Acts, 1954 – 2008 (Professional Indemnity Insurance) (Amendment) Regulations 2010 (SI 495//2010)
Solicitors Acts 1954 (Professional Practice, Conduct and Discipline) Regulations 1955 (SI 151/1955)
Solicitors (Professional Practice, Conduct and Discipline) Regulations 1997 (SI 85/1997)
Solicitors Acts 1954 – 2008 (Professional Practice, Conduct and Discipline – Secured Loan Transactions) Regulations 2009 (SI 211/2009)
Solicitors (Advertising) Regulations 1988 (SI 344/1988)
Solicitors (Advertising) Regulations 1996 (SI 351/1996)
Solicitors (Professional Practice, Conduct and Discipline – Commercial Property Transactions) Regulations 2010 (SI 366/2010)

High Court Directives

High Court Practice Directive 54 'Proceedings involving a litigant in person' 26th July 2010

England and Wales

Courts and Legal Services Act 1990
Legal Services Act 2007

Northern Ireland

Solicitors (Northern Ireland) (Amendment) Order 1989.

United States of America

Glass-Steagall Act 1933
Sarbanes-Oxley Act 2002
Sherman Act 1890

Australia

Legal Profession Amendment (Incorporated Legal Practices) Act 2000.
The Legal Profession Act 2004
The New South Wales Legal Profession Act 2004

The Legal Profession Regulations 2005

Greece

Law no 3910 of 8th February 2011

Zimbabwe

Legal Practitioners Act 1981

European Union

Treaty on the Functioning of the European Union

Article 5 TFEU
Articles 101 – 109 TFEU (Ex Articles 81 – 89 TEC)

Directives

Council Directive 77/249/EEC of 22 March 1977 to facilitate the effective exercise by lawyers
of freedom to provide services [1977] OJ L 078/17
Council Directive 89/48 EEC of 21 December 1988 on a general system for the recognition of
higher education diplomas awarded on completion of professional education and training of at least three years' duration [1989] OJ L 19
Council Directive 91/308/EEC of 10 June 1991 on prevention of the use of the financial
system for the purpose of money laundering [1991] OJ L 166/77
Council Directive 98/5/EC of 16 February 1998 to facilitate practice of the profession of
lawyer on a permanent basis in a Member State other than that in which the qualification was obtained [1998] OJ L 77/36
Directive 2000/3/EC of the European Parliament and of the Council of 8 June 2000 on
certain legal aspects of information society services, in particular electronic commerce
in the Internal Market (Directive on electronic commerce) [2000] OJ L 178/1
Directive 2005/36/EC of the European Parliament and of the Council of 7 September 2005
on the recognition of professional qualifications. [2005] OJ L 255/22.
Directive 2006/123/EC of the European Parliament and of the Council of 12 December 2006
on the services of the internal market [2006] OJ L 376/36

Regulations

Council Regulation No 1/2003 on the implementation of the rules on competition laid down
by Articles 81 and 82 of the Treaty [2003] OJ L1/1

Resolutions

European Parliament Resolution on the legal profession and the general interest in the functioning of the legal system, 23rd March 2006 OJ C292 E/105

Recommendations

Recommendation No R (2000) 21 of the Committee of Ministers to Member States on the Freedom of Exercise of the Profession of Lawyer.

Conventions

Convention against Corruption involving European Officials or Officials of Member States of the European Union OJ C/195 25/6/97

Convention on the Protection of the European Communities Financial Interests OJ C316/48 27/11/1995

Other EU Materials

EU Commission. 'Commission Staff Working Document: Assessment of the 2012 National Reform Programme and Stability Programme for Portugal'. 8

EU Commission. Communication from the Commission to the Council, the European Parliament, the European Economic and Social Committee and the Committee of the Regions 'Professional Services – Scope for More Reform' (5/9/2005) COM (2005)
EU Commission. 'Legal Professions – Portugal'. European Judicial Network.

EU Commission: State Aid N725/2009 – Ireland: Establishment of a National Asset Management Agency (NAMA) Asset Relief Scheme for banks in Ireland. Brussels, 26/2/2010 C (2010) 1155

EU Commission. 'Task force for Greece: Quarterly Report. December 2012'.

EUROPA Treaty of Lisbon: The Treaty at a Glance

European Commission. 'The Economic Adjustment Programme for Portugal: Sixth Review – Autum 2012'. European Economy. Occasional Papers 124/December 2012. 14

European System of Central Banks and Statute of the ECB (The 'ECB Statute'). Arts 2 & 25 (1)

Table of Cases

Ireland

Battle v Irish Art Promotion Centre Ltd [1968] IR 252
Beatty v Rent Tribunal 2 IR 191
Chance v Tanti (1901) 35 ILTR 126
Culhane v O'Maoileoin HC unrep 17th November 1988
Duncan v Governor of Portlaoise Prison [1997] 1 IR

Fraser v Buckle [1996] 1 IR 1

Gregg v Kidd [1956] IR 183

In the matter of Thomas Byrne, a solicitor formerly practising under the style and title of Thomas Byrne and Company, and in the matter of the Solicitors Acts 1954-2002 6095/DT60/06, 6095/DT36/08 and High Court record no 2008 no 52SA

In the Matter of Michael Lynn, a solicitor formerly practicing under the style and title of Capel Law and in the matter of the Solicitors Acts 1954 – 2002 7153/DT/15/08 and High Court Record no 2008 no 32SA

In the Matter of Michael Lynn, a solicitor formerly practicing under the style and title of Capel Law and in the matter of the Solicitors Acts 1954 – 2002 7153/DT/16/08 and High Court Record no 2007 no 50SA

Law Society v Colm Carroll and Henry Colley [2009] 2 ILRM 77

Mackie v Wilde [1995] 1 ILRM 468

McAleenan v AIG (Europe) Ltd [2010] IEHC 128.

McMullen v Carty Supreme Court unreported 28th January 1998

McMullen v Farrell [1993] 1 IR 163

Mulheir v Gannon [2006] IEHC 274

Mulligan v Corr [1925] 1 IR 169

O'Connor v First National Building Society [1991] ILRM 204

O'Donoghue v The Legal Aid Board, the Minister for Justice, Equality and Law Reform, Ireland & the Attorney General [2004] IEHC 413

Re Burke and in the matter of the Solicitors Acts 1954 – 1994 [2001] IESC 13

Re Lane Joynt [1920] 1 IR 228

Re O'Farrell and the Solicitors Act 1954 [1961] 95 ILTR 167

Roche v Pellow [1986] ILRM 189

Sheehan v Mc Mahon Supreme Court unreported 29th July 1993

Tansey v Gill and Others [2012] IEHC 42

Tuohy v Courtney [1994] 3 IR 38

W v Ireland (No 2) [1997] 2 IR 141

United Kingdom

Boardman v Phipps [1967] 2 AC 46

Duchess of Argyll v Beuselinck [1972] 2 Lloyd's Rep 172

Gordon v Gordon [1904] P 163

Hall (Arthur JJ) & Co v Simons [2000] 3 All ER 673

Henderson v Merett Syndicates Ltd [1994] 1 AC 428

Lloyd v Nagle (1747) 1 Dick 129

Meek v Flemming [1961] 2 KB 366

Marsh v Joseph [1895-1899] All ER Rep 977

Mouat v Clark Boyce [1994] 1 AC 428

R v Feely [1973] 1 QB 530 (CA)

R v Ghosh [1982] QB 1053 (CA)

Re A Company [1989] BCLC 13

Re Hunt [1959] 1 QB 37

Re K (minors) (Incitement to Breach of Orders) [1992] 2 FLR 108

Rondel v Worsley [1969] 1 AC 191

Saif Ali v Sydney Mitchell & Co (a firm) [1980] AC 198

Seldon v Wilde [1911] 1 KB 701

Underwood, Son & Piper v Lewis [1894] 2 QB 306

United Mining and Finance Corporation Ltd v Becker [1910] 2 KB 296

Wright v Carter [1903] 1 Ch 27
Young v Power (1862) 14 Jur 388

United States of America

Board of Trade of the City of Chicago v United States 246 US 231 (1918)
Goldfarb v State Bar of Virginia 421 US 773 (1975)
Re Enron Corp Sec Derivative v ERISA Litig 235 F Supp 2d 549 (SD Tex 2002)

European Court of Justice

Case C-550/07 *AKZO Nobel Ltd and Akros Chemicals Ltd v Commission* [2008] OJ C37/19
C-384/93 *Alpine Investments* [1995] ECR I-1141
Case 155/79 *AM & S Europe Ltd v Commission* [1982] ECR 1575
Case C-35/99 *Arduino* [2002] ECR I-1529
C-427/85 *Commission v Germany (Lawyers' Services)* ECR 1123
C-17/00 *De Coster* [2001] ECR I-09445
C-221/89 *Factortame* (No 2) [1991] ECR I-3905
C-2/74 *Jean Reyners v The Belgian State* [1974] ECR 631
Case 313/01 *Morgenesser* [2003] ECR I-13467
Case 33/74 *Van Binsbergen* [1974] ECR 1299
Case 340/89 *Vlassopoulou* [1991] ECR I-2357
Case C -309/99 *Wouters* [2002] ECR 1577
Joined cases C-94/04 & C-202/04 *Cipolla & others* [2006] ECR I-11421

Books

Abel R, *English Lawyers between Market and State: The Politics of Professionalism* (Oxford University Press 2003)
Abel R, *Lawyers in the Dock: Learning from Attorney Disciplinary Proceedings* (Oxford University Press 2010)
Abel R, *Lawyers on Trial: Understanding Ethical Misconduct* (Oxford University Press 2011)
Antonioni P & Flynn S, *Economics for Dummies* (John Wiley & Sons Ltd 2011)
Armour J & McCahary J (eds), *After Enron: Improving Corporate Law and Modernising Securities Regulation in Europe and the US* (Hart Publishing 2006)
Becker L & Becker C (eds), *A History of Western Ethics* (Routledge 2003)
Black J, *Rules and Regulators* (Clarenden Press 1997)
Byrne R & McCutcheon P, *Byrne and McCutcheon on the Irish Legal System* (Bloomsbury Professional 2009)
Carr E, *What is History?* (Palgrave McMillan 2001)
Chalmers D, Davies G & Monti, G *European Union Law* (CUP 2010)
Clarkson C, *Understanding Criminal Law* (3rd edn Sweet & Maxwell 2001)
Crownie F (ed), *Stakeholders in the Law School* (Hart Publishing, Forthcoming), Boon A & Webb J, 'The Legal Professions as Stakeholders in the Academy in England and Wales'
Dawson M (ed), *Reflections on Law and History* (Four Court Press 2006)
Dezalay Y & Sugarman D (eds), *Professional Competition and Professional Power: Lawyers, Accountants and the Social Construction of Markets* (Routledge 1995)
Dine J & Gobert J, *Cases and Materials on Criminal Law* (4th edn OUP 2003)
Elhauge E & Geradin D, *Global Competition Law and Economics* (2nd edn Hart Publishing 2011)

Groppelli A & Nikbakht E, *Finance* (Barrons 2000)

Hall E & Hogan D, (eds) *The Law Society of Ireland, 1852 – 2002* (Four Courts Press 2002)

Hogan D, *The Legal Profession in Ireland 1789 – 1922* (The Incorporated Law Society of Ireland, 1986)

Hogan D & Osborough W (eds), *Brehons, Sergeants and Attorneys: Studies in the History of the Irish Legal Profession* (Irish Academic Press 1990)

Kelly F, *A Guide to Early Irish Law* (Dundalgan Press Ltd 2001)

Kenny C, *Kings' Inns and the Kingdom of Ireland* (Irish Academic Press, 1992)

McGreal C, *Criminal Jusitce (Theft and Fraud Offences) Act 2001* (2nd ed Round Hall 2011)

McMahon B & Binchey W, *Law of Torts* (Butterworths, 2005)

Mackie J, *Ethics: Inventing Right and Wrong* (Penguin 1983)

Mills S, Ryan A, McDowell J & Burke E, *Disciplinary Procedures in the Statutory Professions* (Bloomsbury Professional Ltd 2011)

Mooney-Cotter A-M (ed), *Regulatory Law* (Cavendish Publishing 2004)

Morgan B & Yeung K, *An Introduction to Law and Regulation: Text and Materials* (CUP 2007)

Muncie J, McLaughlin E & Langan M, (eds) *Criminological Perspectives: A Reader* (Sage Publications 1997)

Muncie J & McLaughlin E (eds,) *The Problem of Crime* (Sage Publications 1996)

Napley D, *Are Two Legal Professions Necessary?* (Waterlow Publishers Limited 1986)

O'Callaghan P, *The Law on Solicitors in Ireland* (Butterworths 2000)

O'Malley T, *Sources of Law* (Sweet & Maxwell 2001)

O'Toole F, *Ship of Fools: How Stupidity and Corruption Sank the Celtic Tiger* (London: Faber & Faber 2009)

Pinto A & Evans M, *Corporate Criminal Liability* (Sweet & Maxwell 2003)

Popper K, *Conjectures and Refutations* (Routledge & Kegan Paul 1969)

Rhode D (ed), *Ethics in Practice: Lawyers' Roles, Responsibilites and Regulation* (OUP 2000)

Seneviratne M, *The Legal Profession: Regulation and the Consumer* (Sweet & Maxwell 1999)

Simpson S & Gibbs C, *Corporate Crime* (Ashgate Publishing Ltd 2007)

Stiglitz J, *Globalization and its Discontents* (The Penguin Press 2002)

Ullrich H (ed), *The Evolution of European Competition Law: Whose Regulation, Which Competition?* (Edward Elgar Publishing Limited 2006)

Uzelac A & van Rhee C, (eds), *The Landscape of the Legal Professions in Europe and the USA: Continuity and Change* (Intersentia 2011)

Webley L, *Legal Writing* (Routledge Cavendish 2010)

Journal Articles

Akerlof G, 'The Market for 'Lemons': Quality Uncertainty and the Market Mechanism' (1970) 84 (3) Quarterly Journal of Economics 488 – 500

Andreangeli A, 'Between the public interest and the free market: would the liberalisation of the legal profession bring benefits to the client – and to the market?' (2008) 19 (6) *European Business Law Review* 1031 – 1000

Arjoon S, 'Striking a Balance Between Rules and Principles-based Approaches for Effective Governance: A Risks-based Approach' (2006) 68 Journal of Business Ethics 58

Bamford C, 'Financial Crimes and Misdemeanours' [Autumn 2007] 71 Amicus Curiae 19 – 22

Bell E, 'Judges, Fairness and Litigants in Person' [2010] Judicial Studies Institute Journal 1-45, 42

Binchy D, 'Serious Concerns' (2012) 106 (4) The Law Society Gazette 1

Bindman G, 'An Unsung hero: The actions of one man transformed the regulation of the solicitors' profession' (May 2007) 157 (7274) New Law Journal 746

Blankenship M, Janikowski W & Sparger J, 'The Impact of General Education on Criminal Justice Pedagogy' (1990) 1 (1) Journal of Criminal Justice Education 87 – 98

Boon A, 'From Public Service to Service Industry: The impact of socialization and work on the motivation and values of lawyers' (July 2005) 12 (2) International Journal of Legal Profession 232

Boon A, Earle,R & Whyte A, 'Regulating Mediators?' (2007) 10 (1) Legal Ethics 26 – 50

Boon A & Flood J, 'The Globalization of Professional Ethics? The Significance of Lawyers' International Codes of Conduct' (1999) 2 (1) Legal Ethics 29 – 57

Boon A, Flood J & Webb J, 'Postmodern Professions? The Fragmentation of Legal Education and the Legal Profession' (Sept 2005) 32(3) Journal of Law and Society 473-492

Boon A & Whyte A, 'Icarus Falls: The Coal Health Scandal' [2012] 15 (2) Legal Ethics 227 – 313

Bronstein F, 'The Lawyer as Director of the Corporate Client in the wake of Sarbanes-Oxley' [2003] 23 Journal of Law and Commerce 53 – 67

Cahill D, 'Competition Law and the Regulation of the Legal Profession in Ireland – Where's the Trouble?' (A Critical Analysis of Selected Aspects of the Irish Competition Authority's Report into the Legal Profession in Ireland) (2008) 19 (6) European Business Law Review 1061 – 1078

Collins M, 'Legal Costs: A House Less Bleak' (2008) 13 (8) Bar Review 69 – 76

Cooke J, 'Competition in the Cab-rank and the Challenge to the Independent Bar: Part I' (2003) 8 (4) Bar Review 148 – 152

Cooke J, 'Competition in the Cab-rank and the Challenge to the Independent Bar: Part II' (2003) 8 (5) Bar Review 197 – 210

Daintith T, 'Rule of Law Reform and Development: Charting the Fragile Path of Progress' (Publication Review) [2009] Public Law 657 – 658

Daly C, 'The Dichotomy Between Standards and Rules: A New Way of Understanding the Differences in Perceptions of Lawyer Codes of Conduct by US and Foreign Lawyers' (1999) 32 Vanderbilt Journal of Transnational Law 1117

Davies M, 'Solicitors, dishonesty and the Solicitors Disciplinary Tribunal'(1999) 6 (2) International Journal of the Legal Profession 141 -174

Davies M, 'The Demise of Professional Self-Regulation? Evidence from the 'ideal type professions of medicine and law' (2010) 157 (7276) PN 3

Devlin A, 'Law and Economics' [2011] 46 Irish Jurist 165

Devlin A, 'Questioning the Sole-trader Rule in the Barrister Profession' (2009) 44 (1) Jurist Reports 123

Dingwall R & Fenn P, 'A Respectable Profession? Sociological and Economic Perspectives on the Regulation of Professional Services' (1987) 7 International Review of Law and Economics 53.

Doherty G, 'Commercial Undertakings' Aug/Sept 2010 Law Society Gazette 104 (7) 1

Doherty G, 'No Shortage of Challenges' May 2010 Law Society Gazette 104 (4) 1

Doornbos N & De Groot-Van Leeuwen L, 'Incorrigible Advocates' [2012] 15 (2) Legal Ethics 335 – 355

Edmonds D, 'Seize the Opportunity to Change the Profession' (2009) 23 (47) Lawyer 6

Flood J, 'Lawyers as Sanctifiers: The Role of the Elite Law Firms in International Business Transactions' (2007) 14 (1) Indiana Journal of Global Legal Studies 35 – 66

Flood J, 'The Re-Landscaping of the Legal Profession: Large Law Firms and Professional Re-Regulation' [Forthcoming 2010-2011] Current Sociology

Flood J, 'Will There Be Fallout from Clementi? The Repercussions for the Legal Profession After the Legal Services Act 2007' (2012) Michigan State Law Review 537 – 565

Fournier E, 'The Global Regulation Myth' (June 2009) 28 (6) International Financial Law Review

Freyne E, 'E-Conveyancing Project Update' Oct 2012 Law Society Gazette 106 (8) 14

Furlong J, 'The Law Firm Sector in Ireland: An Overview' [2011] Legal Information Management 172 – 176

Gallagher B, 'Avoiding Professional Negligence Claims in Conveyancing' (December 2002) 96 (10) Law Society Gazette 10

Gallagher P, 'A response to the Competition Authority's recommendation that the sole trader rule be abolished' (2007) 12 (4) The Bar Review 134 – 156

Garoupa N, 'Providing a Framework for Reforming the Legal Profession: Insights form the European Perspective' [2008] European Business Law Review 464 – 495

Gilhooly S, 'Memorandum' (June 2011) 105 (5) Law Society Gazette 19

Grogan P, 'Professional Pitfalls' (July 2003) 97 (6) Law Society Gazette 12 – 17

Guillén M, 'Is Globalization Civilizing, Destructive or Feeble: A Critique of 5 Key Debates in the Social Science Literature' [2001] 27 Annual Review of Sociology 235 – 260

Gurdgiev C, 'NAMA: an Institutional and Operational Failure that Keeps Expanding' October 2011 NAMALab, Dublin School of Architecture, Dublin Institute of Technology

Hadfield G, 'Legal Barriers to Innovation: The Growing Economic Cost of Professional Control over Corporate Legal Markets' [2008] Stanford Law Review (6) 1689

Hanley K, 'Higher Rights: Access all areas' (2007) 4 Law Society Gazette 25

Hellwig H-J, 'The Legal Profession under attack: Part 1' [2004] 40 European Lawyer 24-25

Hellwig H-J, 'The Legal Profession under attack: Part 2' [2004] 41 European Lawyer 42-43

Jiraporn, P & Davidson W, 'Regulation, shareholder rights and corporate governance: an empirical note' (2009) 16 (10) Applied Economics Letters 977 – 982.

Kitchin R et al, 'Unfinished estates in Post-Celtic Tiger Ireland'. (2012) National Institute for Regional and Spatial Analysis Working Paper Series No 67 – Feb 2012. NUI Maynooth

Langdon-Down G, 'Professional Indemnity: Disaster Planning' (2008) 8 Law Society Gazette

Lobo G & Zhou J, 'Did Conservatism in Financial Reporting Increase after the Sarbanes-Oxley Act? Initial Evidence' (March 2006) 20 (1). Accounting Horizons 57 -73

Mac Carthaigh D, 'Criminal Prosecutions under the Market Abuse Regulations More than on way to skin a cat' 2010 15 (6) Bar Review 121-128

Mc Dermott M, 'Changing of the Guard' LSG (December 2011) 105 (10) 26 – 29

Mc Dermott M, 'Debating Change in Castlemartyr' LSG (May 2012) 106 (4) 12 – 15

Mac Maolain C, 'Ramifications of the EU/IMF Loan to Ireland for the Financial Services Sector and for Irish Law and Society' (2011) European Public Law 17 (3) 387-397

Mark S & Cowdroy G, 'Incorporated Legal Practices – A New Era in the Provision of Legal Services in the State of New South Wales' (2004) 22 (4) Penn State Law Review 671 – 693

Martin K, 'Law Society President's Speech: Facing the future' (2005) 35 Law Society Gazette

Martin S, 'Informed Consent in the Practice of Law' [1980] George Washington Law Review 307

Manzoor Z, 'The Legal Services Act – a perspective from the Legal Services Ombudsman for England and Wales and the Legal Services Commissioner' (Winter 2008) 76 Amicus Curiae 7 -10

Millard R, 'Avoiding Apocalypse' (2008) 14 (5) Managing Partner 18 – 20

Murphy K, 'Greek lawyers feel under siege by Troika' (2012) 106 (3) The Law Society Gazette 16 – 17

Murphy S, 'Function of the Complaints and Client Relations Society' (March 2009) 103 (2) Law Society Gazette 10

Murphy S, 'Powers of the Complaints and Client Relations Committee' (2009) 103 (3) Law Society Gazette 12 – 13

Murtagh A, 'Irish Competition Policy Under EU/IMF Spotlight' [2012] Competition Law 62

Neary A, 'Cause and Effect' (2011) 105 (7) Law Society Gazette 33

Ogus A, 'Rethinking Regulation' 1995 (15) 1 Oxford Journal of Legal Studies 97-108

O Higgins K, 'Neary and Rowe announce new 'Q Standard' (2012) 106 (7) The Law Society Gazette 10

O'Mahoney J, 'PII Survey Reveals Average Cost Increase of 56%' (2011) 105 (7) Law Society Gazette 33

Parker C, 'Law firms incorporated: how incorporation could and should make firms more ethically responsible' (2004) 23 (2) University of Queensland Law Journal 347 -380

Parker C, Gordon T & Mark S, 'Regulating Law Firm Ethics Management: An Empirical Assessment of an Innovation in Regulation of the Legal Profession in New South Wales' (September 2010) 37 (3) Journal of Law and Society 466 – 500

Parnham R, 'Crisis looms for Europe's lawyers' [2003] 28 European Lawyer 34 – 40

Parnham R, 'Regulators reluctant to embrace change' [2005] 53 European Lawyer 8 – 10

Pech L & Hinds A-L, 'When the public interest masks lawyers' interests: Luxembourg's failure to adhere to Directive 98/5' (2007) 14 (1), (2) Irish Journal of European Law. 161 – 187

Peppet S, 'Lawyers' Bargaining Ethics, Contract and Collaboration: The End of the Legal Profession and the Beginning of Professional Pluralism' [200004 – 2005] 90 Iowa Law Review 475

Philipsen N, 'Regulation of liberal professions and competition policy: developments in the EU and China' [2010] 6 (2) Journal of Competition Law and Economics 203 – 231

Prasifka W, 'Frozen in time: a critique of the sole trader rule' (2007) 12 (4) The Bar Review 124 – 132

Proctor C, 'The Liability of financial regulators for bank failures' [March/April 2004] 52 Amicus Curiae 23 -28

Rhode D and Woolley A, 'Globalization and the Legal Profession: Comparative Perspectives on Layer Regulation: An Agenda for Reform in the United States and Canada' (2012) 80 Fordham Law Review 2761 – 2790

Rogers J, 'Representing the Bar: how the barristers' profession sells itself to prospective members'. (2012) 32 (2) Legal Studies 202 – 225

Rose C, 'Crystals and Mud in Property Law' (1988) 40 Stanford Law Review 577

Rose N, 'Profession hits back at complaints verdict' (2007) 25 Law Society Gazette 1

Rothwell R, 'Crime agency chairman heads list of appointments to new regulatory board' (2005) 37 Law Society Gazette

Russell G, 'Can American Lawyers get to heaven?' [2004] 36 European Lawyer 62 – 23

Samuel A, 'Carrots and Sticks: Will the new complaint rules make solicitors more accountable?' (June 2007) 157 (7276) New Law Journal 798

Skordaki E & Willis C, Defaults by Solicitors Research Study No 4 (London, The Law Society).

Shapiro S, 'Collaring The Crime, not the Criminal: Reconsidering the Concept of White-Collar Crime' 55 (3) American Sociological Review 346 – 365.

Shinnick E, 'Aspects of Regulatory Reform in the Irish Solicitor Profession: Review and Evaluation' (2003) 2 Quarterly Economic Commentary Special Article (ESRI)

Stulz, 'Securities Laws, Disclosure, and National Capital Markets in the Age of Financial Globalization' (May 2009) 47 (2) Journal of Accounting Research.

Sullivan B, 'The Problems and Possibilities of Professionalism' (1999) 6 (1) Dublin University Law Journal 108

Stephen F, 'Regulation of the legal professions or regulation of markets for legal services: potential implications of the Legal Services Act 2007' (2008) 19 (6) European Business Law Review 1129 – 1139

Sutherland E, 'White Collar Criminality' [1940] V American Sociological Review 1 – 12.

Swift J, 'Greek crisis impacts on legal sector as old-fashioned partnerships buckle' (2010) 24 (20) Lawyer 8

Taylor G, 'Risk and Financial Armageddon in Ireland: The Politics of the Galway Tent' (2011) 82 (4) The Political Quarterly 596 – 608

Terry L, 'A Case Study of the Hybrid Model for Facilating Cross Border Legal Practice: The Agreement between the American Bar Association and the Brussels Bars [1998] 21 (4) Fordham Law Review 1382

Terry L, et al 'Adopting Regulatory Objectives for the Legal Profession' (2012) 80 (6) Fordham Law Review. 2685

Terry L, 'A "How To" Guide for Incorporating Global and Comparative Perspectives into the Required Professional Responsibility Course' (2007) 51 St Louis University Law Journal 1135

Terry L et al, 'Trends and Challenges in Lawyer Regulation: The Impact of Globalization and Technology' (2012) 80 (6) Fordham Law Review 2661

Trevelyan L, 'Regulation: Devil in the details?' (2008) 17 Law Society Gazette 21

Underwood K, 'The Legal Services Bill – Death by Regulation?' [2007] Civil Justice Quarterly 124 – 133

Vatier B, 'A year of living dangerously' [2005] 46 European Lawyer 5

Wald E, 'Lawyers and Corporate Scandals' 7 (1) Legal Ethics 54 – 82

Wendel W B, 'Nonlegal Regulation of the Legal Profession: Social Norms in Professional Communities' (Oct 2001) 54 Vanderbilt Law Review 1955

__ __ 'Case Comment: Host state must consider lawyer's diploma' [2003] 134 EU Focus 17 – 19

__ __ 'Not Even Zimbabwe Has a Model Like This'. LSG (November 2011) 105 (9) 12 – 13

Online Articles

Adamopoulos G, 'The Legal Profession in Greece' 9th Jan 2012. Available at: http://greeklawdigest.gr/topics/legal-profession-in-greece/item/125-the-legal-profession-in-greece Accessed 20th 2013

Alfieri A, 'Risk Management, Law Firm Economics, and Lawyer Integrity' April 2010. University of Miami School of Law. Available at: <http://ssrn.com/abstract=1539130> Accessed 5th Dec 2011

Ascher B, 'The Threat to US Lawyers from Competition by Multidisciplinary Practices (MDPs): Is it Gone?' The American Antitrust Institute. AAI Working Paper No 06-06. Available at: <http://ssrn.com/abstract=1103606> Accessed: 5th Dec 2011

Baker T & Swedloff R, 'Regulation by Liability Insurance: From Auto to Lawyers Professional Liability' University of Pennsylvania Law School. Institute for Law and Economics. Research Paper 13.4 Available at: <http://ssrn.com/abstract=2202314> Accessed 6th June 2013

Bar Council of Ireland 'Submission of the Bar Council of Ireland to the Joint Committee on Justice, Defence and Equality on the Legal Services Regulation Bill 2011'. March 2012. Available at: <http://www.lawlibrary.ie/document/news_events/BarCounciSubmissionJointComm03201 2.pdf>Accessed 7th Jan 2013

Barnhizer D, 'Children of a Lesser God: Lawyers, Economics, and the Systemic Corruption of the Legal Profession' June 2009. Cleveland State University. Cleveland-Marshall School of Law. Research Paper 09-174. Available at: <http://ssrn.com/abstract=1375028> Accessed: 5th Dec 2011

Barnhizer D, 'Golem, "Gollum", Gone: The Lost Honour of the Legal Profession' Cleveland State University. January 2011. Research Paper 11 -203. Available at: <http://ssrn.com/abstract=1734412> Accessed: 5th Dec 2011

Bohrer A, 'The Impact of the Financial Crisis on the Law and the Legal Profession' (Submitted to International Junior Faculty Forum 2009, Harvard Law School & Stanford Law School) Availabe at: <http://ssrn.com/abstract=1511323> Accessed: 20th Nov 2011

Cassens Weiss D, 'Futurist Says Lawyers Will Become Legal Risk Consultants' ABA Journal 14/11/2008. Available at: <http://www.abajournal.com/news/article/futurist_says_lawyers_will_become_legal_risk_consultants/> Accessed 23rd Sept 2012

Cassens Weiss D, 'Legal Futurist: "The Party is Now Over"' ABA Journal 11th Nov 2008. Available at: <http://www.abajournal.com/new/article/legal_futurist_the_party_is_now_over/> Accessed 23rd Sept 2012

Childress S, 'Lawyers' June 2007. Tulane University School of Law. Public Law and Legal Theory Research Paper Series. Research Paper No 07-15. Available at: <http://srrn.com/abstract=1100186> Accessed: 5th Dec 2011

Clarke B & Hardiman N, 'Crisis in the Irish Banking System' 2012. University College of Dublin Working Papers in Law, Criminology and Socio-Legal Studies. Research Paper No 02/2012. Available at: <http://ssrn.com/abstract=2008302> Accessed 20th Oct 2012

Construction Industry Federation 'Construction Industry in need of "intensive care" following CSO Report'. Available at: <http://www.cif.ie/news-events/current-news/cif-warns-construction-industry-in-need-of-intensive-care-following-iso-report/> Accessed 30th April 2013

Cummings S, 'What Good are Lawyers?' Available at: <http://ssrn.com/abstract=1763337> Accessed 5th Dec 2011

Ernst D, 'Lawyers, Bureaucratic Autonomy, and Securities Regulation During the New Deal' September 2009. Georgetown Law Faculty Working Papers. Available at: <http://ssrn.com/abstract=1470934> Accessed: 5th Dec 2011

Fisher D, 'Google Jumps into Online-Law Business with Rocket lawyer' Forbes (11/8/2011) available at: <http://www.forbes.com/sites/danielfisher/2011/08/11/google-jumps-into-online-law-business-with-rocket-lawyer/> Accessed 2nd Mar 2013

Fisher K, 'The Higher Calling: Regulation of Lawyers Post-Enron' (2004) 37 (4) University of Michigin Journal of Law Reform 1017 – 1144. Available at: <http://ssrn.com/abstract=824426> Accessed 5th Dec 2011

FLAC 'Submission on the Legal Services on the Legal Services Regulation Bill 2011'. February 2012. Available at: <http://www.flac.ie/download/pdf/20120220130320.pdf> Accessed 1st Feb 2013

Flood J, 'Ambiguous Allegiances in the Lawyer-Client Relationship: The Case of Bankers and Lawyers' May 2009 Available at: <http://ssrn.com/abstract=962725> Accessed: 5th Dec 2011

Flood J, 'Betting the System and Beating the House?' Gillian Tett's Story of the Financial Crisis: "Fool's Gold – How Unrestrained Greed Corrupted a Dream, Shattered Global Markets and Unleashed a Catastrophe" (Little, Brown 2009) (Available at: <http://ssrn.com/abstract=1462723> Accessed 5th Dec 2011

Flood J, 'From Ethics to Regulation: The Re-Organization and Re-Professionalization of Large Law Firms in the 21st Century' Available at: <http://ssrn.com/abstract=1592324> Accessed: 5th Dec 2011

Flood J & Whyte A, 'Straight There No Detours: Direct Access to Barristers' June 2009 Available at: <http://ssrn.com/abstract=1321492> Accessed: 5th Dec 2011

Flood J, "When the Troika comes to the Rescue" Iberian Lawyer 9/7/12. Available at: <http://www.iberianlawyer.com/panorama/3622-when-the-troika-come-to-the-rescue> Accessed 20th Feb 2013

Fortney S & Horn P, 'Tales of Two Regimes for Regulating Limited Liability Law Firms in the US and Australia: Client Protection and Risk Management Lessons'. Texas Tech University School of Law Legal Studies Research Paper No 2010-15. Available at: <http://ssrn.com/abstract=1427298> Accessed 5th Feb 2011

Gallagher W, 'Ideologies of Professionalism and the Politics of Self-Regulation in the California State Bar' [1995] 22 Pepperdine Law Review 485 – 628. Available at: <http://ssrn.com/abstract =1103723> Accessed: 5th Dec 2011

Goldsmith J, 'Troika forces ABSs on Italy' 21 November 2011. Law Society Gazette <www.lawgazette.co.uk/blogs/blogs/euro-blog/the-phoney-crisis-has-ended> Accessed 1st May 2013

Greenstein R, 'Against Professionalism' 22 (30) The Georgetown Journal of Legal Ethics Available at: <http://ssrn.com/abstract=340094> Accessed: 5th Dec 2011

Hennigan M, 'EU-IMF Bailout: Hope, anger and denial on Ireland's Day of Infamy' Available at: <http://www.finacts.ie/irishfinancenews/Irish_Economy/article_1021128_printer.shtml> Accessed 5th Dec 2011

Honohan P, (2010) 'The Irish Banking Crisis: Regulatory and Financial Stability Policy 2003 – 2008: A Report to the Minister for Finance from the Governor of the Central Bank' Central Bank, Dublin, May 2010. Available at: <http://www.bankingenquiry.gov.ie/The%20Irish%20Banking%20Crisis%20Regulatory%20and%20Financial%20Stability%20Policy%202003-2008.pdf> Last accessed 27th Oct 2012

Irish Human Rights Commission, 'Observations on the Legal Services Regulation Bill 2011' February 2012. Available at: <http://www.ihrc.ie/download/pdf/ihrc_observations_on_lsra_bill_2011.pdf > Accessed 28th April 2013

Joy P, 'The Relationship Between Civil Rule 11 and Lawyer Discipline: An Empirical Analysis Suggesting Institutional Choices in the Regulation of Lawyers' (2004) 37 Loyola Los Angeles Law Review 765 – 817. Available at: <http://ssrn.com/abstract=55272> Accessed 5th Dec 2011

Kelly M, 'The Irish Credit Bubble' (2009) UCD Centre for Economic Research Working Paper Series 2009 WP09/32. 1. Available at: <http://www.ucd.ie/t4cms/wp09.32pdf> Accessed 19th Dec 2012

Long A, 'Attorney Deceit Statutes: Promoting Professionalism through Criminal Prosecutions and Treble Damages' 23/3/2010. Available at: <http://ssrn.com/abstract=1559238> Accessed: 5th Dec 2011

McBarnett D, 'Financial Engineering or Legal Engineering? Legal Integrity and the Banking Crisis. (Forthcoming, McNeil I & O'Brien J eds 'The Future of Financial Regulation' Oxford, Hart 2010) Available at: <http://ssrn.com/abstract=1546486> Accessed 5th Dec 2011

Maniatopoulos S, 'Legal Professional Privilege in Greece and Competition' <http://www.econn.gr/general_docs/Articlee_Maniatopoulos.pdf> Acessed 1st May 2013

Margulies P, 'Lawyers' Independence and Collective Illegality in Government and Corporate Misconduct, Terrorism and Organised Crime' 23/3/2006. Available at: <http://ssrn.com/abstract=893055> Accessed 5th Dec 2011

McMorrow J, et al 'Judicial Attitudes Towards Confronting Attorney Misconduct: A View from the Reported Decisions'. Boston College of Law, Public Law and Legal Theory Research

Papers. Research Paper no.36. 1st April 2004. Available at: <http://ssrn.com/abstract=531223> Accessed: 5th Dec 2011

Neil M, 'Prophet Richard Susskind Predicts the Future of Law; Internet is Key' ABA Journal 17/2/2009. Available at: <http://www.abajournal.com/news/article/prophet_richard_susskind_predicts_the_future_of_law/> Accessed 23rd Sept 2012

Nyberg P, (2011) 'Misjudging Risk: Causes of the Systemic Banking Crisis in Ireland: Report of the Commission of Investigation into the Banking Sector in Ireland'. Dublin. Available at: <http://www.bankingenquiry.gov.ie/Documents/Misjudging%20Risk%20-%20Causes%20of%20the%20Systemic%20Banking%20Crisis%20in%20Ireland.pdf> Accessed 27th Oct 2012

Muzio D & Faulconbridge J, 'The Global Law Firm as a Locus of Professional Education' Available at: <http://ssrn.com/abstract=1516314> Accessed: 5th Dec 2011

Parker C, 'Peering over the Ethical Precipice: Incorporation, Listing and Ethical Responsibilities of Law Firms' (2008). University of Melbourne Legal Studies Paper No 339, 2008. Available at: <http://ssrn.com/sol3/papers.cfm?abstract_id=1132926> Accessed 5th Mar 2013

Pue W, 'Death Squads and "directions over lunch": A Comparative Review of the Independence of the Bar' 28th Aug 2006. Available at: <http://ssrn.com/abstract=1000725> Accessed 5th Dec 2011

Purcell D, 'A Rough Guide to Irish Regulators' 26th November 2008. Available at <http://www.tca.ie/images/uploaded/documents/2008-11-26%20A%20Rough%20Guide%20to%20Irish%20Regulators.pdf > Accessed 2nd Nov 2011

Rayner J, 'Lawyers in UK and Ireland hit hardest by problems in property market' 3rd Dec 2009. Available at: <http://www.lawgazette.co.uk/new/lawyers-uk-and-ireland-hit-hardest-problems-property-market>. Accessed 3rd May 2012

Rayner J, 'Troika's liberalisation drive 'threatens profession'' 30th Nov 2011. The Law Gazette. Available at: <http://www.lawgazette.co.uk/print/63318> Accessed 27th June 2012

Regling K and Watson, M (2010) 'Preliminary Report on the Sources of Ireland's Banking Crisis'. Dublin, Government Publications Office. Available at: <http://www.bankingenquiry.gov.ie/Preliminary%20Report%20into%20Ireland's%20Banking%20Crisis%2031/%20May%202010.pdf> Accessed 27th Oct 2012

Revenue Comissioners' Tax Defaulters' List October – Dec 2007. Available at: <www.revenue.ie/en/press/defaulters/archive/def2-407.pdf> Accessed 7th Dec 2012

Ring S, 'Mishcon to go Beyond Legal with New High-Net Private Client Business' Legal Week (24/2/12). Available at: <http://www.legalweek.com/legalweek/news/2154441/mishcons-legal-net-private-client-business> Accessed 1st Mar 2013

Rochvarg A, 'Enron, Watergate and the Regulation of the Legal Profession' [2003] 43 Washburn Law Journal 61 – 90. Available at: <http://ssrn.com/abstract=1331152> Accessed: 5th Dec 2011

Rose J, 'The Ambidextrous Lawyer: Conflict of Interest and the Medieval Law Profession' Available at: <http://ssrn.com/absract=99988.pdf> Accessed 5th Sept 2011

Russell I, 'The Evolving Regulation of the Legal Profession: The Costs of Indeterminacy and Certainty' University of Tulsa Legal Studies Research Paper No 2009-08. Available at: <http://ssrn.com/abstract=1357609> Accessed 5th Dec 2011

Sako M, 'Global Strategies in the Legal Services Marketplace: Institutional Impacts on Value Chain Dynamics' (July 2009). Available at:

http://www.sbs.ox.ac.uk/research/people/Documents/Mari%20Sako//Global%20Strategies%20by%20LPO%20paper%20June2010.pdf Accessed 29th Jan 2013

Sassen S, 'The Repositioning of Cities and Urban Regions in a Global Economy: Pushing Policy and Governance Options'. Available at: <http://www.oecd.org/dataoecd/11/21/40077412.pdf> Accessed 27th June 2012

Scott C, 'Regulating in Global Regimes' University College Dublin. UCD Working Papers in Law, Criminology & Socio-Legal Studies. Research Paper No 25/2010. Available at: <http://ssrn.com/abstract=1598262> Accessed 5th Dec 2011

Sherr A & Webley L, 'Legal Ethics in England and Wales' Institute of Advanced Legal Studies. Available at: <http://ssrn.com/abstract=1201822> Accessed 5th Dec 2011

Simon W, 'Wrongs of Ignorance and Ambiguity: Lawyer Responsibility for Collective Misconduct' Columbia Law School, Public Law and Legal Theory Working Group Paper. Paper number: 04-80. Available at: <http://ssrn.com/abstract=602627> Accessed 5th Dec 2011

Spigelman A, 'Are Lawyers Lemons? Competition Principles and Professional Regulation' The 2002 Lawyer's Lecture. St James Ethics Centre. Available at: <http://ssrn.com/abstract=1800450> Accessed 5th Dec 2011

Stephen F & Love J, 'Regulation of the Legal Profession' (1999) *Encyclopaedia of Law and Economics* Available at: <http://users.ugent.be/~gdegeest/5860book.pdf> Accessed 5th Dec 2011

Terry L, 'An Introduction to the Paris Forum on Transnational Practice for the Legal Profession' (1999) 18 (1) Dickinson Journal of International Law. 1 – 32 Available at: <http://ssrn.com/abstract=596205> Accessed 5th Dec 2011

Terry L, 'GAT'S Applicability to Transnational Lawyering and its Potential Impact on US State Regulation of Lawyers' [2002] 35 Vanderbilt Journal of Transnational Law 1387. Available at www.ssrn.com/abstract=596023 Accessed 23rd Nov 2011

Terry L, et al, 'Transnational Legal Practice' (2010) 44 (1) The International Lawyer 563 – 576. Available at: <http://ssrn.com/abstract=1673351> Accessed 5th Dec 2011

Terry L, 'The Future Regulation of the Legal Profession. The Impact of Treating the Legal Profession as "Service Providers"'. Available at: <http://ssrn.com/abstract=1304172> Accessed: 5th Dec 2011

Terry L, 'Regulation of Legal Systems and Lawyers' 12th Sept 2009. Harvard-Oxford-Jindal Programme on Globalization of the Legal Profession. Available at: <http://www.personal.psu.edu/faculty/l/s/lst3/presentations%20for%20webpage/Laurel_Terry_Oxford.pdf> Accessed 18th Oct 2012

Tzotzadini A, 'Greek Lawyers Unhappy about New Measures'. Greek Reporter.com 14/9/2010. Available at: <http://greece.greekreporter.com/2010/09/14/provincial-lawyers-face-new-tough-measures/> Accessed 20th Feb 2013

Van den Bergh R, 'Toward Better Regulation of the Legal Profession in the European Union' July 2008. Rotterdam Institute of Law and Economics Working Paper Series No 2008/07. Available at: <http://ssrn.com/abstract=1113310> Accessed. 5th Dec 2011

Vischer R, 'Trust and the Global Law Firm: Are Relationships of Trust Still Central to the Corporate Legal Services Market?' 2010. University of St Thomas. Minnesota School of Law. Legal Studies Research Paper Series. Legal Studies Research Paper No 10-19. Available at: <http://ssrn.com/abstract=1666973> Accessed: 5th Dec 2011

Wald E, 'Should Judges Regulate Lawyers?' [2010] 42 McGeorge Law Review 1 – 26. Available at: < http://ssrn.com/abstract=1734491> Accessed: 5th Dec 2011

Wendel B, 'If Lifelong Learning is the Solution, What is the Problem?: A Perspective From South of the Border' Available at: <http://ssrn.com/abstract=1361695> Accessed: 5th Dec 2011

Wendel B, 'The Jurisprudence of Enron: Professionalism as Interpretation' Cornell Law School. Legal Studies Research Paper Series. Research Paper No 04-012. Available at: <http://ssrn.com/abstract=959860> Acessed 5th Dec 2011

Wood K, 'Are Irish lawyers anti-competitive?' 11th December 2006. Available at: <http://irishbarrister.com/competition.html> 6th Sept 2012

Woolley A, 'Rhetoric and Realities: What Independence of the Bar Requires of Lawyer Regulation' University of Calgary. June 2011 4 (8) The School of Public Policy. SPP Research Papers. 1 – 39. Available at: <http://ssrn.com/abstract=1920921> Accessed: 5th Dec 2011

Zacharias F, 'Integrity Ethics' July 2009 (revised) University of San Diego School of Law. Legal Studies Research Paper Series. Research Paper No 08-056 Available at: <http://ssrn.com/abstract=1221722> Accessed 5th Dec 2011

Zacharias F, 'The Myth of Self-Regulation' [2009] 93 Minnesota Law Review 1147 – 1189. Available at: <http://ssrn.com/abstract=1431723> Accessed: 5th Dec 2011

Zacharias F, 'Why the Bar Needs Academics – and Vice Versa' Public Law and Legal Theory Research Paper Series. Paper no 67 Fall 2003. Available at: <http://ssrn.com/abstract=499122> Accessed 5th Dec 2011

Zacharias F & Green B, 'Reconceptualizing Advocacy Ethics' Oct 2005. University of San Diego School of Law. Legal Studies Research Paper Series. Research Paper No 07-15. Available at: <http://ssrn.com/abstract=829304> Accessed 5th Dec 2011

__ __ 'An Economic Analysis of the Government's Proposed Regulatory Regime for the Legal Profession in Ireland'. Final Report. Compecon – Competition Economics, 3/3/2012. Available at: http://www.lawlibrary.ie/documents/news_events/BarCouncilRegulatoryImpactAssessment 03032012.pdf Accessed 29th Jan 2013

__ __ 'BoI action against solicitor and wife' 17th Jan 2011. RTE News. Available at: <http://www.rte.ie/news/2011/0117/nama-business.html> Accessed 05th Nov 2012

__ __ 'Concluding Statement, Seminar on Reform of the Legal System in Zimbabwe' 1st August 2009. Available at: <http://www.icj.org/dwn/database/ZIM-JudicialReform-FINALRESOLUTION-9August2009.pdf>. Accessed 30th Nov 2011

__ __ 'Exclusive-Michael Lynn Interview'. 24th May 2011. NewsScoops.Org. Available at: <http://www.newsscoops.org/?p=305> Accessed 18th Nov 2012

__ __ 'Ex-solicitor jailed for three-and-a-half years for €750,000 fraud'. 12th June 2012. RTE News. Available at: <http://www.rte.ie/news/2012/0612/ex-solicitor-jailed-following-750-000-fraud.html> Accessed 5th Nov 2012

__ __ 'Greek Lawyers Unhappy about New Measures' 14 September 2010. Greek Reporter <http://greece.greekreporter.com/2010/09/14/provincial-lawyers-face-tough-measures/> Accessed 1 May 2013

__ __ 'Irish bond yields hit new high' irishtimes.com 10th Oct 2010. <http://www.irishtimes.com/newspaper/breaking/2010/1028/breaking15.html> Accessed 4th Nov 2012

__ __ 'Lawyer in Greece' Bridgewest. Available at: http://www.bridgewest.eu/article/lawyer-in-greece Accessed 20th Feb 2013

__ __ 'Legal Ethics and Regulatory Legitimacy: Regulating Lawyers for Personal Misconduct' Available at: <http://ssrn.com/abstract=1331598> Accessed 5th Dec 2011

__ __ 'Quality Solicitors Hits the Big Time as PE Investor Buys Majority Stake' Legal Futures 20th October 2011. Available at: http://www.legalfutures.co.uk/legal-services-act/market-monitor/quality-solicitors-hits-the-big-time-as-pe-investor-buys-majorty-stake Accessed 1st Mar 2013

__ __ 'Return on Investment Case Study IBM SPSS Memphis Police Department' Nucleus Research Inc 2010. Available at: <http://www-01.ibm.com/software/success/cssdb.nsf/CS/SSAO8DJ5CL?OpenDocument8Site=default&cty=en_us> Accessed 8th Oct 2012

__ __ 'Round Up: Ireland's €85 bn EU/IMF bailout' 29/11/2010. Business and Finance. Available at: http://www.businessandfinance.ie/news/roundupirelands85bneu/imfbailout Accessed 4th Nov 2012

__ __ 'SMDF 2009 annual report shows €14.3 million investment loss' 4/8/2010. A Clatter of the Law. Available at: <http://aclatterofthelaw.com/2010/08/04/smdf-2009-annual-report-shows-e14-3-million-investment-loss/> Accessed 6th Dec 2012

__ __ 'Solicitors 'let down' by Law Society' 6/12/2007. RTE News. Available at: <http://www.rte.ie/news/2007/1206/lawsociety.html> Accessed 4th Sept 2012

__ __ 'Structural Reforms: Liberalisation of closed professions in Greece and other reforms' Mourgelas Greek Law Update. February 2012 <http://www.mourgelas.gr/img/x2/collection/pdfs/Greek-law-update/NewsletterFeb2012> Accessed 1st May 2013

__ __ '"The Irish are Stealing our Jobs!"-- Two London BigLaw Firms Setting Up Legal Process Outsourcing Operations in Belfast' 25/2/2011 Law Without Borders: Adventures in Legal Outsourcing t India and Beyond. Available at: <http://www.lawwithoutborders.typepad.com/legaloutsourcing/2011/02/the-irish-are-stealing-our-jobs-two-london-biglaw-firms-setting-up-legal-process-outsourcing-operati.html> Accessed 8th June 2012

Reports

Ireland

Committee of Public Accounts 'Third Interim Report on the procurement of legal services by public bodies' (Dáil Éireann, January 2011) PRN A11/0171

Department of Environment, Community and Local Government 'National Housing Development Survey Summary Report' November 2012 6. Available at: <http://www.environ.ie/en/Publishing/DevelopmentandHousing/Housing/FileDownLoad,31621,en.pdf> Accessed 29th Nov 2012

Department of Justice, Equality and Law Reform *Report of the Legal Costs Working Group* (Stationery Office, Dublin, 2003) Available at: <http://www.justice.ie/en/JELR/leglalcosts.pdf/Files/legalcosts.pdf > Accessed 18th Sept 2012

Department of Justice and Equality *Report of the Special Group on Public Service Numbers and Expenditure Programmes Volume II*. Available at: <http://www.djei.ie/publications/corporate/2009/volume2.pdf>

Department of the Taoiseach, 'Regulating Better: A Government White Paper setting out six principles of Better Regulation' (2001). Available at:

<http://www.taoiseach.gov.ie/eng/Publications/Publications_Archive/Publications2011/Regulating_Better_Government_White_Paper.pdf> Accessed 29th Jan 2013

Fair Trade Commission *Fair Trade Commission Report of Study into Restrictive Practices in the Legal Profession* (Dublin: Government of Ireland Stationery Office, 1990)

Forfas 'Costs of Doing Business in Ireland 2012'. <http://www.forfas.ie/media/08042013-Costs_of_Doing_Business_2012-Publication.pdf> Accessed 1st May 2013

Honohan P (2010) 'The Irish Banking Crisis: Regulatory and Financial Stability Policy 2003 – 2008: A Report to the Minister for Finance from the Governor of the Central Bank' Central Bank, Dublin, May 2010. Available at: <http://www.bankingenquiry.gov.ie/The%20Irish%20Banking%20Crisis%20Regulatory%20and%20Financial%20Stability%20Policy%202003-2008.pdf> Accessed 27th Oct 2012

Houses of the Oireachtas Committee of Public Accounts (PAC) 'Report on the Crisis in the Domestic Banking Sector: A Preliminary Analysis and a Framework for a Banking Enquiry' July 2012. Available at: <http://www.oireachtas.ie/parliament/media/committees/pac/PAC-Report---FINAL.pdf> Accessed 19th Dec 2012

Independent Adjudicator of the Law Society of Ireland '13th Annual Report of the Independent Adjudicator of the Law Society of Ireland: Year ending 30th September 2010. Available at <www.lawsociety.ie/Documents/committees/Complaints/IAAnnualReport.pdf> Accessed 5th Dec 2012

McDowell M, 'Report of the Implementation Advisory Group on a Single Regulatory Authority for Financial Services' (1999). Available at: <http://www.finance.govt.ie/viewdoc.asp?docID=677> Accessed 27th Oct 2012

Moriarty Tribunal of Enquiry (2012) 'The Tribunal of Enquiry into Certain Planning Matters and Payments'. Available at: <http://www.flood-tribunal.ie/asp/Reports.asp?objectid=310&Mode=0&RecordID=504> Accessed 12th Nov 2012

Neary A & O'Toole F *The Blueprint Report: A Review of the Legal Profession in Ireland and a Vision for Irish Law Firms* (Anne Neary Consultations, 2011)

Nyberg P (2011) 'Misjudging Risk: Causes of the Systemic Banking Crisis in Ireland: Report of the Commission of Investigation into the Banking Sector in Ireland'. Dublin. Available at: <http://www.bankingenquiry.gov.ie/Documents/Misjudging%20Risk%20-%20Causes%20of%20the%20Systemic%20Banking%20Crisis%20in%20Ireland.pdf> Accessed 27th Oct 2012

'Programme for Government 2011 – 2016'. (Government for National Recovery 2011 – 2016: Law Reform, Courts and Judiciary) 51. Available at: <http://www.socialjustice/sites/defaut/files/file/Government%20Docs%20etc/2011-13-06%20-%20Programme%20for%20Government%202011-2016.pdf> Accessed 29th Jan 2013

Regling K and M Watson M (2010) 'Preliminary Report on the Sources of Ireland's Banking Crisis'. Dublin, Government Publications Office. Available at: <http://www.bankingenquiry.gov.ie/Preliminary%20Report%20into%20Ireland's%20Banking%20Crisis%2031/%20May%202010.pdf> Accessed 27th Oct 2012

Solicitors Disciplinary Tribunal Annual Reports from 2003 – 2010. Available at: <http://distrib.ie/reports.htm> Accessed 20th Sept 2012

Solicitors Mutual Defence Fund Annual Report 2009. Available at:
<http://www.smdf.ie/pubs/Accounts_as_at_30th_November_2011.pdf> Accessed 3rd Jan
2013

Solicitors Mutual Defence Fund Annual Report 2010. Available at:
<http://www.smdf.ie/pubs/Solicitors_Report_Aug_2011.pdf> Accessed 3rd Jan 2013

Solicitors Mutual Defence Fund Directors' Report and Financial Statements Year Ended
2011. Available at:
<http://www.smdf.ie/pubs/Solicitors_Report_JUN_2010_Solicitors_Report_July_08.pdf>
Accessed 3rd Jan 2013

Special Report by the Comptroller and Auditor General: DIRT. Available at:
<http://www.publicenquiry.eu/Reports/CandGDirt.doc> Accessed 12th Nov 2012

The Competition Authority 'Competition in Professional Services: Solicitors and Barristers'
December 2006. Available at:
<http://www.tca.ie/images/uploaded/documents/Solicitors%20and%20barristers%20full%2
0report.pdf > Accessed 15th Oct 2012

The Law Society of Ireland Annual Report and Accounts 2005/2006 Available at:
<http://www.lawsociety.ie/Global/About%20Us?Annual%20Reports/AR06.pdf> Accessed
2nd Jan 013

The Law Society of Ireland Annual Report and Accounts 2006/2007 Available at:
<http://www.lawsociety.ie/Global/About%20Us?Annual%20Reports/AR%2007.pdf>
Accessed 2nd Jan 2013

The Law Society of Ireland Annual Report and Accounts 2007/2008 Available at:
<http://www.lawsociety.ie/Global/About%20Us?Annual%20Reports/AR08.pdf > Accessed
2nd Jan 2013

The Law Society of Ireland Annual Report and Accounts 2008/2009 Available at:
<http://www.lawsociety.ie/Global/About%20Us?Annual%20Reports/AR08-09.pdf >
Accessed 2nd Jan 2013

The Law Society of Ireland Annual Report and Accounts 2009/2010 Available at:
<http://www.lawsociety.ie/Global/About%20Us?Annual%20Reports/AR09_10.pdf>
Accessed 2nd Jan 2013

The Law Society of Ireland Annual Report and Accounts 2010/2011 Available at:
<http://www.lawsociety.ie/Global/About%20Us?Annual%20Reports/AnnualReport2011.pdf
> Accessed 2nd Jan 2013

The Law Society of Ireland Annual Report and Accounts 2011/2012. Available at:
<http://www.lawsociety.ie/Global/About%20Us?Annual%20Reports/AnnualReport2012.pdf
> Accessed 8th Nov 2012

The Moriarty Tribunal of Enquiry (2012) 'The Tribunal of Enquiry into Certain Planning
Matters and Payments'. Available at: <http://www.flood-
tribunal.ie/asp/Reports.asp?objectid=310&Mode=0&RecordID=504> Accessed 12th Nov
2012

The National Competitiveness Council 'Costs of Doing Business in Ireland 2010 Volume 1'
22nd July 2010. Available at:
<http://www.competitiveness.ie/newsevents/news/title,6542,en.php>

The Solicitors Disciplinary Tribunal 'A Guide to Applicants on How to make an Application to the Solicitors Disciplinary Tribunal for an Inquiry into Alleged Misconduct of a Solicitor'. Issued upon request from the SDT, The Friary, Bow Street, Dublin

'The Solicitors Disciplinary Tribunal Annual Report 2008' Available at <http://www.distrib.ie/documents/Solicitors_Disciplinary_Tribunal_CMS08.pdf> Accessed 10th Oct 2012

'The Solicitors Disciplinary Tribunal Annual Report 2009' Available at <http://www.distrib.ie/documents/Solicitors_Disciplinary_Tribunal_CMS09.pdf> Accessed 10th Oct 2012

England

Clementi D, 'Report of the Review of the Regulatory Framework for Legal Services in England and Wales' December 2004. Available at: <http://www.legal-services-review.org.uk/content/report > Accessed 2nd Jan 2012

The Office of Fair Trading. 'The Office of Fair Trading, Competition in Professions: A Report by the Director General of Fair Trading' (2001) Available at: <http://www.oft.gov.uk/shared_oft/reports/professional_bodies/oft328.pdf> Accessed 13th Jan 2013

The Solicitors Regulation Authority, 'The Regulation of International Practice'. 16th Feb 2012. Available at: <http://www.sra.org.uk/sra/consultations/regulation-international-practice.page> Accessed 21st May 2012

UK Nolan Committee on Standards in Public Life 'The Nolan Principles' are available at: <http://www.public-standards.gov.uk/about-us/what-we-do/the-seven-principles/> Accessed 3rd Mar 2013

Scotland

Stephen F 'An Economic Perspective on the Growth of Legal Service Markets' Evidence submitted to the Justice 1 Committee's Inquiry into the Regulation of the Legal Profession. Available at: <http://scottishparliament.net/business/committees/historic/justice/inquiries02/j1-lps-pdfs/lps-099.pdf > Accessed 13th Jan 2012

Northern Ireland

Bain G, 'Legal Services in Northern Ireland: Complaints, Regulation, Competition' (2006) Legal Services Review Group. Available at: <http://www.lawlibrary.ie/documents/memberdocs/Bainreport.pdf> Accessed 29th Jan 2013

Australia

Council of Australian Governments National Legal Profession Reforms 'Report on key isssues and amendments made to the National Law since December 2010. <http://www.lawlink.nsw.gov.au/Lawlink/Corporate/ll_corporate.nsf.vwFiles/NLPR_Report _key_amendments_LegalProfessionNationalLaw_since_Dec2010.pdf> Accessed 1st May 2013

Other Sources

Codes of Practice

Ireland

The Law Society of Ireland "A Guide to Professional Conduct of Solicitors in Ireland" 2nd ed (2002)

Code of Conduct for the Bar Council of Ireland. (5th July 2010) Available at <www.lawlibrary.ie/documents/memberdocs/Codeof ConductAdopted050710.pdf> Accessed 2nd Aug 2011

Disciplinary Code for the Bar Council of Ireland (5th July 2010) Available at < <http://www.lawlibrary.ie/documents/memberdoc/DisciplinaryCodeAdopted050710.pdf> Accessed 2nd Aug 2012

United Kingdom

The UK Corporate Governance Code (2012) Available at: <http://www.frc.org.uk/Our-Work/Publications/Corporate-Governance-Code-September-2012.pdf> Accessed 29th April 2013

International

ABA Model Rules of Professional Conduct   Available at: <http://www.americanbar.org/groups/professional_responsibility/publications/model_rule s_of_professional_conduct.html> Accessed 26th Aug2012

UK Corporate Governance Code. Available at: <http://www.frc.org.uk/getattachment/a7f0aa3a-57dd-4341-b3e8-ffa99899e154/UK-Corporate-Governance-Code-September-2012.aspx > Accessed 30th Nov 2012

International Organisations

American Bar Associaton

ABA Commission on Ethics 20/20 Proposal- Model Rule 5.5 and Foreign Lawyers. 19th September 2011. Available at: <http://americanbar.org/content/dam/aba/adminitrative/ethics/2020/20110919_ethics_20 _20_foreign_lawyers_and_model_rule_5_5_resolution_report.authcheckdam.pdf > Accessed 17th Oct 2012

ABA Model Rules for Lawyer Disciplinary Enforcement (2002). Avaialbe at: <http://www.americanbar.org/groups/professional_responsibility/resources/lawyer_ethics _regulation/model_rules_for_lawyer_ethics_regulation/model_rules_for_disciplinary_enfor cement.html> Accessed 30th April 2013

ABA Model Rule for the Licensing and Practice of Foreign Legal Consultants. As amended by the ABA House of Delegates, 7-8 August 2006. Available at: <http://www.americanbar.org/content/dam/aba/migrated/cpr/mjp/FLC.authcheckdam.pdf>

CCBE

CCBE Charter of Core Principles of the European Legal Profession and Code of Conduct. Available at: <www.ccbe.eu/fileadmin/user_upload/NTCdocument/EN_Code_of_conductp1_130674821 5.pdf> Accessed 30th Apr 2013

CCBE 'Standing up for Justice and the Rule of Law: The CCBE's Main Goals in 2012'. Available at: <http://www.ccbe.eu/fileadmin/user_upload/NTCdocument/eLeaflet_2012_EN_v_1_13330 92065.pdf> Accessed 18th Oct 2012

Council of Europe

Council of Europe: An Overview. Available at: <http://www.coe.int/AboutCoe/media/interface/publications/tour_horizon_en.pdf> Accessed 18th Oct 2012

Council of Europe Civil Law Convention on Corruption (1999) Available at: <http://conventions.coe.int/Treaty/en/Treaties/Html/174.htm> Accessed 26th Aug 2012

Council of Europe Criminal Law Convention on Corruption (1998). Available at: <conventions.coe.int/Treaty/en/Treaties/html/173.htm> Accessed 26th Aug 2012

Council of Europe Parliamentary Assembly Information Brochure. Available at: <http://www.assembly.coe.int/Communication/Brochure/Bro03-e.pdf> Accessed 8th July 2012

Council of Europe. Parliamentary Assembly Information Brochure. Available at: <http://www.assembly.coe.int/Communication/Brochure/Bro03-e.pdf> Accessed 2nd Jan 2011

Council of Europe Recommendation No R (2000) 21 of the Committee of Ministers to Member States on the Freedom of Exercise of the Profession of Lawyer. Adopted by the Committee of Ministers on 25th October 2000 at the 727th meeting of Ministers' Deputies. Available at: https://wcd.coe.int/com.instranet.InstraServlet?command=com.instranet.CmdBlobGet&Ins tranetImage=533749&SecMode=1&DocId=370286&Usage=2 Accessed 17th Oct 2012

International Association of Lawyers (Union Internationale Des Avocats)

The Turin Principles of Professional Conduct for the Legal Professiona in the Twenty-first Century. 27th Oct2002. Available at: <www.americanbar.org/content/dam/aba/migrated/cpr/gats/uia_ex_1.autcheckdam. pdf> Accessed 11th July 2012

International Bar Association

IBA Council 'Rule of Law Resolution' (September 2006). Available as a pdf document: <www.ibanet.org/PPID/Constituent/Rule_of_Law_Action_Group/Overview.aspx > Accessed 31st July 2012

IBA Financial Action Task Force website. Available at: <www.ibanet.org/LPD/Task_Force_on_the_Financial_Crisis.aspx> Accessed 31st July 012

IBA 'General Principles for the Legal Profession' (September 2006). Available as a pdf document: <www.ibanet.org/About_the_IBA/IBA_resolutions.aspx> Available at: <http://www.ibanet.org/About_the_IBA/IBA_resolutions.aspx> Accessed 14th Oct 2012

IBA-OECD-UNDOC 'Anti-Corruption Strategy for the Legal Profession: Risks and Threats of Corruption and the Legal Profession'. 2010. Available at: <http://www.oecd.org/daf/briberyininternationalbusiness/46137847.pdf> Accessed 18th Oct 2012

IBA Report of the International Bar Association's Human Rights Institute (IBAHRI) September 2011. 'Zimbabwe: time for a new approach' Available at: <http://www.osisa.org/sites/default/files/sup_files/ibhari_report_on_zimbabwe.pdf> Accessed 30th Nov 2011

IBA Resolution in Support of a System of Terminology for Legal Services for the Purposes of International Trade Negotiations (September 2003) Available at: <http://www.ibanet.org/About_the_IBA/IBA_resolutions.aspx> Accessed 14th Oct 2012

IBA Statement of Principles for the Establishment and Regulation of Foreign Lawyers (June 1998)

IBA Survey. 'Anti-Corruption Strategy for the Legal Profession: Risks and Threats of Corruption in the Legal Profession' (2010). Available at: <http://www.oecd.org/investment/briberyininternationalbusiness/46137847.pdf> Accessed 28th Aug 2012

IBA 'Task Force on the Financial Crisis' Available at: <http://www.ibanet.org/LPD/Task_Force_on_the_Financial_Crisis.aspx> Accessed 21st May 2012

International Law Association

Constitution of the International Law Association, adopted at the 74th Conference, 2010. Available at <http://www.ila-hq.org/en/about_us/index.cfm> Accessed 12th July 2012

The Study Group of the International Law Association on the Practice and Procedure of International Courts and Tribunals, 'The Hague Principles on Ethical Standards for Counsel Appearing before International Courts and Tribunals'. 27/9/2010. Available at: <http://www.ucl.ac.uk/laws/cict/docs/Hague_Sept2010.pdf> Accessed 17th Aug 2012

International Monetary Fund

Greece: Memorandum of Economic and Financial Policies accompanying the Letter of Intent of 6/8/10 from George Papaconstantinou (Minister of Finance) and George Provopoulos (Governor of the Bank of Greece) to Dominque Strauss-Kahn (Managing Director of the IMF). Available at: <http://www.imf.org/external/np/loi/2010/grc/080610.pdf>   Accessed 6th Mar 2013

Greece: Memorandum of Economic and Financial Policies accompanying the Letter of Intent of 8/12/10 from George Papaconstantinou (Minister of Finance) and George Provopoulos (Governor of the Bank of Greece) to Dominque Strauss-Kahn (Managing Director of the IMF) para 21, 5. Available at: <http://www.imf.org/external/np/loi/2010/grc/120810.pdf> Accessed 6th Mar 2013

Greece: Memorandum on Specific Economic Policy Conditionality accompanying the Letter of Intent of 8/12/10 from George Papaconstantinou (Minister of Finance) and George Provopoulos (Governor of the Bank of Greece) to Dominque Strauss-Kahn (Managing Director of the IMF). 40. Available at: <http://www.imf.org/external/np/loi/2010/grc/120810.pdf> Accessed 6th Mar 2013

Ireland: Letter of Intent, December 2010. 'Memorandum of Economic and Financial Policies, and Technical Memorandum of Understanding' Available at: <http://www.imf.org/external/np/loi/2010/irl/120310.pdf> Accessed 20th Sept 2012

Ireland: Memorandum of Economic and Financial Policies, attached to Ireland's letter of Intent to the IMF, 3/12/10. Available at: <http://www.imf.org/external/np/loi/2010/irl/120310.pdf > Accessed 31st Oct 2012

Ireland: Memorandum of Understanding on Specific Economic Policy Conditionality 27. Available at: <http://www.imf.org/external/np/loi/2010/irl/120310.pdf> Accessed 20th Sept 2012

Ireland: Transcript of a Conference Call on the Eight Review under Extended Fund Facility Arrangement with Ireland. 25th October 2012. Available at: <http://imf.org/external/np/tr/2012/tr102512.htm> Accessed 30th Apr 2013

Portugal: D Strauss-Kahn. Statement on Portugal by IMF Managing Director Dominique Strauss-Kahn and European Commissioner for Economic and Monetary Affairs Olli Rehn. (Press Release No 11/162). 5th May 2011. <http://www.imf.org/external/np/sec/pr/2011/pr11162.htm> Accessed 21st Feb 2013

Portugal: Memorandum of Economic and Financial Policies accompanying the Letter of Intent of 17/5/2011 from Fernando Teixeira dos Santos (Minister of State and Finance) and Carlos Silva da Costa (Governor of the Banco de Portugal) to Dominque Strauss-Kahn

(Managing Director of the IMF) para 41, 16. Available at:
<http://www.imf.org/external/np/loi/2011/prt/051711.pdf> Accessed 22nd Feb 2013

Organisation for Economic Co-operation and Development

Hook A, 'Domestic Regulation and Trade in Professional Services: Sectoral Study on the
Impact of Domestic Regulation on Trade in Legal Services'. OECD- World Bank. Sixth Services
Experts Meeting. Available at: <http://www.oecd.org/site/tadstri/40778871.pdf> Ac-
cessed 27th June 2012

OECD Anti-Bribery Convention (1997). Available at:
<www.oecd.org/daf/briberyininternationalbusiness/anti-briberyconvention/38028044.pdf>
Accessed 7th Aug 2012

United Nations

United Nations Basic Principles on the Role of Lawyers adopted by the Eighth UN Congress
on the Prevention of Crime and the Treatment of Offenders, Havana, Cuba 27th August to 7th
September 1990. <http://www2.ohchr.org/english/law/lawyers.htm> Accessed 10th July
2012

United Nations Charter. Available at: <http://www.un.org/en/documents/charter/>
Accessed 10th July 2012

United Nations Convention against Corruption (2003) Available at:
<http://www.unodc.org/documents/treaties/UNCAC/Publications/Convention/08-
50026_E.pdf> Accessed 6th Aug 2012

The United Nations Basic Principles on the Role of Lawyers adopted by the Eighth UN
Congress on the Prevention of Crime and Treatment of Offenders, Havana, Cuba, 27th
August to 7th September 1990. Available at:
<http://www2.ohcr.org/english/law/lawyers.htm> Accessed 10th July 2013

World Trade Organisation

Communication from Australia, Canada, Chile, The European Communities, Japan, Korea,
New Zealand, Singapore, Switzerland, The Separate Customs Territory of Taiwan, Penghu,
Kinmen and Matsu and the United States. Joint Statement on Legal Services TN/S/W/37
S/CSC/W/46 24th Feb 2005 Available at:
<http://docsonline.wto.org/GEN.viewerwindow.asp?http://docsonline.wto.org:80/DDFDoc
uments/t/S/CSC/W46.doc> Accessed 10th Dec 2011

Communication from the United States. Legal Services. S/CSS/W/28 18 December 2000.
Available at:
htpp://docsoline.wto.org/GEN.viewerwindow.asp?http://docsonline.wto.org:80/DDFDocum
ents/t/S/CSS/W28.doc Accessed 10th Dec 2011

GATS – Fact and Fiction. Available at:
<http://www.wto.org/english/tratop_e/serv_e/gatsfacts1004_e.pdf>

WTO Joint Statement on Legal Services. 24th February 2005. Available at:
<http://trade.ec.europa.eu/doclib/docs/2008/september/tradoc_140347.pdf > Accessed
10th Aug 2012

WTO Understanding the WTO: The Agreements. Services: Rules for Growth and Investment.
Available at: <http://www.wto.org/english/thewto_e/whatis_e/tif_e/agrm6_e.htm>
Accessed 2nd Aug 2012

Conference Papers/Presentations/Speeches

Ahern D 'Speech by the Minister for Justice and Law Reform Law Society Annual Dinner' 21st
May 2010. Available at:
<http://www.justice.ie/en/JELR/Pages/Speech%20by%20Dermot%20Ahern%20TD,%202020
10> Accessed 10th Sept 2012

Barrosso M, Speech to the EU Parliament, 28/9/2011. Available at:
<http://www.irishtimes.com/newspaper/breaking/2011/0928/breaking40_pf.html>
Accessed 30th Sept 2012

Binchy D, 'Why the Independence of the Legal Profession must be defended in the Public
Interest' Speech. 5th December 2011. Convention Centre, Dublin. Available at:
<http://www.lawsociety.ie/Global/eNewsletters/ebulletin/SpeechLegalServicesBill_DB.pdf>
Accessed 7th Jan 2013

Ferguson G, 'National Legal Profession Reform in Australia: An Overview'. ABA Annual
Meeting International Bar Leader Roundtable Panel. 6th August 2010.
<http://lawcouncil.asn.au/shadomix/apps/fms/fmsdownload.cfm?file_uuid=548BDC85-
BA51-7A06-7B59-417BF7E6FCB7&siteName=1ca> Accessed 1 Feb 2013

Kenny C, 'Changes, Trends and ABS in England and Wales'. Conference Speech, Department
of Justice and Equality, 6th July 2012. Link to presentation available at:
<http://www.justice.ie/en/JELR/Pages/SP12000217> Accessed 28th April 2013

Lamy P. Speech at The China International Fair in Trade in Services, Beijing, 28th May 2012.
Available at: <http://www.wto.org/english/news_e/sppl_e/sppl233_e.htm> Accessed 2nd
Aug 2012

Lenihan B 14/5/2008. Speech to Seanad Eireann during a Private Members' Motion.
Available at <http://www.finance.gov.ie/viewdoc.asp?DocID=5286> Accessed 28/10/2012

McDowell M, 'Speech by an Tanaiste at Regulating the Professions in Ireland Conference'
10th November 2006 Department of Justice and Law Reform. Available at
<http://www.inisgov.ie/en/JELR/PagesSP07000416> Accessed 30th July 2012

Mark S, 'Regulation of the Legal Professions – The Australian Experience with Particular
Focus on New South Wales'. Conference Speech, Department of Justice and Equality, 6th July
2012. Link to presentation available at:
<http://www.justice.ie/en/JELR/Pages/SP12000217> Accessed 28th April 2013

Neary P, 'IFSC 2.0 Conference – The Next Phase' 5/3/2008 UCD. Available at:
<http://www.centralbank.ie/press-area/speeches/Documents/05%20March%202008%20-
%20%20Address%20by%20Patrick%20Neary%20to%20IFSC%202.0%20Conference%20-
%20The%20Next%20Phase%20.pdf> Accessed 28th Oct 2012

Scott C, 'Models of Regulation for the Legal Profession'. Conference Speech, Department of Justice and Equality, 6th July 2012. Link to presentation available at: <http://www.justice.ie/en/JELR/Pages/SP12000217> Accessed 28th April 2013

Shatter A, 'Regulation, Representation and the Future of the Legal Profession' Law Society Annual Conference. 14th April 2012. Available at: <http://www.justice.ie/en/JELR/Pages/SP12000102> Accessed 7th Jan 2013

Shatter A, 'Speech' Conference on Regulatory Reform for a 21st Century Legal Profession'. 6th July 2012. Available at: <http://www.justice.ie/en/JELR/Pages/SP12000204> Accessed 7th Jan 2013

Whelan M, 'Attorney General Address to the Bar Council' 4th June 2011. Available at: <http://www.lawlibrary.ie/documents/membersdocs/GalwayPaperMarieWhelan07062011. pdf >. Accessed 22nd June 2011

Parliamentary Debates

53 *Dáil Debates* Cols 7 – 32 (Second Stage)

147 *Dáil Debates* Cols 992 – 1018 (Second Stage)

147 *Dáil Debates* Cols 1306 – 1327 (Committee and Final Stages)

156 (13) *Dáil Debates* Cols 1087 – 1120 (Second Stage) 15th Oct 1998

169 (18) *Dáil Debates* Cols 1601 – 1615 (Second Stage) 4th April 2002

184 *Dáil Debates* Cols 124 – 157 (Second Stage)

189 (2) *Dáil Debates* Cols 77 – 100 (Second Stage Resumed) 9th Apr 2008

189 (19) *Dáil Debates* Cols 998 – 1016 (Second Stage Resumed) 27th May 2008

190 (2) *Dáil Debates* Cols 153 – 159 (Report and Final Stages) 5th Jun 2008

440 (3) *Dáil Debates* Cols 615 – 622. (Second Stage Resumed) 10th Mar 1994

440 (5) *Dáil Debates* Cols 1196 – 1223 (Second Stage) 23rd Mar 1994

444 (5) *Dáil Debates* Cols 1131 – 1139 (Second Stage) 23rd Mar 1994

496 (7) *Dáil Debates*(Seanad: Second Stage) Cols 1607 – 1647 18th Nov 1998

505 (6) *Dáil Debates* Cols 1230 – 1243 (Second Stage) 1st June 1999

624 (4) *Dáil Debates* Cols 1687 – 1735 (Second Stage Resumed) 4th Oct 2006

624 (5) *Dáil Debates* Cols 1967 – 1975 (Second Stage Resumed) 5th Oct 2006

642 *Dáil Debates* Cols 1 – 7 (Leaders' Questions)

648 (3) *Dáil Debates* Cols 550 – 570 (Report Stage) 27th Feb 2008

655 (4) *Dáil Debates* Cols 785 – 791(Second Stage) 28th May 2008

656 *Dáil Debates* Cols 40 – 63 Second Stage

656 (1) *Dáil Debates* Cols 42 – 63 (Second Stage Resumed) 29th May 2008

750 *Dáil Debates* Col 582 16th December 2011

771 *Dáil Debates* Col 516 Written Answers (1) 3rd July 2012

773 *Dáil Debates* Col 489 – 511 Written Answers (18) 23rd Oct 2012

Oireachtas Discussions and Speeches

Joint Committee on Justice, Defence and Equality Debate 'Legal Services Regulation Bill 2011: Discussion' 21st Mar 2012. Available at: <http://debates.oireachtas.ie/JUJ/2012/03/21/00004.asp> Accessed 6th Sept 2012

Joint Committee on Justice, Equality, Defence and Women's Rights Debate 'Solicitors' Undertakings: Discussion with Law Society and Irish Banking Federation' 5th Mar 2008. Available at: <http://debates.oireachtas.ie/JUJ/2008/03/05/00003.asp> Accessed 4th Sept 2012

'Legal Services Regulation Bill 2011 Closing Statement for Second Stage by Mr Alan Shatter TD Minister for Justice, Equality and Defence' 23rd Feb 2012. Available at: <http://www.justice.ie/en/JELR/Pages/SP12000047> Accessed 6th Sept2012

Lenihan B, Speech to Seanad Eireann during a Private Members' Motion. 14th May 2008. Available at <http://www.finance.gov.ie/viewdoc.asp?DocID=5286> Accessed 28th Oct 2012

Newspaper Articles/Press Releases

Canning M, 'Global legal firm Allen & Overy outsources to Belfast' *Belfast Telegraph* 4 February 2011 Available at: <http://www.belfasttelegraph.co.uk/business/business-news/global--legal-firm-allen-amp-overy-outsources-to-belfast-15073428.html> Accessed 13th July 2013

Canning M, 'US legal firm to bring 100 posts to Northern Ireland' *Belfast Telegraph* 21 March 2012 Available at: <http://www.belfasttelegraph.co.uk/business/business-news/us-legal-firm-to-bring-100-posts-to-northern-ireland-16133947.html>

Carswell S, et al 'Ex-Anglo Irish Bank Chief Charged on Loan Offences' *The Irish Times* 28th July 2012. 1

Carswell S, 'Vico Capital sells block in Washington DC for $155m' 2nd Feb 2012. Irish Times <http://www.irishtimes.com/newspaper/finance/2012/0202/1224311111745.html> Accessed 30th Oct 2012

Carty E, 'Bloxham Stockbrokers ordered to cease trading'. 28/5/2012 Independent.ie. Available at: <http://www.independent.ie/business/Irish/bloxham-stockbrokers-ordered-to-cease-trading-3120187.html> Accessed 6th Dec 2012

Coulter C, 'Shatter abandons plan for legal services ombudsman' *irishtimes.com* 14th May 2011. Available at: <http://www.irishtimes.com/newspaper/Ireland/2011/0520/1224296945402_pf.html> Accessed 17th Aug 2012

Coulter C, 'Council to survey barristers' fees and expenses' *irishtimes.com* 20th May 2011. Available at: <http://www.irishtimes.com/newspaper/ireland/2011/0520/1224297355000-_pf.html> Accessed 9th Oct 2012

Coulter C, 'Court sees human misery after Celtic Tiger demise' *irishtimes.com* 9th April 2012. Available at: <http://www.irishtimes.com/newspaper/ireland/2012/0409/1224314548021_pf.html> Accessed 30th Sept 2012

Coulter C, 'Law groups query effects of troika on impartiality' *irishtimes.com* 29th December 2011
<http://www.irishtimes.com/newspaper/ireland/2011/1229/1224309591774_pf.html> Accessed 7th Jan 2013

Coulter C, 'Legal services Bill should do more to confront costs' *irishtimes.com* 21st March 2012. Available at:
<http://www.irishtimes.com/newspaper/opinion/2012/0321/1224313638558_pf.html> Accessed 9th Sept 2013

Creaton S, 'Former EBS Chairmen invested in O'Donnell Firm' 16th Dec 2011. Independent.ie
<http://www.independent.ie/business/irish/former-ebs-chairmen-invested-with-odonnell-firm-2965946.html> Accessed 16th Nov 2012

Devlin M, 'Time to grab this thief by his dirty white collar'. 22/7/2010. Independent.ie.
Availllable at: <http://www.independent.ie/opinion/columnists/martina-devlin-time-to-grab-this-thief-by-his-dirty-white-collar-2267858.html> Accessed 5th Nov 2012

Drennan J, 'Solicitors default on stamp duty bills' *Independent.ie* 5th July 2009 Available at:
<http://www.independent.ie/national-news/solicitors-default-on-stamp-duty-bills-1806551.html> Accessed 4th Sept 2012

Edwards E, 'Call for changes to legal reform Bill' *irishtimes.com* 27/2/2012. Available at:
<http://www.irishtimes.com/newspaper/breaking/2012/0227/breaking40_pf.html> Accessed 27th Feb 2012

Elliot J, (Registrar of Solicitors and Director of Regulation of the Law Society of Ireland), "Further Changes to the Professional Indemnity Insurance Regulations". Available at:
<http://www.lawsociety.ie/Documents/committees/PII/PII_nov09gazette.pdf > Accessed 30th Aug 2012

Gartland F, 'Independent regulator for legal sector demanded' *The Irish Times* 1st March 2010.

Healy T, 'Are O'Donnells 'Alice in Wonderland?' asks Judge' 18th April 2012 Herald.ie.
Available at: <http://www.herald.ie/news/are-o'donnells-alice-in-wonderland-asks-judge-3084445.html> Accessed 30th Oct 2012

Hope K, 'Greeks strike over professional reforms' 19th Jan 2011 *Financial Times.* Available at: <http://www.ft.com/cms/s/0/82b23910-23d1-11e0-8bb1-00144feab49a.html> Accessed 5th Oct 2012

IBM 'Memphis Police Department Reduces Crime Rates with IBM Predictive Analytics Software' 21st July 2010. Available at: <http://www-03.ibm.com/pressrelease/32169.wss>

IMF 'IMF Executive Board Approves €30 Billion Stand-By Arrangement for Greece' Press Release No 10/187. 9/5/2010. Available at:
<http://www.imf.org.external/np/sec/pr/2010/pr10187.htm> Accessed 22nd Feb 2013

IMF 'Statement by the EC, ECB and IMF on the Review Mission to Ireland' Press Release No 11/136 12th April 2011. Available at:
<http://www.imf.org/external/np/sec/pr/2011/pr11136/htm> Accessed 8th July 2012

Kelly F, 'Two solicitors found guilty of eight charges' *Independent.ie* 6th February 2008.
Available at: <http://www.independent.ie/irish-news/two-solicitors-found-guilty-of-charges-26421414.html> Accessed 7th June 2013

Kelly J, 'Unrepentant Honohan ups Criticism of Solicitors' *Independent.ie*. 27th November 2011. Available at: <http://www.independent.ie/national-news/unrepentant-honohan-ups-criticisms-of-solicitors-2946944> Accessed: 30th Sept 2012

Kerrigan G, 'The Beautiful, The Damned, The Charmed, The Saved and The Disappeared: The Definition of Debt in Absurdistan' *Sunday Independent* 2nd September 2012. 18 – 20

Kilfeather V, 'Alleged Negligent Advice puts Solicitors' Defence Fund in Jeopardy' 8th Dec 2009. irishexaminer.com. Available at: <http://www.irishexaminer.com/business/kfauqlmhojgb/> Accessed 3rd Jan 2013

Law Society of Ireland. News Release. 'Law Society condemns actions of former solicitor Michael Lynn who "disgraced himself and brought disrepute on his profession"' 23rd May 2008. Available at: <http://www.lawsociety.ie/Pages/News-Archive/News-Release---Law-Society-Condemns-Actions-of-Former-Solicitor-Michael-Lynn-Who-disgraced-himself-and-brought-disrepute-on-his-profession/> Accessed 17th Oct 2012

McDonagh M, 'The worst-planned estates in Ireland?' 21st April 2012 Available at: <http://www.irishtimes.com/newspaper/weekend/2012/0421/1224315001367.html> Accessed 17th Nov 2012

McDonald D, 'Bank denies Quinn family phones'. 'independent.ie' 1st Sept 2012. Available at: <http://www.inependent.ie/national-news/bank-denies-tapping-quinn-family-phones-3216527.html> Accessed 8th Oct 2012

McDonald D, 'New rules allow barristers to be struck off' *Independent.ie* 4th June 2010. Available at: <http://www.independent.ie/national-news/new-rules-allow-barristers-to-be-struck-off-2207333.html> Accessed 26th May 2011

McDonald D, 'The day I came face to face with Michael Lynn, the 'Scarlett Pimpernel''. 10th Sept 2010. Independent.ie. Available at: <http://www.independent.ie/entertainment/books/the-day-i-came-face-to-face-with-michael-lynn-the-scarlett-pimpernel-2342798.html> Accessed 3rd Jan 2013

McDonald D & Kelpie C, 'Foster and Allen Barrister Expected to be Struck Off' *Irish Independent* 30th November 2011

Mills S, 'Statutory regulation of many of our professions due for reform' *Irishtimes.com* 23rd May 2011. Available at: <www.irishtimescom/newspaper/ireland/2011/0523/1224297541496_pf.html> Accessed 7th June 2012

Noonan L, 'Collapse of European operations mired in controversy' 2/10/2012. Independent.ie. Available at: <http://www.independent.ie/national-news/collapse-of-european-operations-mired-in-controversy-3247241.html> Accessed 5th Nov 2012

O'Donovan D, ''Maple 10' developers are named in court' Independent.ie 24th July 2012. Available at: <http://www.independent.ie/business/irish/maple-10-developers-are-named-in-court-3179000.html> Accessed 30th Nov 2012

O'Hora A, 'Solicitors not able to pay €80 million Anglo loan' 28th Feb 2011. Independent.ie Available at: <http://www.independent.ie/national-news/solicitors-not-able-to-repay-80m-anglo-loan-2559016.html> Accessed 22nd Nov 2012

O'Kelly S, 'Bailout finally marks the end of insane Irish speculative boom'. 29th Nov 2010. Mailonline. Available at: <http://www.dailymail.co.uk/property/article-1334015/MARKET-WATCH-Bail-finally-marks-end-insane-Irish-speculative-boom.html> Accessed 3rd Jan 2013

Palazzolo J, 'In Europe, Debt Crisis Raises Questions about Regulating Lawyers'. *The Wall Street Journal* 5th January 2012. <http://blogs.wsj.com/law/2012/01/05/in-europe-debt-crisis-raises-questions-about-regulating-lawyers/> Accessed 7 January 2012

Purcell D, 'Change coming for 'archaic' legal profession' *ThePost.ie* 27th March 2011. Available at: <http://www.sbpost.ie/businessoflaw/change-coming-for-archaic-legal-profession-55287.html> Accessed 24th May 2011

Riely J, 'Unrepentant Honohan ups Criticism of Solicitors" *Independent.ie* 27th November 2011. Available at: <http://www.independent.ie/national-news/unrepentant-honohan-ups-criticism-of-solicitors-2946944.html> Accessed 1st Oct 2012

Ryan P, 'Doubling of legal fees is 'outrageous'. *Independent.ie* 15th July 2012. Available at: <http://www.independent.ie/national-news/doubling-of-legal-fees-is-outrageous-3168529.html> Accessed 19th July 2012

Sheahan F, 'Reform of lawyers, chemists 'will make customer king'' *Irish Independent* 18th April 2011 20

Sheeehan M, 'Failure to act on initial complaint was costly error' *Irish Independent* 27th April 2009.

Sheehan M, 'Lynn is taking the Mickey after bunking off to trainrobber haven' 7th Oct 2012. Irish Independent. Available at: <http://www.irishindependent.ie/opinion/analysis/lynn-is-taking-the-michael-after-bunking-off-to-trainrobber-haven-3251455.html> Accessed 31st Oct 2012

Thompson T, "Software that can predict violent crime to help police". The Observer 25th July 2010

Transparency International, 'Government proposals to protect whistleblowers described as misleading' 21st May 2010. Available at: <http://www.transparency.ie/news_events/wbwhitecollar2010.htm> Accessed 13th April 2012

Tremlett G, 'Portugal settles terms of €78 billion bailout with EU and IMF' The Guardian 4th May 2011. Available at: <http://www.guardian.co.uk/business/2011/may/04/portugal-78bn-bailout-imf> Accessed 21st Feb 2013

Terry L, 'The European Commission Project Regarding Competition in Professional Services' European Commission Project: Competition in Professional Services 3rd June 2009 3:58 17 PM

Walsh J, 'Not a stone will stand upon a stone' 9th May 2006. *The Guardian* Available at: <http://www.guardian.co.uk/commentisfree/2006/may/09/notastonewillstandupona> Accessed 22nd Oct 2012

Webb N & McBride L, 'Lifting a Lid on Anglo's links to the docklands' 15th Feb 2009. Independent.ie. Available at: <http://www.independent.ie/business/irish/lifting-a-lid-on-anglos-links-to-the-docklands-1640827.html > Accessed 12th Nov 2012

Wood K, 'Report warns of solicitors' insurance fund collapse' *ThePost.ie* 8th May 2011. Available at: <http://www.sbpost.ie/news/ireland/report-warns-of -solicitors-insurance-fund-collapse-56241.html> Accessed 24th May 2011

Woulfe J, 'Claim some solicitors acting as gang 'intelligence officers'' *Irish Examiner.com* 7th July 2009 Available at: <http://www.examiner.ie/ireland/claim-some-solicitors-acting-as-gang-intelligence-officers-95730.html> Accessed 10th Nov 2011

__ __ 'A Reluctant Transformation'. *irishtimes.com* 4th October 2012. Available at: <http://www.irishtimes.com/newspaper/opinion/2012/1004/1224324835602_pf.html> Accessed 7th Jan 2013

__ __ 'Bank gave 'payment holiday' on €3m loans' 6th Jan 2008. *Independent.ie* Available at: <http://www.independent.ie/national-news/bank-gave-payment-holiday-on-3m-loans-1258802.html> Accessed 4th Dec 2012

__ __ Department of Justice and Equality 'Minister Shatter publishes Criminal Justice Bill 2011' 13th May 2011. Available at: <http://www.justice.ie/en/JELR/Pages/CrimJustBill2011_PR> Last accessed 19th May 2011

__ __ European Parliament. 'Access to lawyers before police questioning essential, say civil liberties MEPs' 10th July 2012. Available at: <http://www.europarleuropa.eu/news/en/pressroom/content/20120709IPR48489/html/Access-to-lawyers-before-police-questioning-essential-say-civil-liberties-MEPs Accessed 13th July 2013

__ __ 'Greek lawyers under seige' *irishtimes.com* 28th May 2012. Available at: <http://www.irishtimes.com/newspaper/finance/2012/0528/1224316801988.html> Accessed 27th June 2012

__ __ 'Judge in call to penalise defamation on internet' *irishtimes.com* 1st Feb 2012. Available at: <http://www.irishtimes.com/newspaper/ireland/2012/0201/1224311048403_pf.html> Accessed 21st Sept 2012

__ __ 'Legal Services Bill' *The Irish Times* 8th December 2011. Available at: http://www.lawsociety.ie/Global/Newsletters/ebulletin/irishtimes8dec11.pdf Accessed 7th Jan 2013

__ __ 'Lifting a lid on Anglo's links to the docklands'. 15th Feb 2009. *Independent.ie.* Available at: <http://www.independent.ie/business/irish/lifting-a-lid-on-anglos-links-to-the-docklands-1640827.html> Accessed 3rd Jan 2013

__ __ 'Lynn case raises questions'. 2nd Oct 2012. *Independent.ie.* Available at: <http://www.independent.ie/opinion/editorial/Lynn-case-raises-questions-3248220.html> Accessed 5th Nov 2012

__ __ 'Priory Hall Residents protest 12 months after evacuation' *irishtimes.com* 13th Octover 2012. Available at: <http://www.irishtimes.com/newspaper/breaking/2012/1013//breaking3.html> Accessed 13th Nov 2012

'Priory Hall residents protest 12 months after evacuation' *Irishtimes.com* 13th Oct 12. Available at: <http://www.irishtimes.com/newspaper/breaking/2012/1013//breaking3.html> Accessed 19th Dec 2012

__ __ 'Quinn denies backdating loans to deprive Anglo of group's assets' *Irishtimes.com* 24th Mar 2012. Available at <http://www.irishtimes.com/newspaer/finance/2012/0324/1224313821680.html> Accessed 29th Nov 2012

__ __ 'Two solicitors fined 25k each by disciplinary tribunal' The Irish Emigrant 10th February 2008. Available at: <http://www.emigrant.ie/index.php?option=com_content&task=view&id=55458&Itemid=32> Accessed 6th Jun 2013

__ __ 'University of Memphis's Janikowski gains distinction as crime 'reducer'' *Update* (Feb 2010) (University of Memphis). Available at: <http://www.memphis.edu/update/feb10/crime.php > Accessed 30th July 2012

__ __ 'Wallace used hitman threat over debt' *irishtimes.com* 6th Ocotber 2011. Available at: <http://www.irishtimes.com/news/wallace-used-hitman-threat-over-debt-1.741032> Accessed 30th April 2013

__ __ 'Which? Wants Law Regulation' 'Which?' 21st March 2005. Available at: <http://www.which.co.uk/about-which/press/press-releases/campaign-press-relaeases/consumer-market/2005/03/which-wants-law-regulation> Accessed 1st Mar 2013

Correspondence

Dal G-A, (CCBE President) and William T (Bill) Robinson III (ABA President) letter to Christine Lagarde, Managing Director of the IMF. 21st Dec 2011. Available at: <http://www.ccbe.eu/fileadmin/user_upload/NTCdocument/CCBE_and_ABA_letter_1_132 5686329.pdf> Accessed 7th Jan 2013

Department of Justice and Equality letter to IMF 31/1/12. Available at: < <http://www.lawlibrary.ie/documents/news_events/IMFResponseToCCBEABALetter030220 12.pdf>   Accessed 7th Jan 2013

Fallon R, Principal Officer, Civil Law Reform Division, Department of Justice and Equality letter to Sean Hagan, IMF. 31st Jan 2012. Attached to the IMF letter of 3rd Feb 2012 from IMF to CCBE and ABA . Available at: <http://www.lawlibrary.ie/documents/news_events/IMFResponseToCCBEABALetter032201 2.pdf> Accessed 7th Jan 2013

Hagan S, (General Council of the Legal Department of the IMF) letter to the CCBE and ABA. 3rd Feb 2012. Available at: <http://www.lawlibrary.ie/documents/views_events/IMFResponseToCCBEABALetter03022 012.pdf> Accessed 7th Mar 2013

IMF Letter to ABA and CCBE. 3rd Feb 2012 Available at: <http://www.lawlibrary.ie/documents/news_events/IMFResponseToCCBEABALetter032201 2.pdf> Accessed 7th Jan 2013

Scott C, letter to the 'Irish Times'. 12th Dec 2011. Available at: <http://www.irishtimes.com/newspaper/letters/2011/1209/1224308798676.html> Accessed 2nd Mar 2013

Other Items

Hackett C, 'Dependent States, Global Capital and the Capacity to Regulate: Why Can't Small Open Economies like Ireland have Robust Corporate Social Responsibility?' (PhD Thesis: Queen's University of Belfast 2010)

Mackay C, (2012) Bloomberg 27th Sept 2009. 'Quotes from the Irish Property Bubble' (Quoting Bertie Ahern). Available at: <http://quotesfromthebubble.blogspot.com/2009/03/bertie-ahern-former-taoiseach.html> Accessed 12th Nov 2012

Helenic National Reform Programme 2012 – 2015. 41 Availabe at: <http://ec.europa.eu/europ2020/pdf/nd/nrp/2012_greece_en.pdf> Accessed 8th Mar 2013

'Programme for Government 2011 – 2016'. Government for National Recovery 2011 – 2016'. Available at: <http://www.socialjustice/sites/defaut/files/file/Government%20Docs%2etc/2011-13-06%20-%20Programme%20for%20Government%202011-2016.pdf> Accessed 29th Jan 2013

Rand Corporation *Million Random Digits* (The Free Press). Available at: http://www.rand.org/publications/classics/randomdigits. Accessed 19th April 2013

Scott C, 'Regulating Everything' UCD Geary Institute Discussion Paper Series (Geary WP/24/2008)

Seasonally Adjusted Standardised Employment Rates (SUR). Central Statistics Office. Available at: <http://www.cso.ie/en/statistics/labourmarket/principalstatistics/seasonallyadjustedstanda rdised employmentratessur/> Accessed 30th April 2013

The National Recovery Plan 2011 – 2014. Available at: <http://www.budget.gov.ie/The%20National%20Recovery%20Plan%202011-2014.pdf> Accessed 30th April 2013

__ __ 'Complaints against Barristers' The Department of Justice and Equality. Available at: <http://www.justice.ie/en/JELR/Pages/Complaints_against_barristers> Accessed 7th Jan 2013

__ __ 'Ex-solicitor jailed for three-and-a-half years for €750,000 fraud' 12th June 2012. RTE News. Available at: <http://www.rte.ie/news/2012/1612/ex-solicitor-jailed-following-750-000-fraud.html> Accessed 22nd Nov 2012

Useful Websites

Ireland

Central Statistics Office <www.cso.ie>

Construction Industry Federation <www.cfi.ie>

Department of Environment, Community and Local Government <www.environ.ie>

Department of the Taoiseach www.taoiseach.gov.ie

Honorable Society of Kings Inns <http://www.kingsinns.ie>

Law Reform Commission <www.lawreform.ie>

Public Appointments Service < http://www.publicjobs.ie/publicjobs>

Rate Your Solicitor <www.Rate_Your_Solicitor.com>

Revenue Commissioners <www.revenue.ie>

RTE <www.rte.ie>

Solicitors Mutual Defence Fund <www.smdf.ie>

The Competition Authority <www.tca.ie>

The International Monetary Fund <www.imf.org>

The Irish Economy <www.irisheconomy.ie>

The Law Library <www.lawlibrary.ie>

The Law Society of Ireland <www.lawsociety.ie>

The Solicitors Disciplinary Tribunal <www.distrib.ie>

Transparency International <www.transparency.ie>

Victims of the Legal Profession Society
<www.d1041561.dotsterhost.com/index.php?s=wst_page4:html> No longer available.

United Kingdom

AA Services <http://www.theaa.com>

Co-Operative Legal Services <http://www.co-operative.coop/legalservices>

Legal Futures <http://www.legalfutures.co.uk>

Legal365 <http://www.legal365.com>

Parabis Group <http://www.parabisgroup.co.uk>

Quality Solicitors <www.qualitysolicitors.com>

The Bar Library of Northern Ireland (The General Council of the Bar of Northern Ireland)
<http://www.barlibrary.com/>

The Law Society <www.lawsociety.org.uk>

The Law Society of Northern Ireland <http://www.lawsoc-ni-org/>

The Solicitors Regulatory Authority <http://www.sra.org/uk>

European Union

EUROPA <http://europa.eu>

International

A Clatter of the Law <www.aclatterofthelaw.com>

American Bar Association <www.abanet.org>

Australian Government Attorney General's Department <http://www.ag.gov.au>

Blue Flag (Linklaters) <http://www.blueflag.com>

CCBE <http://www.ccbe.org>

Complete Case <http://completecase.com>

Council of Australian Governments <http://www.coag.gov.au>

Google Scholar <http://googlescholar.com>

International Bar Association <http://www.ibanet.org>

International Association of Lawyers (Union Internationale des Avocats) <www.uianet.org>

International Law Association <www.ila-hq.org>

International Monetary Fund <www.imf.org>

New South Wales Government Lawlink Attorney General & Justice
http://www.lawlink.nsw.gov.au

OECD <http://www.oecd.org>

Terry, Laurel Website <http://www.personel.psu.edu/faculty/l/s/lst3/>

The Council of Europe <http://www.hub.coe.int>

World Trade Organisation <http://wwww.wto.org>

Blogs

John Flood's Random Academic Thoughts Blog <http://www.johnflood.blogspot.ie>

McGarr Solicitors <http://www.mcgarrsolicitors.ie>

The Irish Economy <http://www.irisheconomy.ie>

ꟼP

Visit us at *www.quidprobooks.com.*

www.ingramcontent.com/pod-product-compliance
Lightning Source LLC
Chambersburg PA
CBHW070556270326
41926CB00013B/2337

Francis Orpen Morris

Records of Animal Sagacity and Character
With a Preface on the Future Existence of the Animal Creation

ISBN/EAN: 9783744767958

Printed in Europe, USA, Canada, Australia, Japan

Cover: Foto ©Andreas Hilbeck / pixelio.de

More available books at **www.hansebooks.com**

RECORDS

ANIMAL SAGACITY AND CHARACTER.

WITH

A PREFACE

ON THE FUTURE EXISTENCE OF THE ANIMAL CREATION.

BY

THE REV. F. O. MORRIS, B.A.

RECTOR OF NUNBURNHOLME, YORKSHIRE,

AND CHAPLAIN TO HIS GRACE THE DUKE OF CLEVELAND.

Author of

A History of British Birds, A Natural History of British Butterflies,
A History of the Nests and Eggs of British Birds,
A Natural History of British Moths, A Natural History of the Bible,
Book of Natural History, Anecdotes in Natural History, &c.

"Thou, LORD, shalt save both man and beast."—PSALM xxxvi. 6

LONGMAN, GREEN, LONGMAN, AND ROBERTS.

1861.